Argumentation and Debate:
Rational Decision Making

Fourth Edition

Argumentation and Debate:
Rational Decision Making

Austin J. Freeley

John Carroll University

Wadsworth Publishing Company, Inc.
Belmont, California

To Trudie

Communications Editor: Rebecca Hayden
Designer: Ann Wilkinson

ISBN 0–534–00420–2
L.C. Cat. Card No. 75–23636
Printed in the United States of America
3 4 5 6 7 8 9 10–80 79 78

Preface

Today's students readily recognize the need for new editions of textbooks, for they have grown up in the greatest era of change in all human history. The world's store of knowledge doubled from 1750 to 1900. It doubled again from 1900 to 1950 and again from 1950 to 1960. Since 1960 the sum total of knowledge has doubled every five years. By the year 2000 there will be over a thousand times more knowledge than there was in 1900. Today's students—who will be mature adults occupying major decision-making positions as we enter the twenty-first century—will be called upon to face problems we cannot even imagine and to reach decisions based on evidence that does not now exist—97 percent of everything known by the start of the twenty-first century will have been discovered since today's students were born.

Knowledgeable teachers of argumentation also recognize that the accelerated rate of change has had marked impact on the field of argumentation and debate. The simple fact is that in many important ways we no longer analyze arguments, build cases, or conduct debates in the way we did ten or even five years ago. Disraeli, speaking in a far more leisurely century, said "Change is inevitable. In a progressive country change is constant." The field of argumentation and debate is certainly a "progressive country" where change is indeed constant.

This fourth edition of *Argumentation and Debate*, hopefully, retains and reinforces those features that have led to its wide use and, at the same time, brings before students the significant changes of our constantly developing field of study. This edition draws on the National Developmental Conference on Forensics (in which the author was a participant). It also draws on the proceedings of major professional conventions, research from the related fields of behavioral science and communication theory, and the "shop talk" of tournaments. These sources have provided new materials on recent development in argumentation theory and changes in debate practices that are added to the foundation of classical and modern principles. For example, new material has been provided on "should," "should-would," "fiat power," "issues," "structural inherency," "attitudinal inherency," "reasoning," "the requirements of consistency in case construction," "alternative justification affirmative cases," and "offensive and defensive casing." New outlines of typical affirmative and negative cases are designed to help the student prepare for debate. A completely new treatment of the negative case, including conditional and hypothetical counterplans, reflects contemporary practice and emerging theory. New materials on nonverbal communication and the application of many of the key recommendations of the National Developmental Conference on Forensics, together with many changes and updating of examples, are included to facilitate students' understanding of argumentation and debate and to enhance their ability to make rational decisions.

This book is for all who are interested in rational decision making. It is designed specifically for the undergraduate course in argumentation and debate, but it may be used in any broadly liberal course designed for students who seek self-realization and who desire to prepare themselves for effective participation in a democratic society.

The instructor may assign the chapters in any order adapted to the needs of the students. The chapter on briefing will be given major emphasis by some; others may omit it. If the students have limited speech communication experience, the chapters on speech composition and speech delivery may be introduced earlier; if they have had considerable experience in speech communication, these chapters may be reviewed briefly or omitted. Some instructors may prefer to assign the chapters on the case and refutation early in the course and begin promptly with full-scale debates.

I wish to record my thanks to Jerry M. Anderson of the University of Wisconsin at Oshkosh and Harold L. Lawson of Capital University who studied the third edition with the greatest care and offered much valuable advice for the fourth edition. I also wish to thank B. Wayne Callaway of the University of Wyoming, Lucy Keele of California State University at Fullerton, and Scott Nobles of Macalester College who read the entire manuscript of the fourth edition and provided many valuable suggestions. I wish to thank, too, Rebecca Hayden of the Wadsworth Publishing Company whose editorial work on this and the previous editions is most sincerely appreciated. Hundreds of my students, too, have contributed to this edition as well as to the earlier editions. By their questions and their discussion in class and in briefing sessions as we prepare for debates, they have helped me refine my thinking and develop more cogent statements on many matters.

Austin J. Freeley

Contents

21.   Modern Procedures: Educational Debate Formats   325

22.   Modern Procedures: The Tournament   343

23.   Parliamentary Debate   360

Appendix A   The First Presidential Debate   371

Appendix B   An Intercollegiate Debate   395

Appendix C   National Intercollegiate Debate Propositions   418

Index   423

Chapter 1

Rational Decision Making

Many of the most significant and critical communications of our lives are conducted in the form of debates. These may be intrapersonal communications, where we weigh the pros and cons of an important decision in our own minds; or they may be interpersonal communications, where we listen to a debate conducted to secure our decision or participate in a debate to secure the decision of others.

Success or failure in life is largely determined by our ability to make wise decisions for ourselves and to secure the decisions we want from others. Much of our significant, purposeful activity is concerned with making required decisions. Whether to join a campus organization, go to graduate school, accept a certain job offer, buy a car or house, move to another city, invest in a certain stock, or vote for Smith—these are just a few of the thousands of decisions we may have to make. Often intelligent self-interest or a sense of responsibility will require us to secure certain decisions from others. We may want a scholarship, a particular job, a customer for our product, or a vote for a certain candidate.

Some people make decisions by flipping a coin. Others act on the whim of the moment or respond unthinkingly to the pressures of the "hidden persuaders." If the problem is trivial—the movies tonight?—the use of these methods is of no consequence. For important matters, however, mature adults require rational means of decision making. They seek the greatest possible assurance that their decisions are wise and based on true evidence and valid reasoning.

Argumentation is reason giving by people in communicative situations. Although argumentation may make some use of psychological methods, motivational techniques, and other extralogical appeals, the paramount emphasis is on *logical* reasoning.

First we will consider debate as a method of rational decision making; and then we will consider other methods—some rational and some non-rational—and see how they relate to argumentation and debate.

I. Debate

Debate is the process of inquiry and advocacy, seeking reasoned judgment on a proposition. Debate may be used by an individual to reach a decision in

1

his or her own mind, or it may be used by an individual or a group seeking to secure a decision from others.

When debate consists of reasoned arguments for and against a given proposition, it is a *rational* means of decision making. It is essential that society, as well as the individual, have an effective method of reaching rational decisions. A free society is so structured that many of its decisions are reached through debate. Our law courts and our legislative bodies are specifically designed to create and perpetuate debate as the method of reaching decisions. In fact, any organization that conducts its business according to parliamentary procedure has selected debate as its method. Debate pervades our society at decision-making levels.

From the earliest times to the present, thoughtful men have recognized the importance of debate for the individual and society. Plato, whose dialogues were an early form of cross-examination debate, defines rhetoric as ". . . a universal art of winning the mind by arguments, which means not merely arguments in the courts of justice, and all other sorts of public councils, but in private conference as well."[1]

Aristotle lists four values for rhetoric.[2] First, it prevents the triumph of fraud and injustice. Aristotle argues that truth and justice are by nature more powerful than their opposites. When decisions are not made as they should be, speakers with right on their side have only themselves to blame for the outcome. Thus, it is not enough to know the right decision ourselves; we must be able to argue for that decision before others.

Second, it is a method of instruction for the public. Aristotle points out that there are people who cannot be persuaded by logic. In such cases the speaker must frame his proofs and arguments with the help of common knowledge and commonly accepted opinions.

Third, it makes us see both sides of a case. By arguing both sides, no aspect of the case will escape us and we will be prepared to refute our opponents' arguments.

Fourth, it is a means of defense. Often a knowledge of argumentation and debate will be necessary to protect ourselves or our interests. Aristotle states: "If it is a disgrace to a man when he cannot defend himself in a bodily way, it would be odd not to think him disgraced when he cannot defend himself with reason. Reason is more distinctive of man than is bodily effort."

Similarly, in the nineteenth century, John Stuart Mill placed great emphasis on the value of debate:

If even the Newtonian philosophy were not permitted to be questioned, mankind could not feel as complete assurance of its truth as they now [1858] do. The beliefs which we have the most warrant for, have no safeguard to rest on, but a standing invitation to the whole world to prove them unfounded. If the challenge is not

---

[1] Plato, *Phaedrus*, 261. Cooper and Jowett use slightly different terms in translating this passage. This statement draws from both translations.

[2] See: Aristotle, *Rhetoric*, I, 1.

accepted, or is accepted and the attempt fails, we are far enough from certainty still; but we have done the best that the existing state of human reason admits of; we have neglected nothing that could give the truth the chance of reaching us; if the lists are kept open, we may hope that if there be a better truth, it will be found when the human mind is capable of receiving it; and in the meantime we may rely on having attained such approach to truth as is possible in our day. This is the amount of certainty attainable by a fallible being, and this is the sole way of attaining it.[3]

In 1957, the United States Senate designated, as Senate Immortals, five senators who had shaped the history of our nation by their ability as debaters: Henry Clay, Daniel Webster, John C. Calhoun, Robert M. La Follette, Sr., and Robert A. Taft. The triumvirate of Webster, Clay, and Calhoun towered over all others and were the near unanimous choice of senators and scholars alike. These commanding figures might well be included in a list of the world's great debaters. As John F. Kennedy, then a freshman senator, pointed out, "For over thirty years they dominated the Congress and the country, providing leadership and articulation on all the great issues of the growing nation."[4] La Follette and Taft were selected as the outstanding representatives of the progressive and conservative movements in the twentieth century. In honoring these "immortals," the Senate recognized the importance of debate in determining the course of American history. John Quincy Adams considered Webster's reply in his debate with Hayne to be "the most significant act since the founding of the Constitution."[5] Indeed, it would be impossible to understand the history of the United States without a knowledge of the great debaters and their debates.

Our laws not only are made through the process of debate but are applied through debate as well. The famous attorney Joseph N. Welch has stated:

America believes in what lawyers call "the adversary system" in our courtrooms, including our criminal courts. It is our tradition that the District Attorney prosecutes hard. Against him is the lawyer hired by the defendant, or supplied by the court if the defendant is indigent. And the defendant's lawyer defends hard. We believe that truth is apt to emerge from this crucible. It usually does.[6]

We need debate not only in the legislative assembly and the courtroom but in all areas of human activity, since most of our liberties are directly or indirectly dependent upon debate. As Walter Lippmann has pointed out, one of our most cherished liberties, freedom of speech, can be maintained only by creating and perpetuating debate:

---

[3] John Stuart Mill, *On Liberty* (New York: A. L. Burt Co., n. d.), pp. 38–39.

[4] John F. Kennedy, Speech in the Senate, May 1, 1957, from a press release.

[5] *Ibid.*

[6] Joseph N. Welch, "Should a Lawyer Defend a Guilty Man?" *This Week* Magazine, December 6, 1959, p. 11. Copyright 1959 by the United Newspapers Magazine Corporation. Reprinted by permission of *This Week* Magazine and Joseph N. Welch.

Yet when genuine debate is lacking, freedom of speech does not work as it is meant to work. It has lost the principle which regulates and justifies it—that is to say, dialectic conducted according to logic and the rules of evidence. If there is no effective debate, the unrestricted right to speak will unloose so many propagandists, pro- curers, and panderers upon the public that sooner or later in self-defense the people will turn to the censors to protect them. It will be curtailed for all manner of reasons and pretexts, and serve all kinds of good, foolish, or sinister ends.

For in the absence of debate unrestricted utterance leads to the degradation of opinion. By a kind of Gresham's law the more rational is overcome by the less rational, and the opinions that will prevail will be those which are held most ardently by those with the most passionate will. For that reason the freedom to speak can never be maintained by objecting to interference with the liberty of the press, of printing, of broadcasting, of the screen. It can be maintained only by promoting debate.[7]

Not only do we need debate to maintain freedom of speech but also to provide a methodology for innovation and judgment about matters related to contemporary problems. As Chaim Perelman, the Belgium philosopher-rhetorician whose works in rhetoric and argumentation have become increasingly influential among the forensic community, has pointed out:

If we assume it to be possible without recourse to violence to reach agreement on all the problems implied in the employment of the idea of justice we are granting the possibility of formulating an ideal of man and society, valid for all beings endowed with reason and accepted by what we have called elsewhere the universal audience.[8]

I think that the only discursive methods available to us stem from techniques that are not demonstrative—that is, conclusive and *rational* in the narrow sense of the term—but from argumentative techniques which are not conclusive but which may tend to demonstrate the *reasonable* character of the conceptions put forward. It is this recourse to the rational and reasonable for the realization of the ideal of universal communion that characterizes the age-long endeavor of all philosophies in their aspiration for a city of man in which violence may progressively give way to wisdom.[9]

Thus we see the age-long concern of philosophers and statesmen with debate as an instrument for dealing with the problems of society. It is easy, then, to understand why debate is pervasive in our society. It is in the interest of the individual to know the principles of argumentation and debate and to be able to apply them in reaching and in securing decisions. It is in the interest of society to encourage debate both to protect the individual and to provide a means whereby society may reach rational decisions.

[7] Walter Lippmann, *Essays in the Public Philosophy* (Boston: Little, Brown & Co., 1955), pp. 129– 130. Reprinted by permission.

[8] C. Perelman and L. Olbrechts-Tyteca, *Traité de l'argumentation, La nouvelle rhetorique* (Paris: Presses Universitaries de France, 1958), Sec. 7.

[9] Ch. Perelman, *The Idea of Justice and the Problem of Argument*, trans. John Petrie (New York: Humanities Press, 1963), pp. 86–87.

II. Individual Decisions

Whenever the conditions necessary to the solution of a problem are within the control of the individual, the problem may be solved by personal decision. If the problem is "Shall I go to the basketball game tonight?" and if the price of admission and a means of transportation are at hand, the decision can be made individually. If, however, a friend's car is needed to get to the game, then his or her decision to furnish the transportation must be secured.

Complex problems, too, are subject to individual decision. When the Ford Motor Company discontinued production of its famous Model T, millions of dollars, hundreds of dealers, and thousands of workers were involved. Henry Ford was in effective control of his company, and by individual decision he determined what type of automobile would be produced. When Eisenhower sent the Marines into Lebanon, when Kennedy and Johnson escalated the war in Vietnam, and when Nixon sent troops into Cambodia, they used different methods of decision making, but the ultimate decision was each President's alone.

Whenever we have to make an individual decision of any importance, we may find it advantageous to debate the matter. This debate may take place in our minds as we weigh the pros and cons of the problem, or we may arrange for others to debate the problem for us. For instance, many governmental decisions can be made only by the President. Walter Lippmann points out that debate is the only satisfactory way by which the great issues of our times can be decided:

A president, whoever he is, has to find a way of understanding the novel and changing issues which he must, under the Constitution, decide. Broadly speaking . . . the president has two ways of making up his mind. The one is to turn to his subordinates — to his chiefs of staff and his cabinet officers and undersecretaries and the like, and to direct them to argue out the issues and to bring him an agreed decision. . . .

The other way is to sit like a judge at a hearing where the issues to be decided are debated. After he has heard the debate, after he has examined the evidence, after he has heard the debaters cross-examine one another, after he has questioned them himself, he makes his decision. This is the method intended by the authors of the National Security Act. . . .

It is a much harder method in that it subjects the president to the stress of feeling the full impact of conflicting views, and then to the strain of making his decision, fully aware of how momentous it is. But there is no other satisfactory way by which momentous and complex issues can be decided.[10]

As Senator Henry M. Jackson has stressed, the most important role of the National Security Council is to provide just this sort of debate for the President.[11]

[10] Walter Lippmann, "How to Make Decisions," *New York Herald Tribune*, March 3, 1960. Reprinted by permission.

[11] See: Henry M. Jackson, "Organizing for Survival," *Foreign Affairs*, Vol. 38 (March 1956), pp. 446–456.

Franklin Roosevelt followed a competitive theory of administration by encouraging vigorous and often public debate among his advisors. This method enabled him to know everything that was going on and to have all important matters of government come to him for decision.[12] Indeed, "he made debate a fundamental method of government."[13] Eisenhower did not believe that a commander could afford to spend his time talking with his advisors one at a time, particularly when they held widely differing views. Rather, he felt that the proponents of conflicting ideas should argue them out in front of the commander in the interest of supplying more complete information and presenting a better perspective.[14]

Kennedy used Cabinet sessions and National Security Council meetings to provide debate to illuminate diverse points of view, expose errors, and challenge assumptions before he reached decisions.[15] As he gained experience in office, he placed greater emphasis on debate. One historian points out: "One reason for the difference between the Bay of Pigs and the missile crisis was that fiasco instructed Kennedy in the importance of uninhibited debate in advance of major decision."[16] Early in his administration Nixon decided to handle foreign policy through the mechanism of the National Security Council. In addition to the NSC, Kennedy, Johnson, and Nixon all had special assistants from the academic world who had access to the White House Situation Room and to most of the secrets of government. Their job was to make sure that the President had all the information and insights he needed and to clarify and define the options open to the President and the consequences likely to flow from them.[17]

We may never be called on to render the final decision on great issues of national policy—but we are constantly concerned with decisions important to ourselves where debate can be applied in similar ways. Youth is increasingly involved in the decisions of the campus, community, and society in general; it is in intelligent self-interest that these decisions be reached after rational debate.

When we reach an individual decision, we can put it into effect if we control the necessary conditions. If we need the consent or cooperation of others to carry out our decision, we must find a means of securing the appropriate response from them by debate—or by group discussion, persuasion, propaganda, coercion, or a combination of methods.

---

[12] See: Arthur M. Schlesinger, Jr., *The Coming of the New Deal* (Boston: Houghton Mifflin Co., 1959), Chap. 32.

[13] Arthur M. Schlesinger, Jr., *The Imperial Presidency* (Boston: Houghton Mifflin Co., 1973), p. 213.

[14] See: "Exclusive Interview with Former President Eisenhower," *U. S. News & World Report,* January 14, 1963, p. 64.

[15] See: Theodore C. Sorensen, *Decision-Making in the White House* (New York: Columbia University Press, 1963), p. 59.

[16] Schlesinger, *Imperial Presidency,* p. 215.

[17] See: David Nevin, "Autocrat in the Action Arena," *Life,* September 5, 1969, pp. 50A–57.

III. Group Discussion

Decisions may be reached by group discussion when the members of the group (1) agree that a problem exists, (2) have compatible standards of value, (3) have compatible purposes, (4) are willing to accept the consensus of the group, and (5) are relatively few in number. When these conditions are met and when all relevant evidence and arguments are carefully weighed, group discussion is a rational means of decision making.

Despite considerable differences, the discussions of Roosevelt and Churchill with their advisors on the conduct of World War II produced many effective decisions. Overriding the differences there was usually agreement on the problem, standards of value, purposes, and a willingness to make considerable concessions. In contrast, the Paris Peace Talks on the Vietnam war dragged on interminably because items (2) and (3) were missing. For instance, the North Vietnamese representatives often began each discussion with demands they knew could not be accepted by the United States.

If the group is much larger than fifteen or twenty, profitable discussion becomes difficult or impossible. A group of senators can discuss a problem in committee, but not on the floor of the Senate. The Senate is too large for discussion; here debate must be used. Of course, informal debate may take place within the discussion process. Discussion may be a precursor of debate.[18] If the differences cannot be solved by discussion, debate is the logical recourse. Or if the group, such as a Senate committee, reaches a decision by discussion, it may then be necessary to debate it on the floor to carry the Senate as a whole.

Like an individual, a group may act upon its decision only insofar as it has the power to do so. If the performance of its plan requires the consent or cooperation of others, the group must use other means to secure their decision to cooperate.

IV. Persuasion

Persuasion is sometimes defined very broadly. In his *Rhetoric*, Aristotle said:

Of the means of persuasion supplied by the speech itself there are three kinds. The first kind reside in the character of the speaker; the second consist in producing a certain attitude in the hearer; the third appertain to the argument proper.[19]

[18] See: James H. McBurney, James M. O'Neill, and Glen E. Mills, *Argumentation and Debate*, (New York: Macmillan Co., 1951), p. 67.

[19] Aristotle, *Rhetoric*, I. 2.

Many contemporary students of persuasion use a similar broad spectrum definition, including almost all communication under the umbrella of persuasion.

Students of argumentation and debate, however, often find it desirable and practical to bring the term into sharper focus as the debater is primarily concerned with "the argument proper." In this context, persuasion is the art and science of using primarily extralogical appeals to secure decisions. Thus the difference between argumentation and persuasion may be seen as one of emphasis: *Argumentation gives priority to logical appeals while taking cognizance of ethical and emotional appeals; persuasion gives priority to ethical and emotional appeals while taking cognizance of logical appeals.*

Persuasion differs from debate in that it consists only of arguments for a proposition or only of arguments against it. Debate, of course, consists of arguments for and against a given proposition.

Persuasion is sometimes criticized because of its use of ethical and emotional appeals, but there can be no reasonable objection to their use as long as the persuader bases them on true evidence and valid reasoning. Indeed, the debater often blends ethical and emotional appeals with logical appeals.

The distinction between argumentation and persuasion is easily understood. We use the method of argumentation when we seek to convince an audience of mature adults who are seeking to reach a rational decision based on true evidence and valid reasoning. This is akin to what has been called the *universal audience.*[20] Persuasion is addressed to a particular audience which may, or may not, consist of mature rational adults seeking a rational decision. For example, an attorney making a final plea before a jury might well seek to persuade by drawing on emotional appeals specifically tailored to the wants, preferences, and beliefs of the specific jury before him or her.[21] If the attorney lost the case and appealed it to the Supreme Court, the plea before the high tribunal would be closely reasoned and fact laden. It would be adapted, of course, to the specific justices on the bench but also addressed to the *universal audience,* since the justices base their decisions on reasons they believe will be convincing to mature rational adults seeking rational decisions.

Persuaders reach a decision on the problem before they begin the process of persuasion. They continue the process of persuasion until they solve the problem by persuading others to accept the decision or until they are convinced that further efforts at persuasion are pointless. In their efforts to influence others, they may find it necessary or advantageous to join with

---

[20] See: Ch. Perelman and L. Olbrechts-Tyteca, *The New Rhetoric* (Notre Dame, Ind.: University of Notre Dame Press, 1966), Part One, Sec. 6 and Sec. 7 *et passim.*

[21] Lawyers have always pleaded so. Contemporary attorneys have greatly escalated the practice by using computer technology and teams of communication theorists, sociologists, and psychologists to select jurors sympathetic to their clients and to choose the appeals most likely to persuade the selected jurors. See: *Time,* January 28, 1974, p. 60.

other persuaders and become propagandists or to face the opposition and become debaters. Thus they must know the principles of argumentation and debate in order to secure the desired judgment. This knowledge is also a defense against the persuasion of others. If we subject their appeals to critical analysis, we increase our opportunity of making rational decisions. If persuaders advocate a decision we believe to be unsound, we may find it necessary to become debaters and advocate the conclusion we believe to be wise.

V. Propaganda

Propaganda is the use of persuasion by a *group,* often a closely knit organization, in a *sustained, organized campaign* for the purpose of influencing others to accept a decision. Propaganda differs from debate in that only one side of the proposition is presented. In popular usage, propaganda is a pejorative term. An official of a women's liberation group recently said: "We've been conducting an extensive educational campaign to inform the public of the necessity of making abortion on demand available to women on welfare. It was going very well until the churches unleashed a bunch of propagandists to work against us." Thus, in everyday language, *we* educate or give information, while *they* propagandize.

Of course, the end does not justify the means. Propaganda, like persuasion, may be viewed as good or bad only in relation to the degree that it is based on true evidence and valid reasoning. Examples of questionable methods may be found in the Allied propaganda in the United States prior to America's entry into the First World War. At that time extensive use was made of distorted or false atrocity stories. Other examples may be found in communist propaganda, which makes extensive use of the technique of the "big lie." During any Middle East crisis both Israel and the Arab countries conducted propaganda campaigns in the United States designed to sway public opinion in their favor. Each side obviously thought of theirs as good and the other's as bad.

Examples of propaganda used for good purposes may be found in the various campaigns designed to get the public to drive safely or to recognize the symptoms of cancer; these examples are usually based on true evidence and valid reasoning. Other examples may be found in churches that conduct campaigns to persuade people to act in accordance with the Ten Commandments or in colleges that conduct campaigns to raise funds.

Propagandists reach a decision on a problem before they begin the process of propaganda. They continue their campaign until they solve the problem by persuading others to accept their decision or they are convinced that further efforts are pointless. In their efforts to influence others, propagandists may find it necessary or advantageous to face their opponents and become debaters. In such cases, they need a knowledge of argumentation and debate. If their evidence is true and their reasoning valid and if their extralogical appeals are carefully selected, the campaign will have the greatest opportunity for success. If any of the conditions is lacking, the opportunity for success is diminished.

On the other hand, a knowledge of argumentation and debate is an important defense against the propaganda campaigns constantly seeking to influence our decisions. Unless we subject propaganda to critical analysis, we will be unable to distinguish the good from the bad. We will lose our ability to make rational decisions and become hapless puppets manipulated by the "hidden persuaders."

VI. Coercion

Coercion is defined as the threat or use of force. Parents use coercion when they take a box of matches from a baby; society uses coercion to confine criminals to a prison; the nation uses coercion when it goes to war. A free society places sharp restrictions on the use of coercion. The amount of coercion parents may use on a child is limited; criminals may be sentenced to prison only after they have an opportunity for debate on the charges against them; the United States may declare war only after the advocates of war win a debate in Congress. Even undeclared wars, such as the Vietnam conflict, require Congressional sanction in the form of joint resolutions and military appropriations. In a free society the use of coercion as a method of solving problems — by private individuals or the state — is generally prohibited except in those special cases where its use has been found necessary after debate. A totalitarian society, on the other hand, is characterized by sharply limited debate and by almost omnipresent coercion.[22]

Coercion may be used to influence a decision. The existence of the coercive powers of the state is a strong logical appeal against a decision to commit a crime; and for some it may be the only effective appeal.

A decision to use coercion is likely to be socially acceptable and effective when that decision is made after full and fair debate. Baron Karl von Clausewitz's classic definition of war as the "continuation of diplomacy by other means" indicates that war, the ultimate form of coercion, is a method of problem solving to be selected after a careful debate on the possible risks and possible advantages.

Brainwashing, a term that became familiar during the Korean War, is a specialized use of coercion as a method of securing a decision. It is defined as the use of coercion in combination with a blend of sound and specious argument, persuasion, propaganda, and rigidly controlled group discussion in a situation where intensive and unremitting pressure is applied by a con-

---

[22] See: Aleksandr I. Solzhenitsyn, *The Gulag Archipelago* (New York: Harper & Row, 1974).

trolling group—an army or a secret police organization—to controlled individuals—prisoners—for the purpose of securing from the prisoners a decision to profess publicly the ideas dictated by their captors. As an essential ingredient of brainwashing the captors punish any "wrong" statement or attitude by physical or mental torture, or conditioning, and reward a "right" statement or attitude by granting some desirable privilege. The first objective is to produce prisoners free from visible signs of torture and so conditioned that they will profess the ideas of their captors in a convincing manner and in an apparently uncontrolled situation. The ultimate objective is to condition the prisoners so thoroughly that they come to believe the ideas dictated to them and to act in accordance with the dictated ideas even after their release. Brainwashing is a form of coercion, because it is dependent upon the complete physical control of the subjects for an indefinite period of time.

A knowledge of argumentation is a basic factor in the administration of brainwashing, for those who administer it seek to convince prisoners by logical and pseudo-logical argument. Endless pressures are designed to condition the prisoners to believe that their side is "logically" wrong and that the captors' side is "logically" right.

The same kind of knowledge may be a defense against brainwashing, in that prisoners can detect the false evidence and invalid reasoning of their captors and thus may prove to be unprofitable subjects. In the cases of prominent persons, however, when a totalitarian state has found it profitable to make extraordinary efforts, even well-educated persons have succumbed to brainwashing.

The decisions of the Supreme Court provide an interesting example of changed social attitudes toward coercion. Until relatively recent years it was accepted practice that the police could arrest a "known criminal," apply the "third degree," and extract a confession that would be admissible in court. As social attitudes toward "known criminals" and the "third degree" have changed, the Supreme Court has made it increasingly difficult for any confession—no matter how "voluntary"—to be admitted as evidence.

The demonstrations so prominent in the civil rights movements of the mid-1960s provide another example of changed social attitudes toward coercion. In the mid-1960s demonstrators, to enforce their demands, used the techniques of sit-ins, pray-ins, marches, and picketing by lying on the ground in front of construction equipment. The sit-in, for example, might be used to coerce the proprietor of a restaurant to serve blacks. The demonstrators would remain in the restaurant and refuse to leave until the proprietor yielded to their demands. A few years earlier, such demonstrators would have been arrested and hauled off to jail with little ceremony. By the mid-1960s, however, the social climate had changed and demonstrators could be moved only by forms of coercion—police dogs, cattle prods, or "police brutality"—which the general public no longer considered acceptable in these situations.

A different, and far less sympathetic, public reaction followed the violent riots of the late 1960s and early 1970s. When riots erupted in Watts, Hough, Detroit, Washington, and other urban areas, and when there was violence in the streets during the Democratic Convention and on the campuses of Columbia, San Francisco State, Harvard, Kent State, and other universities, the public responded to this sort of coercion by voting in increasing numbers for "law and order" candidates. Senator Margaret Chase Smith gave this sober warning:

> Extremism bent upon polarization of our people is increasingly forcing upon the American people the narrow choice between anarchy and repression.
> And make no mistake about it. If that narrow choice has to be made, the American people, even if with reluctance and misgiving, will choose repression.
> For an overwhelming majority of American people believe that:
> Trespass is trespass — whether on the campus or off.
> Violence is violence — whether on the campus or off.
> Arson is arson — whether on the campus or off.
> Killing is killing — whether on the campus or off.
> The campus cannot degenerate into a privileged sanctuary for obscenity, trespass, violence, arson, and killing, with special immunity for participants in such acts.
> Criminal acts, active or by negligence, cannot be condoned or excused because of panic, whether the offender be a policeman, a National Guardsman, a student, or one of us in this legislative body.[23]

VII. Combination of Methods

It is often necessary to use a combination of methods in reaching a decision to a problem. The social context will determine the methods most suitable for reaching decisions on a given problem.

The solution to a problem requiring the consent or cooperation of others may well extend over a considerable period of time and may require use of all the methods of decision making. For example, through *individual decision* a person may determine that "the pollution of streams in this state must be stopped."

Because that person is powerless to put a decision into effect alone, he or she must use *persuasion* to influence some friends and associates to join in the decision. They may use the process of *group discussion* to decide how to proceed toward their objective. They might conduct a *propaganda* campaign directed toward getting the Chamber of Commerce to support their decision; in turn, the Chamber of Commerce, as a result of parliamentary *debate,* might decide to support this decision.

As a result of further *group discussion* and *debate,* the Chamber of Commerce might decide to conduct a *propaganda* campaign directed toward the

---

[23] Speech in the Senate, June 1, 1970.

voters of the state. During this campaign many individuals might serve to *persuade* or *debate*. Eventually, a bill might be introduced into the state legislature.

After *discussion* in committee hearings and a number of *debates* on the floor of the legislature, there would be a final *debate* to determine the disposition of the bill. If enacted into law, *coercion* would be provided to insure compliance. The validity of the law would probably be tested by *debates* in the law courts to determine its constitutionality. In cases of violation of the law, *coercion* could be applied only as the result of *debates* in the law courts.

How do we reach a decision on this problem or on any other matter of importance? We are all under constant pressure to make nonrational decisions. Unquestionably many people often use nonrational means to make decisions. What is the method most likely to lead to a wise decision? Our only assurance of wise judgments is in the use of a rational approach. In many situations argumentation's emphasis on logical considerations and debate's confrontation of opposing sides give us our best or our only opportunity to reach rational conclusions. The point of view here is that it is in the public interest to promote debate and that it is in the intelligent self-interest of the individual to know the principles of argumentation and to be able to apply them in debate.

Exercises

1. List ten types of business or professional activities in which a knowledge of argumentation and debate would be an important asset. Explain why.

2. Can you find any significant business or professional activities in which a knowledge of argumentation and debate would not be an important asset? Explain why.

3. Prepare a brief paper in which you list recent examples of the following:
a. A debate in a campus organization to which you belong.
b. A group discussion in a campus organization to which you belong.
c. A persuasive speech which you have heard on campus.
d. Evidence of a propaganda campaign you have seen on campus.
e. Evidence of the use of coercion you have heard of on a campus.

4. Prepare a brief paper in which you list recent examples of the following:
a. An individual decision, apparently made after debate, on an important public matter.
b. A group discussion in which a decision of public importance was made.
c. A persuasive speech by a national figure on a matter of public importance.
d. A current propaganda campaign on a matter of national importance.
e. The use of coercion to enforce a decision on a matter of public importance.

5. Prepare for a class discussion on the question "How important was their debating ability to the careers of the 'Senate Immortals'?"

6. Prepare to participate in a class discussion in which you explain why you agree or disagree with one or more of the following statements:

a. Mill, as quoted on pages 2–3

b. Welch, as quoted on page 3

c. Lippmann, as quoted on page 4

d. Perelman, as quoted on page 4

e. Smith, as quoted on page 12

7. Prepare to participate in a class discussion on the following statements. What do you think prompted the speaker to make the statement? Do you agree with his view?

a. "If all my possessions and powers were to be taken from me with one exception, I would choose to keep the power of speech, for by it I could soon recover all the rest." —Daniel Webster

b. "The most valuable form of public speaking is debate." — William Jennings Bryan

c. "It seems to me that stronger than any other group, tougher in intellectual fiber, keener in intellectual interest, better equipped to battle with coming problems, are the college debaters." — Alexander Meiklejohn, late President of Amherst College

d. "The training I received in speech and debate has been more valuable to me than all the rest of my training put together." — William O'Neill, Chief Justice, Ohio Supreme Court

e. "I believe that training in debate should be a most valuable preparation for a career in business. Forty years in the business world certainly indicates to me that the ability to present a position clearly and forcefully, to detect the flaws or weaknesses in the presentation of an opposite position and rapidly decide how to bring these flaws or weaknesses to light and then counter them convincingly is of the utmost value to most businessmen. It is an ability which is essential in almost every form of negotiations, whether it be contract negotiations, labor negotiations, negotiations with Government agencies or representatives, or in fact any sort of negotiations. This ability is inherent in every successful salesman. It is essential in dealing with organizational matters in a person's own business. It is not too much to say that such ability—objectively applied to one's own personal problems—can spell the difference between personal success and failure." — M. J. Rathbone, former President, Standard Oil Company of New Jersey

f. "As I have remarked before, it seems to me that the mark of an educated man is an ability to think intelligently, to hold convictions, and to be able to speak clearly and persuasively on public issues. For this reason it is good to observe how many college students are interested in debating." — Nathan M. Pusey, former President, Harvard University

Chapter 2

Substantive and
Educational Debate

Debate may be classified into two broad categories: substantive and educational. *Substantive debate* is conducted on propositions in which the advocates have a special interest; the debate is presented before a judge or audience with power to render a binding decision on the proposition; and the purpose of the debate is to establish a fact, value, or policy. *Educational debate* is conducted on propositions in which the advocates usually have an academic interest; it is presented before a judge or audience usually without direct power to render a decision on the proposition — indeed, in educational debate the judge is instructed to disregard the merits of the proposition and to render the decision on the merits of the debate; and the purpose of the debate is to provide educational opportunities for the participants.

I. Substantive Debate

Substantive debate may be classified as special debate, judicial debate, parliamentary debate, and nonformal debate. This chapter will consider each of these classifications of debate briefly; educational debate will then be considered in more detail.

A. Special Debate

Special debate is conducted under special rules drafted for a specific occasion. Perhaps the best-known examples are the Lincoln-Douglas debates of 1858 and the Kennedy-Nixon debates of 1960. These were formal debates; yet they were neither judicial nor parliamentary, and they were conducted under special rules agreed upon by the debaters. Although this type of debate is most frequently associated with political figures and campaign issues, it may be used by anyone on any proposition; it merely requires the agreement of opposing advocates to come together under the provisions of a special set of rules drafted for the occasion. The televised debate of the House Judiciary Committee on the impeachment of President Nixon occupies a unique place in American history. Conducted under the special rules of the committee, the debate lasted for six days and nights on network television and was seen by more people than any other Congressional debate in history.

It served to educate the public not only on the facts of the case but also on such vital but unfamiliar concepts as what is impeachment and what is the burden of proof in an impeachment case. Ten days after the committee voted articles of impeachment, Nixon took the unprecedented step of resigning from the Presidency.

B. Judicial Debate

Judicial debate is conducted in the law courts or before quasi-judicial bodies. It is conducted under the rules of a court of law and has as its purpose the prosecution or defense of individuals charged with violation of the law or the determination of issues of law alleged to be applicable to specific cases before the court.

Judicial debate may be observed in any law court from the Supreme Court of the United States to a local court. In its educational form, judicial debate (known as moot-court debate) is used by law schools as a method of preparing students for their later debates in court.

The principles of argumentation and debate apply to judicial debate. Since judicial debate is also very much concerned with sometimes highly technical rules of procedure—which may vary considerably from federal to state courts, from one state to another, and from one type of court to another within a given state—the specific methods of judicial debate are not considered here.

C. Parliamentary Debate

Parliamentary debate is conducted under the rules of parliamentary procedure. It has as its purpose the passage, amendment, or defeat of motions and resolutions that come before a parliamentary assembly.

The practice of parliamentary debate may be observed in the Senate or House of Representatives of the Congress, the legislatures of the several states, city councils, town governing bodies, and at the business meetings of various organizations, such as the national convention of a major political party or a meeting of a local fraternity chapter. In its educational form, parliamentary debate may be known as a model Congress, a model state legislature, a model United Nations Assembly, a mock political convention, or other similar designations.

The principles of argumentation and debate apply to parliamentary debate. The special provisions of parliamentary procedure that also apply to this type of debate are considered in Chapter 23.

D. Nonformal Debate

Nonformal debate is conducted without the formal rules found in special, judicial, parliamentary, and educational debate. This is the type of debate newspapers are usually referring to when they speak of the "foreign policy debate," "the farm problem debate," and other controversies that engage public interest. The term "nonformal" has no reference to the formality or informality of the occasion in which the debate may take place. A President's State of the Union Address—a very formal speech—may be a part of a nonformal debate; or a rap session in a college fraternity—a very informal situation—may also be part of a nonformal debate.

Examples may be found in national political campaigns, in community debates about pollution of water or a new school bond issue, in business debates about the policies of a corporation, in colleges on matters of educational policy or the allocation of the college budget, or in the contests for the various offices in student politics. On the family level, nonformal debates may revolve about such matters as who will have the car tonight or the choice of a college.

II. Educational Debate

Educational debate is conducted under the direction of an educational institution for the purpose of providing educational opportunities for its students. Most schools and colleges today conduct programs of educational debate; it is almost inevitable that every educated person at some time will be a participant in some form of debate. Clearly the question before us is not whether or not we will participate in debate—our participation as decision renderers or advocates is inevitable. The only question is whether our participation be effective. The purpose of educational debate is to enable us to become effective in this essential art.

Sometimes educational and substantive debate may overlap. As we saw earlier, the substantive special debate of the House Judiciary Committee also served an important educational function. The League of Women Voters and similar civic groups often schedule debates between candidates for public office. From the point of view of the sponsors, the debates are educational, for the purpose is to provide information for the voters. From the point of view of the participants, the purpose is to win votes.

A. Backgrounds of Educational Debate

A history of educational debate would fill many volumes. There are, however, a few salient facts we may consider here. The beginnings of debate are lost in the remote reaches of the earliest recorded history. Civilized man began debating at least 3,000 years ago: Chinese scholars conducted important philosophical debates during the Chou Dynasty (1122–255 B.C.). Homer's (c. 900 B.C.) epic poems, the *Iliad* and the *Odyssey*, contain speeches, which Quintilian cites as examples of the arts of legal pleading and deliberation, that may be regarded as embryonic debates. The *Rhetoric* of Aristotle (384–

322 B.C.) laid the foundation of argumentation and debate and is influential even to the present day.

Educational debate began at least 2,400 years ago when the scholar Protagoras of Abdera (481–411 B.C.), known as the father of debate, conducted debates among his students in Athens. Corax and Tisias founded one of the earliest schools of rhetoric, specializing in teaching debate so that students might plead their own cases in the law courts of ancient Sicily.

Debate flourished in the academies of the ancient world and in the medieval universities, where rhetoric was installed as one of the seven liberal arts. Perhaps the first intercollegiate debate in the English-speaking world took place in the early 1400s at Cambridge University between students of Oxford and Cambridge. The debating programs at British universities have long been a principal training ground for future members of Parliament.

Debating has been an important part of the American educational scene from the earliest times. Debating flourished in the colonial colleges; disputations were a required part of the curriculum, and debates were frequently a featured part of the commencement ceremonies. Almost all of the leaders of the Revolution and the early national period were able debaters, who had studied argumentation in the colonial colleges or in the innumerable community debating "societies," "lyceums," and "bees" that flourished throughout the land.

The New England town meeting established public debate on the widest possible base, and the tradition of debate moved westward with the pioneers. Lincoln's early training in the New Salem debate club was typical of his time. After the Civil War, the lyceum and lecture bureaus flourished, sending such great speakers as Wendell Phillips, William Lloyd Garrison, Susan B. Anthony, and Henry Ward Beecher on extensive tours. The ideas expounded by these and other speakers stirred up countless debates in thousands of communities. The Chautauqua movement, widely popular in the late 1800s and early 1900s, brought the great speakers of that day— William Jennings Bryan, William McKinley, Theodore Roosevelt, Robert La Follette, and others—to vast audiences and encouraged extensive public debate.

Intercollegiate debating began in the later part of the 1800s, and interscholastic debating followed soon after. In the early part of this century, however, intercollegiate debates were relatively rare events. Normally a college would schedule only a few intercollegiate debates during an academic year, and large audiences would assemble to watch the few students who were privileged to participate in these unusual events. Recognition of the value and importance of educational debate has increased steadily during this century, however. The Committee on Intercollegiate Debate and Discussion has identified over 1,100 colleges with reasonably active debate programs; and thousands of secondary schools also conduct educational debate programs. The American Forensic Association has identified well over 400 intercollegiate debate tournaments that are conducted annually. In contrast with the very limited number of intercollegiate debates at the turn of the century, many colleges today participate in 300 to 400 intercollegiate debates annually through tournaments. Developed in the 1920s, tournament debating became the dominant form of intercollegiate and interscholastic debating after World War II. Howe reports that there are college tournaments on every weekend from mid-September to late May (with the exception of the week including Christmas) and that on a busy weekend over 3,000 college students will be participating in tournaments.[1]

B. Organization of Educational Debate

Educational debate is by no means limited to the classroom and the argumentation course. Most colleges and schools conduct a program of educational debate through the organization of a debating team, which provides a means for students to obtain additional opportunities beyond the traditional course offerings. Academic credit is often given for participation in the debate program—a program usually open to any qualified undergraduate. The director of forensics conducts the program so as to provide training opportunities for students new to debate and maximum challenge for the more experienced students.

As the designation "director of forensics" suggests, most debating teams today have been broadened to include other forensic activities in addition to debate. *Forensics is an educational activity primarily concerned with using an argumentative perspective in examining problems and communicating with people.*[2] Although debating continues to form the still-expanding base of the forensic program, extemporaneous speaking, original oratory or persuasive speaking, discussion, speakers' bureaus, oral interpretation of literature, or almost any other form of speech activity may be included. *Forensic activities, from this perspective, are laboratories for helping students to understand and communicate various forms of argument more effectively in a variety of contexts to a variety of audiences.*[3]

Much of the important work of educational debate is carried on through the programs and publications of various associations. Some of these, with which the student should be familiar, include: the Speech Communication Association, an organization composed primarily of speech communication teachers and professors, and interested students, in American schools and colleges (this association includes a Division of Forensics); the American Forensic Association, an organization of directors of forensics in American schools and colleges; the Committee on Discussion and Debate Materials

---

[1] Jack H. Howe, *Intercollegiate Speech Tournament Results,* Vol. 13 (1974), p. 95. Privately published.

[2] This definition was adopted by the National Development Conference on Forensics at meetings in Sedalia, Colorado, 1974.

[3] Ibid.

and Interstate Cooperation of the National University Extension Association, an organization that facilitates and encourages secondary school forensics; and the various honorary organizations for which the outstanding debater may be selected. The honorary organizations include: Delta Sigma Rho–Tau Kappa Alpha and Pi Kappa Delta for colleges; Phi Rho Pi for junior colleges; and the National Forensic League and the National Catholic High School Forensic League for secondary schools. In addition to these national organizations, there are a large number of local, state, and regional associations. Names and addresses of the current officers of these associations may be found in the *Directory of the Speech Communication Association,* a publication available in most libraries.

C. Values of Educational Debate

Because debating is an ancient discipline that is thriving in modern educational institutions, it may be well to consider briefly some of the values of educational debate that are responsible for its increasing prominence on the educational scene. Although not all these values are unique to debate, the well-conducted educational debate program is an important means of attaining these values. Indeed, for many students it is the best or sometimes the only means of attaining full realization of these values.

1. Debate provides preparation for effective participation in a free society. Debate is an inherent condition of a free society. Our Constitution provides for freedom of speech. Our legislatures, our courts, and most of our private organizations conduct their business through the medium of debate. Because debate is so widespread at decision-making levels, the citizen's ability to vote intelligently or to use his or her right of free speech effectively is limited without a knowledge of debate. As we know from history, freedoms unused or used ineffectively are soon lost. Citizens educated in debate can have hopes of attaining truly effective participation in a free society (*see inset*).

2. Debate offers preparation for leadership. The American Telephone and Telegraph Company once defined executive ability in these words:

> The ability to state a goal and reach it—
> Through the efforts of other people—
> And satisfy those whose judgment must be respected—
> Under conditions of stress.

Business and industry are never able to find enough men and women with this ability, and this ability is developed by educational debate. Our society is in great need of articulate men and women trained in the logical analysis of problems, able to win the decision of others under competitive stress, and able to persuade others to make the necessary effort to implement the decision. Students who can fulfill these qualifications often rise to positions of leadership in college and in their business, professional, or civic undertakings after college.

A very high percentage of persons who have achieved leadership positions have had school or college debate experience, and they regard that experience as a significant factor in their attainment of those positions. A survey of 160 senators, congressmen, governors, Supreme Court justices, Cabinet members, and other leaders revealed that 100 of the leaders had high school or college debate experience. All of the 100 found their debate experience helpful in their careers, and 90 classified the experience as "greatly helpful" or "invaluable." Of the 60 who did not have debate experience, 26 expressed regret that they had not gone out for the debating team while in school or college.[4] President Kennedy said:

I think debating in high school and college a most valuable training whether for politics, the law, business, or for service on community committees such as the PTA

[4] For further details of the survey, see: "100 of 160 Leaders Began Careers as Student Debaters," *Freedom & Union*, November 1960, pp. 6–7.

American Forensic Association: Statement of Principles

Recognizing that the free interchange and objective evaluation of ideas through such forensic activities as public speaking, discussion, and debate are essential to the maintenance of a democratic society, the American Forensic Association herewith records this statement of principles, which it believes should govern academic training in these disciplines.

☐ We believe that forensic activity should create opportunities for intensive investigation of significant contemporary problems.

☐ We believe that forensic activity should promote the use of logical reasoning and the use of the best available evidence in dealing with these problems.

☐ We believe that forensic activity should develop the ability to select, arrange, and compose material clearly and effectively.

☐ We believe that forensic activity should train students in the sincere and persuasive presentation of this material to the appropriate audience.

☐ We believe that forensic activity should stimulate students to honest and original effort.

☐ We believe that interscholastic and intercollegiate competition should be used to motivate students to their best efforts in attaining these objectives.

☐ We further believe that forensic activities should be under the responsible direction of a qualified faculty member, whose duty it should be to maintain and support the above principles.

and the League of Women Voters. A good debater must not only study material in support of his own case, but he must also, of course, thoroughly analyze the expected arguments of his opponent.

The give and take of debating, the testing of ideas, is essential to democracy. I wish we had a good deal more debating in our educational institutions than we do now.[5]

President Johnson was a high school and college debater and was for a time a high school debate coach. After he reached the White House, he spoke of how valuable this experience had been in his career in government.

3. Debate offers training in argumentation. From classical times to the present, argumentation professors have found that debate is the best method of providing training in this discipline. Debate provides an unexcelled opportunity for students to apply the theories of argumentation under conditions designed to increase their knowledge and understanding of these theories and proficiency in their use. As an educational method, debate provides excellent motivation for learning, since the student has both the short-term goal of winning a decision or an award in a tournament and the long-term goal of increasing knowledge and ability. This combination of short-term and long-term motivations provides for an optimum learning situation. The constant evaluation of student achievement, in the form of decisions rendered on debates, provides frequent opportunities to encourage growth and progress and to detect and remedy misunderstandings or misapplications.

4. Debate provides for investigation and intensive analysis of significant contemporary problems. Thoughtful educators have long been concerned that students and the general public often have only a superficial knowledge of significant contemporary problems. In addition to acquiring a knowledge of the principles of argumentation, debaters also have the opportunity to investigate in depth and to analyze intensively the various significant contemporary problems that form the basis of the propositions under debate. In the course of a debating career, students will acquire a better than average knowledge of current problems, as well as skill in applying methods that will enable them to analyze critically the problems they will encounter in the future. As Baldwin points out, the true aim of rhetoric—the energizing of knowledge—is necessarily correlated with inquiry and with policy.[6] In debate, students learn both to acquire knowledge and to energize that knowledge.

5. Debate develops proficiency in critical thinking. Through study of argumentation and practice in debate, students participate in an educational

---

[5] *Ibid.* Reprinted by permission.

[6] See: Charles Sears Baldwin, *Medieval Rhetoric and Poetic* (New York: Macmillan Co., 1928), p. 3.

process specifically designed to develop their proficiency in critical thinking. Winston Brembeck investigated whether a college course in argumentation and debate, as taught at eleven different colleges, improved critical thinking scores on a standardized test and found that the argumentation students outgained the control students by a statistically significant amount. Ted R. Jackson found that the critical-thinking ability of 100 college debaters (in comparison with 147 nondebaters) improved by a statistically significant amount after one season of intercollegiate debating.[7] The debater learns to apply the principles of critical thinking not only to problems that emerge in the relative leisure and comfort of research or the briefing session but also to problems that arise in the stress of debate.

6. Debate is an integrator of knowledge. Educators are constantly searching for methods of synthesizing knowledge. Debate has long served as a means of achieving this goal. Baird comments: "Again the exponents of a synthesis of knowledge and the broader view of a problem can well take a leaf from the practical experience and method of the arguer and discussant. Almost any problem at which the debater works cuts across these fields of knowledge."[8] For example, in debating the proposition dealing with the problem of guaranteed annual wages, debaters must have at least a minimal acquaintance with the principles of argumentation, economics, political science, sociology, psychology, finance, business management, labor relations, government, history, and philosophy. They will, of course, learn the principles and details of these disciplines through the appropriate departments of the college or through independent study; however, through debate they can integrate their knowledge of these various problems and bring them to bear upon a significant contemporary problem. For many students debate is their first, and often their most intensive and valuable experience, in interdisciplinary studies.

7. Debate develops proficiency in purposeful inquiry. Debate is preceded by inquiry. Of necessity the debater must be well informed of all the relevant aspects of the problem to be debated. The extent to which debate motivates the student to undertake purposeful inquiry in the form of the study of significant contemporary problems, to apply the principles of critical thinking to those problems, and to integrate the knowledge acquired from various disciplines is suggested by a former college debater:

[In just six years] high school and college debaters were introduced to such vital and contemporary issues as compulsory arbitration of labor disputes, world govern-

---

[7] Both the Brembeck and the Jackson studies are reported in: Richard Huseman, Glen Ware, and Charles Gruner, "Critical Thinking, Reflective Thinking, and the Ability to Organize Ideas: A Multi-Variate Approach," *Journal of the American Forensic Association* Vol. 9 (Summer 1972), pp. 261–262.

[8] A. Craig Baird, "General Education and the Course in Argumentation," *The Gavel*, Vol. 38 (March 1956), p. 59. Reprinted by permission of Delta Sigma Rho.

ment, electoral college reforms, price and wage controls, FEPC, and tariff revision. Each of these big topics raised subsidiary, but equally important public questions.

Study and debate of such topics serves as an introduction to the social sciences for many undergraduates whose major studies are in the humanities or the sciences. My first reading in *Foreign Affairs, American Economic Review, American Political Science Review, The Annals,* law reviews, regional quarterlies, and other social science journals was in search of materials relevant to debate topics. I suspect that many an undergraduate relies on debating for his important contact with social science. . . .

While I do not mean to say that thoroughness can be measured by length, I think it interesting and significant that the volume of my and my colleague's research on FEPC and free trade was about equal to that which went into my master's thesis of two hundred thirty pages on a question of public law.[9]

The recognition of the necessity to conduct inquiry in sometimes unfamiliar fields, and the knowledge of principles that will make that inquiry purposeful and effective, will serve the student well in many of his later undertakings.

8. Debate emphasizes quality instruction. Debate is based on a close tutorial relationship between faculty and students. Concerned educators are worried about the implications of mass classes and impersonal teaching. The debate program provides an effective solution to this problem by providing a tutorial relationship between the faculty and the student. Most of the educational activity of the debate program is carried out in a tutorial situation where the Director of Forensics or one of the assistants works with the two members of the debate team as they plan their research, develop their affirmative case, and plan their negative strategies or with a group of four students after a practice debate as they critique the debate in-depth and plan for further improvement. As this tutorial relationship is rarely limited to one quarter or semester, and often extends over four years, it provides a valuable opportunity for a personal education in the all too often impersonal world of higher education.

9. Debate encourages student scholarship. Debate establishes high standards of research and scholarly achievement that are rarely equaled in undergraduate courses. Some students fear that the time spent on debate may have an adverse effect on their grades. Experience proves the contrary to be true. Intercollegiate debaters report that their work in debate is a significant factor in helping them write better exams, prepare better term papers, and obtain better results in graduate school admission examinations. This, of course, is the predictable result of the values considered in this section. The scholarly skills the debater develops through research, organization, and presentation and defense of a debate case are directly transferable to many areas of

---

[9] James Robinson, "A Recent Graduate Examines His Forensic Experience," *The Gavel,* Vol. 38 (March 1956), p. 62. Reprinted by permission of Delta Sigma Rho.

scholarly endeavor. Added to this is the challenge to do one's best that debate provides. In the classroom the professor typically makes "reasonable" assignments that the "average" student can fulfill. In intercollegiate debate the student's opponent is rarely "reasonable" or "average." As we recognize in point 7 above, good debaters will do far more research than a reasonable professor would ever assign for a term paper and will present it with far more skill, and defend it far more ably than would be required in a classroom report. Preparing for and participating in major tournaments can truly be a mind-expanding experience that gives students the incentive to work at the very maximum of their capabilities and enables them to discover their real potential.

Argumentation courses and participation in intercollegiate debate are traditional training grounds for pre-law students. In a study of 98 law school deans, Swanson found that 69.9 percent would advise pre-law students to take a course in argumentation, and 70.3 percent recommended participation in intercollegiate debate. The deans also indicated that pre-law students "needed training in the skills of public speaking" (81.9 percent), "practical experience in the use of research techniques" (84.2 percent), "training in the application of the principles of logical reasoning" (89.6 percent), and "training in the techniques of refutation and rebuttal" (75.8 percent).[10]

While such training and experience are of obvious value to the pre-law student, it is easy to see that they would be important assets in many areas of graduate study and business and professional endeavor.

10. Debate encourages mature judgment. Scholars in the field of general semantics tell us that many problems in human affairs result from the misevaluation and misunderstanding that come from considering complex problems in the context of a one- or two-valued orientation. Educational debate provides an opportunity for students to consider significant problems in the context of a multivalued orientation. They learn to look at a problem from many points of view. As debaters analyze the potential affirmative cases and the potential negative cases, including the possibility of negative counter plans, they begin to realize the complexity of most contemporary problems and to appreciate the worth of a multivalued orientation; as they debate both sides of a proposition under consideration, they learn not only that most problems of contemporary affairs have more than one side but also that even one side of a proposition embodies a considerable range of values.

Sometimes at the start of an academic year some debaters may, on the basis of a hastily formulated opinion, feel that only one side of a proposition is "right." After a few debates, however, such students usually request an assignment on the other side of the proposition. By the end of a year, in which they have debated on both sides of the proposition, they learn the

---

[10] From a paper by Don R. Swanson, "Debate As Preparation for Law: Law Deans' Reactions," presented at the Western Speech Communication Association convention, 1970.

value of suspending judgment until they have investigated and analyzed a reasonable amount of evidence and reasoning. The necessity of advocating one side of the proposition in a debate has also taught them that decisions may not be postponed indefinitely. When, at the end of the year, they finally formulate their personal position on the proposition, it may or may not be the same as it was at the start of the season; but this time it will be a position that they have reached after due consideration and that they can defend logically.

11. Debate develops courage. Debate helps students to develop courage by requiring them to formulate a case and defend it against strong opposition. In debate, students' cases will come under attack. Opponents may seem to be ten feet tall, to speak with the tongues of angels, and to think with the brains of genius. It would be easy to push the panic button, beat a disorderly retreat, and avoid the problems. They can't do this, however. The situation requires that they defend their position. They must have the courage of their convictions. They must discipline themselves, concentrate on the problem, organize thoughts, and present refutation. Well-prepared debaters find that they *can* defend their position, that their opponents are only human; they thus gain new confidence in themselves and in their ability to function in a competitive situation.

12. Debate encourages effective speech composition and delivery. Since composition and delivery of the debate speech are among the factors that determine the effectiveness of arguments, debaters are encouraged to select, arrange, and present their materials in accordance with the best principles of public speaking. Debating places a premium on extemporaneous delivery, requiring speakers to think on their feet. Typically, debaters will speak before many different audiences: a single judge in the preliminary round of a tournament, a group of businessmen at a service club, or a radio or TV audience. Each of these situations provides new challenges for students. Constant adaptation to the audience and to the speech situation develops flexibility and facility in thinking and speaking.

13. Debate develops social maturity. Debate provides an opportunity for the student to travel to different colleges and meet students and faculty members from various parts of the country. With the dawning of the jet age, many colleges developed continental debate programs, and it is by no means unusual for a team to participate in tournaments on the East Coast, the West Coast, the Deep South, the New England States, and many points in between in the course of a year. Previously there used to be Eastern, Midwestern, Southern, and Western cases and styles of debating. Now that debating is a continental activity these regional differences have largely disappeared. Association in both the businesslike atmosphere of the debate and the pleasantly informal social situations that accompany most debates and tournaments help students to acquire social amenities, poise, and assurance. Amid the competition of a tournament, they learn that they must accept victory or defeat gracefully and that they must respond courteously to the criticism of a judge regardless of the decision. The incidental educational benefit that comes from the opportunity of meeting professors from a number of different colleges in an informal social situation has significant value.

III. Ethical Standards for Debate

Because we use debate as a means of influencing human behavior, the mature, responsible advocate will be concerned with ethical standards for debate. The form of educational debate itself provides strong incentives for ethical conduct. Form alone, however, is not self-enforcing and the format of educational debate is frequently not available in substantive debate. The following may be regarded as minimum ethical standards for the responsible advocate:

1. He must know his subject; he must be thoroughly prepared; and he must base his case on the best available evidence and argument.

2. He must present facts and opinions accurately.

3. He must reveal the sources of his information.

4. He must welcome dissent and seek to maintain and promote debate as a means of rational decision making.[11]

There are, of course, scores of specific problems that arise in applying these ethical standards to the practice of educational debate. The responsible debater would, for example, reject as unethical any use of fabricated or distorted evidence. The responsible director of debate would refuse, as an unethical practice, to render a decision on an educational debate on any basis other than an honest and rational answer to the question "Which team did the better debating?" There are other problems where the decision is not so clear cut. There are honest differences of opinion within the forensic community as to whether certain practices should be considered ethical or unethical.[12] The surest guide to the debater and the director may be found in answering this question: "Am I more concerned with enduring ethical standards and educational objectives than with the short-term goal of winning a debate?" If the answer is an honest "yes," the decision about a particular practice will probably be an ethically sound one.

---

[11] For a thoughtful treatment of ethical standards for the teacher of speech, see: Karl R. Wallace, "An Ethical Basis of Communication," *Speech Teacher*, Vol. 4 (January 1955), pp. 1–9.

[12] For a more detailed treatment of some of the ethical problems of educational debate, see: Donald Klopf and James McCroskey, "Ethical Practices in Debate," *Journal of the American Forensic Association*, Vol. 1 (January 1964), pp. 13–16, and Stanley G. Rives, "Ethical Argumentation," *Journal of the American Forensic Association*, Vol. 1 (September 1964), pp. 79–85.

Exercises

1. Find an example of a special debate in a recent political campaign. Prepare a brief report in which you describe the procedures used by the debaters.

2. Attend a court trial. Prepare a brief report in which you describe the judicial debate. How was it similar to educational debate? How different?

3. Analyze a nonformal debate currently in the news. Prepare a brief report in which you identify the leading debaters on each side and the principal issues of the debate.

4. Prepare a brief report on the history of educational debate at your college. By special arrangement with your instructor, you may present a longer report on this subject as a term paper.

5. Find a recent article on the values of debate in the publications of the speech associations or forensic honoraries. (Your instructor will give you the names of the publications available in your library.) Prepare a brief report on the article.

6. Prepare a five-minute speech, suitable for presentation at a freshman orientation program at your college, in which you set forth the values of educational debate.

7. Prepare a history of the educational debate program at your college. If this project involves significant research, your instructor may grant extra credit.

Chapter 3

Stating the Problem

Problems, to be considered intelligently, must be clearly stated. Vague understanding results in vague "solutions." A man disturbed by the problem of inflation might say, "Mortgage rates are too high—everything is too expensive," and arrive at an unprofitable "solution," such as "We ought to do something about this." But if a precise question is posed—such as "What can be done to curb inflation?"—then a profitable area of discussion is opened up. One or more solutions can be phrased in the form of debate propositions, motions for parliamentary debate, or bills for legislative assemblies.

The statement "Resolved: That the federal government should adopt a program of compulsory wage and price controls" clearly identifies one of the possible ways of dealing with inflation in a form suitable for debate.

I. Defining the Problem

In order to have a profitable debate, the basis for argument must be clearly defined. If we merely talk about "dissent," "abortion," or "them," we are likely to have a rap session, providing a pleasant way to spend a few hours but not affording the most profitable basis for argument. For example, the statement "Resolved: That the pen is mightier than the sword" fails to provide a basis for argument. If this statement means that the written word is for some purposes more effective than physical force, we can identify a problem area: the comparative effectiveness of writing or physical force for a specific purpose.

Although we now have a general subject, we have not yet stated a problem. It is still too broad, too loosely stated to promote well-organized argument. What sort of writing are we concerned with—poems, novels, government documents, or what? What does "effectiveness" mean in this context? What kind of physical force—fists, dueling swords, military occupation, hydrogen bombs, or what? A more specific question might be "Would a mutual defense treaty or a visit by our fleet be more effective in assuring Lower Slobbovia of our support in a certain crisis?" The basis for argument could be phrased in a debate proposition such as "Resolved: That the United States should enter into a mutual defense treaty with Lower Slobbovia." Negative advocates might oppose this proposition by arguing that fleet maneuvers would be a better solution.

II. Phrasing the Debate Proposition

In argumentation and debate the term *proposition* means a *statement of judgment that identifies the issues in controversy.* The advocate desires to have others accept or reject the proposition. Debate provides for organized argument *for* and *against* the proposition: those arguing in favor of the proposition present the affirmative side; those arguing against it, the negative side. To promote intelligent and effective argumentation, a debate proposition must have certain characteristics.

A. Controversy

Debate is a means of settling differences. Therefore, there must be a difference of opinion or a conflict of interest before there can be a debate. If everyone is in agreement on a fact, or value, or policy, there is no need for debate; the matter can be settled by unanimous consent. Thus it is pointless to attempt to debate "Resolved: That two plus two equals four" — there is simply no controversy about this statement. Controversy is an essential prerequisite of debate.

B. One Central Idea

If a proposition contains more than one central idea, it may lead to needless confusion. Consider the proposition "Resolved: That the Circle K Club should hold a tobogganathon on the weekend of February 1 and 2 and donate the proceeds to the American Cancer Society." There are two subjects for argument here — the most advantageous date for the tobogganathon and the most worthy recipient for the proceeds. Some might favor the proposed date, but want to use the money for the Heart Fund; others might favor a different date, but support the American Cancer Society. Two such central ideas should be placed in separate propositions and debated separately.

C. Neutral Terms

The proposition should be stated in impartial terms. It should not include emotional language giving special advantage to the affirmative or the negative. Consider the proposition "Resolved: That cruel, sadistic experimenters should be forbidden to torture defenseless animals pointlessly." The heavily loaded emotional language gives the affirmative an unreasonable advantage. "Resolved: That vivisection should be illegal" states the proposition in neutral terms. Although emotionally loaded terms have persuasive value, they have no place in a debate proposition.

"Resolved: That everyone should have the right to work" places an almost impossible burden on the negative — who can oppose the right to work? "Resolved: That the requirement of membership in a labor organization as a condition of employment should be illegal" states the problem in neutral terms. The wording of the proposition must be such that reasonable participants on either side will accept it as accurately describing the problem to be debated.

D. Precise Statement of the Affirmative's Desired Decision

The proposition should represent a statement of the decision the affirmative desires. It should set forth the decision clearly and precisely so that, if adopted, the affirmative advocates will have achieved their purpose. The proposition "Resolved: That the power of the federal government should be increased" is vague and indefinite. If the affirmative should win a debate on such a proposition, what would they have won? Actually nothing. Once it was agreed that the powers of the federal government should be increased, it would be necessary to proceed to another debate on the specific power in question. People who might favor increasing the power of the federal government by allowing it to make military appropriations for three, rather than two, years might well oppose an increase in the power of the federal government that would allow it to abolish the states.

A proposition such as "Resolved: That the President of the United States should be permitted to veto individual items in appropriation bills" states a specific decision clearly. The phrasing of the proposition must be clear, specific, devoid of ambiguous terms, and precise in the statement of the desired decision.

Although the decision desired by the affirmative must be stated with precision, the proposition sometimes allows the affirmative considerable latitude in its analysis of the status quo and permits the option of several plans in implementing that decision. For example, in debating the proposition "Resolved: That the federal government should grant annually a specific percentage of its income tax revenue to the state governments" indicated the plan to be used, but allowed the affirmative considerable latitude in its analysis of the status quo and in developing the details within the plan. Thus some affirmatives called for the plan to improve the financing of general state and local services, while others focused on such specific problems as improved financing of the administration of criminal justice, mental health, or health care generally, while still others developed a quite different analysis and called for adopting the proposition as a means of checking the power of the military-industrial complex.

Such "open-ended" propositions realistically reflect the fact that different persons may support one policy for a variety of reasons. As the saying goes, "Politics makes strange bedfellows," and in substantive debate we often find unlikely combinations of legislators supporting a bill for widely different reasons.

The statement of the proposition must be affirmative in both form and intent. The proposition "Resolved: That the United States should not give direct economic aid to foreign countries" is in negative form. The use of negative phrasing would violate sound debate practice, since it would confuse the audience and needlessly complicate the problem of the advocates in presenting their cases.

The proposition "Resolved: That the jury system should be abolished" is negative in its intent. The flaw here is that the proposition represents an interim goal and does not provide a clear and precise statement of the decision desired by the affirmative. If the jury system were abolished — and nothing provided in its place, all accused criminals would go free as there would be no means of trying them. The proposition "Resolved: That juries should be replaced by a panel of three judges" represents a statement of a decision some affirmatives might advocate.

E. Presumption and Burden of Proof Placed

The proposition must be so stated as to place the burden of proof on the affirmative. The presumption favors the status quo.

Phrasing the Proposition for Educational Debate

The additional requirements for propositions used in educational debate are as follows:

Significant Contemporary Problem In choosing a problem for educational debate, directors of forensics seek not only a well-phrased proposition but one that will provide an opportunity for exploring a significant problem of current interest to students, judges, and audiences. Since the topic should be one on which information is readily available, national debate propositions deal with matters of current national or international concern. Educators also seek a problem that will remain in the news during the academic year so that the topic will remain challenging and the debaters can continue to find new evidence and argument.

When "right-to-work" laws were the subject of a national debate proposition, the educators who chose that problem expected that neither Congress nor the majority of the states would enact "right-to-work" legislation during the time the proposition was being debated. Had such laws been enacted, the status quo in the field of labor legislation would have changed and the debate proposition would have required rephrasing. Even on such a rephrased proposition, debates would have been anti-climactic.

Sometimes the status quo may change dramatically and require substantial changes in affirmative cases without necessitating a change in the proposition. During the academic year in which the proposition concerning "federal control of the supply and utilization of energy" was debated, there were a number of such changes. Early in the season some affirmative teams argued "the Arab nations might embargo

In addition to the criteria for any debate proposition considered here, there are certain additional requirements for a proposition to be used in educational debate. (*See inset.*)

III. Presumption and Burden of Proof

The concepts of "presumption" and "burden of proof" are more easily understood through another term often used in connection with them — *status quo*.

Status quo means the existing state of things. At one time capital punishment was legal in the United States. It was the *status quo*. Then the Supreme Court ruled the existing capital punishment statutes unconstitutional. The *status quo* then became one of no capital punishment. Subsequently, some states have begun to enact new capital punishment laws designed to meet the Supreme Court's requirements. If these laws are upheld, the *status quo* would then change to permit capital punishment under certain circumstances in certain states.

---

oil." Negative teams confidently denied this possibility; but the Arabs did in fact embargo oil early in the season. Some affirmative teams then argued for gas rationing as the only means of dealing with the oil embargo. As the academic year went on, however, it became apparent that, although some states imposed limitations on gas sales, no federal rationing program was deemed necessary. During that year many teams found it necessary to redraft their affirmative cases for almost every tournament, for the status quo changed repeatedly as new policies became operative or as new evidence became available.

Equal Conflicting Evidence and Reasoning In substantive debates the evidence and reasoning may strongly favor one side. In the law courts, attorneys may defend clients when the evidence against them is almost overwhelming. In the legislative assembly, the minority leader may fight for an almost hopeless cause. In educational debate, however, the objective is not to secure, or prevent, the adoption of a proposition. Rather, it is to use the proposition to provide opportunities to learn about argumentation and debate, as well as about the subject itself. For educational purposes, preference is given to propositions that give both sides an approximately equal opportunity to build a strong case.

Single Declarative Sentence In the interests of clarity, and because of the limited amount of time available, educational debate propositions are limited to a single declarative sentence. In substantive debates, the proposition may be as long as necessary; for instance, a bill in Congress is a specialized form of debate proposition and may extend for many printed pages.

The concept of "presumption" assumes that the policy in effect at the present time will continue in effect; the value accepted at the present time will continue to be accepted; and what is acknowledged to be fact at the present time will continue to be accepted as fact. *Presumption* favors the status quo. The existing state of affairs will continue until good and sufficient reason can be given for changing it.

Now that brings us to "burden of proof." The "burden of proof" is the risk of the proposition. It is the obligation of advocates who affirm the proposition to prove their case. They must provide good and sufficient reason for adopting the proposition and must convince those who render the decision. If they do not carry the burden of proof, they will lose all that they hoped to gain were the proposition adopted.

Let us now look at a few examples to see how these concepts operate. The concept of presumption does not mean that the present policy is the best possible policy, or even that it is a good policy. It merely indicates that *the established policy is the status quo. It is in effect, and it will continue in effect until changed—until someone presents good and sufficient reason for changing it.* The same concept applies to any *presently accepted* value or fact.

The intensity with which a presumption favors the status quo may vary enormously. Whately points out: "A presumption evidently admits of various degrees of strength, from the very faintest, up to a complete and confident acquiescence."[1]

[1] Richard Whately, *Elements of Rhetoric* (New York: Sheldon & Co., 1872), p. 145.

Choosing the Proposition for Educational Debate

Each year a national intercollegiate debate proposition is chosen for use by colleges and universities throughout the United States. The vast majority of all intercollegiate debates are conducted on this proposition. Colleges, of course, may debate any proposition they wish, and some debate several propositions in the course of a year. The growth of tournament debating and the expansion in the number of intercollegiate debates scheduled by colleges, however, makes the use of a national debate proposition indispensable. Many college teams today schedule well over three hundred debates each year. If the students attempted to debate a different proposition each time, or even if they attempted to debate a number of different propositions, they would acquire considerable experience in research methods but very limited experience in sound debating. The first few educational debates on a new proposition are often tentative and experimental. After a number of debates on a proposition, the learning situation is far more profitable.

Since most educational debating is on a national intercollegiate debate proposition, it is well to know how such propositions are chosen. The care devoted to the selection of these propositions suggests something of the care that the individual should exercise in phrasing propositions for his own use.

The status quo may be passionately defended by devoted supporters or it may remain in existence merely through inertia. For example, there is a presumption favoring the Constitution as it exists at any given time. People would give their lives to preserve some portions of the Constitution unchanged; yet they would willingly enough agree to changes in other portions of the Constitution if only someone else would do the necessary work.

The proponents of prohibition had to conduct a hard-fought, century-long campaign to change the status quo by securing the passage of the Eighteenth Amendment. The presumption then changed, and it required another hard-fought campaign (lasting thirteen years) before the status quo was again changed with the passage of the Twenty-first Amendment. Prohibition and its repeal were major issues of political campaigns for many years; and the status quo could be changed only with the greatest effort.

On the other hand, there was little intensity of support for the one-time status quo that Congress should convene on the first Monday in December and that the President should begin his term on March 4. The dates were obviously arbitrary, but they seemed convenient enough. No one really supported them, no one really opposed them, and so they remained in effect for over a century. In 1932, when the evils of the lame-duck session were pointed out along with the advantages of having Congress convene and the President take office in January, Congress passed the Twentieth Amendment almost without opposition, and the states ratified it unanimously in less than a year.

Is the present immigration policy of the United States good or bad? Good

---

The national intercollegiate debate proposition is published by the Committee on Intercollegiate Debate and Discussion. Members of the committee are representatives of Delta Sigma Rho–Tau Kappa Alpha, Phi Rho Pi, and Pi Kappa Delta (the national forensic honorary organizations), the American Forensic Association, and the Speech Communication Association. Each year the committee asks the directors of forensics in colleges and universities to recommend potential propositions suitable for educational debate for the next year. After careful study and research the committee submits several propositions having the greatest potential as *national* propositions to a preferential ballot by the nation's directors of forensics. The proposition receiving the greatest preferential vote is announced as the national proposition. The national discussion question is chosen in the same manner and at the same time. The national high school debate proposition and discussion question are chosen by somewhat different procedures through the National University Extension Association Committee on Discussion and Debate Materials.

or bad, it is the status quo. It will continue in effect until those who believe it is bad can, by showing good and sufficient reason for changing it, convince a majority of the House and the Senate to agree to pass a new bill and convince the President to sign the bill, creating a new policy.

The concept of presumption is a vital part of our legal system. Did Richard Roe rob the Cook County National Bank? Our laws explicitly require that a man must be presumed innocent until proved guilty. The status quo is that Richard Roe is innocent, and the police department and the district attorney must convince a jury that he is guilty before he can be sentenced. (Unfortunately, this principle of law is sometimes distorted. The accused in a well-publicized case may have a "trial by news media" and be "proved guilty" in the minds of prospective jurors before the courtroom trial begins. British law is much stricter than American law in prohibiting pre-trial publicity of an accused.)

The lobbyist who would change our immigration policy has the burden of proof of convincing the House, the Senate, and the President. The district attorney who would convict Richard Roe has the burden of proof of convincing all of the jurors.

In some cases change may be inherent in the status quo. In such cases, there is a presumption in favor of *a* change, but *not* in favor of any *particular* change. A typical example may be found in the automobile industry. Most companies have a policy of making annual model changes. This is the status quo. Thus there is a presumption in favor of making *some sort* of a change next year. (Yet certain foreign auto manufacturers are known for their policy of not changing models annually — they have decided to buck the *status quo*.) But while new models come out each year, the designer advocating model X has the burden of proof to convince his company that model X is better than model Y or model Z or any other model under consideration.

Thus, when the status quo provides for a change or a change is inherent in the status quo, the advocates of a new policy or of a possible change have the burden of proof. In similar circumstances, the advocates of a new fact or a new value have the burden of proof.

The correctly stated debate proposition calls for a departure from the *status quo*. The affirmative thus has the *burden of proof*. Since the affirmative must carry the burden of proof, the question arises as to what amounts to satisfactory proof. The answer to this depends upon the rules governing the debate and the judgment of the person or group empowered to decide. As a minimum the affirmative must go more than half way in convincing those who render the decision. If 49 percent of the members of your club vote *for* a motion and 51 percent vote against it, the motion fails. If 50 percent vote for the motion and 50 percent against it, the motion fails unless the chair casts one additional vote *for* the motion.

In our law courts different standards prevail for the burden of proof in different circumstances. Before a grand jury, only "probable cause" need be proved to secure an indictment; in a criminal trial, the prosecutor must establish proof "beyond a reasonable doubt" to secure a guilty verdict; in a civil case, the verdict is based on a "preponderance of evidence." Outside the courtroom, reasonable persons usually apply this standard and base their decisions on important matters on a "preponderance of evidence."

In certain situations in parliamentary debate, the affirmative must obtain a two-thirds or a three-quarters majority to carry its burden of proof. In order to convict Richard Roe of robbing the Cook County National Bank, the prosecutor must convince 100 percent of the jury. If one juror is not convinced of Roe's guilt, he cannot be convicted.

If we want to obtain a new federal law, we must convince a majority of the House, a majority of the Senate, and the President. If the President vetoes the law, we must convince two-thirds of the House and two-thirds of the Senate. If the law is challenged in the courts, we may have to convince a majority of the Supreme Court of its constitutionality. This is the burden of proof we place on those who seek new federal legislation.

A tie is thus impossible in debate. The affirmative either carries its burden of proof or it does not. Even in a debate with one judge, a common situation in educational debate, a tie is impossible. If the judge discerns that both teams have done an equal job, he or she must render a decision for the negative because the affirmative has failed to carry its burden of proof. Reasonable people follow this principle in making individual decisions. If the arguments pro and con on a matter are equal — if they just cannot make up their minds — they tend to continue with the status quo. They require that a new proposal provide at least some advantage over the status quo before they will bother changing their usual way of doing things.

Note that there is a distinction between *the* burden of proof and *a* burden of proof. *The* burden of proof always rests on the affirmative; it must prove that the proposition should be adopted. However, *a* burden of proof may rest on either the affirmative or the negative. Whoever introduces an issue or a contention into the debate has *a* burden of proof. The advocate must support the argument he introduces. During a trial, for example, the prosecution may allege that Richard Roe committed a robbery in Chicago. Richard Roe may claim that he was in New York at the time of the robbery. Richard Roe now has assumed a burden of proof; he must prove his alibi.

Either side may have a *burden of refutation.* A burden of refutation rests on advocates whose case is weakened by an argument advanced by their opponent. They must refute that argument or suffer damage to their case. In Richard Roe's case, if Roe introduces evidence to establish that he was in New York at the time of the robbery, the prosecution has a burden of refutation. The Chicago district attorney must refute that evidence or Richard Roe will go free.

IV. The Prima Facie Case

The minimum burden of the affirmative is the necessity of establishing a *prima facie case.* The prima facie case is defined as one which in and of itself establishes good and sufficient reason for adopting the proposition. It must be both structurally and qualitatively strong enough to be logically self-sufficient—unless it is successfully refuted or weakened.

The requirements of a prima facie case in courtroom debates are usually explicitly stated in the law. Let us return once more to the case of Richard Roe. The prosecution has charged that Roe committed a robbery in Chicago. Since the defendant is presumed innocent, the prosecution must prove, among other things, that the defendant was in Chicago when the robbery took place. If the prosecution does not prove that Roe was in Chicago, it has not established a prima facie case and the case may be dismissed for lack of evidence.

In debating outside the courtroom, there are no fixed rules defining a prima facie case. It is not necessary to satisfy the sometimes rather technical requirements of legal debate. It is necessary, however, to satisfy the logical requirements of a case strong enough to convince reasonable people unless that case is refuted. In an early season educational debate on the proposition "Resolved: That the requirement of membership in a labor organization as a condition of employment should be illegal," an affirmative team established with irrefutable evidence that some unions were corrupt and then urged the adoption of "right-to-work" laws. This was not a prima facie case, because this particular affirmative team did not demonstrate that a "right-to-work" law would solve the problems of corruption that they had raised. Later in the season the same affirmative team modified their case and did not advocate "right-to-work" laws as a solution to corruption. Instead they advocated "right-to-work" laws as a means of protecting the individual worker from compulsory support of corrupt activities. This, together with the introduction of other issues, enabled them to present a prima facie case. Unless the affirmative team establishes a prima facie case, they cannot logically win a debate.

It is not enough to present merely the *structure* of a prima facie case. If the affirmative is using a needs analysis case, it is not sufficient to present merely arguments suggesting need, plan, and advantages. Rather, they must continue and support these issues with enough evidence and analysis to make the case qualitively strong enough to overcome the presumption.

The prima facie case must, of course, be *propositional*. It must stem directly from the proposition and also give good and sufficient reason for adopting the proposition. It is not sufficient to give reasons for adopting part of the proposition or to claim advantages for the proposition which could be achieved in other ways.[2] Actually the negative need not even reply until the affirmative has established a prima facie case. In most debates, however, the affirmative will present either a prima facie case or a case that comes close to being one. Therefore, the prudent negative advocate is well advised to be prepared to refute any case that may appear to the average audience to be a prima facie case.

[2] See Chapter 16 on "Attack Propositionality."

In some situations the requirement that the affirmative present a prima facie case may be waived. In nonformal or special debates[3] the negative may choose to answer an argument before it is fully established, or the participants may choose to focus on only one or two issues, even though additional issues would be necessary to establish the affirmative's case logically. Student debaters appearing on radio or television or before a service club may find themselves confronted with sharply reduced time limits and agree to limit the debate to only the need issues or to clash only on the plan-advantages versus plan-disadvantages arguments. In similar fashion political speakers appearing in campaign debates may agree that a particular debate shall be limited to "the land-use issue" or "the Middle East issue."

In educational debate, except by mutual consent in the type of situation just described, the presence of a well-prepared negative and a qualified judge will force the affirmative to present a prima facie case or face defeat. In substantive debate on important matters the mature adult will require that a prima facie case be presented as the basis for rational decision.

V. Types of Debate Propositions

Debate propositions may deal with decisions of *fact, value,* or *policy.*

A. Propositions of Fact

In a debate on a proposition of fact, the affirmative maintains that a certain thing is true, while the negative maintains that it is false. Our law courts are almost entirely concerned with propositions of fact. Typical propositions of legal debates are, in effect, "Resolved: That John Doe is guilty of murder," or "Resolved: That this is the last will and testament of Sam Smith," or "Resolved: That the plaintiff's constitutional rights were violated in this trial." Typical debates on propositions of fact, outside the courtroom, would include "Resolved: That some labor unions are corrupt" or "Resolved: That direct economic aid to foreign countries serves the national interest of the United States."

B. Propositions of Value

In a debate on a proposition of value, the affirmative maintains that a certain thing is good, beneficial, proper, virtuous, or admirable, while the negative maintains either that the same thing is undesirable or that something else is better. One long-lived debate in the United States centered about the proposition "Resolved: That it is immoral for the United States to wage war

---

[3] See Chapter 2 on "Substantive Debate."

in Vietnam." A bitter United Nations debate focused on the proposition "Resolved: That the terrorist activities of the Palestine Liberation Organization are morally justified." Other typical propositions of value are "Resolved: That it is morally unjustifiable to require a man to join a corrupt labor organization as a condition of employment" or "Resolved: That preemptive war is justifiable."

C. Propositions of Policy

In a debate on a proposition of policy, the affirmative maintains that a policy or course of action should be adopted, while the negative maintains that this policy should be rejected. Most debates in legislative assemblies are on propositions of policy. Typical debates in Congress, state legislatures, and city councils are, in effect, "Resolved: That the proposed tax bill should be enacted" or "Resolved: That the Senate does advise and consent to the nomination of Joseph Doakes as Ambassador to France." In private organizations as well, most debates are on propositions of policy: "Resolved: That the Speech Communication Association should hold its annual convention in Chicago," or "Resolved: That Compact Motors, Inc., should pay a quarterly dividend of fifty cents per share of common stock," or "Resolved: That more coed dormitories should be established on this campus."

Educational debates are conducted almost exclusively on propositions of policy. In such debates propositions of fact and of value often arise as important contentions. In debates on the proposition of policy "Resolved: That the requirement of membership in a labor organization as a condition of employment should be illegal," it was sometimes necessary to debate as essential subpropositions "Resolved: That some labor unions are corrupt" (a proposition of fact) and "Resolved: That it is morally unjustifiable to require a man to join a corrupt labor organization as a condition of employment" (a proposition of value).

Exercises

1. Examine the following "propositions." Which are well phrased? Which violate the criteria of a well-phrased proposition? What criteria do they violate? Rephrase the incorrect propositions so that they meet the requirements for educational debate.

a. Inadequate parking facilities on campus

b. The threat of communism today

c. Should our college abandon intercollegiate athletics?

d. The present method of electing the President of the United States should be improved

e. The United States should reject a system of socialized medicine

f. The federal income-tax rate should be limited to a maximum of 25 percent, and labor unions should be subject to the antitrust laws

g. College entrance requirements should be stricter

h. A federal world government should be established

i. Washington was a greater President than Lincoln

j. The present agricultural price support program is beneficial to the American people

2. Phrase one proposition of fact, one of value, and one of policy in each of the following areas:

a. Federal agricultural programs

b. Labor-management relations

c. Federal fiscal policies

d. United States foreign policy

e. A current campus problem

3. From the newspapers, newsmagazines, radio and television broadcasts of the past week, discover what problems are currently being debated in Congress or in the nation. Phrase propositions of fact, value, and policy on five problems currently being debated nationally. Phrase these fifteen propositions in a manner suitable for educational debate.

4. Prepare a five-minute speech for delivery in class in which you state a proposition of policy and demonstrate how it meets the criteria for a well-phrased proposition for educational debate.

Chapter 1

Analyzing the Problem

The proposition for debate may be formulated by one of the advocates in the debate, by agreement between the opposing advocates, or by someone other than the actual advocates. If a student at a business meeting of a college organization introduces a motion, "Resolved: That the dues of this organization should be increased five dollars a semester," he or she is formulating a proposition for debate. Before Lincoln and Douglas held their famous debates, they agreed on the propositions they would use when they met. Frequently, an attorney first learns of the proposition to be debated in a court case when retained by a client.

Regardless of how the proposition is chosen, our first task as advocates is to analyze the proposition and the total problem area from which it is derived. We must define the terms of the proposition and discover the issues involved. Analysis of the proposition's relationship to a problem area may reveal further terms that require definition and that will aid in the development of issues.

I. The Importance of Defining Terms

The *prompt definition of terms* is essential to a profitable debate. In educational debate the first affirmative speaker should present the team's definitions early in the first speech. The first negative speaker must then either accept these definitions or present the negative's definitions and provide reasons for believing them to be superior. If the plan is presented in the first affirmative speech, the debater may find it convenient to define the terms operationally with the presentation of the plan. In any debate an early definition of terms is necessary in order to permit the debate to proceed to the essential issues.

Many emotion-charged arguments about abortion never become intelligent debates because of the inability of the participants to agree on a definition of life. Physicians, clergymen, and ethicists have never been able to agree on the point at which human life begins. Does it start — at conception, when the fetus becomes capable of survival outside the womb, when brain life begins, or at the moment of birth?

Exactly the opposite problem has clouded the debate over the use of transplants. When does death occur—when breathing stops, when the heart stops, or when the brain ceases to function?

Virtually all of us are, or will be, affected by the provisions of the Employee Retirement Income Security Act passed in 1974. The law now requires pension-fund fiduciaries to invest *prudently* and *diversify* their investments. Wise objectives surely—but *the law does not define these crucial terms.* Thus the ability of your parents—and later you—to collect retirement funds may well hinge on future debates in the law courts, where the definitions of these terms in the context of this law will have to be hammered out.

It is easy to see that the definition of terms is often critical to the debate. If the participants in a debate have defined their terms carefully, the debate is likely to be a profitable one concerned with the real matters of contention; if not, the debate is likely to degenerate into a quibble and never get to the real issues.

Terms which do not actually occur in the proposition itself, but which an advocate expects to occur in the course of the debate, should also be defined. The words "cyclical," "frictional," and "hidden" did not appear in the proposition "Resolved: That the federal government should establish a national program of public work for the unemployed." Yet since references to these types of unemployment recurred in debates on the proposition, it was necessary for the debaters to define them.

In debates on this same proposition, dictionary definitions of the individual words "public" and "work" did little to provide a profitable explanation of the meaning of the proposition or to furnish a basis for argument. Advocates found it necessary to define the term "public work" rather than the individual words; and, by referring to the use of this phrase in legislation, they were able to provide a useful definition.

In analyzing the problem, advocates must carefully consider all possible definitions of all the terms. In presenting their cases, however, they will define only those terms that might be unfamiliar to their audience or about which they and their opponents might differ. In debating the proposition "Resolved: That Congress should be given the power to reverse decisions of the Supreme Court," it would probably be unnecessary to define "Congress" and "Supreme Court." It would be necessary, however, to define "reverse" and "decisions," since the legal usage of these terms is different from the popular usage, and opposing advocates sometimes differ in their interpretations of these words within the context of this proposition.

The terms of a debate proposition may be defined in a variety of ways. In order to make the basis of the argument explicit, advocates should choose the method or combination of methods best suited to the requirements of the proposition and to the interests of the audience. It is important to define terms carefully to avoid peripheral argument and to move to a profitable debate on the essential issues.

II. Methods of Defining Terms

A. Basic Methods

1. Example Giving an example is often an effective method of defining terms. In debates on the national program of public work proposition, affirmative teams sometimes defined terms by saying "By a national program of public work we mean a program similar to the WPA of the 1930s," thus giving their audiences a specific example of the type of program they proposed.

2. Common Usage In the interest of accuracy and precision, debate propositions must sometimes contain technical terms. Often these terms can be defined effectively by referring to common usage. In debates on the proposition "Resolved: That the requirement of membership in a labor organization as a condition of employment should be illegal," some affirmative teams defined an important term by saying "By 'labor organizations' we mean the type of organizations popularly referred to as unions." This reference to common usage usually served to establish a definition acceptable to both teams and clear to the audience. Although the word "unions" served well as a definition, it would not have been an acceptable term for use in the proposition. Many important "unions" operate under the legal title of "brotherhoods," "associations," "federations," or other names; and most important legislation regulating unions speaks of "labor organizations." Had the word "unions" been used in the proposition, it might have led to some pointless quibbles on whether or not such legislation would apply to organizations such as the Railroad Brotherhoods.

3. Authority Some terms may be defined most effectively by referring to an authority qualified to state the meaning and usage of the term. Dictionaries, encyclopedias, and books or articles by recognized scholars are often used as authority for a particular definition. In debates on nationalization of the basic nonagricultural industries, some debaters defined "nationalization" by quoting *Webster's Dictionary, Black's Law Dictionary,* or various encyclopedia articles. In debates on "tax sharing," advocates often defined "a specific percentage of federal income tax revenue" by quoting Walter Heller, who had done much of the basic writing on this subject, or other economists who had written about this problem or who had testified before Congressional committees.

4. Operation Some terms are best defined if the advocate provides an operational definition and explains the function or special purpose represented by the terms in a specific context. Debates on the proposition "Resolved: That the nonagricultural industries should guarantee their em-

ployees an annual wage" required careful definition of the term "guarantee
. . . an annual wage." Some affirmative advocates chose to provide an
operational definition, defining these terms by presenting their plan. One
debater said:

We propose a plan whereby the employer places the sum of five cents per employee
hour worked in a trust fund until that fund equals 50 percent of the average annual
payroll of that company for the past five years. When an employee is laid off, he may
then draw from his fund a sum equal to 75 percent of his average weekly pay for the
previous year less such state unemployment compensation as he may receive for 52
weeks or until he is rehired.

The use of operation as a method of definition is often linked with the
presentation of a plan and is a helpful way of explaining a complex matter.
The plan, of course, must be compatible with the context of the resolution —
not only the literal word context, but most importantly the "real world"
context in which the debate takes place. Many in the forensic community
were outraged when a team debating the proposition "Resolved: That the
federal government should adopt a program of compulsory wage and price
controls" proposed wage and price controls for migrant farm workers only.
The "real world" context was such that the entire country was facing a
serious problem of inflation and a few months later full scale wage and price
controls were actually instituted. Three years later the national debate proposition was "Resolved: That the powers of the Presidency should be significantly curtailed." While the literal word context might admit of plans to limit
the powers of the president of France, or of the president of International Telephone and Telegraph, the "real world" context — this proposition was debated in the academic year following Nixon's resignation — was such that the
forensic community, most reasonably, concentrated on debating the Presidency of the United States. In defining terms one must be aware of and adapt
to the contextual constraints reasonable men and women will impose on the
definitions.

5. Negation Sometimes a term may be defined effectively by indicating
what it does not mean. In debates on nationalization of basic industries,
some teams defined "basic industries" by combining negation with example,
saying "We do not mean the corner drugstore, we do not mean retail businesses, we do not mean service businesses; we mean steel, autos, transportation, mining, oil, and gas."

6. Comparison and Contrast Some terms may be best understood if they are
compared to something familiar to the audience or contrasted with something within the common experience of the audience. In debates on the
proposition "Resolved: That a federal world government should be established," students often defined "federal world government" by comparing

their proposed plan to the government of the United States. The method of contrast was used by advocates in debates on this same proposition when they said, "Unlike the United Nations, a federal world government would have the following powers . . ."

7. Derivation One of the standard methods of defining words is to trace their development from their original or radical elements. Thus, in a debate on fair employment practices, it would be possible to define the word "prejudice" by pointing out that the word derived from the Latin words "prae" and "judicium" meaning "before judgment." Definition by derivation has limited use in argumentation and debate, because the advocate is usually concerned with the contemporary usage of the word within a specific context.

8. Combination of Methods Since most propositions of debate contain several terms that must be defined, no one of the methods mentioned is likely to be satisfactory for the definition of all of the terms. If any term is particularly difficult to define, or if it is of critical importance in the debate, the advocate may find it desirable to use more than one method of definition in order to make the meaning clear.

B. Problems in Handling Unusual Definitions

Sometimes advocates offer unusual definitions—definitions that are not consistent with the expectations of the opposing advocates. The use of "trick" definitions to avoid the burden of proof, or to gain some advantage, is specifically *not recommended*. The advocate who has to resort to such tricks is usually quickly exposed and defeated by competent opposition. Not every unusual definition, however, should be regarded as a "trick" definition. The apparently unusual definition might be a perfectly reasonable one, and it might take the opposing advocates by surprise only because they had failed to do a thorough job of analyzing the proposition.

Two methods are available to advocates confronted with an unusual definition: (1) They may demonstrate, by using the methods of defining terms already discussed, that their definition of terms is a more reasonable one than that of their opponents. (2) They may accept the definition of terms offered by their opposition and proceed to attack the case presented by their opposition. An example of the latter method occurred in a debate on the proposition "Resolved: That the further development of nuclear weapons should be prohibited by international agreement." The affirmative, seeking to escape the burden of proof, defined "international agreement" as an agreement between any two nations and proposed that Andorra and San Marino should enter into a treaty prohibiting the further development of nuclear weapons. The competent negative meeting this case did not waste time crying "foul" or seeking to redefine terms. Rather, the negative accepted the affirmative's definition and pointed out that there was no need for such an agreement because both Andorra and San Marino lacked the capability of producing nuclear weapons; furthermore, they made clear that no advantages could result from the plan since Andorra and San Marino would be unable to force other nations to abide by their agreement.

Sometimes advocates offer a plan that is not related to or does not directly stem from the proposition or claim advantages that do not flow from adopting the resolution or that could be obtained without adopting the proposition. In such cases the negative should "attack propositionality" (see Chapter 14).

C. Problems of the Stipulated Definition

The terms of many debate propositions are subject to more than one reasonable and legitimate definition. As was noted in the discussion on "Phrasing the Proposition" (Chapter 3), some propositions give the affirmative considerable latitude in their analysis of the status quo and permit the option of several plans. In such cases it is the privilege of the affirmative to stipulate which legitimate definition of terms it will use, and the negative must debate on the basis of the definition elected by the affirmative. What, for example, is a "guaranteed annual wage"? A number of corporations have programs known by this name, and these programs differ greatly in important details. In debates on this proposition, the affirmative could reasonably advocate a program similar to any of those in existence, or it could advance a program of its own devising which approximated some existing programs.

There are a number of similar examples in recent intercollegiate debate propositions. In debates on "curtailing the power of the Presidency," some affirmatives stipulated they were concerned only with the power of the Presidency to control the office of the Attorney General or with Presidential control of the CIA. In debates on the "energy" proposition, some affirmatives stipulated that "energy" should be limited to nuclear power reactors or to coal produced through strip mining. In debates on "comprehensive medical care," some affirmatives stipulated the debate was concerned with catastrophic illnesses or with mandating the delivery of medical care through health maintenance organizations rather than the traditional delivery modes.

When the affirmative stipulates a reasonable definition, it is usually wisest for the negative to accept it and to proceed with the debate. If the affirmative has stipulated too limited a definition, the negative can usually demonstrate that the affirmative's plan is too limited to meet the needs cited by the affirmative or that its advantages are so limited that a change in the status quo is unnecessary.

In organized debates between students or individuals being trained in the practice of argumentation, it is the commonly accepted practice for the affirmative to offer its stipulated definition in the first affirmative speech; the negative must then accept or reject this definition in its first speech. In other debates, the definition of terms may be stipulated by agreement between the advocates or by some party or agency outside the debate. In debates in law courts, the definition of terms is frequently stipulated by legislation. When the Supreme Court ruled many state abortion laws unconstitutional, some indignant citizens mounted bumper stickers on their cars proclaiming "Abortion Is Murder." That statement has no standing in law, however. Abortion and murder are what the laws, as interpreted by the courts, define these terms to be. To convict anyone of murder, it is necessary to prove that his or her activities were consistent with the legal definition of murder.

Sometimes in political campaigns the definition of terms is deliberately confused. Politicians may accuse their opponents of favoring "left-wing" or "reactionary" programs, while avoiding any definition of these labels. Fortunately, in some instances, definitions become more clear as the campaign progresses.

D. The Meaning of "Should"

Most propositions on matters of policy contain the word "should"—for example, "Resolved: That such-and-such *should* be done." In a debate on a policy proposition, "should" means that intelligent self-interest, social welfare, or the national interest prompts this action, and that it is both desirable and workable. When the affirmative claims a policy "should" be adopted, it must show that the policy is practical—but it is under no obligation to show it *will* be adopted. The affirmative must give enough detail to show it would work. It may be impossible, within the time limitations of the debate, for the affirmative to give all the details, but it must at least show the outline of its policy and indicate how the details could be worked out. For example, in a debate on federal aid to education, the affirmative could not reasonably be expected to indicate how much money each state would receive under its plan, but it would be obliged to indicate the method by which the amount of the grants would be determined. It is pointless for the negative to seek to show that the affirmative's plan could not be adopted by demonstrating that public opinion is against it or that the supporters of the plan lack sufficient voting strength in Congress.

Public opinion and a majority of congressmen were opposed to the income tax at one time; yet, when the advocates of the income tax demonstrated that it *should* be adopted, the Sixteenth Amendment was enacted. In the same way it could be demonstrated that at a given time the Eighteenth, Nineteenth, Twenty-first, or Twenty-sixth Amendments of the Constitution could not possibly have been passed—too many people were opposed to prohibition, opposed to women's suffrage, opposed to the repeal of the

Eighteenth Amendment, opposed to lowering the voting age to eighteen —
yet all these amendments were passed after the advocates of these measures
won debates showing they *should* be adopted. Thus, in an educational debate on a policy proposition, *constitutionality is never an issue.* If the affirmative proves that a certain policy *should* be adopted, it has also proved that,
if necessary, the Constitution should be amended. In the same way, if the
affirmative's proposal is presently illegal or outside the scope of existing law,
it has, by showing that its proposal should be adopted, demonstrated that
the necessary enabling legislation should be enacted.

Thus the negative, in educational debate, cannot argue "Congress will
never pass the affirmative's plan" and proceed to prove that because of
attitudinal barriers, political interest, or for some other reason the affirmative
plan can never get enough votes to enact their proposal. The affirmative may
simply "fiat" their proposal and reply that Congress *should* enact the plan.
The affirmative need only demonstrate that its proposal ought to be adopted
and need not consider the political or attitudinal barriers that thus far have
prevented its enactment.

The negative must avoid the pointless, in educational debate, "should–
would" argument.[1] The point is not *would*—but *should*—the affirmative's
proposal be adopted. The negative may, of course, focus on the workability
of the policy and seek to demonstrate that a given policy, if adopted, would
not work or would produce significant disadvantages.

For example, in debating the "government control of the supply and
utilization of energy" proposition, the negative could not argue that Congress would not pass gasoline rationing because it was so unpopular with
members of Congress and their constituents. The affirmative could simply
"fiat" rationing, that is, argue that it *should* be passed. The negative could,
however, argue that because rationing was so unpopular it would not work;
that there would be widespread violations and black markets; that the system would break down; and thus that the affirmative could not achieve any
advantage.

The advocate must consider the question of *who* should. In debating
the higher education proposition, affirmative advocates are urging that "we,
the people of the United States," acting through our federal government,
should adopt a certain policy. They should seek to prove that such a policy
is in the national interest of the United States. Some affirmatives sought to
demonstrate that we in the United States would benefit from such a policy
because it would put us in a better position vis-à-vis the USSR. A policy that

---

[1] "Should–would" arguments may be of considerable importance in substantive debate. A
political leader might feel that a certain policy *should* be adopted but, recognizing that it would
be impossible to marshal sufficient support, decide not to make the fight for it, feeling it is
better to conserve energy and credibility for the possible. For example, some of President
Franklin D. Roosevelt's advisers urged that the United States *should* declare war on Germany
a year or so before Germany declared war on us. Roosevelt rejected such proposals, however, in
the no doubt accurate belief that Congress *would* not declare war at that time.

would put us ahead of the USSR in the space race, or the arms race, would be seen as a very real benefit by many Americans.

In debating the proposition "Resolved: That the further development of nuclear weapons should be prohibited by international agreement," affirmative advocates are urging that the nuclear powers and those nations with the capability of becoming nuclear powers should adopt a certain policy. Thus they would not seek to prove, for instance, that such a policy would place the United States in a better position vis-à-vis the USSR; this, of course, would be an excellent reason why the USSR should *not* enter into an international agreement. Rather, they would seek to demonstrate that the national interest of the United States, the USSR, and other powers coincided on this matter; that it would serve the vital interests of all nations to enter into such an agreement; and that all would derive advantages from it.

III. Issues

Issues are those critical claims *inherent* in the proposition that the affirmative must establish. The negative must defeat at least one issue in order to win. Issues may be readily recognized since they are claims with answers that *directly* prove or disprove the proposition. If the issues are established, then the proposition must prevail. As debaters begin analysis of the proposition, they phrase the issues as questions—"Did John Doe kill Richard Roe with malice?" Issues, in the analysis stage, are phrased in the form of questions to which the affirmative must answer *yes;* and the negative must answer *no* to at least one issue or there is no debate. When the issues are presented in a debate, the advocate phrases them as declarative sentences—"John Doe killed Richard Roe with malice."

Contentions are statements offered in support of an issue. Pertinent evidence is organized into cogent argument to support each contention. Usually several contentions are required to establish an issue. The affirmative may fail to establish several supporting contentions and still win its case, providing that the remaining contentions have enough probative force to establish the issue.

Potential issues are all the issues relevant to a particular proposition. In any given debate, however, it is unlikely that all the potential issues will be used. Time may preclude the consideration of all possible issues, or the negative may concede certain issues.

Admitted issues are those issues that the negative concedes or admits are true. For example, in debates on right-to-work laws, some affirmatives introduced the issue "Are some labor unions corrupt?" In view of the evidence the affirmative could produce to support this issue, some negative advocates admitted this issue and concentrated their attack on other issues they felt they had a better chance of defeating.

The *issues of the debate* are those issues on which the debate is actually conducted, that is, issues introduced into the debate on which the opposing advocates clash. For example, the potential issues on a certain proposition might be: A, B, C, D, E, F, G, H, I, and J. The affirmative might introduce issues A, B, C, D, and E. The negative might admit issues B and E, introduce issue F, and seek to refute issues A, C, D, and F. The potential issues G, H, I, and J were not introduced by either side and thus did not enter into the debate. The issues of this debate were: A, C, D, and F.

The *ultimate issue* is the one issue remaining in dispute. In some debates the clash may narrow down to one undecided issue, known as the ultimate issue. In the above example, the affirmative might win issues A, C, and D early in the debate, leaving only issue F in dispute.

Stock issues are standard questions that are applicable to almost any proposition. They will be discussed next.

A. Discovering the Issues

One of the first problems confronting the advocate in preparing to debate on a proposition is discovering the issues. In a courtroom debate, the issues are usually stated explicitly in the law applicable to the case before the court. For example, if the proposition before the court is, in effect, "Resolved: That John Doe murdered Richard Roe," in most jurisdictions the issues would be:

1. Is Richard Roe dead?
2. Did John Doe kill Richard Roe?
3. Did John Doe kill Richard Roe unlawfully?
4. Did John Doe kill Richard Roe following premeditation?
5. Did John Doe kill Richard Roe with malice?

If the prosecution fails to prove any one of these issues, John Doe cannot be convicted of murder; however, he might be convicted of manslaughter or some other lesser charge if some of the issues were proved.

In debates outside the courtroom, the issues are seldom so explicitly stated. It is up to the advocates to discover them by one of several possible methods. First of all, a careful definition of the terms of the proposition will aid the advocate in discovering some of the issues of the debate. As the terms are defined, important aspects of the proposition will become apparent and reveal at least some of the issues. In debates on "a national program of public work for the unemployed," the definition of the word "unemployed" was important. If "unemployed" was defined as including housewives who were seeking part-time work, this definition suggested the issue "Do the unemployed have the skills necessary for a public work program?"

In addition, stock issues—the standard questions applicable to many propositions—may be used profitably in the early analysis of the problem. As standard questions, they are not sufficiently specific to be the issues of a particular proposition; but they often aid the advocate in the formulation of the actual issues.

1. Stock Issues for Propositions of Policy The stock issues for the proposition of policy are drawn from the three potential elements of the affirmative case: need, plan, and advantages. Some of the stock issues are as follows:

Is there a *need* for a change in the status quo? (Are there certain evils, undesirable factors, or shortcomings in the status quo? Are these significant enough to warrant a change in the status quo? Are these inherent in the status quo? Is it impossible to eliminate them by repairs, adjustments, or improvements within the framework of the status quo? Is any negative proposal to repair or adjust the problems of the status quo unsatisfactory?)

Is the *plan* propositional? (Is it directly related to the proposition?) Will the plan proposed by the affirmative solve the need? (Is the plan proposed by the affirmative workable? Is any possible negative counter plan unworkable? Is the plan proposed by the affirmative the best possible way to achieve the agreed goals of the status quo?)

Will the affirmative's plan achieve the claimed *advantages?* (Will the plan proposed by the affirmative solve the *needs* of the status quo? Will it achieve the agreed goals of the status quo in a more advantageous way? Will the plan produce no disadvantages as great or greater than those existing in the status quo? Will any possible negative counter plan produce greater disadvantages than the status quo or the plan?) Are the advantages claimed inherent in the plan? (Will they necessarily flow from the adoption of the plan?) Are the advantages unique to the plan? (Can they be obtained without adopting the plan?) Are the advantages significant?

2. Stock Issues for Propositions of Fact The stock issues in a debate on a proposition of fact derive from the subject matter of the alleged fact. In legal debates the stock issues are usually rather neatly spelled out in the applicable legislation. In scientific debates the discipline of the science involved usually provides the framework for the stock issues. Two of the more important stock issues for the proposition of fact are these:

Are certain specific questions available to establish the truth of the "fact" alleged in the proposition?

Do the answers to these questions establish the "fact" as truth?

It should be noted that, although legal debates are almost always *supposed* to be debates on propositions of fact, in reality they are sometimes debates on propositions of policy or value. Some bootleggers may have been acquitted because certain juries disagreed with the prohibition law as a matter of policy, and some murderers acquitted because certain juries had moral objections to capital punishment.

3. Stock Issues for Propositions of Value The stock issues in a debate on a proposition of value derive from the moral, aesthetic, or other value-judgment areas applicable to the proposition. To show that a certain abstract painting is a "good" painting, for example, it would be necessary first to establish aesthetic standards favorable to abstract painting. Some of the important stock issues for the proposition of value are these:

Are certain specific questions available to establish that the subject matter of the proposition is good, beneficial, proper, virtuous, or desirable?

Do the answers to these questions establish the subject matter of the proposition as good, beneficial, proper, virtuous, or desirable?

4. Using Stock Issues After carefully defining the terms of the proposition, as well as the related terms from the problem area, and applying the appropriate stock issues, the advocate will formulate a preliminary statement of the issues of the debate.

The following example shows how the stock issues may be used: Some debaters started their analysis of the proposition "Resolved: That law-enforcement agencies in the United States should be given greater freedom in the investigation and prosecution of crime" by asking "Is there a need for a change in the status quo?" In their preliminary reading, some of them came across a number of articles arguing that law enforcement agencies needed more money to upgrade the quality of police personnel and to purchase more equipment. They tentatively phrased the issue "Law-enforcement agencies need more money to fight crime." As they continued their analysis, defined the term "greater freedom," and considered the stock issue "Is this inherent in the status quo?" they decided that "more money" was not consistent with their definition of "greater freedom" and that a shortage of funds was not inherent in the status quo. Thus they rejected the issue they had tentatively selected and continued their analysis.

As these debaters continued their preliminary research, they decided that the major evil in the status quo was organized crime and that it was a serious enough problem to warrant a change. Further study led to the conclusion that the use of the telephone was essential to the operation of organized crime. They also concluded that status quo legislation inherently prevented law-enforcement agencies from using wiretap evidence in court and that if the police were given "greater freedom" — by the legalization of wiretaps and making evidence thus obtained admissible in court — they would be able to combat crime more successfully. These conclusions led to formulation of the following *need* issues:

Organized crime is a major national problem.

The use of the telephone is essential to the operation of organized crime.

Present restrictions on the use of wiretaps reduces the effectiveness of law-enforcement agencies in combatting organized crime.

Next the debaters asked "Is there a plan to meet this need? Will it be practical? Will it provide the necessary safeguards?" After considering a number of alternatives, they decided that a pending Senate bill provided the best possible solution and stated the *plan* issue as follows:

Senate Bill 2813 should be enacted. (They would, of course, present the principal provisions of the bill in the debate.)

The debaters continued their analysis by asking "Will this plan produce advantages?" Their analysis led them to claim the following advantages:

The plan will provide an effective weapon against organized crime.

The plan will have the additional advantage of reducing all crime.

The plan will extend the right of privacy of law-abiding citizens by providing effective regulation against unauthorized wiretapping.

These issues represent the debaters' preliminary analysis of the problem. At this point they have moved from general stock issues to issues specifically adapted to the proposition. These issues must now be tested by further research to determine whether the evidence will in fact support the claimed needs. The debaters must discover whether there are effective objections to their plan—whether their plan will produce disadvantages greater than the claimed advantages. On the basis of further study, they will no doubt modify their issues. They may try them out in a few practice debates. Experience may lead them to rethink some or all of the issues. They have, however, taken the essential first step: they have moved from the general to the specific and have begun a meaningful analysis of the proposition.

It is interesting to note that less than four years after this case was debated the federal government adopted legislation similar to the plan proposed to meet the same needs as these debaters cited.

In similar fashion, the advocate debating propositions of fact or value must analyze the subject area and move from the general stock issues to the specific issues inherent in the proposition.

B. Introduction of Issues

1. Introduction by Either Side The affirmative must introduce the issues necessary to establish a prima facie case. If the negative detects flaws in the affirmative case, it has the responsibility of introducing the appropriate issues to refute the affirmative. For example, the affirmative case *should* be so clearly propositional that it is unnecessary for the affirmative to prove that it is. In such a case, it is clearly pointless for the negative to attack it, and this issue will not be argued. If it is not propositional, however, the negative must "attack propositionality." (See Chapter 14, "The Refutation Negative

Case," for a consideration of the issues the negative may introduce.) If the affirmative is using a "needs analysis" case, it will certainly introduce one or more "need" issues. In proving these issues, the negative might argue that the status quo cannot be repaired, or it might wait to see if the negative seeks to provide repairs and then argue the specific negative repairs. "Workability," for example, might or might not become a critical issue, and it might or might not be introduced by either side. In debates on the Twenty-sixth Amendment, "workability" was never argued — it was self-evident that the voting age *could* be lowered to eighteen — the affirmative did not have to prove it, and it would have been pointless for the negative to attempt to disprove it. In debates on the "further development of nuclear weapons" proposition, workability was almost invariably a critical issue. The negative was almost certain to introduce the issue. Recognizing this, some affirmatives sought to preempt the argument by introducing the issue first. The affirmative will claim "advantages" for their plan and be prepared for a negative attack on this issue. The issue of "disadvantages," however, will probably be argued only if the negative introduces it.

It is readily apparent that advocates must discover and prepare to deal with *all* potential issues of the proposition — not just those issues they find it most convenient to deal with. Any potential issue may become an issue of the debate.

2. The Counter Plan One of the potential issues of any policy debate is "Is the plan proposed by the affirmative the best possible way to solve the problems of the status quo?" If the negative denies that there are any serious problems in the status quo, this potential issue does not become an issue of the debate. The negative, however, may find it desirable to admit that there are certain problems in the status quo and may introduce a counter plan to meet these problems, as is shown in Chapter 14. In such a case the negative then introduces this issue, and the debate may be narrowed to the ultimate issue of which is the better plan. (Of course, the negative wins if it merely proves its plan to be equally as good as the affirmative's. In such a case the affirmative has failed to carry its burden of proof. As a practical matter, however, each side seeks to prove that its plan is better.)

C. The Number of Issues

The number of issues varies from one proposition to another and can be discovered only by careful analysis of the problem. In general, the number of issues is rather small. There are usually four to six issues in dispute in the typical intercollegiate debate. If advocates claim a large number of "issues," they may be confusing supporting contentions with issues. It is usually to the advantage of the affirmative to try to narrow the number of issues of the debate. If the affirmative can secure the admission of the negative, or if it can quickly establish three out of four issues, for example, then it can concentrate its efforts on proving the remaining issue.

It is usually to the advantage of the negative to seek to establish as many issues of debate as possible. The negative hopes, by keeping the maximum possible number of issues in dispute, to force the affirmative to prove every issue and to deny the affirmative the opportunity of concentrating on a few issues of its own choosing. For this reason, negative advocates seldom admit any issue.

As mentioned previously, in debates on right-to-work laws it was rather easy for the affirmative to produce evidence of corruption in unions, because this proposition was debated at a time when a Senate committee was investigating this very problem and the newspapers were carrying daily reports of relevant testimony. Although some negative advocates admitted the issue in the face of such evidence, others continued throughout the debate to seek to minimize the importance of this evidence or to refute the affirmative's generalizations based on specific examples, thus forcing the affirmative to spend time reestablishing this issue at the cost of devoting less time to the defense of other issues. Although the negative cannot manufacture issues just to waste the affirmative's time — a capable advocate would quickly expose such a trick — the negative has an obligation to develop the objections to the proposition, and it should never concede or abandon an issue unnecessarily.

In some situations both the affirmative and the negative will develop "spread cases"; that is, the affirmative will present an inflated number of need or advantage issues, while the negative counters with an inflated number of plan objections. This proliferation of issues usually produces a "shallow" debate. The skilled debater knows how to slough over a superfluous issue by quickly demonstrating its lack of significance and getting to the roots of the case.

D. Phrasing the Issues

The issues must be so phrased as to provide maximum logical and persuasive impact on those who render the decision. First, the well-phrased issue will preview and then bring into focus the line of argument to be developed. Second, the issue must be phrased persuasively. Third, the issue must be phrased concisely. Fourth, taken as a whole, the issues must be so phrased as to provide a coherent organization for the case and admit of smooth transition from one issue to another. Students will find it worthwhile to review Chapter 18 (Presenting the Case: Speech Composition) and Chapter 19 (Presenting the Case: Delivery) as they begin to put their phrasing of the issues into final form.

Some students debating "Resolved: That executive control of United States foreign policy should be significantly curtailed" wanted to curtail executive control by prohibiting the executive from carrying out covert operations in foreign countries. They *might* have phrased the first need issue as "American foreign policy objectives of combatting communism, protecting the innocent, and preserving peace are seriously impeded when it becomes a matter of public knowledge that the United States has in fact engaged in covert operations to overthrow hostile regimes." They *might* have phrased the second issue as "Neither reducing the number of covert operations nor limiting covert operations to those most likely to succeed will effectively avoid the adverse publicity that will follow when the operations become public knowledge." *Instead,* they wisely phrased the issues as "Discovery of covert operations undermines American objectives" and "The only way to prevent discovery is to end all operations."

The phrasing actually used is clearly superior and meets the criteria considered earlier in this section. Most often, however, the issue will first occur to an advocate in a rambling, disjointed form. The experienced advocate knows that well-phrased issues are the result of careful rewriting and skillful editing.

Well-phrased issues give advocates in educational debate one of the best opportunities to "take control of the flow sheet" and lodge their arguments, *exactly as they want them stated,* in the mind of the judge. The importance of phrasing issues with precision is by no means limited to students in educational debate. In almost any circumstances, advocates are more likely to achieve their objective if the issues are crisply and coherently stated rather than buried in a discursive presentation. The importance of well-phrased issues becomes more critical if advocates attain enough prominence to be quoted on even a local radio or television news program. The advocates quickly learn that their entire speech is almost never presented; rather, they feel lucky if as much as a sixty-second "clip" of their speech is used. In such circumstances, wise speakers quickly learn to phrase their issues effectively. The same considerations, although to a somewhat lesser degree, apply to newspapers, which often quote portions of a speech but only infrequently publish full texts.

E. The Substructure of the Issues

The same considerations that apply to the phrasing of the issues also apply to the substructure of the issue. The contentions—that is, the supporting arguments used to establish an issue—must be phrased with care so that they too will provide the maximum logical and persuasive impact on those who render the decision.

Consider the substructure of the issues cited in the previous section:

I. Discovery of covert operations undermines American objectives.
  A. Discovery strengthens communism.
  B. Discovery injures the innocent.
  C. Discovery threatens peace.

II. The only way to prevent discovery is to end all operations.
    A. Discovery of some operations is inevitable.
    B. Discovery is unpredictable.

The reiteration of the concept of "discovery" on which the advocate wished to focus and the concise phrasing of the contentions helped the advocate to establish the case more effectively.

F. The Issues and the Decision Makers

Advocates must consider the attitudes and values of those who render the decision as they decide what issues they will introduce and how they will handle them. In debating the "comprehensive medical care for all citizens" proposition, some debaters quickly discovered the issue: "Comprehensive medical care for all citizens will inflate taxes by prolonging lives." The argument was irrefutable. If the plan worked as well as the affirmative would claim it would, the negative could prove that vast numbers of elderly indigents would linger on for years in an unproductive state consuming more and more tax dollars in medical and welfare costs. Despite the overwhelming logical force of the argument, the debaters decided against introducing the issue. They felt the values of most American audiences are such that they would reject the idea of denying poor people medical care so that they might die earlier and thus save taxes.

Before a group of business managers, the "cost issue," if the plan requires the expenditure of tax monies, is one that the negative will almost certainly argue. The negative will maximize the tax burden, while the affirmative will seek to minimize it. Many business people are well aware of the enormous taxes they are already paying and are predisposed to resist any new or additional taxes. Cost may well become the critical issue of the debate and provide the negative with its best opportunity of winning. Before student groups, negatives often find that the "cost issue" is less critical. Many students are beneficiaries of tax-spending programs and have not yet felt the personal burden of paying heavy taxes. Before such audiences the negative may decide to drop the cost issue or to transform its material and argue that the affirmative plan will "distort social priorities" because its cost is so great that it precludes or reduces other more desirable programs. Thus, in arguing the "medical care" proposition, some negatives maintained that, rather than spend the money on medical care, more lives would be saved and the quality of life improved if the money were spent to provide better food and housing for the poor.

Audiences sometimes have expectations as to what the issues of the debate will be. On the "gathering and utilization of information" proposition, some affirmative teams introduced the issue that information gathering and utilization should be controlled to implement the legalization of marijuana. On the tournament circuit some judges accepted this rationalization. When the same case was presented before a service club, some of the audience walked out in disgust, saying "They're crazy, that subject has nothing to do with marijuana; they're supposed to be talking about data banks and credit ratings." The moral of that story is this: one can ignore the expectations of the audience only at one's own risk.

Even the highly qualified professional judge, ideally found in educational debate, cannot totally divorce himself from his value system. Thus, if in a debate on the "medical care" proposition, a negative introduced as a counterplan the issue "euthanasia for anyone who is hospitalized more than once a year," it must expect that the judge will evaluate almost any affirmative objection as sufficient to defeat the counter plan.

As students begin to make final selection of issues and to plan their handling of those issues, they may find it helpful to study Chapter 17 (The Role of Motivation), especially sections III ("Analysis of the Audience") and IV ("Analysis of the Key Individual").

Exercises

1. Prepare a brief paper in which you define the terms of the current national intercollegiate debate proposition. Your instructor may call for a class discussion of your definitions.

2. From the newspapers and newsmagazines of the past month find an example of an argumentative speech on a proposition of policy by a public figure. Prepare a brief paper in which you identify the speaker and the occasion on which he spoke, state the proposition, and state the issues he set forth. If necessary, rephrase the speaker's words to form a clear and correct statement of the proposition and issues; be careful, however, to preserve the speaker's ideas. Do you agree with the speaker's choice of issues?

3. Prepare a three-minute speech for delivery in class in which you (a) state a proposition of policy, (b) define the terms, (c) state the issues. The class will be asked to evaluate your statement of the proposition, definition of terms, and statement of the issues. Prepare an outline of this speech to hand to your instructor.

4. Prepare a brief paper in which you formulate a preliminary statement of the issues of the current national intercollegiate debate proposition. Your instructor may call for a class discussion of these issues.

5. Your instructor will divide the class into groups of two students. Each group will select a proposition of fact, value, or policy. One student, acting as an affirmative speaker, will present a three-minute speech in which he (a) states the proposition, (b) defines the terms, and (c) states the issues. The other student, acting as a negative speaker, will (a) accept the definitions or offer superior ones, (b) accept the statement of issues, revise the issues if he thinks this advisable, or offer additional issues if he thinks this advisable.

6. Attend an intercollegiate debate and prepare a brief paper in which you report the definition of terms and statement of issues presented in the debate. Evaluate the ability of the debaters in defining terms and discovering issues. Evaluate the ability of the debaters in phrasing the issues and contentions.

Chapter 5

Exploring the Problem

"They don't know what they're talking about" is one of the worst indictments that can be brought against would-be advocates. Advocates who seek to defend their position intelligently and to persuade others to accept their proposal must be thoroughly familiar with the problem. They must undertake an organized program of research so that they may explore fully all relevant aspects of the proposition. Careful research will not only give them a firm foundation for their case; it will also give them confidence in the case. The issues formulated in the analysis of the problem will help to give direction to the research. The processes of analyzing and exploring the problem are interwoven, and advocates will continue to move from one to the other of these two processes as long as they are concerned with the proposition. They must be innovative and creative in their search for evidence and issues and then be coolly and dispassionately analytical in evaluating findings and planning further research. On the basis of their exploration, they may find it necessary to rephrase the issues they originally developed or to develop new issues or, if the proposition is subject to rephrasing, they may find it desirable to revise the proposition.

In formal debate, a restatement of the proposition cannot be done unilaterally; it requires the consent of all parties concerned. The intercollegiate debater, the attorney in the law court, and other advocates must often debate on a proposition that is not subject to revision. In informal debate in government and business, advocates—for persuasive purposes—often make serious and sometimes successful attempts to change the wording and meaning of the proposition unilaterally. For example, opponents of abortion prefer to speak of the "right to life," and supporters of euthanasia prefer to state their proposal as "death with dignity" rather than as "mercy killing." In parliamentary debate, the proposition may be amended by a simple majority vote; in many conference and discussion situations, the problem may be revised by informal action. In any event, the advocate will continue exploration, constantly revising the case on the basis of new information.

I. Sources of Material

Most often the advocates turn to the library as their first source of material. Resources, physical arrangements, and loan policies of libraries vary enormously, and advocates are well advised to spend some time browsing through the library in order to acquire a general familiarity with its collections and organization so that later search for information may be purposeful and effective. Librarians are usually eager to assist a person doing serious research, and their help can be a valuable asset to the advocate.

A. General References

Exploration usually begins with an effort to acquire general information on the problem. As the advocate acquires a general knowledge of the problem, he or she is in a position to develop more specific lines of inquiry and to seek more specialized information. Among the more important general references are the *card catalogue*, the various *encyclopedias, almanacs,* and *yearbooks,* and such reference guides as Winchell's *Guide to Reference Books* and Shore's *Basic Reference Books.*

Important references for periodical literature include *Readers' Guide to Periodical Literature* and *International Index to Periodicals.* A valuable reference for newspapers is the *New York Times Index.* Although this publication indexes only the *New York Times,* it may be used in connection with almost any daily newspaper since major news stories usually appear in all daily newspapers on approximately the same date.

Often the advocate will wish to learn more about specific individuals to establish the expertness of "witnesses." Useful biographical references are *Who's Who* (worldwide in scope, but primarily British), *Who's Who in America, Who's Who in the East* (and similar publications for other geographic regions of the United States), *Who's Who of American Women, Dictionary of American Biography,* and the *Biography Index.*

B. Special References

General references perform a valuable function by providing the advocate with important information on the proposition and by suggesting further avenues of exploration. Almost invariably, however, the general references do not provide the depth of specialized information the advocate needs; further information may be sought in special reference works. Some of the more specialized references include Black's *Law Dictionary,* the *Congressional Record* indexes, the *Statistical Abstract of the United States,* and the *Monthly Catalogue of U.S. Government Publications.* Many debaters use these as a starting point for their research and then move on to a broader and deeper exploration of the problem.

Special biographical directories list individuals prominent in certain fields. *Who's Who in American Education* and the *Directory of American Scholars* list educators and scholars; and similar directories may be found for other professions.

Sources of information on contemporary problems include the *Con-*

gressional Record, the official record of debates in the Senate and the House, and *Congressional Digest,* a commercial publication that records the views of Congressional and other public leaders.

One of the best methods for locating special references is to answer certain questions. The answers to these questions will suggest many sources of information (*see inset*).

Information secured from sources suggested by answers to the "who is for it or against it" questions must be viewed with special care. It is often easy information to obtain, because those whose interests are affected by the proposition are usually anxious to give the widest possible dissemination to their arguments. At the same time, the very fact that their interests are affected by the problem may mean that the information they distribute is not completely objective or accurate.

Problems of possible bias, conflicting evidence, and conflicting interpretations of the same evidence are, of course, inherent in argumentation. If there were no controversy, there would be no debate. Information from interested parties cannot be rejected out-of-hand merely because of possible bias. Frequently, parties to a dispute are the best — indeed sometimes the only — sources of information about the dispute. The clash of conflicting evidence and opinion is the lifeblood of argumentation and gives advocates

---

Locating References: Questions

1. Who is concerned with the proposition? We may find that persons and organizations concerned with a problem include those with an academic interest in it, those interested in the potential influence of the proposition, and even those unwilling as yet to take a public stand on the problem. For example, if we are seeking information on the "higher education" proposition, our answer to the question "Who is concerned with the proposition?" would include the various associations of educators, economists, political scientists, business people, labor organizations, and organizations in other related fields. The scholarly associations and their journals seldom take an official position for or against legislation, but their journals carry significant articles about contemporary problems in the area of their special interest. The education journals, in particular, yielded a number of significant articles on this proposition.

2. Who is interested in securing the adoption of the proposition? The answer to this question will often lead the advocate to one of the most prolific sources of information. A search for information on "higher education" would lead the advocate to the Office of Education, for example, which took the lead in presenting the administration's arguments in favor of the proposition.

3. Who is interested in preventing the adoption of the proposition? The answer will often lead the advocate to another prolific source of information. The advocate interested in "higher education" found, for example, that the National Association of Manufacturers published a good deal of material opposed to the proposition.

excellent opportunities to get to the root of the matter. In studying conflicting evidence and opinion, advocates must apply the tests of evidence and reasoning considered in later chapters. A searching and rigorous examination of the conflict will help to separate fact from wishful thinking and logical issues of the debate from emotion-laden slogans.

If labor and management *disagree* about a certain proposal to aid the unemployed and if reports issued by the Bureau of Labor Statistics, the AFL–CIO, and the NAM all *agree* that the unemployment rate is x percent, the advocate is probably safe in deciding that the unemployment rate will not be an issue of the debate. The real issue may be "Is x percent too high?" The search for the answer to this question may lead to the profitable exploration of previously overlooked economic and sociology journals. If the AFL–CIO and the NAM disagree about the cost of the proposal, the advocate may well conclude that cost will be a major issue of the debate and may decide to search the conflicting arguments to find the reasons for the differences in the cost estimates. Does the labor report speak only of the first-year cost while the management report speaks of a ten-year total? A precise analysis of the conflicting figures, together with a careful checking of relevant data from impartial sources, may lead to accurate cost estimates.

C. Current Periodicals and Newspapers

Because advocates are most often concerned with a proposition of current interest, they may expect that information relating to the proposition will appear from time to time in the daily press, weekly newsmagazines, and monthly magazines. Resourceful advocates will maintain a constant program of scanning current publications for articles related to their problem. Their daily reading should include the *New York Times* and at least one other metropolitan daily. The Sunday *New York Times*' "News of the Week in Review" section is a helpful summary of current events. Weekly reading should include such newsmagazines as *Time, Newsweek,* or *U.S. News & World Report.* If the proposition is related to a particular field, advocates should add the special publications of that area to their research list. For example, if they are concerned with a business problem, they should read the *Wall Street Journal, Business Week, Fortune,* the *AFL–CIO News,* and the *Monthly Labor Review,* together with some of the trade papers and newsletters of the specific area under consideration.

New books may appear from time to time on the problem of interest to the advocate. A quick scanning of the book reviews will advise advocates of any new publications of interest to them and help them decide whether they should include the new books in their research. The *New York Times Book Review,* the *Chicago Tribune Books,* and the *Saturday Review World* offer reviews of books of general interest. More specialized books are reviewed in scholarly or special interest publications.

Advocates should make a special point of reading publications with many different editorial policies. Much of their opponents' evidence and argument may come from publications with which they disagree. If they study this information in its original source, they will be in a better position to deal with it in the debate.

D. Other Sources

Information may also be obtained through interviews and correspondence. The answers to the three questions in the inset will suggest persons the advocate should seek to interview or with whom he should institute correspondence.

1. Interviews Interviews with subject-matter experts are often very valuable sources of information. The value of any interview depends to a considerable extent on our advance preparation; carefully planned preliminary research will enable us to ask meaningful questions. The student debater is in an excellent position to secure interviews with faculty members, and often interviews can be arranged with congressmen, business executives, labor leaders, and others who have special knowledge of the subject of the debate proposition.

Sometimes debating teams are able to arrange for a group of experts to come to the campus and present a panel discussion. College debaters enjoy a special advantage in securing interviews, for the national debate proposition always deals with an important contemporary problem; and public officials and community leaders are usually willing to aid in an educational undertaking.

There are many other important interviews the advocate can study. Radio and television stations often present interviews with national or world figures on problems of contemporary importance ("Meet the Press," "Issues and Answers," "Face the Nation," and "Bill Moyers' Journal" are examples). Magazines also often publish such interviews; *U.S. News & World Report* regularly has question-and-answer articles in which prominent persons are quizzed about important problems—and these can serve as important sources of information.

2. Correspondence Correspondence is often a fruitful source of information. A helpful starting point in the search for information is the list of associations and societies in the United States published in the *World Almanac*. Hundreds of organizations are listed, ranging from "Abolish Capital Punishment, American League to," through "Zoologists, American Society of." Most of these organizations and other special-interest groups are willing to answer thoughtful letters asking intelligent questions in the area of their concern.

Often advocates will discover organizations that strongly support or oppose the proposition under consideration. Some of these maintain elaborate propaganda agencies and will furnish extensive literature or provide speakers on matters of interest to them. Members of Congress are excellent sources of information on matters within the sphere of the federal government. The representative from the advocate's home district or the senators from his state are usually most responsive to such requests. Congressmen receive so many requests for information about the national debate proposition each year that the Legislative Reference Service of the Library of Congress annually prepares a special government document on the current proposition, which congressmen make available free of charge to intercollegiate debaters. Through correspondence, advocates can often obtain press releases, special papers, data sheets, pamphlets, booklets, and other materials not ordinarily available through libraries.

II. Brainstorming for Ideas

Traditionally, advocates seek to develop a case by a careful, orderly, deliberate, logical process. Although the case they finally present must be logically sound, advocates sometimes finds it advantageous to shorten the logical processes while gathering ideas for their case. Sometimes the solution to a problem is found by means of an "intuitive leap," a "hunch," a "lucky break," an "inspiration," or serendipity. The advocate may just happen to look into an obscure reference and find exactly the piece of evidence needed to complete a chain of reasoning; or consider a seemingly improbable plan "just for the fun of it" and find that it meets the needs perfectly; or follow up an apparently irrelevant lead and uncover an important precedent; or consider an impractical proposal that will lead to a highly practical solution.

It is for the express purpose of uncovering ideas that might otherwise be ignored or delayed that the advocate uses *brainstorming*. There are many situations in which it may be profitable to use brainstorming: in defining terms or discovering issues, in finding materials for the argument, in connection with the problems of evidence or reasoning, in building the case, or in many other areas. Although brainstorming is not a substitute for the ways of dealing with problems considered in other chapters, it is a supplement that may help in many situations.

In a typical brainstorming session, the participants sit around a table. They make a deliberate effort to create an informal atmosphere in which everyone is encouraged to contribute and no one is permitted to criticize. They are usually most successful when following certain guidelines (*see inset*).

Brainstorming is often deceptively simple. The idea evolved may evoke the comment "Why, anyone could have thought of that." This is often true. The point is that in many cases no one had thought of the idea earlier, and perhaps no one would have thought of that particular idea had it not been for the brainstorming session. Many of the ideas evolved in brainstorming sessions are pure "fluff." However, if only one important idea is evolved that otherwise might never have been considered, the technique is worthwhile.

One group of college students debating "a national program of public work for the unemployed" found that early in the season their affirmative teams were having a great deal of difficulty with their plan, which called for a massive program of urban renewal to provide jobs. Their negative opponents were defeating the plan by pointing out that few of the unemployed had the skills necessary for construction work. The debaters held a brainstorming session from which they evolved the idea that the affirmative plan did not have to call for construction work. Then they proceeded to develop a new plan which called for conservation, service, and maintenance work unskilled persons could easily perform. This plan might have been evolved by some other means, of course, but this particular group of advocates was unable to develop an effective plan until they brainstormed the problem.

Method of Brainstorming

1. The size of the group is limited. Brainstorming has been found to work better in small groups. Fifteen is usually considered to be a maximum workable size. Groups as small as two or three have been effective, and it is even possible for an individual to apply the method of brainstorming alone.

2. The time devoted to a brainstorming session is limited. Because the objective of brainstorming is to produce a large number of ideas and to avoid any critical evaluation *during the session*, it is usually desirable to limit a session to one hour or less; many profitable sessions have been limited to between twenty and forty minutes.

3. The problem is announced in advance. The person calling the brainstorming session announces the problem he wishes the group to consider, either at the start of the session or a day or two in advance.

4. All participants are encouraged to contribute. Since the objective is to secure the maximum possible number of ideas, everyone is urged to participate. The leader can encourage contributions by creating a friendly, informal atmosphere. Participants are urged not only to originate ideas but also to modify and extend ideas presented by others.

5. No organized pattern is followed. Whereas traditional discussion follows a careful pattern of reflective thinking, brainstorming deliberately follows no pattern. The objective is to provide an atmosphere for the *trigger effect* in which an idea, even a bad or irrelevant one, once expressed, may trigger a good idea.

III. Reading with a Purpose

Advocates can make brainstorming work by preparing a carefully drafted outline of the ideas and sources suggested in brainstorming. From this list, they should develop a selected bibliography for use in research and a selected list of publications for monitoring. While doing research and monitoring, they can revise and refine the bibliography and list of monitored publications. This process of brainstorming, research, and revising will continue until the first debate, which will often trigger further brainstorming and research that will continue as long as the proposition is debated.

When students are asked to monitor the daily press or weekly newsmagazines they sometimes protest: "But I don't have time to read all those newspapers and magazines." Perhaps they do not have time to read an entire newspaper every day; but when they read for the purpose of finding information on a specific problem, they are not asked to read an entire newspaper. It takes only a few minutes to scan even the bulky *New York Times* to determine whether it contains an article on inflation, unemployment, population stabilization, or an international conflict.

---

6. No criticism is permitted. No criticism or evaluation of ideas should be permitted *during the session*. Since criticism, at this stage, tends to discourage contributions and decreases the possibility of the "trigger effect," the leader must suppress criticism and strive to maintain an atmosphere in which everyone feels free to contribute.

7. All ideas are recorded. All ideas, including those that seem worthless at first glance, must be recorded. The most widely used method is probably that of assigning two or three members of the group to write ideas on a blackboard as rapidly as they are expressed. Other methods include the use of an "idea tree"—a short pole is set in the center of the table and each participant writes out his ideas and attaches them to the "tree" with scotch tape—or the "cracker barrel"—a basket is placed on the table and each participant writes his ideas on a piece of paper and tosses them into the "barrel." No matter which method is used, all ideas should be recorded and forwarded to the person or group responsible for evaluation.

8. The ideas are subject to rigorous evaluation. Once the brainstorming session is over and the ideas have been recorded in some usable form, they are then subjected to thorough evaluation. Sometimes the ideas are duplicated and sent to the participating individuals for their evaluation. In many cases they are forwarded to a policy-making group or to the individual responsible for making decisions for screening and testing. The ideas gathered during brainstorming may serve as springboards for concepts which will be developed more fully during evaluation.

IV. Reading Critically

There is probably more literature available on any contemporary, controversial problem than advocates can possibly read in the time available. Research, then, must be planned for both breadth and discrimination, so that time is used efficiently. Advocates must seek out sources representative of the various points of view related to the problem in order to understand possible lines of argument. Since much writing on any contemporary problem is likely to be a restatement of other writings, or a highly superficial treatment, discriminating advocates will seek out original sources, articles in scholarly or professional journals, writings by qualified authorities, reports by competent and objective persons, giving preference to sources with established reputations for accuracy.

An article on nuclear weapons appearing in the *Bulletin of the Atomic Scientists*, for example, is more likely to contain accurate and significant information than is an article on the same subject in the Sunday supplement of a local newspaper. The full text of the Secretary of State's speech on a foreign policy problem may contain some carefully phrased qualifications that are omitted in the brief summary appearing in a newsmagazine.

The advocate cannot read everything written about his problem. He must be critical in his reading to select representative, authoritative, accurate, and significant material for careful, detailed study.

V. Recording Materials

At the start of the exploration of a problem, advocates will find it desirable to adopt a systematic method of recording materials so they may readily use the information assembled from many different sources.

Candidates for the Presidency and other major political offices have developed an effective solution to this problem. They have scores of thousands of items of information from their own speeches, articles, and newspaper interviews and those of their opponents fed into a computer. These data are so organized that in seconds the computer can produce all of the candidates', or a selected opponent's, statements on a specific subject on a printout. This method is one of the contributing factors to today's high campaign costs and is available only to well-financed candidates.

Advocates may use any method—3 x 5 cards, $8\frac{1}{2}$ x 11 sheets, material assembled in steel filing cabinets, on IBM cards, and so on—that their needs require and their resources permit. Many advocates find that they must develop a portable library they can take with them on the campaign plane or into the board room, the courtroom, or the classroom.

Intercollegiate debaters have evolved a successful method of recording materials by using a thousand or more 4 x 6 file cards, assembled in a file box. Although the advocate will use only a relatively few cards in any one debate, experienced varsity debaters find it desirable to have thousands of pieces of information immediately available to meet the possible arguments of their opponents. The file is usually supplemented by one or two attaché cases in which the debater carries bulkier material. Rather than copying lengthy material, the advocate often finds it desirable to clip a table or a statement from a newspaper or magazine article. These sheets are often carried in lightweight transparent plastic jackets to protect them from wear and tear. Sometimes it is desirable to have available the full text of key Senate Committee Hearings, a particularly authoritative book, or other frequently cited documents.

While reading source material, advocates should have at hand a supply of 4 x 6 cards on which to record (1) all information that may help in supporting their stand on the proposition and (2) all information that may be of help to opponents. They should record the information shown on the annotated sample card.

If advocates record only one piece of information on each card, they will be able to handle the material more flexibly. Such flexibility will be an asset when they organize their material. The sample card (page 70) shows a convenient method of recording information.

If several advocates are working together, as a college debating team, members of a law firm, or a group of congressmen, the task of exploring the problem may be divided, with each member of the group being assigned the responsibility of covering thoroughly a certain segment of the source material. Under this system the information recorded by each member is pooled in a central file. Although executives and attorneys often delegate much of the "spade work" to secretaries or law clerks, they often find, as advocates, they must do much of the research personally. Only the person who actually presents the case can fully appreciate the implications of certain information and determine which avenues of exploration must be more fully developed.

The more important a message, the more intensive must exploration of the problem be. Presidential candidates must be knowledgable on a wide variety of subjects. From the "kitchen cabinets" and "brain trusts" of earlier times, they have now developed vast staffs of researchers, speech writers, and subject-matter experts to brief them on every potential issue and to develop position papers on every potential problem. A large staff obviously enables the advocate to cover more ground. The method of exploring the problem, however, is the same for the student debater and the Presidential candidate.

It must be noted that when a speaker uses a piece of evidence he must accept full responsibility for it. Thus, while much of the "nitty gritty" research may be done by a law clerk, a justice of the Supreme Court—and not the clerk—is responsible for what is said in the justice's opinion. Consequently, whenever an advocate finds an important piece of evidence that has

Sample File Card

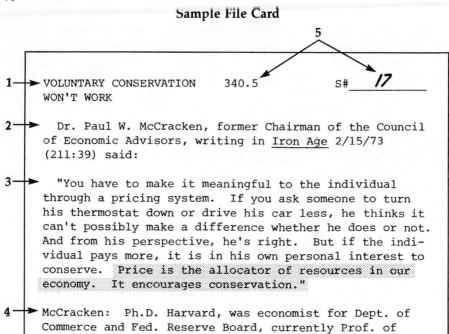

1. **Subject Heading** (This heading will aid advocates when they later organize their material.)

2. **Statement of the Source of Information** This statement should include the title of the publication, the name of the author if known, the publisher, the page number, the date of publication, and the date of the information if it is different from the date of publication.

3. **Statement of Desired Information** A verbatim quotation of the source material is always preferred. It is permissible to omit irrelevant material by ellipsis (. . .) or to paraphrase. The use of ellipsis or paraphrase must always be indicated when the information is recorded and must always be acknowledged when the information is presented; and the advocate must be careful to preserve the intention of the source quoted. Material to be emphasized may be highlighted by marking it with a yellow felt-tip marker.

4. **Relevant Supplementary Information** Sometimes the value of the material is enhanced by supplementary information. Consequently, the advocate may wish to include some information on the author's qualifications, the nature of the organization publishing the material, or other significant details.

5. **A Quick Retrieval Number** Each card should be assigned a number so that the advocate may classify and organize the cards in a manner that permits quick retrieval. (See VI, "Organizing Materials.") Later selected cards may be pulled from the file and assigned a sequence number (S #) indicating the sequence in which the advocate plans to use the card in a particular debate. This number is often penciled in.

come from someone else, he or she should, for both ethical and practical reasons, go back to the original source and verify the quotation.

Consider the case of a debater arguing the "comprehensive health care" proposition. He came across a card, researched by a colleague, which quoted an excellent source as saying:

The AFL–CIO and Senator Kennedy have been outspoken in condemnation of the United States as being listed as fifteenth or sixteenth in the infant mortality tables as compared to such other nations as Sweden, Denmark, France, England, etc.

Without verifying the quotation, he used this apparently "devastating" evidence to indict American health care. Imagine his embarrassment when his better prepared opponent turned to the original source and read the next two sentences:

However, as the Medical Year Book of the World Health Organization points out, the figures on which these statistics are based are not truly comparable. In many European countries an infant mortality is recorded as a stillborn child if the infant did not survive for as much as five days and hence the death does not appear in the infant mortality tables.

VI. Organizing Materials

Advocates must not only have a wealth of information, but that information must be instantly available to them. The method used by intercollegiate debaters will be considered here; however, it may be adapted to any type of advocacy.

As a first step, the advocate should classify recorded information cards as *affirmative or negative*, indicating this classification by an abbreviation placed on each card, or by different colors of cards.

The second step is to classify the cards according to the *issues* the advocate has developed. A readily recognized abbreviation for each issue should be devised and placed on each card.

A system of indexing the file cards should be developed to enable the advocate to locate any card quickly. At the beginning of a season of debating "Resolved: That the federal government should establish a national program of public work for the unemployed," an affirmative team used the following eight main divisions in preparing their affirmative file:

Affirmative

100   Rationale

200   Definitions

300   Need
        310 Unemployment harmful
        320 Unemployment increasing
        330 Unmet need for public work
        340 Status quo cannot solve need

400   Plan

500   Advantages

600   Answers to negative attacks

700   Unemployment statistics

800   Qualifications of authorities

As the advocates built their case, they developed further refinements for their classifications of information cards. Under "Unemployment harmful," for instance, the debaters quickly established subheadings of "310.1 harm to the individual," "310.2 harm to families," "310.3 harm to society," "310.4 harm to economy." This decimal system of organizing materials makes it convenient for advocates to add new information to their file.

A negative team preparing to debate the "comprehensive medical care" proposition used the following ten main divisions to organize their file:

Negative

100   Rationale

200   Not propositional

300   Other goals more important

400   Quality of medical care satisfactory

500   Method of financing medical care satisfactory

600   Method of delivering medical care satisfactory

700   Minor repairs

800   Plan not workable

900   Plan not achieve advantages
        910   not remove economic barrier
        920   not remove other barriers — fear, ignorance
        930   not provide physicians in ghettos or rural areas

1000 Disadvantages

The objective is to provide as many subheadings as are necessary to make essential information instantly available. Index cards may be used to indicate subdivisions, and colored metal "flags" may be used to indicate cards with particularly important information. While the examples shown here are drawn from the files of student debaters, it is obvious that any advocate who must organize a large mass of data must develop some comparable system.

In some cases advocates will find that a given piece of information might appropriately be placed under more than one classification. Multiple cards recording the same information should be prepared and inserted in the proper places, with a cross reference to other locations to avoid repetition.

Careful exploration of the problem is essential to intelligent advocacy. Reasonable and prudent people will give little time and less credence to the person who "doesn't know what he's talking about." Debaters who thoroughly study the appropriate sources of information, who organize their research effectively, who read purposefully and critically, who record materials accurately, and who organize them effectively are taking an important step toward responsible and effective advocacy. Only well-prepared advocates can hope to gain and hold the attention of a critical audience, contend against well-informed opposition, and secure a decision from reasonable and prudent men.

Exercises

1. Find the answers to each of the following questions and indicate the source of your information:

a. What percentage of college students are black?

b. What percentage of college and university faculty members are women?

c. What percent of the current federal budget is spent on defense? On welfare?

d. Define poverty.

e. How has the value of the dollar changed since one year ago? Since five years ago? Since ten years ago?

f. What are the qualifications of Paul A. Samuelson to speak on economic matters?

g. How many nuclear power reactors are there in the United States?

h. How much does pollution cost?

i. How many abortions were performed in the United States last year?

j. How much oil did the United States import last year? How much oil did the United States export?

k. What has been the cost to the United States of its involvement in Vietnam?

l. How much military aid has the United States given to Israel?

2. Select a proposition which may be used for the following exercises and for later classroom debates:

a. Prepare a list of general references useful in exploring this specific problem.

b. Prepare a list of special references useful in exploring this specific problem.

c. Hold a brainstorming session in class on this proposition, and record the ideas suggested. At the next meeting of the class evaluate the ideas. Did the ideas suggested in the brainstorming session "trigger" any additional ideas? What percentage of the ideas had practical value?

d. Prepare a number of information cards (the number to be specified by your instructor) on this specific problem.

e. Organize the information cards according to a system that will provide for the effective use of this information in a debate.

Chapter 6

Evidence

The phrase "Just give us the facts, Ma'am" was made famous by a popular television detective. He used it to cut short verbose comment in an effort to get to the core of the problem. The facts, after all, are what the detective needs to solve a crime. Indeed, the facts, or evidence, are what we all need in order to arrive at an intelligent solution to a problem.

Consider a typical problem in argumentation. In a debate on price and wage controls, one student says controls are urgently needed now. Her opponent, another student, says controls are unnecessary and harmful. Both are pleasant young students, both seem to be equally intelligent, both may have had about the same courses in economics and political science. Which are we to believe? Logically, we will believe the one who does the better job of presenting evidence to establish his or her position.

Evidence is the raw material of argumentation. It consists of facts, opinions, and objects that are used to generate proof. The advocate brings together the raw materials and, by the process of reasoning, produces new conclusions.

In previous chapters we have considered how advocates assemble and organize information as they analyze and explore the problem. In this chapter we consider the evidence itself, and in the next chapter we will consider the tests that must be applied to evidence. By understanding evidence, we will be in a better position to evaluate arguments presented for our decision or to construct sound arguments designed to secure the decision of others.

Evidence may be classified as direct or presumptive. *Direct evidence* is evidence that tends to show the existence of a fact in question without the intervention of the proof of any other fact. In a debate on "tax sharing," the claim that "forty-four states now have state income taxes" could be established or refuted by reference to the *World Almanac* or some other reliable source. In argument, direct evidence is most frequently used to establish supporting contentions rather than to prove the proposition itself. If irrefutable evidence existed in proof of the proposition, there would be no point in debating it. At one time, for example, the proposition "Resolved: That the United States can land men on the moon" was debatable. Today there is simply no point in debating the proposition.

Presumptive evidence, or indirect or circumstantial evidence, is that evidence that tends to show the existence of a fact in question by proof of another or other facts from which the fact in question may be inferred. In debates on the strategic arms limitations treaties, opponents of the SALT agreements argued that the United States should not enter into such agreements with the USSR because "Russia will violate the agreements by secretly increasing the number of or the quality of her nuclear missiles." Since there was no direct evidence in support of this claim, opponents of SALT sought to establish it by presumptive evidence. They sought to establish supporting arguments such as (1) the USSR has violated many international agreements in the past; (2) it would be to the USSR's advantage to have more improved nuclear weapons: (3) it would be difficult or impossible to detect any Russian violations of SALT; and (4) there would be no effective penalty against the USSR even if a violation were detected. From these supporting arguments, opponents of SALT would then infer that "Russia will violate the SALT agreements and gain a nuclear superiority."

Although the subject matter of these debates was highly specialized, they nonetheless illustrate a typical argumentation problem. In this example we see that one important argument — "Russia will violate the agreements" — must be established by presumptive evidence. The subarguments used to establish this claim involved both direct and presumptive evidence. For example, it would probably be possible to find direct evidence that the USSR has violated many international agreements. Presumptive evidence would probably be needed to establish the other subarguments.

As a practical matter, much time and effort is spent on presumptive evidence. "But you can't convict a man on circumstantial evidence!" students sometimes protest. On the contrary — many people are convicted on circumstantial evidence. If there is strong direct evidence of the guilt of the accused, the case seldom comes to trial; under such circumstances the accused usually finds it advisable to plead guilty, "throw himself on the mercy of the court," and hope for a lighter sentence.

I. Sources of Evidence

Evidence is introduced into an argument from various sources. By understanding the uses and limitations of the sources of evidence, we will be more discerning in reaching our own decisions or in developing arguments for the decision of others.

A. Judicial Notice

Judicial notice is the quickest, simplest, and easiest way of introducing evidence into an argument. Judicial notice (the term is borrowed from the law courts) is the process whereby certain evidence may be introduced without the necessity of substantiating it.

In almost any argument, it is necessary to refer to various matters of common knowledge, in order to lay the foundation for other evidence to be introduced later and to set the argument in its proper context. Certain matters, which we might reasonably expect any well-informed layman to know, may be presented as evidence simply by referring to them. Certain cautions, however, must be observed in the use of judicial notice.

1. The evidence must be introduced. Advocates cannot expect those who render the decision to build a case for them; they cannot plead, "But I thought everybody knew that." If it is important to know certain evidence in order to understand the case, then the advocate must introduce that evidence. The Supreme Court summed up this principle, which applies to legal pleadings as well as other types of argumentation, when it ruled: "A judge sees only with judicial eyes and knows nothing respecting any particular case of which he is not informed judicially."

2. The evidence must be well known. The instrument of judicial notice may be used only for those matters which are really common knowledge. When the "energy" proposition was debated, the existence of an oil shortage could be established by judicial notice; the extent of the shortage was another matter, however. To establish this, the debater had to produce evidence that would very likely be attacked with conflicting evidence. If advocates introduce little-known evidence merely by judicial notice, they may anticipate that there will be some doubt in the minds of those who render the decision. The Supreme Court made this sound principle of argumentation a part of our legal structure when it ruled: "Courts should take care that requisite notoriety exists concerning the matters on which they take judicial notice, and every reasonable doubt upon the subject should be resolved in the negative."

3. The evidence may be refuted. Evidence offered by judicial notice is usually presented in the expectation that it will be accepted without question by the opposition. Such evidence, like all evidence, is subject to possible refutation. In debates on "right to work" laws, some affirmative debaters sought to establish by judicial notice that "there is widespread corruption in labor unions." Negative debaters, however, usually refused to allow this claim, and introduced evidence designed to refute it.

In presenting evidence through judicial notice, the advocates ask, in effect, that their opponents and those rendering the decision suspend the tests of evidence and accept their assertion as an established fact not requiring proof. The opposing advocates allow such evidence to go unchallenged at their peril. If the evidence actually is irrefutable, there is no point in raising an objection. If the evidence is refutable and the opposing advocates fail to raise an objection, then they have only themselves to blame if those who render the decision accept the evidence as an established fact.

The use of judicial notice is not uncommon in educational debate. It is most likely to be found toward the end of the academic year, when there is a certain body of evidence and argument related to the current national debate proposition that has become common knowledge to "everybody" in the forensic community. In these circumstances judicial notice will be effective if (1) the evidence is so well known to the opposing team that they will concede the point by failing to attempt to refute it and (2) the evidence is so well known to the judge, or judges, that it will weigh in the decision as if it were fully developed rather than merely asserted.

Judicial notice is not limited to the courtroom or educational debate, however. It may be used in any circumstances where the evidence is, in fact, well known to those who render the decision. Thus an executive at a board meeting might argue, "We can't use this incentive plan—remember Ernst and Ernst's report on how it would affect our tax situation?" If the report is well known to the board, and all accept its conclusion that the incentive plan would hurt the company's tax position, the proposal may well be defeated by this brief use of judicial notice.

The advocate must remember that what is well known to the "in group" may be unfamiliar to others. Thus, the use of a critical piece of evidence by judicial notice might be devastating in the final round of a major tournament and limply ineffective in an exhibition debate before a Kiwanis Club. The brief reminder that might clinch an argument before knowledgeable board members might be meaningless at a stockholders' meeting; the stockholders of a large corporation could not be expected to be familiar with the details of every report submitted to the board of directors.

B. Public Records

Public records are often used as a source of evidence. Indeed, on many matters they are the most important evidence, since private individuals or organizations lack the authority or resources to assemble much of the evidence that can be found only in public records. Public records include all documents compiled or issued by or with the approval of any governmental agency. In this category are such diverse materials as the *Congressional Record*, federal and state statute books, birth certificates, deeds, reports of Congressional investigations, and the minutes of a town meeting. Official records are usually highly regarded. The fact that they are public records, however, does not mean that they should be accepted uncritically. A public record containing the report of a Congressional committee might be the best possible source of information on the amount of money the United States spent on direct economic aid to foreign countries in a certain year, since a committee has power to compel officials to produce their records and testify under oath. The same report might contain the testimony of witnesses on the value of this economic aid. Their testimony would not necessarily be the best possible expert opinion on that subject, however. They might be great and impartial authorities, or they might be highly prejudiced lobbyists.

C. Public Writings

Public writings, another fequently used source of evidence, include all written material, other than public records, made available to the general public. In this category are such diverse materials as the *Encyclopaedia Britannica* and the sensational scandal magazine, the college textbook and the campus humor magazine, the *World Almanac* and fiction, or a Brookings Institution report and an astrologer's chart. Some public writings command high prestige and are likely to be accepted readily; others are more likely to be disbelieved than believed. Obviously, the value of public writings varies tremendously.

D. Private Writings

Another source of evidence, private writings, includes all written material prepared for private rather than public use. Some private writings are designed to become public records at a later date. Wills, for example, become public records when they are probated; contracts become public records if they are brought into court for adjudication. Any private writing may become a public record if it is included in the records of a court or a governmental agency, or it may become a public writing if it is made available to the general public. Most private writings, however, are prepared for a limited circulation among selected individuals. In this category are such diverse materials as a company's financial statement prepared by a certified public accountant, a student's class notes, a diary, or a personal letter.

Private writings may be carefully prepared documents designed to report events with great precision and to reflect carefully considered judgments, or they may be incomplete and studded with offhand comments or facetious remarks. Since private writings constitute an important source of evidence, care should be taken to determine who prepared the document and under what circumstances. It should be noted here that personal letters are not customarily introduced as evidence in educational debate. The reason for this may be that it is usually impossible to authenticate a personal letter within the limitations of an educational debate.

E. Testimony of Witnesses

The testimony of witnesses is one of the most common sources of evidence. Testimony given in court or before a governmental body is usually presented under oath and is subject to the penalties of perjury or contempt. Testimony outside the courtroom is not subject to the same legal restrictions and is usually more informal: management officials usually give testimony on the operation of their company at a stockholders' meeting; the president of a company may ask the plant superintendent for an oral report on the utility of a new machine; the freshman may ask a sophomore for advice on what courses to take. In fact, much of our day-to-day business and social activity is based on the testimony of witnesses. Clearly, the value of such testimony may vary considerably.

F. Personal Inspection

When personal inspection is used as a source of evidence, something is presented for examination to the persons rendering the decision: the automobile salesperson may invite customers to lift the hood and inspect the motor; a stockbroker may show the financial statement of a company to a client; or a senator may bring a bag of groceries into the Senate chamber for use during a speech on inflation. The college student is frequently asked to perform personal inspection: the geology professor may offer a sample of rock for the inspection of the class; the economics professor may sketch a supply-and-demand curve on the blackboard; or the music professor may play a portion of a recording for a music appreciation class.

Personal inspection is frequently used in courtroom debates: attorneys often show juries and judges the murder weapon, arrange for them to visit the scene of the crime, or show them the plaintiff's injuries. Evidence presented through personal inspection has been carefully selected and arranged by someone to support a particular argument; it must therefore be examined with care.

II. Types of Evidence

A. Judicial or Extrajudicial Evidence

Evidence is usually classified as judicial or extrajudicial. *Extrajudicial evidence* is also known as "extralegal" or "incompetent" evidence. The word "incompetent" has no bad connotation when used in this sense; it merely means "not admissible in court." Extrajudicial evidence is used to satisfy persons about the facts requiring proof in any situation other than a legal proceeding and is subject only to the usual tests of evidence. *Judicial evidence*, also known as "legal" or "competent" evidence, is that evidence which is admissible in court. Such evidence must satisfy not only the usual tests of evidence but also the various technical rules of legal evidence.

In legal proceedings, certain otherwise perfectly good evidence is excluded. For example, if we are trying to decide whether a certain man's testimony is trustworthy, we are interested in knowing whether or not he has a criminal record. Such evidence, however, is often excluded from courtroom debates. Thus, if someone says, "That evidence couldn't be admitted in court," the objection is irrelevant unless the debate actually is taking place in court.

B. Primary or Secondary Evidence

Evidence is often classified as primary or secondary. *Primary evidence* is the best evidence that the circumstances admit. It affords the greatest certainty of the matter in question; and it is original or firsthand evidence. *Secondary evidence* is evidence that falls short of this standard, since by its nature it suggests there is better evidence of the matter in question. Thus an examination of Chapters 6 and 7 of this book is *primary* evidence that this book contains two chapters on evidence; a friend's statement that this book contains two chapters on evidence is *secondary* evidence.

In debating the "law enforcement" proposition, students came across many newspaper and magazine stories that quoted the FBI's *Uniform Crime Reports* as reporting that the crime rate had gone up 16 percent that year. These sources were, of course, *secondary evidence* of the FBI's report. Thoughtful debaters checked the *primary evidence*, the FBI report itself. There they found the caution that the statistics should not be used for year-to-year comparisons. (One reason for this caution was that at the time this proposition was debated many police departments had just recently computerized their record keeping. The fact that they were much more efficient in counting and reporting crime was not in itself statistically valid evidence of any change in the number of crimes actually committed.) Many secondary sources omitted this caution, and debaters who depended on secondary evidence sustained embarrassing defeats at the hands of debaters who sought out the primary evidence.

Primary evidence is stronger than secondary evidence because there is less possibility of error. Secondary evidence is weaker than primary evidence because it does not derive its value solely from the credibility of the witness, but rests largely on the veracity and competence of others. In any argument the prudent advocate seeks to use primary evidence whenever possible.

C. Written or Unwritten Evidence

Written evidence is evidence supplied by writings of all kinds: books, newspapers, and magazines, as well as less frequently used types of writing such as roman numerals carved on the cornerstone of a building. *Unwritten evidence* includes both oral testimony and objects offered for personal inspection.

In arguments outside the courtroom, written evidence generally is given greater weight than oral evidence because it is easier to substantiate. In a recent intercollegiate debate, a negative speaker introduced unwritten, secondary evidence by saying:

Last week I had the opportunity to talk with Senator _____ when he visited in my home town, and he told me that . . .

Then the negative debater quoted a statement strongly critical of the affirmative's position. An affirmative speaker replied to this by using written evidence:

We have no way of knowing how accurately the negative quoted Senator ____ nor of knowing what the senator said in a private interview. However, we do have a record of the considered opinion of the senator on this subject as he expressed it in an article in the *New York Times Magazine* of last week when he stated . . .

The affirmative debater then quoted a carefully qualified statement which indicated only minor reservations about the affirmative's position. Which of the speakers quoted the senator correctly? Perhaps both. The senator may have changed his mind; or, more likely, the two statements represented the difference between an offhand comment and a considered opinion. In any event, the judge accepted the statement of the affirmative speaker, since he could better substantiate his evidence.

On the other hand, we often accept and act upon oral evidence even when it is hearsay. If a professor says to some students "Last night the dean told me that the president told him that the trustees have decided to raise the tuition next year," the students might well decide immediately that they will have to raise more money for next fall's tuition.

D. Real or Personal Evidence

Real evidence is furnished by objects placed on view or under inspection. In the courtroom, real evidence may consist of fingerprints, scars, or weapons. Outside the courtroom a farmer may be asked to inspect test plots in which different types of seed are used; a customer might be invited to taste a new grocery product; a student might be invited to examine a famous painting in a museum; or an executive might be asked to examine a new data-processing machine.

The use of real evidence is probably as old as argumentation itself. In recent years, however, new developments have greatly increased the potential of real evidence. Motion pictures and other audio-visual materials, long familiar as training aids in schools, are being used increasingly, in sales and public relations campaigns and even in political campaigns, as a means of presenting approximations of real evidence. Franklin D. Roosevelt was the first to use visual material in a major Presidential address when, in a speech on February 23, 1942, he made frequent reference to a map of the world—having requested, several days in advance of the speech, that his audience have a world map at hand when they listened to his radio broadcast. This request was widely publicized, and apparently millions had maps in view as they listened to his speech. Because television sets became widely available during his Administration, Dwight D. Eisenhower was the first

President to make regular use of visual materials in his speeches. Since then, Presidents have used visual materials extensively on television.

Although private citizens rarely have the financial resources to provide elaborate visual materials for their own arguments, they constantly must render decisions on debates in which such aids are used. However, effective visual materials can be produced very inexpensively, and they are frequently used today in many argumentative presentations. Intercollegiate debaters, for example occasionally use world maps when debating foreign economic aid or bar graphs when debating price and wage controls.

Obviously, real evidence or audio-visual materials are selected and prepared by someone. Consequently, we must apply the appropriate tests of evidence both to the real evidence or the visual materials and to the person who prepared it.

Personal evidence is evidence furnished by persons, and it may be in the form of oral or written testimony. The credibility which we attach to personal evidence depends in large part upon the competence and honesty we attribute to the person providing the testimony.

E. Lay or Expert Evidence

Evidence is usually classified as lay or expert. As a practical matter, however, it is often difficult to distinguish between the well-informed layman and the expert. Representatives and senators, for example, may or may not be experts on the subjects they speak about. However, because their official position gives them unusual opportunities to acquire special knowledge on many subjects, they are often regarded as experts by popular audiences. The able intercollegiate debater who has spent an academic year in a superior forensic program studying the national intercollegiate debate proposition might be qualified as a minor expert on that proposition.

Lay evidence is provided by persons without any special training, knowledge, or experience in the matter under consideration. Such evidence is useful in areas that do not require special qualifications. In debates on "right-to-work" laws, the testimony of "rank-and-file" union members or small businesspersons was often important. These people often had no special knowledge of law, economics, sociology, or even of unions generally. They were, however, able to give important evidence as to how certain union practices had affected them.

In general, the courts will allow laypersons to testify on matters of fact, but will not allow them to testify as to their opinion. This limitation may well be followed in argumentation outside the courtroom as well. Lay persons, assuming they meet the qualifications of a good witness, are usually competent to testify on a matter of fact they have observed; their opinion of the significance of the fact, however, is another matter. The testimony of a "rank-and-file" steelworker as to how many members of his local attended the meeting at which a strike vote was taken would be good evidence, assuming he is an honest and competent man. His opinion about the effect of a steel strike on the national economy, however, cannot be considered as more valuable than that of any other layman of comparable education and intelligence. Only an expert, in this case probably an economist, could give us a meaningful opinion.

Expert evidence is evidence provided by persons with special training, knowledge, or experience in the matter under consideration. In the courtroom, expert testimony is permitted only when the inference to be drawn requires something more than the equipment of everyday experience. This, too, is a wise limitation to follow in argumentation outside the courtroom. Although the testimony of an expert is essential in certain matters, the expert should not be used unnecessarily.

The courts further require that the special competence of experts be established before they are allowed to offer opinion evidence. It is advisable to follow this practice in all argumentation. It should be remembered that an expert is an expert in certain areas only, and that he or she is a lay person in all other areas.

The qualifications of a witness should be studied carefully before that person is accepted as an expert. The fact that persons are well known or that their views appear in print does not establish them as experts. Intercollegiate debaters are constantly required to distinguish between the expert and the pseudo-expert. Each year the national debate proposition deals with some subject of contemporary significance. A number of articles on this subject appear in the press. Some are thoughtful analyses written by experts; others are superficial treatments turned out under the pressure of a deadline by writers who may know less about the subject than the typical college debater.

"Argument from authority" is a phrase sometimes used to indicate that expert opinion is presented to establish a contention in an argument. Expert opinion should be used only when a matter at issue cannot be established readily by other evidence. Intercollegiate debaters and others who cannot establish themselves as experts often find it advantageous to introduce the opinions of experts to sustain certain contentions. In debates on the "compulsory wage and price controls" proposition, some negative speakers contended that controls merely intensified inflationary pressures, while affirmative speakers maintained they were the solution to inflation. The judges in these debates had little basis for accepting the opinion of one college student in preference to that of another. Consequently, the debaters found it necessary to introduce as evidence the opinion of experts who commanded the respect of the judges.

In any matter likely to be the subject of a debate, there will probably be expert opinion on both sides. Economists will differ on the merits of a certain tax policy; physicians will differ on the merits of a certain drug; lawyers will differ in their opinion about whether or not a certain merger violates the antitrust laws; advertising men will differ on the merits of a certain advertising campaign. An important problem in both substantive and educational debates is that of establishing a preponderance of expert opinion—not by simply marshaling *more* experts than the opposition but by using testimony from *better-qualified* experts whose opinions may be related directly to the matter at hand.

F. Prearranged or Casual Evidence

Prearranged evidence is created for the specific purpose of recording certain information for possible future reference. Many public records and public writings are of this type. Political leaders often make an effort to get their views "on the record," so that at election time they will have evidence that they supported measures of interest to their constituents. The average person has a considerable amount of prearranged evidence: birth certificates, driver's licenses, marriage certificates, deeds to property, Social Security cards, insurance policies, receipts, canceled checks, contracts, military discharge papers, or a transcript of college records. Prearranged evidence is valuable because it is usually created near the time that the event in question took place; and, since it is intended for future reference, it is usually prepared with care. On the other hand, since this kind of evidence is *arranged*, it may be subject to the influence of those arranging it.

Casual evidence is created without any effort being made to create it and is not designed for possible future reference. When a newspaper photographer snapped a human-interest picture of a "good Samaritan" helping a motorist whose car had broken down and was blocking rush-hour traffic, he had no intention of creating evidence. It just happened to be a light news day, and the editor decided to run the picture with the names of the motorist and the good Samaritan together with a brief story about the traffic tie-up. Some months later that casual evidence became important evidence in a criminal trial. The good Samaritan was accused of bank robbery. The circumstantial evidence against the good Samaritan was strong; his car matched the description of the robber's car even to a similar dent on the left-rear fender, and his physical description matched that of the robber. The accused had no alibi; he could not remember where he had been at the time of the robbery four months earlier. These facts, together with other circumstances made his future look very bleak until his attorney, doing research on an unrelated case, just happened to come across the newspaper story, which established that at the time of the robbery his client had been in a city a hundred miles away.

This casual evidence led to a prompt acquittal. Casual evidence is valuable because the party concerned did nothing to create the evidence. The accused did not know a photographer was coming to the scene of the traffic jam, and he did not ask him to take his picture or to publish it. As the accused did nothing to create the evidence, the jury was all the more ready to believe it was genuine and not a prepared alibi. The weakness of casual evidence is that its value is usually not known at the time it is created, often no effort is made to preserve it, and a later effort to recall events may be subject to uncertainty. In this case, it was just sheer luck that the picture appeared in the paper together with the accused's name and the fact that it was taken at the height of the morning rush hour on a particular day.

G. Negative Evidence

Negative evidence is the absence of that evidence that might reasonably be expected to be found were the issue in question true. For example, if the name of a man cannot be found in an official list of graduates of your college, this absence of evidence is negative evidence that he did not graduate from your college. Negative evidence played an important part in at least one Presidential election. In 1884, a New York clergyman called the Democrats the party of "rum, Romanism, and rebellion" in a speech at a reception attended by Blaine, the Republican candidate. Blaine's failure to repudiate this statement was taken by many voters as negative evidence that he agreed with it. Some historians regard this as the critical turning point in the election in which Blaine was defeated and Cleveland elected.

Highly important use of negative evidence may be found in the report of the Warren Commission, which investigated the assassination of President Kennedy. Many of the most important findings were based on negative evidence. Myths have traditionally surrounded the dramatic assassinations of history. Wherever there is any element of mystery in such dramatic events, misconceptions often result from sensational speculations. One of the urgent duties of the Warren Commission was to consider all the rumors and speculations following President Kennedy's death and to seek to prove or disprove them. For example:

Speculation: The shots that killed the President came from the railroad overpass . . .
Commission Finding: There is *no evidence* that any shots were fired at the President from anywhere other than the Texas School Book Depository Building.

Speculation: It is probable that Oswald had prior contacts with Soviet agents before he entered Russia in 1959 . . .
Commission Finding: There is *no evidence* that Oswald was in touch with Soviet agents before his visit to Russia. Had Oswald been recruited as a Russian agent while he was still in the Marines, it is most improbable that he would have been encouraged to defect. He would have been of greater value to Russian intelligence as a Marine radar operator than as a defector.

Speculation: Oswald or accomplices had made arrangements for his getaway by airplane from an airfield in the Dallas area.

Commission Finding: Investigation of such claims revealed that they had not the slightest foundation. The Commission found *no evidence* that Oswald had any pre-arranged plan for escape after the assassination.

Negative evidence must be introduced into the argument with care; advocates should claim negative evidence only when they are certain that there is an absence of the evidence in question. Clearly the "man in the street" could not have made any of the claims of negative evidence made by the Warren Commission. The Commission prudently recognized the limitations of negative evidence when it cautioned:

Because of the difficulty of proving negatives to a certainty the possibility of others being involved with either Oswald or Ruby cannot be established categorically, but if there is any such evidence it has been beyond the reach of all the investigative agencies and resources of the United States and has not come to the attention of this Commission.[1]

Even if careful investigation establishes that the evidence is indeed missing, is it missing for the reason you claim? This difficulty of negative evidence can be illustrated by a case from World War II. Germany developed and stockpiled huge amounts of the deadly nerve gases Tabun, Sarin, and Soman.[2] German scientists who studied Allied scientific journals found no reference to these chemicals. Since this absence of any reference to these chemicals was exactly what one would expect to find as the result of efficient censorship, the Germans concluded that the Allies had discovered the gases and probably had large supplies on hand. The fear of retaliation apparently led the Germans to decide not to use their gases during the war. Actually the chemicals were not mentioned in the Allied journals simply because no Allied scientist had discovered the gases. Their existence was unknown until advancing Allied troops stumbled on the German supplies after VE-Day.

Fortunately, we are rarely faced with such complex tasks as confronted the Warren Commission or German wartime intelligence. A typical use of negative evidence in everyday affairs might be as follows. An executive receives an attractive opportunity to purchase some merchandise from an out-of-town firm. The price is very favorable, but he does not know the firm—will they really deliver merchandise of the quality claimed? The executive directs an assistant to look into the matter. The assistant calls the Better Business Bureau in the firm's city and inquires. The reply indicates that the firm has been doing business in that city for twenty-five years and that only six complaints have been received about the firm in the past year, with all adjusted to the satisfaction of the customers. The executive would

[1] These excerpts are taken from the *Report of the President's Commission on the Assassination of President John F. Kennedy* (Washington, D.C.: U.S.Government Printing Office, 1964).

[2] These compounds are designated GA, GB, and GD in the United States; the less volatile liquid counterparts are known as V-agents.

probably take this lack of unsettled complaints as satisfactory negative evidence that the firm is reputable.

H. Evidence Aliunde

Evidence aliunde, also known as "extraneous" or "adminicular" evidence, is used to explain or clarify other evidence. Often the meaning or significance of evidence is not apparent upon the presentation of the evidence per se; therefore, that evidence must be explained by the presentation of other evidence.

In debates on free trade, some debaters introduced as expert evidence the opinion of certain economists that free trade would be beneficial because it would permit the operation of the principle of comparative advantage. Unless those who rendered the decision understood the principle of comparative advantage, this evidence was of little value until the debaters introduced additional evidence to explain the concept.

Evidence is used in extraordinarily complex combinations in argumentation. One piece of evidence may often be classified under several types. In a debate on the proposition "Resolved: That Congress should be given the power to reverse decisions of the Supreme Court," an affirmative speaker offered the following evidence:

The *Congressional Record* of June 21, 1922, quotes Thomas Jefferson as saying ". . . the germ of dissolution of our Federal Government is in the judiciary — the irresponsible body working like gravity, by day and by night, gaining a little today, and gaining a little tomorrow, and advancing its noiseless step like a thief over the field of jurisprudence until all shall be usurped."

The identification of the types of evidence represented by this statement will help us to analyze it. Obviously, it is *secondary* evidence, since Jefferson certainly didn't make this statement in 1922. We would want to know the primary source. It is *written* evidence, and from a public record. It is *personal* evidence, but who is the person? Did Jefferson really say this, or are we asked to take the word of another person? Is it *expert* evidence? Jefferson was probably an expert on the Supreme Court of his day, but is he an expert on the court of today? Nothing in the statement tells us if it is *prearranged* or *casual.* It may have been Jefferson's considered opinion prepared for posterity, or it may have been an offhand remark delivered in a pique. Certainly we need evidence aliunde to clarify this evidence.

III. The Probative Force of Evidence

We are concerned not only with the sources and types of evidence but also with its probative force. Evidence may only partially substantiate a matter at issue, or it may be strong enough to prove the matter conclusively.

A. Partial Proof

Partial proof is used to establish a detached fact in a series of facts tending to support the issue in dispute. In debating the proposition of guaranteed annual wages, affirmative debaters sometimes sought to introduce evidence of seasonal fluctuations in employment as partial evidence in support of their need issue. In a murder trial, the prosecution would usually have to introduce evidence to prove malice on the part of the accused toward the murdered person—partial evidence in the series of facts the prosecution would seek to establish to prove the charge of murder. Evidence that only partially substantiates the advocate's contention is of little value in itself. However, when several pieces of partial evidence are brought together, their combined effect may be very strong. Indeed, taken together they might become conclusive.

B. Corroborative Proof

Corroborative proof, also known as "cumulative" or "additional" proof, is strengthening or confirming evidence of a different character in support of the same fact or proposition. In debates on free trade, some advocates sought to show that free trade would harm domestic industry. Evidence showing one industry that would be harmed was of some value in establishing this contention. Evidence that a number of industries would be harmed made the contention stronger. A defendant in a trial might claim he was out of town on the day the crime took place. One witness who saw him in another city on the day in question could furnish evidence of his alibi. His alibi would be stronger, however, if he could produce several witnesses to corroborate the fact that he was in another city.

C. Indispensable Proof

Indispensable proof is that evidence without which a particular issue cannot be proved. In courtroom debates it is relatively easy to identify indispensable evidence. In a murder trial, for example, the prosecution must introduce evidence to establish the actual death of the person alleged to have been murdered.

In argumentation outside the courtroom, the indispensable evidence necessary to establish the proposition is usually less well defined than in legal proceedings, but careful examination of the proposition will indicate certain matters that must be proved. In a debate on "wage and price controls," the affirmative must introduce evidence showing that such controls will work to control inflation.

D. Conclusive Proof

Conclusive proof is evidence that is incontrovertible, either because the law will not permit it to be contradicted or because it is strong and convincing enough to override all evidence to the contrary and to establish the proposition beyond reasonable doubt. Evidence that may not be contradicted in legal proceedings varies from one jurisdiction to another. Outside the courtroom no evidence is arbitrarily safe from refutation and is conclusive only on its merits. The advocate always seeks to find such evidence; but on matters likely to be the subject of debate, conclusive evidence that applies directly to the proposition is seldom available. Obviously, once conclusive evidence is presented on a proposition, that proposition is no longer debatable. More often such evidence is found to support subsidiary matters related to the proposition. In debates on "right-to-work" laws, for example, some advocates were able to introduce conclusive evidence of corrupt practices in labor-management relations; they were not able, however, to introduce conclusive evidence that "right-to-work" laws would eliminate such corrupt practices.

Evidence is an essential ingredient in all argumentation. We cannot make intelligent decisions without evidence. The value of one piece of evidence, however, may vary considerably from that of another piece of evidence. Therefore, when we evaluate evidence presented to us for our decision, we must accept the good and reject the defective. In the same manner, when we seek the decision of others, we must evaluate evidence carefully so that we may use sound evidence in our case; and we must be able to evaluate the evidence of our opponents so that we may expose their defective evidence. Evidence is evaluated through the application of the *tests of evidence*, considered in the next chapter.

Exercises

1. Select one contention related to the current national intercollegiate debate proposition. Bring to class two examples of each of the following classifications of evidence:

a. Direct evidence to prove this contention

b. Presumptive evidence in support of this contention

2. From newspapers or newsmagazines published within the past week, find examples of the use of the following sources of evidence to support a contention:

a. Judicial notice

b. Public records

c. Public writings

d. A source that was originally a private writing

e. Testimony of a witness

Bring to class a brief paper in which you classify the evidence, identify the contention advanced by the writer, and attach a clipping of the supporting evidence.

3. Obtain the text of a recent public speech by a well-known national figure on a matter of current importance. Prepare a brief paper in which you classify the evidence (1) by type and (2) by probative force.

4. Attend an intercollegiate debate, and take careful note of the evidence presented in the debate. Prepare a brief paper in which you classify the evidence (1) by type and (2) by probative force. Compare this with the paper you prepared for exercise 3. Who used *more* evidence, the public figure or the debaters? Who used *better* evidence, the public figure or the debaters?

Chapter 7

Tests of Evidence

Evidence is the raw material of argumentation. It provides the building blocks with which the advocate constructs the case. If the evidence is valid, the advocate can construct a strong case. If the evidence is weak or invalid, the case can never be sound. Thus we must consider the tests of evidence.

I. Uses of Tests of Evidence

The previous chapter considered the sources and the types of evidence; this chapter considers tests that may be applied to evidence. There are three important uses for such tests.

A. To Test The Credibility of One's Own Evidence

In the construction of their cases, advocates will discover a great deal of evidence. Before they include any of it in their cases, they must apply the tests of evidence, rejecting what is weak and inconclusive and using only what stands up under examination. By applying the tests of evidence, they may also anticipate the probable refutation of their opponents and prepare to meet it.

The tests of evidence must also be applied to problems outside the debate situation. The statesman must weigh intelligence reports that come to him, the executive must evaluate reports of market trends, the college student must appraise studies of employment opportunities in various fields. Throughout life, we are all required to formulate propositions, gather evidence on those propositions, and evaluate that evidence as a part of the process of making decisions. Intelligent self-interest and our sense of responsibility to those affected by our decisions require that we apply the tests of evidence with care.

B. To Test the Credibility of Evidence Advanced by an Opponent

While preparing their own cases, advocates must also seek out evidence that will be of value to opponents, apply the appropriate tests to it, and plan refutation. As a debate develops, they will discover the evidence actually used by opponents, and be prepared to test and refute it, if possible, during the debate. It should be noted that the responsibility of applying the tests of evidence and of refuting evidence rests on the party whose case is damaged by the evidence. If our case is adversely affected by certain evidence used by our opponents and we do not refute it, we may find that the decision renderers will accept even weak evidence at its face value. Indeed, the absence of refutation may enhance the value of the evidence.

C. To Test the Credibility of Evidence Advanced for a Decision

Although we may participate in debates only on rare occasions, there are innumerable occasions on which we are required to render decisions. As citizens, as consumers, and simply as social beings, we find that evidence is constantly directed to us for our evaluation. If we fail to evaluate the evidence of a candidate's qualifications, we may share the responsibility for a poor government; if we fail to evaluate the evidence of the merits of a product, we may suffer inconvenience or financial loss. In fact, any time we fail to apply the tests of evidence, we run the risks inherent in an unwise decision. The rewards of applying such tests are correspondingly great. As we apply them, we increase our opportunities for making sound decisions and gaining all the benefits that come with wise decisions.

II. Tests of Logical Adequacy

The tests of evidence can be stated in the form of questions (*see inset*). As indicated in the previous chapter, all evidence obviously does not have the same degree of validity, and thoughtful persons will want to test the degree of validity found in the evidence they consider. Let us now discuss the tests in detail.

A. Sufficient Evidence

The advocate must provide enough evidence to support the matter at issue. How much is enough? Logically, advocates must provide evidence which is more convincing than the opposing evidence. Naturally, they seek conclusive evidence, but, since such evidence is often not available, they must settle for a fair preponderance of evidence. In the civil courts, the verdict is based on a "preponderance of evidence." In important matters outside the civil courtroom, reasonable men and women usually apply this standard and base their decisions on a "preponderance of evidence." The national intercollegiate debate propositions, for example, always have some evidence — but less than conclusive evidence — on each side. Usually the ability of the advocates determines which side will establish a fair preponderance of evidence. It should be remembered that in an argumentative situation the advocates seek to convince those who render the decision rather than to convince their opponents.[1] They need to persuade only those who judge the debate that they have a fair preponderance of evidence.

B. Clear Evidence

The advocate must provide evidence that is clear or that, by means of evidence aliunde, can be made clear. Examples of unclear evidence were the many Japanese code messages which the United States intercepted and decoded in the months before Pearl Harbor in 1941. For instance, just eight days before Pearl Harbor, the United States intercepted a message from Tokyo to Berlin in which the Japanese Ambassador was instructed to arrange an interview with Hitler and Ribbentrop, and to say:

. . . very secretly to them that there is extreme danger that war may suddenly break out between the Anglo-Saxon nations and Japan through some clash of arms, and add that the time of the breaking-out of this war may come quicker than anyone dreams.[2]

[1] In some argumentative situations, the opponent may render the decision by conceding; e.g., in a civil suit for personal injury damages, the defense attorney may seek to convince the plaintiff's attorney that his or her case is so weak that it would be better to accept a modest out-of-court settlement rather than to run the risk of the jury awarding no damages. Or, of course, vice versa.

[2] See: Winston S. Churchill, *The Second World War,* Vol. 3: *The Grand Alliance* (Boston: Houghton Mifflin Co., 1951), p. 600.

Questions for Testing Evidence

In general, affirmative answers to these questions imply that the evidence is sound; negative answers imply a weakness in the evidence.

☐ Is there enough evidence? (*See II-A.*)

☐ Is the evidence clear? (*See II-B.*)

☐ Is the evidence consistent with other known evidence? (*See II-C.*)

☐ Is the evidence consistent within itself? (*See II-D.*)

☐ Is the evidence verifiable? (*See II-E.*)

☐ Is the source of the evidence competent? (*See II-F.*)

☐ Is the source of the evidence unprejudiced? (*See II-G.*)

☐ Is the source of the evidence reliable? (*See II-H.*)

☐ Is the evidence an index of what we want to show? (*See II-I.*)

☐ Is the evidence statistically sound? (*See II-J.*)

☐ Is the evidence the most recent available? (*See II-K.*)

☐ Is the evidence cumulative? (*See II-L.*)

This message was certainly evidence of Japan's plans, but what did it mean? Was the evidence clear? As late as December 2, 1941, even so astute a leader as Winston Churchill thought it might refer to a Japanese attack on the Kra Isthmus, the Dutch possessions, Thailand, or British possessions; and few if any responsible leaders considered these messages as evidence that Japan would attack Pearl Harbor.

Thus it is easy to see that if the evidence is not clear it will be of little value.

C. Consistent with Other Known Evidence

Advocates must determine whether the evidence is consistent with other known evidence. If it is, they may be able to strengthen their evidence by corroborative evidence; if it is not, they must be prepared to demonstrate that their evidence is more credible than other known evidence, or that other known evidence is not applicable in this particular case. If business executives offer evidence that the unit cost of a certain product will decrease as production increases, their evidence is consistent with the experience of many manufacturing firms. Thus this evidence will be consistent with other known evidence.

This test, however, clearly does not prohibit the advocates from using or considering evidence that is inconsistent with other known evidence. For example, early in the Second World War some scientists presented evidence that an atomic bomb could be built in time to be used in the war. This was inconsistent with a vast body of respected scientific evidence. Many felt the existing evidence indicated that all the money and brainpower a wartime government could mobilize would not achieve the necessary scientific breakthroughs in time. In this case the new evidence proved to be correct; the old evidence proved to be irrelevant or incorrect, and the atomic bomb was built. Consequently, the advocate should not disregard evidence merely because it is inconsistent with other known evidence, but should recognize that it must be studied with particular care. Of course, in most matters of human affairs, some known evidence is available on either side of a proposition. For example, will the stock market go up next month? There is probably some evidence indicating a rise, some indicating a decline.

D. Consistent within Itself

Advocates must study the evidence carefully and determine whether it is consistent within itself. During a debate on United States recognition of the communist government of China, an advocate supporting recognition introduced as evidence the headline and opening paragraph of a news story which stated that a national church organization favored such recognition. An opposing advocate pointed out that, in later paragraphs, the news story indicated the recommendation actually had been made by a *committee* of the national organization and that the national organization would not even consider the proposal until its meeting of the following year. This evidence lost much of its force when it became apparent that the full report was not consistent with the headline and opening sentences.

As another example, a group opposed to a new salary schedule for teachers issued a pamphlet in which they maintained that the increased salaries would cause a higher tax rate. An examination of tables printed in the pamphlet, however, revealed that additional taxes from new industrial expansion in the city would more than offset the cost of the higher salaries.

E. Verifiable Evidence

Advocates must always be able to verify their evidence; that is, authenticate, confirm, and substantiate it. In gathering evidence, the advocates should be careful to check evidence against other sources to satisfy themselves about its validity before presenting it, and they should present whatever supporting evidence may be necessary to their audience. They should also be careful to identify the source of their evidence so that those who render the decision may verify it themselves if they wish. For example, in a debate on nuclear weapons, the statement "It has been estimated that the use of the atomic bomb against Japan in World War II saved America one million casualties" would carry little weight in this form because it provides no opportunity for identification and thus verification. The same statement would be much more meaningful if it were rephrased as follows:

Winston Churchill, Prime Minister of Great Britain during the Second World War, stated on pages 638 and 639 of his book *Triumph and Tragedy* that the use of the atomic bomb against Japan in World War II saved one million American and half a million British casualties.

This sentence, of course, is a paraphrase of Churchill's longer statement. The advocates would have the exact passage from Churchill's book available so that they might quote the source verbatim should the need arise.

F. Competent Source

Advocates must determine whether or not the source of the evidence is actually qualified to testify on the matter at issue. When the source of evidence is a *lay person*, the following tests should be applied:

1. *Did the witness have an opportunity to observe the matter in question?* Once a popular journalist spent a week in Russia and upon his return wrote an article entitled "What's Going On Inside the Kremlin," in which he reported secret foreign policy

decisions of the communist leaders. One might reasonably ask if the writer, who as an expert journalist but a layman on matters of foreign policy or espionage, actually had an opportunity to learn about secret decisions made inside the Kremlin.

2. Was the witness physically capable of observing the matter in question? In a trial a witness once claimed that he would be able to identify a robber he had seen at a distance of approximately one hundred yards; yet he was unable to read a clock in the courtroom only thirty yards from the witness stand. One might reasonably ask if the witness were physically capable of seeing the man he claimed he saw.

3. Was the witness mentally capable of reporting his or her observations? Even a normal person may be questioned when claiming that he or she can perform unusual mental feats. For example, at a certain trial a defendant testified in great detail about the routine events of a business day five years previous, but he was unable to recall any details of other business days at approximately the same time. One might reasonably ask if the witness were mentally capable of recalling all of the details he claimed he remembered.

A person's powers of observations may be influenced by circumstances surrounding the event. A standard psychology-class experiment involves two students who rush into the classroom, fight, and then rush out. When the professor asks the class to describe the incident, he or she often receives widely differing reports. We must know too whether the witness had any interest in making a mental effort to observe and remember the event. How many people attended last year's commencement ceremonies at your college? Ask a few people who were present. Probably very few made any effort to count the audience.

If the source of evidence is an *expert*, then the following tests would be applied in addition to the tests applicable to a lay witness.

4. Does the witness have official signs of respectability? If claiming to be a physician, does the witness have a medical degree? If claiming to be an economist, does he or she have a doctorate in that field? In other words, does the witness have expert credentials? The fact that a physician has all the proper credentials of a surgeon does not, of course, guarantee that the operation will be a success. However, even though some persons without proper credentials have performed successful surgery, few of us would care to entrust our lives to an amateur brain surgeon.

5. Is the witness well regarded by other authorities? If an expert witness is highly regarded by others in the field in which he or she claims special competence, then the opinions have added weight. If a physician is an officer of the appropriate medical associations, is accredited in a specialty, has presented papers at medical conventions, is a professor of medicine at an accredited medical school—then it is reasonable to conclude that this person is well regarded by other authorities in medicine. Similar signs of professional regard should be sought in other areas.

G. Unprejudiced Source

Advocates must be careful to determine whether the source of evidence is prejudiced. In many cases persons testify about matters in which they have an interest; in some cases those who are personally interested in the matter at hand are the only witnesses available. Are these persons free from prejudice? Do they report matters objectively or in a manner most favorable to their own interests? The advocate must determine whether the witness has an interest in the matter at issue and whether this interest is likely to influence his testimony. In a debate on direct foreign economic aid, a negative debater quoted the administrator of the aid program in a certain country as testifying "The program is highly efficient; waste is less than one-tenth of 1 percent." An affirmative debater replied:

Of course he said the program was efficient. What could you expect him to do, admit that the program was inefficient and get fired? Let's see what a Congressional committee found when they investigated this program. . . .

Whenever possible, it is better to do what the affirmative debater did in this case; that is, introduce testimony from a disinterested source.

The *reluctant witness* is a witness who furnishes evidence against his or her own interests or prejudices. This, of course, is even stronger evidence than that coming from a disinterested source. Throughout his long fight against impeachment, President Nixon had counted on Republican loyalists who had ably defended him in the House Judiciary Committee proceedings. When new evidence was released after the committee hearings concluded, Nixon at first glossed over its importance. But within hours of the release of the transcripts, all Republican members of the committee indicated that the new facts "were legally sufficient to sustain at least one count against the President" and that they would vote for impeachment. Apparently, this reluctant reversal of their previous position was a major factor in convincing Nixon his case was hopeless. Three days later he resigned.

H. Reliability

Advocates must be careful to determine whether the source of evidence is trustworthy. Does the source of evidence have a reputation for honesty and for previous accuracy in similar matters? Presidential elections afford interesting examples of the reliability of sources of evidence. Official results of Presidential elections are not known for several days following the election; yet the national news services have established such a reputation for reliability in reporting results that we invariably accept and act upon their unofficial returns, which are announced the night of or the day following the election. The polls predicting the results of Presidential elections, however, have a different reputation. The famous *Literary Digest* poll of 1936 was wrong, and shortly thereafter publication of that once well-known magazine ended. In 1948, many polls predicted the victory of Dewey, but Truman actually won the election. In 1970, Britain had a similar experience. The polls all reported such high popularity for the Labor Party that Prime Minister Harold Wilson called for an early election anticipating an easy victory. The voters, however, supported the Conservative Party, and Edward Heath became Prime Minister. For some time after each of these elections, the predictions of public opinion polls were received with some reservation.

If advocates can demonstrate that the source of their evidence is reliable, they increase the credibility of that evidence; if they can demonstrate that the source of their opponent's evidence is not reliable, then they have cast doubt on that evidence.

I. Relevance

Advocates must be careful to determine whether or not the evidence is actually related to the matter at issue. Sometimes evidence is offered which is not relevant to the issue or has only the appearance of relevancy. The *Literary Digest* poll failed partly because the evidence gathered was not an index of the matter at issue. The announced purpose of the poll was to predict who would be elected President in 1936. The *Literary Digest* gathered evidence by mailing postcards to persons listed in large-city telephone directories and asking them to indicate how they would vote and return the card. The evidence gathered by this method was probably useful for the purpose of predicting how telephone subscribers in large cities would vote. However, many people did not live in large cities. Moreover, 1936 was a year of severe depression, and many people did not have telephone service. Further, the type of person who would make the necessary effort to reply to a post card survey was not necessarily a typical voter. Therefore, the evidence gathered was not an index of how the general public would vote. This was clearly demonstrated when the poll predicted Landon's election, and the voters elected Roosevelt by a landslide.

J. Statistically Sound

Occasionally advocates may find it necessary to use evidence in the form of statistics; however, such evidence should be introduced into a speech only when absolutely necessary. President Franklin D. Roosevelt, for example — although he had a resident statistician at his service in the White House and could draw upon all the resources of the federal government for statistical evidence — would use statistics in a speech *only* if he could not make his point without them. When he did use statistics, he would "round off" figures and simplify and dramatize the statistics as much as possible. This is a sound practice for all speakers to follow, since most audiences find statistics dull, uninteresting, difficult to follow, and easy to forget. Statistical evidence is always prepared by someone, is almost always written evidence, and is usually expert or allegedly expert; it is therefore subject to the usual tests of evidence. Strictly speaking, there are no special tests for statistics which are not implied in the other tests of evidence. However, since the form of statistical evidence is specialized, the following tests will aid the advocate in evaluating this evidence.

1. Have accurate statistics been collected? An advertising firm once wanted to survey reading habits in a certain residential area. They hired a group of college students to ring doorbells and ask housewives what magazines they purchased. An amazingly large number of housewives reported that they read newsmagazines, the better-known opinion magazines, and the more expensive fashion magazines. Very few of the housewives admitted that they purchased the "confession" or "love-story" type of magazine. The responses collected in this survey were not consistent with the known circulation of the magazines, and the advertising firm finally concluded that the responses were inaccurate. Many of the housewives apparently had named the magazines they thought the pollsters expected them to name, or would approve of, rather than the magazines they actually purchased. Polling organizations have developed methods to produce more accurate data. For example, the housewife would be asked, in exchange for some small gift, to show the pollster the magazines she actually had in the house. The advocate must search for evidence that will establish the accuracy of the statistics collected.

2. Have the statistics been classified accurately? Suppose you wish to compare the grades of athletes with those of nonathletes: How would you classify Bill, who plays semiprofessional baseball each summer but does not play on any college team? You are told that a middle-income family does such and such—but what is a middle-income family? Such questions point up the need for clear and accurate classifications of statistical evidence.

Students debating the proposition on direct foreign economic aid came to realize the importance of accurate classification of statistics. Some sources listed foreign aid expenditures as amounting to billions; others listed these expenditures as 700 million, 500 million, or other amounts. The difference depended on how the person preparing the statistics classified military aid, defense support, technical assistance, and other types of aid.

3. Has the sampling been accurate? The ratings of television programs are based on such tiny samples that some Congressional observers wonder if they are meaningless. Some statisticians claim they can predict a Presidential election with only a few thousand samples—if they have just the right number of urban residents, farmers, Northerners, Southerners, college graduates, manual laborers, native Americans, naturalized citizens, and so on.

Getting such a sample, however, is very difficult. Many pollsters would rather interview prosperous-looking people who live in good residential areas than go into the slums to find the requisite number of unskilled laborers. Some ghetto dwellers view pollsters as representatives of "the Establishment" and refuse to reply to questions or give misleading answers. A number of psychological studies are based on responses given by college sophomores—mainly because many sophomores are enrolled in psychology classes, and it is convenient to test them. But one may question whether college sophomores are representative of the general public.

4. *Have the units been accurately defined?* A kilowatt hour is a reasonably well-defined unit, but what is a "work week"? Students debating the proposition on guaranteed annual wages discovered that there were many different definitions for this phrase. It is reported that Russia has more military divisions than the United States, but how does the reporter define the unit "division"? Russian and American divisions differ in size and power; there are also differences between combat and service divisions. Similar definitions are needed for statistics on "the family": that unit is defined one way for tax purposes, another way in housing statistics, and in still other ways in other statistics.

5. *Are the data statistically significant?* Almost any set of statistics will show certain variations. Are the variations significant? Statistical differences are considered significant only if the sample is sufficiently large and representative, and if allowance has been made for the necessary margin of error, seasonal fluctuations, and other factors. If one student has a score of 120 on an IQ test and another student has a score of 121, the difference is not statistically significant. If you toss a coin ten times and it comes up heads eight times, the result is not statistically significant. Figures showing the extent of unemployment in December and June are not significant unless allowance has been made for seasonal differences.

6. *Is the base of the percentage reasonable?* Whenever statistical evidence is reported in percentages, the advocate must be careful to discover the base from which the percentage was determined. In debates on foreign economic aid, it was sometimes necessary to establish the extent to which Marshall Plan aid had helped British industry. It made quite a difference whether industrial production at the end of the Marshall Plan program was compared with that of 1938—the last prewar year—or 1942—a year when industrial plants were heavily bombed. Has the value of the American dollar gone up 10 percent, gone down 50 percent, or remained at 100 percent? It all depends upon the year used as the base.

7. *Do the visual materials report the data fairly?* Statistical evidence is often reported in the visual form. Visual materials are helpful in overcoming audience apathy toward statistics and, when prepared fairly, in clarifying complex data. However, visual materials can also be used to distort statistical evidence. Therefore, the advocate must be careful to determine whether the various charts, diagrams, pictograms, and other visual materials presented really interpret the data fairly. For example, assume that the following figures for the production of a certain type of machine tool are absolutely accurate:

	United States	Russia
Last year	1,000,000	5,000
This year	1,010,000	10,000

Now consider the diagrams (*see inset*) and how they slant these figures. In the first two, the choice of units used on the vertical axis of the graph produces two quite different pictures; in the third graph the height of each bar is reasonably accurate, but a distorted picture is created by using a much wider bar for Russia. The caption above each diagram adds to the distortion.

Visual Materials: Examples

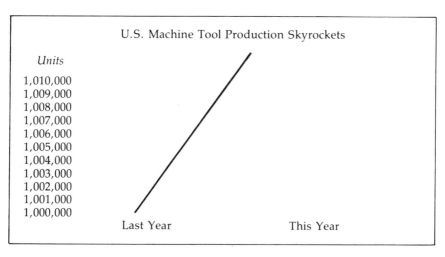

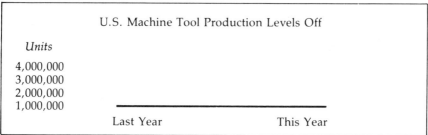

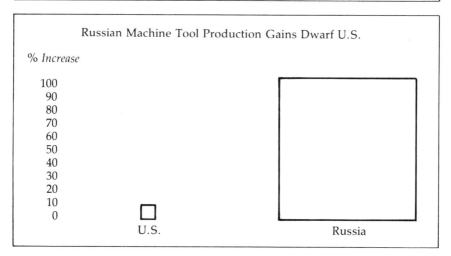

These few simple examples only begin to suggest the possibility of distortion in visual materials. The advocate must study carefully each visual aid presented in the argument to determine whether it is an accurate or a distorted presentation of the data.

8. Is only reasonable precision claimed for the statistics? If greater precision is attributed to the statistics than they deserve, we may reach unwarranted conclusions. One of the 1948 polls, which predicted Dewey's election over Truman, correctly showed Dewey to be in the lead. Dewey's lead, however, was less than the margin of error in the poll. Those who predicted that Dewey would win on the basis of this poll were attributing unreasonable precision to the poll. Sometimes claims of unreasonable precision are made for statistics, and evidence which may merit little consideration is often given undue weight when it is presented in statistical form.

In their desire to satisfy the demand for quantification, journalists, legislative reference clerks, and others often provide us with "imaginary numbers."[3] Consider the following examples of imaginary numbers as they appeared in the press:

1,750,000 Cheered Candidate as He Drove through New York

U.S. Has Coal Reserves for 400 Years

17 Million Americans Go to Bed Hungry Every Night

The thoughtful reader will immediately recognize that unreasonable precision has been claimed for all of these figures. No reporter, riding in a press car behind a candidate could count 1,750,000 people as the motorcade drove along, and some of the people in the crowd certainly were not cheering—they were just waiting to cross the street. The coal reserves statement probably means "at the present rate of consumption." But no one knows what the demand for coal will be in 10, 50, or 100 years, let alone what it will be in 200, 300, or 400 years. The statement about the 17 million hungry Americans overlooks the fact that on any given day 20 million Americans are on a diet and should be going to bed hungry. Thus this figure proves that 3 million Americans cheat on their diets. (If you agree with the conclusion in the previous sentence, please reread this entire section.)

9. Are the data interpreted reasonably? Sometimes "the thing speaks for itself" and no interpretation is necessary.[4] Usually, however, someone reports the data and draws conclusions from them; and that someone may have an interest in supporting a particular point of view. For example, assume that the following figures on the cost of widgets are absolutely accurate:

---

[3] The term is used here to indicate that the numbers come from the writer's imagination, with little or no warrant from the real world. In higher mathematics an imaginary number is a multiple of the square root of minus one.

[4] The legal maxim is *res ipsa loquitur*. A classic example would be that of a patient who, after undergoing surgery, is found to have a sponge in his abdomen. The patient, who was under anesthesia at the time, cannot testify that the surgeon did wrong. Usually there are no witnesses to the wrongdoing; if any of the other physicians or nurses present at the operation had noticed the error, they would have told the surgeon and he would have corrected the situation before the incision was closed. The plaintiff's lawyer would argue *res ipsa loquitur*—sponges simply are not supposed to be left in a patient's abdomen; therefore, the surgeon must have done wrong. The *res ipsa loquitur* argument, while very powerful in this case is not necessarily conclusive. Now, however, the surgeon's lawyer would have the burden of proving that the sponge had somehow been introduced into the patient's abdomen by some other surgeon at some other time.

Month	Cost of Widgets	Increase from January	Increase from Previous Month
Jan.	$1.00	—	—
Feb.	1.10	10%	10%
Mar.	1.20	20%	9.1%
Apr.	1.30	30%	8.3%
May	1.40	40%	7.8%
June	1.50	50%	7.1%
July	1.60	60%	6.7%
Aug.	1.70	70%	6.2%

With these data before them, the advocates may make a number of accurate, but different statements. On one hand they might say, "The price of widgets has increased by seventy cents in eight months." Or they might say, "The price of widgets soared a staggering 70 percent in runaway inflation in just eight months." On the other hand, the advocates might take a more sanguine view and say, "Last month the price of widgets rose only 6.2 percent." Or he might report, "Inflation is ending; for the sixth consecutive month there has been a decreasing rate of increase in the cost of widgets."

Thus it is clear that the advocate should review statistical data in as much detail as possible and determine if the interpretation is reasonable or are other equally reasonable interpretations possible?

K. The Most Recent Evidence

Old evidence may sometimes be more valuable than recent evidence. If we want to know certain facts about the voyage of the *Mayflower*, a document dated 1620 may be more valuable than one dated 1920. A map made in 1000 A.D. was important evidence supporting the claim of many scholars that Leif Ericson's Norsemen reached Labrador, the New England coast, and Martha's Vineyard long before Columbus discovered the New World. Often, however, the recency of evidence is an important factor in establishing its value. If the facts of a situation are subject to change, or if opinions about a certain matter are subject to revision, then we want the most recent information available. For example, this month's estimate by the Bureau of the Census of the population of the United States is more valuable evidence of the size of the population than a report issued by the same bureau a year ago.

In many cases more recent evidence, merely because it is more recent, is sufficient to refute older evidence. In debates on direct foreign economic aid, for example, affirmative teams sometimes cited as expert opinion the criticisms of American aid made by a certain Asian premier. The value of the evidence sharply depreciated when, halfway through the debate season, this same premier came to Washington to ask for economic aid. In debates on federal aid to education, some affirmative teams offered evidence to prove that certain states could not increase their support of education. In the midst of the debate season, new evidence became available showing that these states had actually increased their support of education, thus obviating the older evidence. Since new evidence is constantly being developed on matters that are likely to be subjects of debate, the advocates must make a special point of assembling the most recent evidence and making proper allowance for it in their case.

L. Cumulative Evidence

Although one piece of evidence is sometimes sufficient to establish a given contention, advocates are usually in a stronger position if they can offer several pieces of evidence from different sources or of different types to substantiate their contentions. In a debate on nuclear weapons, for example, the opinion of one eminent scientist might be offered as evidence to establish a certain contention. This contention would be more firmly established, however, if the advocate could show that the same conclusion was shared by the Atomic Energy Commission, the National Academy of Sciences, the President of the United States, the Medical Research Council of Great Britain, the Joint Congressional Committee on Atomic Energy, and other sources.

III. Tests of Audience Acceptability

In addition to the tests of logical adequacy, the advocate must also apply the tests of audience acceptability. We know that decisions are not always rendered on the basis of logic alone; therefore, the advocates must consider the acceptability of their evidence to the audience. The audience, of course, may be a single judge in an educational debate, the whole voting population of the United States in a Presidential election, or any group of decision renderers. A method of audience analysis is considered in Chapter 17; certain tests of audience acceptability are considered here. These tests can be stated in the form of questions (*see inset*). Let us now discuss these tests in detail.

Questions for Testing Audience Acceptability

In general, affirmative answers to these questions indicate that the evidence will probably be acceptable to audiences; negative answers indicate that it probably will not be acceptable to audiences.

☐ Is the evidence consistent with the beliefs of the audience? (*See III-A.*)

☐ Is the source of the evidence acceptable to the audience? (*See III-B.*)

☐ Is the evidence suited to the level of the audience? (*See III-C.*)

☐ Is the evidence consistent with the motives of the audience? (*See III-D.*)

☐ Is the evidence documented for the audience? (*See III-E.*)

A. Consistency with Audience Beliefs

A negative answer to the tests of evidence previously considered implies some weakness in the evidence. A negative answer to this question does not carry such an implication; obviously, advocates occasionally must use evidence that is not consistent with audience beliefs. However, when they use such evidence, the advocates must anticipate audience resistance to this particular evidence and make special provisions to overcome this resistance. Therefore, the advocates must analyze their audiences and determine their beliefs on the various pieces of evidence they plan to use.

For example, three speakers recently participated in a symposium on higher education at a Midwestern university. One speaker presented evidence to show that college tuition costs were too high. This evidence gained uncritical acceptance from the student audience. Another speaker maintained that college building costs were too high and presented evidence to show that a certain type of architecture would be less expensive than the type favored on that particular campus. Since most of the students had no established beliefs about styles of architecture, they considered this evidence objectively. A third speaker addressed the same audience and presented evidence to show that college tuition was far too low; and he proposed a plan whereby tuition would be paid over a period of many years in the same way one might pay for a house. Many students in the audience, who tended to believe that their tuition was already very high, expressed the opinion that the speaker had not proved his contention. They maintained that his evidence was wrong or that it dealt with special cases inapplicable to their university.

B. Source Acceptable to the Audience

Again, a negative answer to this question does not imply any weakness in the evidence itself; rather, it indicates a problem the advocate must overcome. We know that audiences tend to believe some sources more readily than others.[5] If evidence comes from a source which has high prestige in the minds of the audience, it is likely to be accepted with little or no question; if it comes from a source without special prestige for the audience, it must stand on its own merits; if it comes from a source held in low regard by the audience, it may be discredited regardless of its intrinsic merits. The advocates, then, should try to use sources of evidence that are acceptable to the audience. If they find it necessary to use sources with low prestige, they must establish the credibility of the source, at least in this special case. When they find it absolutely essential to use sources toward which the audience is hostile, then they must overcome this hostility.

An excellent example of this problem occurred when the "federal government should control the supply and utilization of energy" proposition was

[5] See Chapter 16 for a discussion of ethos.

debated. When the Arabs embargoed oil and raised prices, there were serious shortages in many parts of the country and prices rose sharply. How much of the shortage was due to the Arab embargo? How much of the price increase was caused by the increase in the price of imported oil? The oil companies had one answer. Government agencies had another. Consumer advocates had still a third answer. Which source would the audience believe? It depended almost entirely on the audience's attitude toward the various sources. One debater solved the problem by citing figures from consumer advocate Ralph Nader and argued that, as even Nader admitted that imports were down x percent, the audience should accept that figure as accurate. The proconsumer members of the audience felt they had to agree with their hero and the probusiness members of the audience, while feeling the actual figure was much higher, were pleased to see an old rival admit there was some truth on their side. As Hovland, Janis, and Kelley point out:

> The debater, the author of scientific articles, and the news columnist all bolster their contentions with quotations from figures of prestige. . . . When acceptance is sought by using arguments in support of the advocated view, the perceived expertness and trustworthiness of the communicator may determine the credence given them. . . . Sometimes a communication presents only a conclusion, without supporting argumentation, and its acceptance appears to be increased merely by attributing it to a prestigeful or respected source.[6]

If, for example, advocates wished to cite certain evidence that had appeared in the *New York Times, National Geographic, Ladies Home Journal,* and *Field and Stream,* they would be well advised to cite the source with the highest prestige for their audience. Janis, Hovland, and Kelley found that the credibility of a message seems to be related to the particular magazine in which it appears.[7] Students debating the "law enforcement" proposition found confirmation of this fact. Some excellent articles relating to the proposition, written by highly regarded, well-qualified sources appeared in *Playboy* magazine. When the debater said, "As Superintendent Parker said in last month's *Playboy* . . . ," audiences usually interrupted the quotation with chuckles. Apparently, the audiences associated the magazine more readily with the centerfold for which it was famous than with the quality articles it sometimes published.

C. Suited to Audience Level

Is the evidence too technical or too sophisticated for the audience to understand? In debates on the proposition about prohibiting nuclear weapons

[6] Carl L. Hovland, Irving L. Janis, Harold H. Kelley, "Credibility of the Communicator" in *Dimensions in Communication,* 2nd ed., eds. James H. Campbell and Hal W. Hepler (Belmont, Calif.: Wadsworth Publishing Co., 1970), p. 146 ff.

[7] Ibid, p. 147.

testing, advocates found a good deal of evidence on the problem of radiation in the fallout from such tests. Some of the primary evidence was so technical that it could be understood only by physics professors. When debating before lay audiences, the advocates were forced to discard the primary evidence and turn to secondary evidence that made approximately the same point in simpler terms.

D. Consistent with Audience Motives

Advocates occasionally must use evidence not in keeping with the motives and attitudes of the audience. In such cases, they must expect audience resistance. Advocates debating the proposition "Resolved: That Congress should be given the power to reverse decisions of the Supreme Court" before groups of lawyers found that the dominant attitude of many lawyers was a desire to preserve the courts unchanged. Evidence that the Supreme Court had made unwise, contradictory, or socially harmful decisions was not evaluated by the audience. They simply ignored it, saying "You just can't change the courts."

E. Documented for the Audience

We saw earlier that the evidence must be verifiable. In order to give the audience the opportunity to verify the evidence, the speaker must provide documentation within his speech at the time he presents the evidence. In an educational debate, the judge expects such documentation, and the wise debater will fulfill the judge's expectations. Indeed, the American Forensic Association in its statement of "Standards" adjures:

Debaters should document their evidence accurately and completely. Complete documentation should generally consist of author, credentials, publication, and year. This information in addition to page numbers should be available when requested by the judge or opponents.

To avoid any misunderstanding, it is emphasized that this information should be presented *in the speech* and also made available if requested by the judge or opponents.

As the student of communication theory knows, not only the debate judge but the general public as well reacts to documentation. Rosenthal points out:

In short, verifiability is the primary linguistic factor in enforcing a statement's credibility, not because the listener *will* verify the statement but because he or anyone else *can* verify it. . . . This opens up the possibility that measurement of the degree of verifiable content in a message may provide an index of its credibility to the receiver.[8]

An experimental study by Fleshler, Ilardo, and Demoretcky led them to conclude:

... it is evident that message documentation was the primary variable that determined evaluations of message and speaker. Concrete message documentation resulted in significantly more positive evaluations of the message and the speaker.[9]

Exercises

1. Find three advertisements in newspapers published within the past week in which the advertiser uses evidence to support his argument. Prepare a brief paper in which you apply the appropriate tests of evidence to the advertisements. Attach copies of the advertisements to your paper.

2. Find three editorials in newspapers published within the past week in which the writer uses evidence to support his or her argument. Prepare a brief paper in which you apply the appropriate tests of evidence to the editorials. Attach copies of the editorials to your paper.

3. Find three examples of the use of statistical evidence in newspapers or newsmagazines published within the past week. Prepare a brief paper in which you apply the appropriate tests of evidence to the statistics. Attach copies of the statistics to your paper.

4. Find three examples of the use of visual aids to present statistical evidence in newspapers or newsmagazines published within the past week. Prepare a brief paper in which you apply the appropriate tests of evidence to the visual aids. Attach copies of the visual aids to your paper.

5. Attend an intercollegiate debate and prepare a brief paper in which you report three examples of evidence used in the debate. Apply the appropriate tests of evidence to each of these examples.

6. Attend an intercollegiate debate and prepare a brief paper in which you report three examples of evidence used in the debate and the way in which the opposing team applied the tests of evidence to refute this evidence. Evaluate the effectiveness with which the tests of evidence were applied.

7. Prepare a three-minute speech for presentation in class, in which you develop one contention supported by carefully chosen evidence. Other members of the class will be invited to apply the tests of evidence to see if your evidence is sound. Prepare an

[8] Paul I. Rosenthal, "Specificity, Verifiability, and Message Credibility," *Quarterly Journal of Speech*, Vol. 57 (December 1971), p. 400. Italics in original. Note again the interrelation of evidence and ethos.

[9] Helen Fleshler, Joseph Ilardo, and Joan Demoretcky, "The Influence of Field Dependence, Speaker Credibility Set, and Message Documentation on Evaluations of Speaker and Message Credibility," *Southern Speech Communication Journal*, Vol. 39 (Summer 1974), p. 400.

outline of your speech in which you indicate the types of evidence used and hand this outline to your instructor.

8. Prepare a three-minute speech for presentation in class, in which you develop one contention supported by evidence. In your speech deliberately include some carefully concealed unsound evidence. Other members of the class will be invited to apply the tests of evidence to see if they can discover the invalid evidence. Prepare an outline of your speech in which you indicate the types of evidence used and the invalid evidence and hand this outline to your instructor.

Chapter 8

Reasoning

Reasoning is the process of inferring conclusions from premises; and the premises may be in the form of any of the various types of evidence. They may be stated as propositions, or they may be statements of conclusions reached through previous reasoning. Thus advocates use the premises they have previously established or asserted, and by a process of reasoning seek to establish something new — a conclusion they wish their audience to accept. If advocates use well-grounded premises, and if the reasoning is logical, they will produce sound conclusions. The advocates' conclusions will be sound to the degree that their premises are true and their reasoning valid. The combination of premises with reasoning is the *proof* of the conclusion.

I. The Degree of Cogency

Logical proof is the degree of cogency arising from the combination of premises with reasoning. Logical proof may be said to establish certainty, probability, plausibility, or possibility. These degrees of cogency may be thought of as existing on a continuum, represented by this diagram:

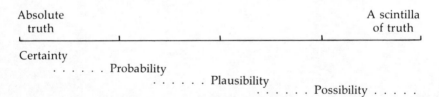

These degrees of cogency are not discrete compartments. Rather they are terms used to suggest the relative compelling force of various logical proofs.

Certainty is associated with absolute truth. If a conclusion is a certainty, all competent observers are in agreement. Relatively little of the advocates' time is concerned with this degree of proof. Few matters of human affairs are subject to proof as certainty. Most of the advocates' efforts are in the realm of probability; they seek to demonstrate that their conclusions have a degree of credibility warranting acceptance. For example, the Secretary of the Treasury, even with all of the resources of the federal government at his or her disposal, cannot establish as a certainty the proposition that a given tax bill will raise x number of dollars in revenue. Students who debated "tax sharing" and "higher education" found that estimates of state sales tax revenues and the yield from school tax levies were often inaccurate. Furthermore, matters which are a certainty are, by definition, not suitable subjects for debate. Matters which are a certainty, however, are often used as part of the evidence and with reasoning are used to establish new conclusions.

It must be noted that it is not only the evidence, but how the evidence is perceived that will determine certainty and the other degrees of cogency. If our ego, politics, finances, or other interests are involved in the matter, our evaluation of the evidence will vary. The hearings of the House Judiciary Committee on the impeachment of President Nixon provided a classic example of this. Very early in the hearings it was apparent that the Democratic members and some of the liberal Republicans perceived the evidence presented to the committee as establishing to a "certainty" grounds for voting for articles of impeachment. A hard core of Republican members, however, argued that the evidence lacked "specificity" and maintained that "certainty" could be established only if—to use the idiom which became popular during the debate—they could produce a "smoking pistol" to establish Nixon's complicity. The "smoking pistol" was never produced during the hearings. It was not until critical transcripts were released after the hearings ended that the Republican members accepted the new evidence as the "smoking pistol" necessary to establish certainty and announced that they would vote for impeachment. While few of us will ever be required to decide on a matter of such historic importance as the impeachment of a President, the example is instructive for all decision making. While the judge or audience can consider some matters dispassionately and with great objectivity (fortunately, this is usually the case with the judge in educational debate), there are other times when the advocates must be very aware of audience attitudes and adapt their cases, reasoning, and evidence to their listeners' interests (see Chapter 17).

Probability is associated with a high degree of likelihood that a conclusion is true. As advocates, we will spend much of our time seeking to prove that our propositions have a high degree of probability, and that our propositions are more probably true than those of our opponents. For example, medical developments are usually subject to the most rigorous scientific tests; yet we cannot establish as a certainty the proposition that Salk vaccine will prevent polio—it is not 100 percent effective. We can say only that, at a given moment in medical history, the probability of Salk vaccine's preventing polio was sufficiently high for most competent medical authorities to recommend its use. At another moment in medical history, most competent authorities recommended the use of Sabin oral vaccine, and public health authorities continue to debate the relative effectiveness of the two vaccines. In medicine and in the physical sciences, the degree of probability of a proposition's being true can be established with great precision; often, thousands of cases can be examined under carefully controlled conditions. In other areas of human affairs, however, it is not always possible to measure so accurately and to control so precisely the variables affecting the proposition. For example, the Secretary of the Treasury, in seeking to establish the proposition that a given tax bill will raise x number of dollars in revenue, will have to qualify his statement by saying that *if* the present level of employment is maintained, *if* spending is continued at the present level, *if* there isn't an international crisis, and *if* various other relevant factors don't change — then it is reasonable to assume that the tax bill will raise x number of dollars.

Plausibility is associated with a lesser degree of likelihood that a proposition is true. The advocate will use arguments having this degree of proof only when no better arguments are available. This type of proof was often used by the ancient Sophists and is often used today by modern propagandists. Arguments of this type are sometimes superficial or specious, and have limited probative force for the thoughtful listener or reader. Sometimes, of course, we are forced to make decisions simply on the basis of plausibility, if this relatively low degree of cogency is the best available. Many life-or-death surgical decisions are made on this basis. When a new surgical procedure is first developed (heart transplants, for example), the surgeon tells the patient, in effect, "If you go on as you are all our experience indicates that your condition will continue to deteriorate and you will die within a few months. We've developed a new surgical procedure that *could* help you. We've had some successes with this new procedure, but frankly it is still experimental and we do not have enough data to make firm estimates. We believe, however, that this new operation will give you a 50 percent chance of living out a normal life span with normal physical activity." Given this set of circumstances would you take the gamble?

Possibility is associated with a very low degree of likelihood that a proposition is true. The advocate has only limited use for proofs with this degree of cogency and will always seek proofs having greater logical force. Until the closing weeks of the major league baseball season, there usually exists a mathematical possibility that the last-place team could win the pennant. If such a possibility requires, however, that the last-place team win all its remaining games and that the top three teams lose all their remaining games, this possibility would not warrant serious consideration. Sometimes, of course, we are forced to make decisions when proofs with this low degree of likelihood are the best available. In debating the proposition "Resolved: That the federal government should establish a national program of public work for the unemployed," some affirmative teams argued that the proposition should be adopted because a major recession might occur in the future and that such a program should be established and held in readiness to put into effect at the onset of the recession. At the time the proposition was debated, the country was enjoying a period of great prosperity and there was no evidence of a recession in the foreseeable future. Nonetheless, some affirmative teams were successful in arguing that on the basis of all our previous experience a recession was a possibility for which we should be prepared.

Often a number of variables must be brought together to establish the degree of cogency of a conclusion. In a famous criminal case in San Pedro, California, an elderly woman was mugged. Shortly afterward a witness saw a blond woman, her ponytail flying, run from the scene of the crime and get into a yellow car driven by a bearded black. On the basis of this circumstantial evidence a blond woman and her black husband who owned a yellow car were arrested and brought to trial. The prosecutor used the laws of statistical probability to establish his case. He asked the jury to consider the six known factors of the case: a blond white woman, a ponytail hairdo, a bearded man, a black man, a yellow car, an interracial couple. He suggested probability factors ranging from 1 to 4 odds that a woman in San Pedro would be a blond to 1 to 1,000 odds that a couple would be black–white. Multiplying all the possibility factors together he arrived at odds of 1 to 12 million that any other couple matching all of these factors could have been at the scene of the crime. The jury was convinced beyond a reasonable doubt and brought in a verdict of guilty.

The balance of this chapter will consider the types and uses of the tests of reasoning. General tests applicable to all types of reasoning will be considered. Finally, specific tests will be indicated for (1) reasoning by example, (2) reasoning by analogy, (3) causal reasoning, and (4) sign reasoning.

II. Tests of Reasoning and Their Uses

Obviously, all reasoning does not have the same degree of cogency. Therefore, the thoughtful person will want to test reasoning to determine the degree of probability of the conclusions. Often more than one type of reasoning is involved in a given line of argument; therefore, the thoughtful person will apply all of the appropriate tests to each piece of reasoning that he considers. There are three uses for the tests of reasoning.

A. To Test the Validity of One's Own Reasoning

In the construction of a case, advocates will discover much reasoning advanced by others and will develop tentative lines of reasoning of their own. Before incorporating any of this reasoning into their case, they must apply the tests of reasoning so that they may reject invalid reasoning and include only what will stand up under scrutiny. By applying the tests of reasoning, they can anticipate the probable lines of refutation by their opponents and prepare their counter refutation.

These tests of reasoning must also be applied outside the debate situation. As college students weigh the propositions that they should enter law school, or medical school, or a certain business, their future happiness and success require that they carefully apply the tests of reasoning to the arguments supporting these propositions.

B. To Test the Validity of the Reasoning Advanced by the Opposition

In preparing cases, advocates must try to discover the probable lines of reasoning their opponents will use, apply the appropriate tests to this reasoning, and plan refutation of it. In the course of the debate, they must be prepared to apply the appropriate tests as their opponent's actual lines of reasoning are presented and to develop their refutation accordingly.

C. To Test the Validity of Reasoning Presented for Personal Decision

Often we may seek neither to advance our own arguments nor to refute arguments of others; rather, we function as decision renderers to whom various lines of reasoning are directed. As citizens, we are the target of arguments advanced by both political parties. To function as responsible citizens, we must apply the tests of reasoning to these arguments. If we plan to buy a car, purchase stock, buy a house, or undertake any significant purchase, our own self-interest compels us to apply the tests of reasoning to the arguments advanced by the salesman. In fact, at any time when we are required to make a decision of any significance, prudence dictates that we must apply the tests of reasoning to the factors relating to that decision with a degree of rigor directly related to the importance of the decision.

III. General Tests of Reasoning

There are two general questions that must be applied to all types of reasoning: (1) *Are the evidence and propositions on which the reasoning is based true?* (2) *Is the conclusion relevant?* In general, an affirmative answer to these questions implies that the reasoning is sound; a negative answer may imply the presence of a fallacy.

A. Truth of Evidence

Since reasoning is the process of inferring conclusions from other propositions or from evidence, the advocate must be careful to determine whether the evidence and the propositions on which the reasoning is based are true. In doing this, the advocate must apply the appropriate tests of reasoning and of evidence to the premises on which the argument is built.

In debating federal aid for higher education, some affirmative advocates stated that since states and local communities lacked the financial resources to provide new public colleges or the expansion of existing public colleges, the federal government was the only practicable source of the necessary financing. In refuting this argument, some negative advocates did not concern themselves with the contention that the federal government was the only practicable source of revenue. Rather, they focused on the premise that states and local communities lacked these resources and introduced counter evidence designed to refute the base of the affirmative argument.

Thus, advocates must be certain that the evidence and the propositions on which their reasoning is based are true. The soundness of their later reasoning is irrelevant if their original premise is incorrect.

B. Relevance of Conclusion

The advocate must be careful to determine that the conclusion is relevant to the proposition under consideration. In debating on guaranteed annual wages, some affirmative advocates developed a closely reasoned argument that seasonal fluctuations in the labor force are inherent in our economy, and they offered this conclusion as a need for the adoption of their plan. Some negative advocates did not seek to refute the argument on seasonal fluctuations, which successfully met the other tests of reasoning, but focused their refutation on the conclusion. They sought to demonstrate that the conclusion was irrelevant since the plan proposed by the affirmative did not provide for seasonal workers. The advocate must make sure that a conclusion is relevant to the proposition under consideration.

IV. Types of Reasoning and Tests for Each Type

Reasoning is often classified as inductive or deductive. *Inductive* reasoning may be defined as the process of reasoning from specific cases to a generalization; *deductive* reasoning, as the process of reasoning from a generalization to a specific case. While it is sometimes convenient to make this distinction, the advocate in actual practice moves from induction to deduction to induction, and back and forth many times while developing or analyzing an argument. Some logicians maintain that all processes of reasoning are ultimately inductive. John Stuart Mill, for instance, points out:

Although . . . all processes of thought in which the ultimate premises are particulars, whether we conclude from particulars to a general formula, or from particulars to other particulars according to that formula, are equally Induction; we shall yet, conformably to usage, consider the name Induction as more particularly belonging to the process of establishing the general proposition, and the remaining operation, which is substantially that of interpreting the general proposition, we shall call by its usual name, Deduction. And we shall consider every process by which anything is inferred respecting an unobserved case as consisting of an Induction followed by a Deduction; because, although the process needs not necessarily be carried on in this form, it is always susceptible to the form, and must be thrown into it when assurance of scientific accuracy is needed and desired.[1]

The intermingling of induction and deduction will become apparent as we consider each of the principal types of reasoning and the related tests.

A. Reasoning by Example

The process of reasoning by example consists of inferring conclusions from specific cases. This process may be represented as follows:

$$\left.\begin{array}{l} \text{Case}_1 \\ \text{Case}_2 \\ \text{Case}_3 \\ \text{Case}_n \end{array}\right\} \text{Conclusion}$$

Sometimes a single case may be used to establish the conclusion or generalization. More frequently, however, a number of cases will be offered as the basis for the conclusion. Reasoning by example is a form of inductive reasoning and involves either cause or sign reasoning, since the advocate seeks to show that the examples or cases are a cause or a sign of the conclusion he presents.

The advocate makes frequent use of reasoning by example. In debating the proposition "Resolved: That the United States should discontinue direct economic aid to foreign countries," some affirmative teams sought to establish the argument that recipient nations resented direct economic aid. They offered as examples a series of statements by various foreign leaders, maintained that these statements showed resentment toward direct economic aid, and from these cases drew the conclusion that resentment against such aid was widespread. Other affirmative teams debating this proposition maintained that direct economic aid was wasteful. They offered examples of expenditures of direct economic aid monies, maintained that these expenditures were unwise, and from these cases drew the conclusion that direct economic aid was wasteful.

The following questions serve as tests for reasoning by example.

1. Is the example relevant? The advocate must be careful to determine whether the cases offered are relevant to the matter under consideration. Some negative teams, refuting the argument that recipient nations resented direct economic aid, were quick

[1] John Stuart Mill, *A System of Logic* (London: Longmans, Green, & Co., 1895), pp. 133–134.

to point out that some of the statements quoted by the affirmative were criticisms of American foreign policy generally and not of direct economic aid specifically; or that the statements quoted by the affirmative were criticisms of American military aid, not of direct economic aid. Thus, these negative teams demonstrated that the examples offered by the affirmative were not relevant examples of criticism of direct economic aid, however accurate they might be as examples of criticism of other aspects of American foreign policy. Consequently, they refuted the conclusion drawn from the examples.

2. *Are there a reasonable number of examples?* Although a single example may be used to establish a generalization or conclusion, the advocate's position is usually stronger with supporting examples. Even a very carefully controlled laboratory experiment is usually not accepted as establishing a conclusion until it has been repeated with the same results by other competent scientists — and in medicine, not until thousands of cases have been studied.

How many cases are enough? One method of obtaining enough cases is to make a complete enumeration. You could ask students in your argumentation class whether they own typewriters, and then, on the basis of complete enumeration, draw the conclusion that x percent of the students own typewriters. Complete enumeration, however, has obvious limitations, since it is often impracticable or impossible to consider every case; therefore, the advocate must seek to present enough cases to convince a reasonable and prudent man that there is a high degree of probability that a conclusion is correct.

Some negative teams, answering the argument that direct economic aid was wasteful, did not attempt to refute the examples. Rather, they maintained that three or four examples of waste among thousands of projects were not sufficient to justify the conclusion that such aid, as a whole, was wasteful. Some negative teams carried this refutation a step further; they introduced reports of Congressional committees that had studied large numbers of projects and had concluded that such projects were, on balance, useful. Thus, although time limitations will often prevent our citing a large number of examples directly, we may give a few examples to illustrate our point and then, to substantiate our conclusion further, offer the testimony of persons who have studied large numbers of cases.

3. *Do the examples cover a critical period of time?* In many instances, the time at which the examples were studied, or the period of time covered by the examples, may be of critical importance. The advocate must seek to find examples representative of the period of time critical to the argument. If, in debating direct economic aid, the affirmative had chosen all of its examples of waste from the first year or two of the operation of the aid program, the negative might have maintained that some errors in administration could be expected at the start of a new program, and that the affirmative had offered no examples of waste in the recent or current operation of the program. Perhaps the classic example demonstrating the importance of time in selecting examples is to be found in the Dewey-Truman-Wallace Presidential campaign of 1948. Many observers feel that the error in the polls occurred partly because some pollsters based their final conclusions on data gathered too far in advance of election day. Thus, although the polls may have accurately reported public opinion as of early October, they failed to reflect a small but important shift of voters to Truman in the closing days of the campaign.

4. Are the examples typical? The advocate must be careful to determine whether the cases offered are really representative. In Senate debates on labor legislation, some senators have cited examples of corrupt labor practices and called for legislation to regulate labor unions. Other senators have opposed such legislation, maintaining that the few examples of corruption were not typical of labor unions generally.

5. Are negative examples noncritical? Advocates must discern whether the negative examples they discover are critical or noncritical. In matters of policy, it is unlikely that all of the examples will support one conclusion. Some examples may well be negative or contrary to the conclusion. In considering direct economic aid, advocates will find examples of waste and examples of excellent management; in considering employment practices, advocates will find examples of firms that practice discrimination and others that do not. They are well advised to remember that they are concerned more often with probability than certainty. They should not attempt to show that *all* direct economic aid projects are wasteful; rather, they should seek to show that the examples of wastefulness warrant the conclusion that waste is inherent in the program and that direct economic aid should be discontinued. On almost any proposition the opponents are likely to have negative examples; advocates must anticipate these and be prepared to offer adequate evidence that the examples are noncritical and do not invalidate their conclusion.

B. Reasoning by Analogy

The process of reasoning by analogy consists of making a comparison between two similar cases and inferring that what is true in one case is true in the other. Reasoning by analogy is a form of inductive reasoning, in which the advocate seeks to show that the factors in his or her analogy are either a cause or a sign of the conclusion presented. This process may be represented as follows:

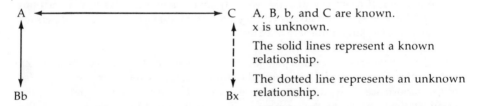

In the above diagram, A might represent Megalopolis, Bb might represent the type of city income tax in effect in Megalopolis, C might represent Gotham, and Bx might represent a type of city income tax proposed for Gotham. An advocate using reasoning by analogy might argue that, since a certain type of city income tax was desirable in Megalopolis, a similar city income tax would be desirable in Gotham. Similarly, in debating the proposition "Resolved: That the federal government should grant annually a specific percentage of its income tax revenue to the state governments" some negative teams sought to show that, as state income taxes were effective revenue producers for some states, such taxes could be used effectively by other states.

Analogies may be literal or figurative. The analogy is *literal* when the cases compared are in the same classification, as are Megalopolis and Gotham (if we will accept these as metropolitan cities for the purposes of our illustration) or the various state governments. The analogy is *figurative* when the cases compared are in different classifications. The classic example of this was provided by President Roosevelt when, just before America's entry into World War II, he used a figurative analogy when he compared the Lend-Lease Bill to the act of lending a garden hose to a neighbor whose house is on fire. Lending a garden hose to a neighbor and lending billions of dollars in goods and munitions to other nations at war are not in the same classification.

Carefully developed literal analogies may be used to establish a high degree of probability. Figurative analogies, on the other hand, have no value in establishing *logical* proof. If well chosen, however, they may have considerable value in establishing *ethical* or *emotional* proof, in illustrating a point, and in making a vivid impression on the audience.

The following questions serve as tests for reasoning by analogy.

1. Are there significant points of similarity? The advocate must be careful to determine whether significant points of similarity exist between the cases compared. In making an analogy between Megalopolis and Gotham, the advocate might be able to discover a number of significant points of similarity; both might have approximately the same population; both might have comparable inner city problems; both might have suburbs of about the same size and affluence; both might have about the same ratio of heavy industry to service businesses. Unless the advocate can demonstrate some significant points of similarity between the cases he seeks to compare, he cannot make an analogy.

2. Are the points of similarity critical to the comparison? It is not sufficient that the cases merely have some significant similarities. The existence of significant points of similarity makes an analogy possible; but the analogy cannot have a reasonable degree of cogency unless it can be demonstrated that the cases are similar in *critical* points. We could easily demonstrate, for example, that there are some points of similarity between a water pump and the human heart. We would not conclude, however, that any skilled amateur mechanic is qualified to repair both of them. As indicated, we could find many significant similarities between Megalopolis and Gotham; however, in arguing that a certain type of city income tax is equally desirable in both cities, we would find these similarities noncritical. To support an analogy involving a city income tax, we would have to determine, for example, whether similar state income tax laws applied in both cities or whether there were similar state and city sales taxes in effect in both cities, similar reciprocity provisions for suburban city income taxes, similar taxes of other types, similar financial policies. In other words, we would have to demonstrate that the two cities were similar in critical points.

3. *Are the points of difference noncritical?* The advocate will discover that no two cases are identical in every respect. Even when two cases are similar in critical points, there will still be certain points of difference. The task of the advocate, then, is to determine whether the points of difference are critical or noncritical. This very often depends on the context within which the comparison is made. For example, "identical" twins are usually similar in many respects, yet they have different fingerprints. This apparently minor difference might become critical and outweigh all similarities in a case where the identity of one of the twins was the issue and fingerprint evidence was available.

As another example, one might point to the very low level of malpractice suits against British physicians and the soaring rate of malpractice suits against American physicians and argue that British physicians must be providing far better medical care. In support of this, one could argue that an injured British patient would be just as willing to sue as an injured American patient, so the only possible reason for the difference in the ratio of malpractice suits must be the quality of medical care. However, there are critical differences in British and American law. In Britain, the lawyer's contingency fee is expressly forbidden; in America, it is almost the sole means of financing malpractice suits. Another critical difference is that in Britain all malpractice suits are held before a judge; in America almost all such suits are heard by juries. In order to defend an analogy, the advocate must be prepared to demonstrate that the similarities outweigh the differences in the cases compared and that the differences are not critical to the matter at issue.

4. *Is the reasoning cumulative?* An analogy is strengthened if it can be demonstrated that more than one comparison may be made in support of the conclusion. For instance, in defending the proposition that a city income tax would be advantageous in Gotham, the advocate would strengthen his case by making analogies not only between Gotham and Megalopolis, as mentioned, but also between Gotham and other comparable cities having city income taxes. If we were able to demonstrate that the similarities between the cities compared were critical and that the differences were noncritical, we would strengthen our case by using cumulative analogies.

5. *Are only literal analogies used as logical proof?* The advocate must remember that only literal analogies may be used to establish logical proof. Figurative analogies are useful as illustrations, but have no probative force. Roosevelt's figurative "garden-hose" analogy, used in the debate on the Lend-Lease Bill, is credited with having played an important part in securing public acceptance for this legislation. Although this analogy suggested a certain identity of principle in the cases compared, the qualitative and quantitative differences were so great that they precluded logical proof. When confronted with a figurative analogy, the advocate must be prepared to demonstrate its shortcomings as logical proof.

C. Causal Reasoning

In the process of reasoning by cause one infers that a certain factor (a cause) is a force that produces something else (an effect). This process may be represented as follows:

$$C \longrightarrow E$$
$$\text{(known)} \qquad\qquad \text{(inferred)}$$

The same process may be used in reverse. If an effect is known to exist, it may be reasoned that it was produced by a cause. This process may be represented as follows:

$$\underset{\text{(inferred)}}{C} \longleftarrow \underset{\text{(known)}}{E}$$

Causal reasoning may be cause-to-effect or effect-to-cause reasoning, and usually involves generalization. In using causal reasoning, the advocate seeks to show *why* his proposition is valid. The National Weather Service regularly reports the existence of low-pressure areas and other phenomena (causes) and predicts that we will have rain (an effect) tomorrow. The fact that the weather service is not always right emphasizes the point considered earlier. We often deal with matters in the realm of probability because we cannot establish certainty in many areas of concern to us. In debates on the discontinuance of direct economic aid, some affirmative teams tried to show that such aid was a cause of criticism among recipient countries. Continuing this argument, those advocates reasoned that if direct economic aid (the cause) were discontinued, then criticism (the effect) would also be eliminated. Conversely, the proponents of such aid argued that it was producing desirable effects.

Advocates must, of course, recognize that many causes are at work in any problem under consideration; at the same time, they must try to discern the practical effective cause or causes in the matter at issue. Many debates on human affairs revolve about causal matters. The supporters of a "national program of public work for the unemployed," for example, saw such a program as a cause that would produce many desirable effects, while the opponents of this program saw it as a cause that would produce many undesirable effects. Causal reasoning influences our thinking on personal matters as well. Students may go to college because they see a college education as a cause that, hopefully, will produce desirable effects in later life.

The problem, as we apply the tests of causal reasoning, is to discern the significant, practical, and effective causes in the matter at issue. The following tests of reasoning may be applied either to cause-to-effect or to effect-to-cause reasoning.

1. Is the alleged cause relevant to the effect described? Some observers have claimed that an increase in sunspot activity causes a rise in the stock market. Is there a relevant cause-and-effect relationship between these two phenomena? Most competent authorities have not been able to discern it. One college debater recently informed her professor that she expected to win because it was snowing the day the tournament began and she had previously won a tournament when snow had fallen at the start of the event. Her remark was facetious, of course, because she recognized that there was no causal relationship between snowfall and the winning of a tournament. Yet this very kind of reasoning has formed the basis of many superstitions. The superstition that breaking a mirror will cause seven years of bad luck, for example, is based on the assumption that a cause-to-effect relationship exists where, in fact, there is no such relationship. Unless and until a causal link can be established between an alleged cause and an alleged effect, one cannot hope to develop causal reasoning.

2. *Is this the sole or distinguishing causal factor?* It is necessary to determine whether the alleged cause is the only causal factor in producing the effect under consideration or, if not, whether it is the distinguishing causal factor. In debates on direct economic aid, some affirmative advocates used cause-to-effect reasoning to demonstrate that there was considerable criticism of the United States by nations receiving such aid, and they argued that this criticism was caused by the aid. In refuting this line of reasoning, some negative advocates granted that recipient nations were critical of the United States, but argued that other causes besides direct economic aid had produced this criticism. In support of this argument, they pointed out, among other factors, that military aid, the stationing of American troops abroad, and the identification of the United States with colonial powers all caused criticism.

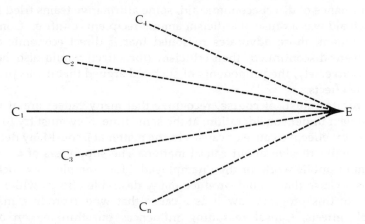

Is this the sole or distinguishing causal factor—or are there
other causes that produce the effect under consideration?

Some negative advocates then extended their refutation by pointing out that nations not receiving economic aid were also critical of the United States—for example, Canada, the USSR, mainland China—and hence direct economic aid was not the distinguishing causal factor in producing criticism. Thus, negative advocates using this line of argument demonstrated that direct economic aid was neither the sole nor the distinguishing causal factor in criticism. The advocate must therefore be prepared to demonstrate that the alleged cause is the sole or distinguishing factor producing the effect at issue.

3. *Is there reasonable probability that no undesirable effect may result from this particular cause?* Usually a given cause will produce various effects in addition to the effect under consideration. Will these other effects be desirable, unimportant, or undesirable? If desirable, they will aid those advocating this particular cause; if unimportant, they will have no adverse impact; if undesirable, they may provide good reason for rejecting the arguments in support of this cause. In debates on federal

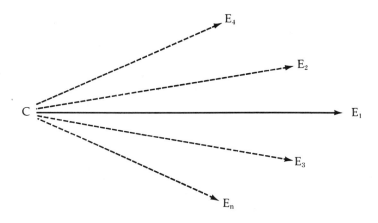

Are any of the other effects undesirable?

aid for higher education, many affirmative advocates argued that such aid would increase the number of college graduates — an effect they maintained to be desirable. Some negative advocates contended that such aid would cause overcrowding in the colleges and thus reduce the quality of higher education — an effect that would be undesirable. Negative advocates using this type of refutation claimed that the disadvantages of federal aid (lowering the quality of education) outweighed any advantage that might come from increased numbers of college graduates (the effect claimed by the affirmative). Some readers of this book can verify the following example from their own experience. Penicillin is a very effective cause for producing certain very desirable effects in some types of illness. Yet, in some persons, penicillin causes effects that are so undesirable that its use is contraindicated. The possible good effects are outweighed by the undesirable effects. Thus, the advocate must determine what other effects will be produced by the cause he speaks for and be prepared to demonstrate, at least, that these other effects are not undesirable.

4. Is there a counteracting cause? When an effect that will take place in the future is the factor under consideration, it is necessary to determine that no counteracting cause, or causes, will offset the alleged effect. In debating the proposition on guaranteed annual wages, some affirmative teams argued that automation would cause future unemployment and that guaranteed annual wages were necessary to protect employees when this future unemployment came. Some negative teams maintained

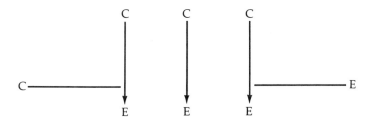

Do other counteracting causes prevent the operation of the cause under consideration?

that there were other causes at work which would prevent serious future unemployment. They argued that rapid population growth would increase the demand for goods and thus actually produce a labor shortage rather than a labor surplus or unemployment; they also cited the Full Employment Act, military procurement policies, and various other causes they maintained would prevent serious future unemployment. Thus, advocates must be prepared to demonstrate that other causes at work in a situation will not counter the effect they claim a certain cause will produce.

5. Is the cause capable of producing the effect? Often various factors occur prior to a given event; yet these factors cannot be considered as causing the effect until it can be established that they are capable of producing it. For example, did the assassination of Archduke Ferdinand at Sarajevo cause World War I? Although this incident did immediately precede the outbreak of that war, the assassination of European royalty was not an altogether unusual occurrence and such occurrences did not cause wars. Most thoughtful historians do not regard this assassination as a cause capable of producing World War I and assign other causes to that war.

In debating diplomatic recognition of the communist government of China, some affirmative teams argued that recognition could cause a breach between the communist governments of China and the USSR. Some negative teams maintained that diplomatic recognition is not capable of causing such a change in the foreign policy of the government recognized. In support, they maintained that our diplomatic recognition of the USSR has not caused any change in Soviet foreign policy. Thus, the advocate must be prepared to demonstrate that the cause is capable of producing the effect under consideration.

6. Is the cause necessary and sufficient? A necessary cause is a condition that is essential to producing the effect. Oxygen, for instance, is a necessary condition for fire. Oxygen alone will not cause fire, but we cannot have fire without it. Once we have identified the necessary condition for an event, we can *prevent* that event from occurring by removing one of the necessary conditions. In debating the "curtail executive control of foreign policy" proposition, some affirmatives argued that, when exposed *necessarily*, covert operations caused harm to American foreign policy and thus they advocated prohibiting the executive from carrying out covert operations.

A sufficient cause is a condition that automatically produces the effect. Decapitation, as the inventor of the guillotine well knew, is sufficient cause for death. The difference between a necessary and sufficient cause is that, although a necessary condition must be present, it will not by itself produce the effect. The sufficient cause is by itself enough to produce the effect. Most often a sufficient cause is a collection of necessary causes all present at one time and place. For instance, oxygen, a combustible material, and the combustion point are all necessary conditions to fire. Together, all three constitute the sufficient cause for a fire. Once we have identified the sufficient conditions for an event, we can *produce* the event by bringing the sufficient conditions together. In debating the "comprehensive health care" proposition, some affirmatives argued that if the government provided free medical care, trained more physicians and other medical personnel, and built more medical facilities, the *necessary* result would be better health for all citizens.

7. How does a new cause affect the system? As we have seen, the world is not a simple place, and we rarely have linear, one-to-one cause-to-effect relationships. As the

Feedback Loops of Population, Capital, Agriculture, and Pollution

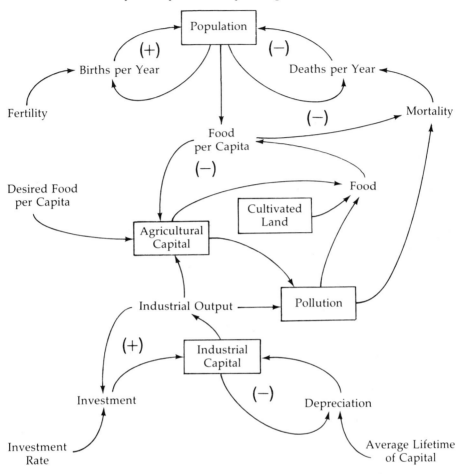

Some of the interconnections between population and industrial capital operate through agricultural capital, cultivated land, and pollution. Each arrow indicates a causal relationship, which may be immediate or delayed, large or small, positive or negative, depending on the assumptions included in each model run.

diagram above indicates, we live in a world of complex interrelationships.[2] If one "simply" wishes to increase food per capita, this diagram shows some of the interconnections and some of the many causes and effects that must be considered. In debates on the "comprehensive medical care" proposition, some affirmatives claimed as a need better medical care for slum residents and cited tragic cases of

[2] Donella H. Meadows, Dennis L. Meadows, Jørgen Randers, William W. Behrens III, *The Limits to Growth*. A Potomac Associates book published by Universe Books, New York, 1972, p. 97. Based on Graphics by Potomac Associates. Reprinted by permission.

children bitten by rats as a need for providing medical care in slums. Some negatives countered this by arguing that there will be little point in treating the rat bite and then sending the child back to his slum home to be bitten again by another rat. Instead of spending the money on medical care, they argued it would be better spent on providing better housing, better food, and other improved conditions for slum dwellers.

D. Sign Reasoning

The process of reasoning by sign consists of inferring relationships or correlations between two variables. One argues that two variables are so related that the presence or absence of one may be taken as an indication of the presence or absence of the other. This process may be represented as follows:

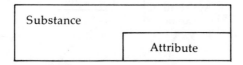

Reasoning by sign involves reasoning by analogy, by example, or from effect to effect as the advocate seeks to show that a proposition *is* valid. In causal reasoning, it will be remembered, the advocate seeks to show *why* a proposition is valid.

We use sign reasoning when we note that the leaves are falling from the trees and take this as a sign that winter is coming soon. The attribute is a part or a characteristic of the substance or totality with which we are concerned. In sign reasoning, the advocate may reason either from the attribute to the substance or from the substance to the attribute.

If one variable may be taken as a sign of another, the relationship between the variables is *reciprocal.* The relationship between the variables is *nonreciprocal* when one variable may be taken as a sign of the other, but the second variable is *not* a reliable sign of the first. For instance, if a man is President of the United States, we may take this as a sign that he is at least thirty-five years old. Obviously, we cannot take the fact that a man is thirty-five years old as a sign that he is President of the United States.

In debating the proposition "Resolved: That the United States should extend diplomatic recognition to the communist government of China," some negative advocates argued that we should not adopt the proposition because diplomatic recognition was a sign of approval of the government recognized.

The following questions serve as tests of sign reasoning:

1. *Is the alleged substance relevant to the attribute described?* It is necessary to determine whether there really is a sign relationship between the substance and the

attribute under consideration. Some affirmative advocates, in meeting the argument that diplomatic recognition would be a sign of approval, maintained that diplomatic recognition is not a sign of approval. They pointed out, in support of this, that the United States extended diplomatic recognition to Communist Russia and to other dictatorships of which we did not approve; they maintained that there was no sign relationship between approval of a government and extending diplomatic recognition to that government. Unless and until advocates can demonstrate that a sign relationship exists between the substance and the attribute under consideration, they cannot develop sign reasoning.

2. Is the relationship inherent? The advocate must determine whether the relationship between the substance and the attribute is inherent or merely incidental. A political commentator once noted that the communist government of China had greatly increased the number of cultural attachés at its embassy in a certain Asian country. He took this action as a sign that the Chinese communists were planning to invade that country. But was the relationship inherent? On some occasions, this type of action has been a sign of an invasion; on other occasions, it has merely meant an increased propaganda or trade campaign.

3. Is there a counter factor that disrupts the relationship? It is necessary to determine that no counter factor or factors disrupt the relationship. An increase in the number of cultural attachés one country assigns to another may, under some conditions, be a sign that the nation so increasing its embassy plans to invade the other. But in 1965 the United States greatly increased its cultural activities in the USSR. No one took this as a sign that the United States planned to invade the USSR; too many counter factors disrupted that sign relationship.

4. Is the sign reasoning cumulative? Sign reasoning is strengthened by demonstrating that more than one sign relationship can be presented in support of the conclusion. An upturn in durable goods orders might be a sign that an economic slump is ending. This sign is a relatively weak indicator when taken alone. If other signs could be found — such as increases in a number of indicators (productivity rate, orders for plants and equipment, orders for consumer goods, work week in industry, and new residential building permits) — the accumulation of a series of signs may add up to a conclusion with a high degree of cogency.

Exercises

1. Prepare a three-minute speech for presentation in class in which you develop one closely reasoned argument. Other members of the class will be invited to apply the tests of reasoning to your argument and see whether it is valid. Prepare an outline of your speech in which you indicate the types of reasoning and hand this outline to your instructor.

2. Prepare a three-minute speech for presentation in class in which you develop one argument. In your speech, deliberately include some carefully concealed violations of sound reasoning. Other members of the class will be invited to apply the tests of reasoning and see whether they can discover the violations. Prepare an outline of your speech in which you indicate the types of reasoning used and the violations of good reasoning and hand this outline to your instructor.

3. Prepare a three-minute speech for presentation in class in which you develop a closely reasoned argument. After you have presented the speech, your instructor will designate another member of the class to present a three-minute refutation of your argument in which he applies the tests of reasoning. Prepare an outline of your speech in which you indicate the types of reasoning used and hand this outline to your instructor.

4. Bring to class five examples of each of the four types of reasoning considered in this chapter. Draw your examples from newspapers or newsmagazines published within the past week. Apply the appropriate tests of reasoning to each example.

5. Attend an intercollegiate debate and prepare a brief paper in which you report four examples of reasoning used in the debate. Apply the appropriate tests of reasoning to each of these examples.

6. Attend an intercollegiate debate and prepare a brief paper in which you report four examples of reasoning used in the debate and the way in which the opposing team applied the tests of reasoning to refute them. Was the refutation effective or not? Justify your answer.

7. Bring to class one example of each of the four types of reasoning considered in this chapter. Draw your examples from recent public speeches by well-known national figures. Consult current publications for the full text of their speeches. Apply the appropriate tests of reasoning to each example.

Chapter 9

The Structure of Reasoning

For centuries philosophers, rhetoricians, debaters, and others have been concerned with the structure of reasoning. In this chapter we will consider the two structures most widely used today. First, we will turn to the structures of Aristotle, whose *syllogism* and *enthymeme* have been standard tools of reasoning for centuries and are still the basis of much reasoning today. Next, we will turn to the concepts of a contemporary logician, Toulmin, whose structural model of argument is now widely used and whose tools— *data, claim,* and *warrant*—have come into common usage.

The formal structure of these methods of reasoning gives us special opportunities to make piercing and precise *analyses* of lines of reasoning and to *test* their validity. The methods and terminologies of both the classical and contemporary structures are widely used in present-day argumentation, and the student is well advised to have a working knowledge of both.

I. The Classical Structures

Two special forms of deductive reasoning are the *syllogism* and the *enthymeme*. By using these structures for the purpose of analysis, we can apply the appropriate tests of formal validity to the reasoning we encounter as we explore the problem, to the reasoning we develop for our own case, and to the reasoning we meet in our opponent's case.

A. Syllogisms

We will consider three types of syllogisms: (1) categorical, (2) disjunctive, and (3) conditional. First, however, let us consider the structure of all types of syllogisms. The *syllogism* is a systematic arrangement of arguments:

1. A *major premise,* which is a proposition stating a generalization ("All A's are B's")

2. A *minor premise,* which is a proposition stating a specific instance related to the generalization ("C is an A")

3. A *conclusion,* which necessarily must follow from these premises ("Therefore, C is a B")

The following statement is an example of syllogistic reasoning:

All legally insane persons are incompetent to make binding agreements (*major premise*).

John Doe is legally insane (*minor premise*).

Therefore, John Doe is incompetent to make a binding agreement (*conclusion*).

In the various examples of syllogisms that follow, assume for the present that each premise is absolutely true. First, we will give consideration only to the structure of the argument. Later, we will consider the truth of the premises in the section on "Formal Validity and Material Truth."

1. The Categorical Syllogism In the categorical syllogism, the major premise is an unqualified proposition. Such propositions are characterized by words

---

Tests: Categorical Syllogism

1. The categorical syllogism must have three terms—no more and no less. These terms may be represented by the letters A, B, and C, as follows: Major Term: B; Middle Term: A; Minor Term: C. *Example:*

Major Premise:	All A's are B's.	Middle Term
Minor Premise:	C is an A.	Minor Term
Conclusion:	Therefore, C is a B.—	Major Term

2. Every term must be used twice in the categorical syllogism—no more and no less.

3. A term must be used only once in any premise.

4. The middle term must be used in at least one premise in an unqualified or universal sense. In the syllogism on legal insanity, the middle term was correctly *distributed,* referring to *all* legally insane persons. The middle term is incorrectly distributed in the following example, because (A) is qualified (*some*). Consequently, the conclusion of this syllogism is invalid.

Major Premise: Some politicians (A) are corrupt (B).

Minor Premise: Richard Roe (C) is a politician (A).

Conclusion: Therefore, Richard Roe (C) is corrupt (B).

5. A term may be distributed in the conclusion only if it has been distributed in the major or minor premise. The following is an example of an *illicit major*—a major term that is distributed in the conclusion but not in the major premise.

Major Premise: All communists (A) want the United States to cut defense spending (B).

Minor Premise: Congressman Zilch (C) is not a communist (A).

Conclusion: Therefore, Congressman Zilch (C) does not want the United States to cut defense spending (B).

like *all, every, each,* or *any,* either directly expressed or clearly implied.

Some thoughtful scholars object to this aspect of the categorical syllogism, maintaining that it is very difficult to make unqualified generalizations. It might be pointed out, for example, that all legally insane persons are not alike: the nature and degree of their illnesses, the types of treatment they require, and the possibilities for their recovery are quite different. They are identical, however, in that they are all incompetent to make binding agreements as long as they are legally insane. Thus, for the purpose of making binding agreements, we treat all legally insane persons in the same manner.

When the major premise is fully stated — "All communists are *among those* who want the United States to cut defense spending" — it becomes readily apparent that the major term (B) is not used in a universal sense in the major premise and thus may not be distributed in the conclusion. Congressman Zilch might be a pacifist. The following is an example of an illicit minor — distributed in the conclusion but not in the minor premise.

Major Premise: All union presidents (A) favor the union shop (B).
Minor Premise: All union presidents (A) are members of unions (C).
  Conclusion: Therefore, all members of unions (C) favor the union shop (B).

In this example, the minor term (C) is not distributed in the minor premise, but is distributed in the conclusion. When the minor premise is fully stated — "All union presidents are *some* members of unions," it becomes readily apparent that the minor term (C) has not been distributed and that consequently the conclusion is invalid. The only conclusion that could be drawn from these premises is that *some* union members favor the union shop.

6. At least one of the premises must be affirmative. Obviously, no valid conclusion can be drawn from two negative premises. *Example:*

Major Premise: No Democratic Senators (A) will vote for this bill (B).
Minor Premise: Senator Eliot (C) is not a Democratic Senator (A).
  Conclusion: Therefore, Senator Eliot (C) will ____?

7. If one premise is negative, the conclusion must be negative.

Major Premise: No Republican Senators (A) voted for this bill (B).
Minor Premise: Senator Eliot (C) is a Republican Senator (A).
  Conclusion: Therefore, Senator Eliot (C) did not vote for this bill (B).

As a practical consideration, we treat many matters as identical and make unqualified generalizations about them. The problem of the advocate is to determine when it is practical or necessary to make unqualified generalizations, within a specific context and when it is prudent or necessary to recognize the differences in apparently identical matters.

Certain tests may be applied to the categorical syllogism (*see inset, pages 130–131*).

2. The Disjunctive Syllogism The disjunctive syllogism is one with a major premise containing mutually exclusive alternatives. The separation of al-

---

Tests: Disjunctive Syllogism

1. The major premise of the disjunctive syllogism must include all of the possible alternatives. In debates on the "energy" proposition some affirmative advocates cited the shortage of gasoline and maintained:

Major Premise: We must either have gas rationing or gas shortages.
Minor Premise: We don't want gas shortages.
   Conclusion: Therefore, we must have gas rationing.

Negative advocates meeting this syllogism recognized that the major premise did not include all possible alternatives. They were quick to point out other ways of dealing with gas shortages and they maintained that voluntary allocations, car pools and a 55 mile an hour speed limit would solve the problems of the gas shortage.

2. The alternatives presented in the disjunctive syllogism must be mutually exclusive. Some of the negative advocates meeting the above syllogism were quick to point out that gas rationing and gas shortages were not mutually exclusive. They argued that gas rationing merely exacerbates the gas shortage by adding the problems of bureaucracy and blackmarkets.

3. The minor premise must affirm or contradict one of the alternatives given in the major premise. If the minor premise neither affirms nor contradicts one of the alternatives in the major premise, no valid conclusion is possible. *Example:*

Major Premise: Congress must either raise taxes or reduce federal expenditures.
Minor Premise: Congressmen will not cut their own salaries.
   Conclusion: Therefore, Congress must ____?

Since Congressional salaries are only a minor part of all federal expenditures, the premise that congressmen will not cut their own salaries might more accurately be phrased as "Congressmen will not reduce *some* federal expenditures." Even though congressmen will not cut their own salaries, it is possible for them to reduce *other* federal expenditures; therefore, this premise neither affirms nor contradicts one of the alternatives in the major premise.

ternatives is usually indicated by such words as *either, or, neither, but,* and *although,* either expressly stated or clearly implied.

Major Premise: Either Congress will amend this bill or the President will veto it.
Minor Premise: Congress will not amend this bill.
Conclusion: Therefore, the President will veto it.

Certain tests may be applied to the disjunctive syllogism (*see inset, page 132*).

3. The Conditional Syllogism The conditional syllogism, also known as the hypothetical syllogism, is a syllogism in which the major premise deals with uncertain or hypothetical events that may or may not exist or happen. The conditional event is usually indicated by *if, assuming, supposing,* or similar concepts, either expressly stated or clearly implied. For example, the following conditional syllogism was used in debates on the proposition "Resolved: That the federal government should adopt a program of compulsory wage and price controls":

Major Premise: If the present measures have checked inflation, then we will not need compulsory wage and price controls.
Minor Premise: Present measures have not checked inflation.
Conclusion: Therefore, we will need compulsory wage and price controls.

The major premise of the conditional syllogism contains an *antecedent* statement, which expresses the conditional or hypothetical event under consideration, and a *consequent* statement, which expresses the event that is maintained as necessarily following the antecedent. In the above example, the antecedent statement begins with the word *if* and the consequent statement begins with the word *then.* The *if — then* relationship is a convenient way of expressing the major premise in a conditional syllogism.

Certain tests may be applied to the conditional syllogism (*see inset, page 134*).

B. The Enthymeme

There are two definitions of the *enthymeme,* both of which are important to the advocate (*see inset, page 135*).

1. Definitions of the Enthymeme The rigorous rules of the syllogism make it a valuable instrument for testing arguments. At the same time they limit the situations in which it can be used. We rarely talk in syllogisms — we are more likely to express our arguments in less than complete syllogisms. Further, there are many situations in which we must deal with probabilities rather than certainties. In these circumstances we make use of the *enthymeme.*

Tests: Conditional Syllogism

1. The minor premise must affirm the antecedent or deny the consequent. If the minor premise affirms the antecedent, the conclusion must affirm the consequent; if the minor premise denies the consequent, the conclusion must deny the antecedent:

Major Premise: If the interest rate on treasury notes increases, then more of these notes will be purchased.

Minor Premise: The interest rate on treasury notes will increase.

  Conclusion: Therefore, more of these notes will be purchased.

Note that, in this case, the minor premise affirms the antecedent and the conclusion affirms the consequent. The following example does just the opposite:

Major Premise: If compulsory wage and price controls are to be effective, then black-marketing must be prevented.

Minor Premise: Blackmarketing cannot be prevented.

  Conclusion: Therefore, compulsory wage and price controls cannot be effective.

2. If the minor premise denies the antecedent or affirms the consequent, no valid conclusion can be drawn. *Example:*

Major Premise: If the interest rate on treasury notes increases, then more of these notes will be purchased.

Minor Premise: The interest rate on treasury notes will not increase.

  Conclusion: Therefore, ____?

In this example, the absence of an increase in interest rates will not lead to more of these notes being purchased; but (since a change in any of a number of fiscal or monetary policies might lead to more of these notes being purchased), one cannot conclude that more notes will *not* be purchased. Thus, when the minor premise denies the antecedent, no valid conclusion can be drawn. Now consider this example:

Major Premise: If compulsory wage and price controls are to be effective, then black-marketing must be prevented.

Minor Premise: Blackmarketing can be prevented.

  Conclusion: Therefore, ____?

Even if blackmarketing could be prevented, there are numerous other factors that might prevent the effective operation of a program of compulsory wage and price controls. Thus, when the minor premise affirms the consequent, no valid conclusion can be drawn.

As there are two discrete concepts involved, there are two definitions of the *enthymeme* (*see inset below*).

This first definition of the enthymeme—as a *truncated syllogism*—is of great importance to the advocate. As we have noted earlier, people usually do not talk in syllogisms. Many of their arguments are expressed in the form of enthymemes. In a debate on federal aid for higher education, we might hear the following argument: "This plan would lead to federal control and is undesirable." Expressed in the form of an enthymeme, this argument would look like this:

Minor Premise: This plan leads to federal control.

Conclusion: Therefore, this plan is undesirable.

As advocates encountering this enthymeme, we would promptly seek out the unstated major premise. If the unstated major premise were "*Some* forms of federal control are undesirable," we would recognize that the middle term is not distributed and that therefore the conclusion is formally invalid. If the unstated major premise were "All forms of federal control are undesirable," the conclusion would be formally valid, but we might wish to raise a question about the material truth of the major premise.

Thus, when we encounter enthymemes in an argument—and we will encounter them frequently—we should seek out the unstated premise and determine whether the conclusion logically follows that premise or whether the unstated premise is materially true. In discovering the unstated premise, we may open up important avenues of analysis.

Sometimes advocates may find it psychologically advantageous to omit the conclusion. If the major and minor premises are clearly stated, the audience or judges will draw the conclusion and may hold it more firmly because they reached it "on their own"; or advocates may be able to make an unpleasant point without actually stating it. Thus a professor might say to a student, "Anyone who failed the midterm exam must get a B or better on the final to pass the course. You failed the midterm." The professor would, no doubt, "get the message across" without verbalizing it; and the student, drawing the inevitable conclusion, might be motivated to put extra effort into preparing for the final exam.

Two Definitions of the Enthymeme

1. The enthymeme is a *truncated* syllogism in which one of the premises or the conclusion is not stated.

2. The enthymeme is a modified form of syllogism that deals with *probability* rather than with *certainty*.

The enthymeme—as the term is used in the second definition (a modified form of syllogism dealing with *probability*)—may or may not omit one of the premises or the conclusion. This definition of the enthymeme is also of very real importance to the advocate, who is often concerned with probability rather than certainty.

Many negative debaters use this objection to the cost of an affirmative plan:

Major Premise: All plans that cause inflation should be rejected.
Minor Premise: This plan *may* cause inflation.
  Conclusion: Therefore, this plan should be rejected.

Syllogistically, this argument proves absolutely nothing. It has a formal validity of zero. The syllogism is a logical instrument for dealing with certainty; it is concerned with all of the factors in a certain classification and with matters that necessarily and inevitably follow from certain premises. However, many problems the advocate must consider are not subject to certainty or to absolute proof. If the negative can establish a reasonable degree of cogency for its argument—if it can establish a reasonable probability that the plan will cause inflation—it might well win the decision. Another enthymeme was used in some debates on the "tax-sharing" proposition:

Major Premise: All tax programs which impede urban renewal are undesirable.
Minor Premise: The affirmative's plan of tax sharing *may* impede urban renewal.
  Conclusion: Therefore, the affirmative's plan of tax sharing is undesirable.

At the time of these debates the negative could cite some evidence to support the minor premise, and the affirmative could cite some evidence to refute it. As neither side could establish certainty, the decision on this clash would go to the side establishing a fair preponderance of evidence.

Enthymemes, like syllogisms, may be classified as categorical, disjunctive, and conditional. The same tests that would be used to determine the formal validity of a syllogism may be used to determine the formal *validity* of an enthymeme. Although the above-cited enthymemes are invalid as syllogisms, they are formally valid as enthymemes. Thus, if advocates can establish a preponderance of probability to support their arguments, they may well persuade reasonable and prudent persons to accept their conclusions.

The following enthymeme, however, is formally invalid; and thus, regardless of the degree of probability attached to the premises, the conclusion is worthless:

Major Premise: Some domestic industries are not harmed by Japanese imports.
Minor Premise: Textiles are a domestic industry.
  Conclusion: Therefore, textiles are probably not harmed by Japanese imports.

The fallacy of an undistributed middle term — *some* domestic industries — renders the conclusion of this enthymeme formally invalid.

2. Chain of Enthymemes Frequently, arguments are stated in the form of a chain of enthymemes. A speaker may state only the conclusion of an enthymeme, use that as one premise of a second enthymeme, state the conclusion to the second enthymeme without indicating the other premise, and continue in this manner to build a chain of enthymemes. The omitted portion of the enthymeme sometimes will be readily evident and uncontestable; at other times, however, it may not be readily apparent or may be subject to refutation. Consequently, the advocate should recognize and analyze a chain of enthymemes, seek out the omitted portions of the argument, restructure the argument in syllogistic form, and apply the appropriate tests.

The advocate will frequently find it advantageous to begin to build a chain of enthymemes in the minds of the listeners. As Aristotle advised:

Our speaker, accordingly, must start out from . . . the [actual] opinions of the judges [audience], or else the opinions of persons whose authority they accept. And the speaker must make sure that his premises do appear in this light to most, if not all, of his audience. And he must argue not only from necessary truths, but from probable truths as well.[1]

Thus, if the advocate were speaking before a civil liberties group, analysis of the audience might lead him or her to conclude that the group would support the major premise "No law should abridge the freedom of the press." Building on this premise in the minds of the audience, the advocate might begin the argument by stating, in effect:

Minor Premise: The Decent Literature Act abridges the freedom of the press.
   Conclusion: Therefore, the Decent Literature Act must be repealed.

Or, if the speaker were addressing a gun club, analysis of the audience might lead him or her to conclude that the group would support the major premise "The right of the people to keep and bear arms shall not be infringed." Building on this premise in the minds of the audience, the speaker might begin the argument by stating, in effect:

Minor Premise: The Gun Registration Act infringes on our right to keep guns.
   Conclusion: The Gun Registration Act is unconstitutional.

Advocates should analyze their decision renderers carefully and seek out opportunities to build a chain of enthymemes on the premises already established in the minds of the audience or judge.[2]

[1] Aristotle, *Rhetoric*, II, 22.
[2] See Chapter 17 ("Analysis of the Audience" and "Analysis of the Key Individual"), pp. 266–275.

C. Formal Validity and Material Truth

In the syllogisms and enthymemes considered thus far in this chapter, it has been assumed that each premise of each syllogism is absolutely true, and that each premise of each enthymeme is probably true. If they are true, the conclusions drawn from the formally valid syllogisms are matters of absolute certainty, and the conclusions drawn from the formally valid enthymemes must be accorded the degree of cogency appropriate to the probability found in the premises. If, however, any of these premises is false, then its conclusion is worthless regardless of the formal validity of the construction:

Major Premise: Any child can make a spaceship.
Minor Premise: John is a child.
   Conclusion: Therefore, John can make a spaceship.

This syllogism is formally valid; there is no question about that. Assume that John really is a child; the minor premise is then materially true. The major premise, however, has no foundation in fact. Obviously, the conclusion is worthless.

It must be noted that a materially true conclusion is not proof that the premises are materially true or that the syllogism is formally valid, as the following syllogism shows:

Major Premise: All nations that have received direct economic aid from the United States are now military allies of the United States.
Minor Premise: Canada has not received direct economic aid from the United States.
   Conclusion: Therefore, Canada is a military ally of the United States.

The proof of this conclusion must come from a source other than this syllogism.

In order to establish the material truth of a premise, the advocate must apply the tests of reasoning and the tests of evidence, considered earlier. Since many premises are, in fact, conclusions from other syllogisms or enthymemes that may or may not have been stated in the argument, the appropriate tests of formal validity should be applied to them.

II. A Structural Model for Argument

For centuries Aristotle's syllogism and enthymeme have been *the* methods of analyzing arguments. Recently, however, the English logician Toulmin presented a structural method of analyzing arguments, based on his jurisprudential analogy.[3] The student of argumentation should be familiar with both classical and recent methods.

Toulmin analyzes argument in terms of *claim* or conclusion (C); *data* or evidence (D); and *warrant* or supporting argument (W), which allows one to move from data to claim.

In debating the "energy" proposition, some affirmative advocates sought to establish that the federal government should encourage the construction of more nuclear power plants. Consider this argument within the structural method of analysis:

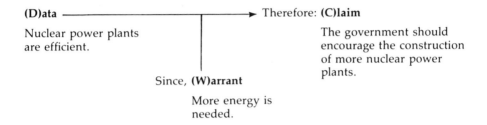

(D)ata ⎯⎯⎯⎯⎯⎯⎯⎯⎯⎯⎯⎯⎯⎯⟶ Therefore: **(C)laim**

Nuclear power plants are efficient.

The government should encourage the construction of more nuclear power plants.

Since, **(W)arrant**

More energy is needed.

In addition to the essential elements of *data, claim,* and *warrant,* one or all of the following supporting elements may become necessary: *backing, rebuttal,* and *qualifier.*

Backing (B) consists of additional argument, supporting evidence, or evidence aliunde, needed to establish the *warrant* when the *warrant* will not be accepted by judicial notice.[4]

Rebuttal (R) indicates exceptions, limitations, special conditions, counter argument, or counter evidence that may refute the *claim,* discount it, or restrict or qualify it in some way.

Since *warrants* vary considerably in their value, the *qualifier* (Q) indicates the degree of cogency[5] that may be attributed to the warrant.

The next example continues the argument on nuclear power plants, using *backing, rebuttal,* and *qualifier.*

The structural model of argument expands and becomes increasingly complex as the argument develops. For example, further *rebuttal* may be introduced as refutation of the original rebuttal; the *claim* may become the *data* in the next step of argument, just as a conclusion in one argument may become a premise in another argument in a chain of enthymemes. *Example:*

---

[3] See: Stephen Toulmin, *The Uses of Argument* (Cambridge, England: Cambridge University Press, 1958), Essay III.

[4] See Chapter 6, "Evidence."

[5] See Chapter 8, "Reasoning" (Continuum of Cogency).

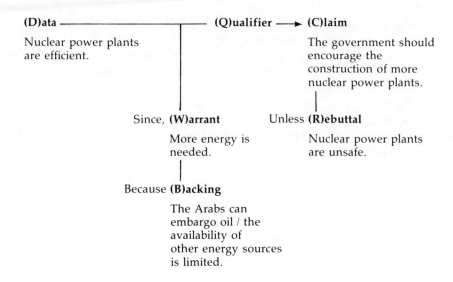

Arguments analyzed in the form of the structural model may also be analyzed in the form of a syllogism or enthymeme:

Major Premise: More efficient energy plants are needed.
Minor Premise: Nuclear energy plants are efficient.
   Conclusion: Therefore, the government should encourage the construction of nuclear power plants.

In analyzing an argument in the form of a syllogism or enthymeme, we should consider the warrant, the qualifier, the backing, and the rebuttal, which are omitted in the syllogism. The structural model, with its specific provision for these parts of the argument, focuses attention on elements that might be obscure in syllogistic form.

The structural model does not establish either the formal validity or the material truth of the elements analyzed. Formal validity may be established by applying the appropriate tests considered in this chapter. In order to establish material truth, we must return to the tests of reasoning and evidence considered earlier.

In using the structural model, the advocate draws on the types of reasoning considered in Chapter 8 (*see insets, pages 141–142*).

By laying out his arguments in the form of the structural model, the advocate gains an additional opportunity to analyze the whole complex of the argument and to select certain portions of the argument for further examination by application of appropriate tests of evidence and reasoning.

Structural Model: Types of Reasoning

Reasoning by Example Assume that the advocate claims there are practical alternatives to nuclear power:

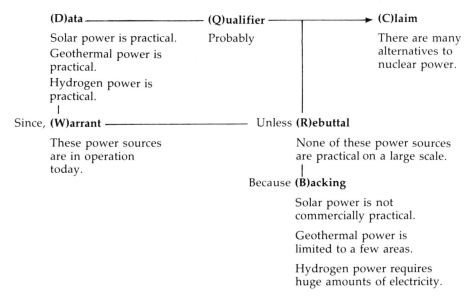

(D)ata —————————— **(Q)ualifier** —————┬—————→ **(C)laim**

Solar power is practical.   Probably   There are many
Geothermal power is   alternatives to
practical.   nuclear power.
Hydrogen power is
practical.

Since, **(W)arrant** ——————————————— Unless **(R)ebuttal**

These power sources   None of these power sources
are in operation   are practical on a large scale.
today.
                        Because **(B)acking**

                                 Solar power is not
                                 commercially practical.

                                 Geothermal power is
                                 limited to a few areas.

                                 Hydrogen power requires
                                 huge amounts of electricity.

Reasoning by Analogy Assume that the advocate claims that covert operations by the CIA will be successful in the future:

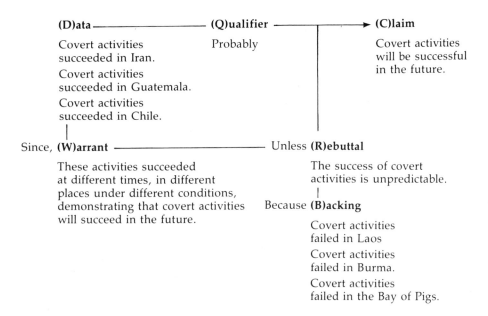

(D)ata ——————————— **(Q)ualifier** —————┬—————→ **(C)laim**

Covert activities   Probably   Covert activities
succeeded in Iran.   will be successful
Covert activities   in the future.
succeeded in Guatemala.
Covert activities
succeeded in Chile.

Since, **(W)arrant** ——————————————— Unless **(R)ebuttal**

These activities succeeded   The success of covert
at different times, in different activities is unpredictable.
places under different conditions,
demonstrating that covert activities Because **(B)acking**
will succeed in the future.
                                 Covert activities
                                 failed in Laos
                                 Covert activities
                                 failed in Burma.
                                 Covert activities
                                 failed in the Bay of Pigs.

Causal Reasoning Assume that the advocate claims the Cost of Living Index will go up because of a recent increase in the price of meat:

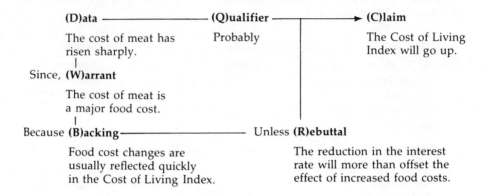

Sign Reasoning Assume that the advocate claims the economy will improve in the next few months:

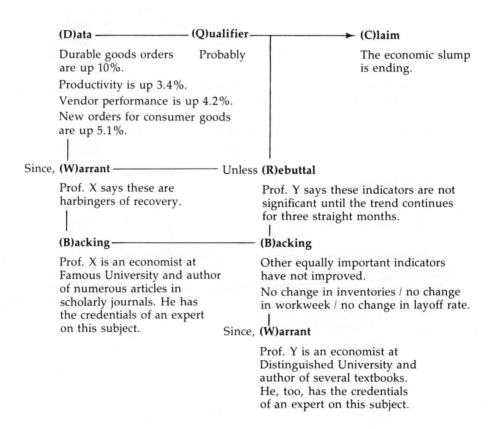

Exercises

1. Find an argumentative editorial that has been published in a daily newspaper within the past month. Restate the arguments in the form of enthymemes or syllogisms. Analyze these arguments. Show why they are or are not formally valid.

2. Find an argumentative editorial as in exercise 1. Lay out one of the major arguments in the form of the structural model. Does the warrant justify the movement from data to claim? Has the editor qualified his claim accurately? Is sufficient backing given for the warrant? Has proper consideration been made for rebuttal?

3. Prepare a five-minute speech for presentation in class in which you support or oppose a proposition of policy. Use the structural model for argument as you prepare your speech. Do not state your arguments in the form of the structural model, but present them in your usual manner of speaking. Hand an outline of your speech to your instructor. Attach to the outline a structural model layout of your major arguments. Invite your classmates to locate your data(s), claim(s) and warrant(s) and apply the questions listed in exercise 2 to them.

4. Select a major argument from one of the constructive or rebuttal speeches in Appendix B of this book, and analyze it in the form of the structural model. Apply the questions listed in exercise 2.

5. Prepare a speech similar to the one described in exercise 2. As soon as you have presented your speech, your instructor will designate another member of the class to present a five-minute speech in which he or she seeks to refute your arguments by applying the questions listed in exercise 2.

Chapter 10

Obstacles to Clear Thinking

Clear thinking is essential to all intelligent decision making. From the moment we begin to explore a problem until the end of the final debate on that problem, we must constantly be on guard against obstacles to clear thinking. The obvious obstacles are readily detected. One type of obstacle, however, which is more subtle and hence more deceptive, is called a *fallacy*. At first glance the error, unreasonableness, or falseness of the fallacy is not apparent, for the statement has the appearance of truth or reasonableness. Whately defined a fallacy as "any unsound mode of arguing, which appears to demand our conviction, and to be decisive of the question in hand, when in fairness it is not."[1]

Fallacies are usually recognized easily in isolation, but woven into the context of an argument they may pass unnoticed unless we are on guard against them. Debate affords those who render decisions one of the strongest protections against fallacies, since they not only have the opportunity to detect fallacies themselves but they also have the added safeguard that it is in the interest of the opposing advocates to point out fallacies in one another's cases.

Fallacies may be used accidentally or deliberately. Some advocates deliberately introduce fallacies into their arguments in order to exploit their listeners or readers and secure an unfair decision. A contemporary example of the apparently deliberate use of fallacies can be found in communist propaganda. Much of this propaganda is prepared by persons sufficiently intelligent to recognize the fallacies they are using; yet these men and women deliberately introduce fallacies into their arguments. Some fallacies, on the other hand, may be introduced into argument unintentionally by honest people. Therefore, the advocate must be alert for obstacles to clear thinking at all times and from all sources.

For convenience, fallacies are classified here under various headings. In argument fallacies often are interwoven, and a fallacious argument may be a complex of several fallacies. In exposing fallacies in our opponent's case, we will do little good by declaiming "Ah, ha, in his last statement my opponent has committed the fallacies of *circulus in probando* and *per negationem consequentiae!*" Although we may wish to identify and classify a fallacy for our own convenience, our task in the debate is not to name the fallacy but

---

[1] Richard Whately, *Elements of Logic* (Boston: James Munroe and Co., 1848), p. 143.

to be able to demonstrate to those who render the decision how or why the matter in question is fallacious.

It is probably impossible to assemble a complete list of the obstacles to clear thinking, since the ways in which communicators can make mistakes or create deceptions are probably unlimited. Nonetheless, it is possible to identify many of the more common fallacies and to suggest ways of avoiding them in our own arguments and of exposing them in arguments of others.

I. Fallacies of Evidence

Theatre or film advertisements sometimes afford instances of fallacious use of evidence. For example, one critic wrote of a Broadway musical:

Interlude represented an inept effort to make a dull story palatable by adding music. Unfortunately one brilliantly executed dance number in the first act was not enough to keep the show moving. Lavish costuming could not overcome the basic fact that the female lead simply does not have an adequate voice for the theater. The comedy routines showed brief flashes of inspiration, but they could not relieve the overall pedestrian pace of *Interlude*.

The newspaper advertisements quoted the reviewer as saying "*Interlude* . . . brilliantly executed . . . lavish costuming . . . flashes of inspiration." We can guard against this kind of fallacious use of evidence by asking "Is any evidence omitted?"

One of the most common fallacies of evidence is the use of the unsupported assertion. Here, the speaker offers no evidence to support a statement; rather, he or she asks us to assume that something is so merely because he or she says it is so. The high-pressure used-car salesman may tell a customer, "This car is in perfect condition. You'd better buy it now before someone else gets it." The prudent buyer would not accept this unsupported assertion, but would look for evidence of the condition of the car. We can guard against this fallacy by asking "Is the contention an unsupported assertion?"

The tests of evidence in Chapter 7 can help us guard against other fallacies of evidence.

II. Fallacies of Reasoning

Not only must we guard against fallacies of evidence, we must also be alert to fallacies that may occur in each of the types of reasoning we considered earlier.

A. Example

A speaker who maintained that college students are "going to the dogs" offered as proof the following examples of their depravity:

Last week college kids burned an ROTC building on a West Coast campus. Just two days ago some graduate students were arrested for selling drugs on a Chicago campus. This morning's paper tells of rioting and looting in Harvard Square. I could cite a dozen more examples similar to these, but this is enough to show what kind of hoodlums we have in our colleges today.

Are you willing to agree that this paints an accurate picture of American college students? We can quickly expose this fallacy by asking "Are the examples given typical of the whole?"

Another common fallacy of reasoning by example is committed by the person who knows two or three long-haired persons to be homosexuals and concludes that "all long-haired types are homosexuals." Here, one should ask, "Have sufficient examples been given?" A hasty generalization based on insufficient examples often leads to unsound conclusions.

Additional questions that will aid us in guarding against other fallacies of reasoning by example may be found under "The Tests of Reasoning by Example" in Chapter 8.

B. Analogy

A communist leader once told an American visitor to the USSR, "We're a completely democratic country; we have elections just as you do." The American exposed the fallacy in this analogy by replying "In my country, however, we have at least two political parties." In this case the American applied the question "Are there critical differences in the factors compared?" and his reply pointed out one of the essential differences between American and Soviet elections.

See Chapter 8 for other questions that will help in detecting fallacies in reasoning by analogy.

C. Cause

There are many causal factors at work in most situations. Although some of these minor causal factors may contribute to the effect under consideration, they alone are not capable of producing the effect. For example, the fact that Rockefeller was divorced and remarried probably caused him to lose some support in his efforts to secure the Republican Presidential nomination in 1964, but this factor is not considered by political analysts as the sole or distinguishing causal factor in his defeat. Fallacies of this type may be detected by asking "Is a minor causal relationship treated as the sole or distinguishing causal factor?"

Another common fallacy of causal reasoning is the assumption that, because two events occur in sequence, the first event is the cause of the second. For example, Herbert Hoover was elected President in 1928, and a great depression began in 1929. Did Hoover cause the depression? Economists assign other causes to the depression, but many voters apparently noted only the sequence of events and assumed a causal relationship. In cases such as this, one should ask, "Is a sequential relationship treated as a causal relationship?"

Additional questions we may ask to expose fallacies of causal reasoning may be found under "Tests of Causal Reasoning" in Chapter 8.

D. Sign

The ability to use sign reasoning effectively is an essential part of the work of all who seek rational decisions. The physician, for example, must constantly be on guard against fallacies in interpreting signs. In diagnosing a case, the neurologist may look for the Babinski sign, a certain type of movement of the toes after stimulus. This sign is apparently inherent in certain types of illness and, when found in adults, is taken as an indication of the presence of disease of the corticospinal pathway. The Rossolimo sign, a certain type of flexing of the toes after stimulus, indicates disease of the pyramidal tract. It is a much less reliable sign, however, because it is sometimes absent when the disease is present and it is sometimes found in normal patients. All who use sign reasoning should be on guard against fallacies that might lead to such false conclusions.

Questions that can help us to detect fallacies in sign reasoning in argumentative situations are considered in Chapter 8.

III. Fallacies of Language

The fallacies of language are often interwoven with other fallacies. Some of the more common fallacies of language that the advocate must guard against are cited here.

A. Ambiguity

Ambiguity arises when the meaning of a word, phrase, or passage may be reasonably interpreted in two or more ways. For example, what does a

speaker mean when saying "I favor the American way of doing things"?
A candidate for public office once campaigned on the slogan of "more teamwork in government." "Teamwork" may sound good, but what does it
mean? A government official recently testified that he had not received any
"improper" gifts from a constituent and that he had not made any "unreasonable" requests of governmental agencies on behalf of this constituent.
His opponents viewed these same activities as "corruption" and "influence."
Such terms as "New Deal," "New Frontier," "Great Society," "Win," and
even "Democrat," "Republican," "Conservative" and "New Left," have so
many different meanings to so many different people that they are often
ambiguous.

B. Verbalism

Verbalism arises when words are used so that they obscure meaning. *Time*
magazine reported an example of this from a Senate committee hearing:

Shedding less useful light than a firefly at noon, Yankee Manager Casey Stengel, 68,
long used to watching his hirelings clobber the Washington Senators, flummoxed
singlehanded a different sort of Senator with his favorite weapons: syntax. As a witness before a subcommittee hearing testimony on a bill to exempt baseball from
antitrust action, Stengel was asked by Tennessee Democrat Estes Kefauver why the
bill should be passed. "Well," said Casey, clarifying things, "you can retire with an
annuity at 50, and I further state that I am not a member of that plan. You'd think, my
goodness, why not, and him 48 years in baseball." "I'm not sure I made my question
clear," said the Keef, doubtfully. "I would say that I wouldn't know," droned Stengel
again, "but I imagine to keep baseball going as high as baseball is a sport that has
gone into baseball from the baseball answer." Murmured defeated Senator Kefauver,
changing the subject, "I see."[2]

C. Loaded Language

Loaded language provides many possibilities for obstacles to clear thinking.
Emotionally charged words are often used in an effort to establish a contention without proof. In a recent political campaign one candidate declared,
"The time has come to throw this do-nothing, corruption-riddled Administration out of office." Obviously, such an administration should be
thrown out of office, but the mere use of these labels did nothing to prove
that the Administration was guilty of either of the charges. Consider the
examples of loaded language in the following "conjugations":

[2] *Time*, July 21, 1958, p. 33. Reprinted by permission of *Time* Magazine. Copyright Time Inc.
1958.

I am economical.	I am a playboy.
You are a tightwad.	You are oversexed.
He is a miser.	He is a pervert.
I am revising my plans.	I am a freedom fighter.
You are impetuous.	You are a hijacker.
He is irresponsible.	He is a terrorist.

Are these extreme cases? Perhaps. Is a man who solicits memberships for a labor organization a "field representative," an "organizer," an "agitator," a member of a "goon squad," or a "hired thug"? It may depend on what paper we read. Is a successful businessman a "robber baron," a "manipulator," an "exploiter," a "dynamic executive," or a "self-made man"? Once again, it may depend on what paper we read.

Loaded language, or name calling, is used all too often in political campaigns. *Time* magazine reported this example from a Florida Senatorial campaign:

Word-wise George Smathers was said to have won over back-country Floridians by malapropian innuendo. Gasped Smathers righteously: "Claude Pepper is known all over Washington as a shameless extrovert! Not only that, but this man had to matriculate before he could go to college, and he has a sister who was once a Thespian in wicked New York. Worst of all, it is an established fact that Mr. Pepper, before his marriage, habitually practiced celibacy!"[3]

D. Poor Grammatical Structure

The use of poor grammatical structure may alter the meaning of a passage, often rendering it ambiguous or unintelligible. The sentence " 'The Secretary of State,' said the senator, 'would issue a statement tomorrow' " takes on quite another meaning if the commas and quotation marks are omitted— "The Secretary of State said the senator would issue a statement tomorrow." The ambiguous reference of the word "it" leaves the speaker's meaning in doubt in this sentence: "When we weigh the dangers of inflation against dangers of increased unemployment, we can only conclude that it is a risk we must take." The false double capacity of the word "they" in the following passage creates confusion: "The American delegation believed the Russians would veto the proposal. The British delegation concurred in this view. At the conclusion of the debate, they vetoed it."

Incomplete comparison is another grammatical fallacy—for example, "The present foreign aid program is unquestionably more effective." More effective than what? The advocate must guard against these and all of the other hazards of grammatical usage.

[3] *Time,* September 8, 1958, p. 20. Reprinted by permission of *Time* Magazine. Copyright Time Inc. 1958.

IV. Fallacies of Pseudo Arguments

Pseudo arguments are fallacies created, by accident or design, by distortion, confusion, manipulation, or avoidance of the matters at issue or by substitution of matters not germane to the issue. Some of the more common fallacies are considered here.

A. Extension

The fallacy of extension carries an argument beyond its reasonable limits. For example, some opponents of "right-to-work" laws argued that these laws did not provide jobs for the unemployed. These laws were not intended to provide jobs, but merely to eliminate the requirement of union membership as a condition of employment. It would be just as reasonable to criticize Salk vaccine, a serum designed to prevent polio, because it does not prevent pneumonia.

B. Arguing in a Circle

The fallacy of arguing in a circle occurs when two unsupported assertions are used to "prove" each other. For example: "Because abortion is immoral, it should be prohibited. Because abortion should be prohibited, the practice of abortion is immoral."

C. Ignoring the Issue

In a debate on the proposition "Resolved: That the United States should adopt a program of compulsory health insurance for all citizens," an affirmative team proposed a particularly weak and ineffective plan. In a thoughtful, closely reasoned refutation, the negative demonstrated that the affirmative's plan was completely unworkable. In their remaining speeches, the affirmative speakers ignored the issue of the workability of their plan; instead, they spent their time describing pitiful cases of widows and orphans without medical care (persons whom the negative had demonstrated would not be helped by the affirmative plan) and demanding that something be done to alleviate this suffering. By ignoring the issue, the affirmative lost this debate.

D. Baiting an Opponent

Sometimes advocates will bait their opponents by insulting them, attacking them personally, criticizing their friends, or doing anything that will cause them to lose their tempers. Once advocates lose their "cool," they are very likely to lose control of the argument and make reckless statements that will expose their case to defeat. Advocates can defend themselves against this kind of baiting only by holding their tempers during the argument; later, they may be able to "blow off steam" without damaging the case.

E. Repeated Assertion

The fallacy of repeated assertion occurs when an argument is repeated, with the repetition treated as proof. In a debate on guaranteed annual wages, members of the affirmative team stated repeatedly, without offering any proof, that American working persons need a guaranteed annual wage. A negative speaker, exposing this fallacy, pointed out that saying something three times did not make it true. This fallacy is not always so easily brushed off, however. Hitler developed to a fine art the technique of repeating a "big lie" so often that many came to believe it.

F. Structured Response

This fallacy is often found in cross examinations or in any situation where the advocate has an opportunity to ask a series of questions. Using this fallacy, the advocate first asks a series of unimportant questions, which the respondent must answer in a predetermined way, until the pattern of a response has been established — then the critical question is asked. An old routine of insurance salespersons, for example, goes something like this: "You love your wife, don't you?" "You love your children, don't you?" "You want your children to go to college, don't you?" "You want your wife to continue to live in this lovely house, don't you?" "If something should happen to you, you want your family to be provided for?" "You would still want your children to go to college?" "You want to provide protection for them?" "To be safe, hadn't you better write your name on this routine form today?" If the prospect has been lulled into a series of "yes" responses, he may find that he has signed an application for insurance without fully realizing the commitment he has undertaken.

G. Special Pleading

The fallacy of special pleading occurs when advocates accept a line of reasoning and its conclusions but urge a special exception for their case. Examples of special pleading are sometimes found in Congress. A representative may favor a general reduction of tariffs on the ground that they raise prices for the consumer; at the same time, he may demand an increase in the tariff on some product of special importance in his own district.

H. Substituting the Person for the Argument

This fallacy consists of the attempt to have an argument accepted or rejected, not because of any merit or defect intrinsic to the argument but because of the character of the person advancing the argument. For example, some people said that compulsory wage and price controls should be rejected because socialists favored them. Conversely, it may be argued that because someone is good in some respect, his arguments on some other matter must also be good. The defense attorney in a murder trial—as argument against the prosecution's claim that his or her client shot a business rival—sometimes tries to present the client as a kindly man who helps old ladies across busy streets, is good to his wife, kind to his children, generous to charities, and a member of the church choir. During the "One Hundred Days" of Franklin D. Roosevelt's first term and the early part of Eisenhower's first term, the popularity of these men was so great that many laws were enacted by Congress simply because "the President wants this bill passed—therefore, it must be good."[4] The Civil Rights Bill undoubtedly moved through Congress far more quickly after President Kennedy's assassination than it would have had he lived. Many argued: "We must pass this bill to show our support of the new President in a time of crisis," or "We must pass this bill as a tribute to our martyred President."

It should be noted that argument about a person is legitimate when the character of the person is intrinsic to the matter at issue. Evidence that John Doe is a convicted embezzler would be legitimate evidence if the issue were his employment as an accountant. Evidence that Jane Doe is a communist would be germane if she were urging that the United States adopt a certain foreign policy toward the USSR.

I. Substituting Bombast for Argument

When no evidence or reasoning is available, advocates may sometimes attempt to support their argument by sheer noise and histrionics. In a debate on guaranteed annual wages, for example, a novice debater inserted in his affirmative case the impromptu claim that industry has a moral obligation to provide its workers with a guaranteed annual wage. The next negative speaker denied that any industry has a moral obligation to drive itself into bankruptcy and, quite reasonably, asked that the affirmative define what was meant by moral obligation. The second affirmative speaker searched his card file and was unable to find a single scrap of evidence defining moral obligation, nor any notation of lines of argument that might support his colleague's impromptu claim. There may have been some arguments to support this assertion, but they were not available to the advo-

[4] For one interesting example, see: Stanley High, *Roosevelt—And Then* (New York: Harper & Row, 1937), p. 89.

cate at that moment. In desperation he decided to bluff his way by bombast. He approached the lectern, wearing a well-simulated expression of deadly seriousness. In a voice seemingly choked with emotion he said, "The negative has asked us to define 'moral obligation.'" Eyes flashing with apparent righteous indignation he glared at his opponents: "We all know what 'moral obligation' is!" With a stern thump on the lectern, with ringing resolution, and an air of absolute finality, he cried, "A 'moral obligation' is a 'moral obligation'!" The negative, cowed by these histrionics, never dared mention the subject again. Had the next negative speaker assumed a calm and thoughtful air, providing a sharp contrast with the bombast of the affirmative, and quietly pointed out the absurdity of the affirmative's definition, he might well have punctured the balloon the affirmative speaker had used so effectively to conceal his lack of an adequate answer to a reasonable question.

J. Denying a Valid Conclusion

The fallacy of denying a valid conclusion occurs when an advocate admits or cannot refute the premises of an opponent, yet denies the conclusion that logically follows from these premises. For example, in a debate on federal aid for higher education, one negative team admitted that more money was needed for education and that the money must come either from federal aid or from increased aid by state and local governments; furthermore, the negative was unable to refute the affirmative's argument that many states and many local governments could not increase their aid to education. The logical conclusion from the admitted and unrefuted premises was that the federal government was the only source of the needed money; but the negative attempted to deny this valid conclusion.

The negative team's error was twofold. They admitted too much and failed to advance arguments they could have used. Other negative teams successfully argued that state and local governments could increase their aid to education and that the dangers of federal control outweighed the benefits of federal funds.

K. Popular Appeal

The fallacy of popular appeal occurs when an advocate seeks to gain support for a position by maintaining he or she is just an "ordinary human" like everyone else. This device was particularly popular with rural politicians at the turn of the century and still has considerable currency today. Some observers felt that much of Harry Truman's effectiveness in political campaigns was due to his popular image as an "ordinary man" who just happened to be a candidate for high office. At some of his "whistle stop" speeches in the 1948 campaign, President Truman is reported to have said, "How do you do, friends! My name is Harry Truman, and I'm trying to keep

my job. I'm your hired hand, and I want to tell you what I've been doing for
you in Washington." He concluded some of these speeches by saying, as he
presented Mrs. Truman to the audience, "And now I want you to meet my
boss."

Mr. Truman, of course, was not an "ordinary man." An ordinary person
would not be capable of running for the Presidency or of conducting the
affairs of government.

Another aspect of the same fallacy is the "bandwagon" technique—or
arguing that something should be done because "everybody" is doing it.
In many political campaigns, both candidates will announce their confidence
that they will win by an overwhelming majority. They hope by this method
to induce many undecided voters to vote for Doakes because Doakes is going
to win anyway. Only one brand of cigarettes or soap or any other type of
product can be the most popular; yet note the number of companies that
claim their product is the "most popular." They hope their product will be
bought because "everyone" is buying it.

L. "Straw Man"

The fallacy of the "straw man" occurs when advocates set up an issue just
so they can knock it down. Sometimes they attack a minor argument of their
opponents and claim that they have refuted the whole case, or else they refute an argument their opponents did not advance and claim that they have
thus refuted their opponents' position.

An example of this fallacy occurred in a debate on free trade. A frequently
used affirmative argument was that the economic theory of comparative
advantage demonstrated the need for the adoption of a policy of free trade.
Most negative advocates were prepared for this argument and had considerable refutation available. In one particular debate, the affirmative
speakers did not mention comparative advantage in their case. A negative
team meeting this affirmative had what they considered to be some rather
effective refutation for comparative advantage available, so they introduced
this refutation into the debate anyway. Theirs was an attack on a "straw
man."

M. Appeal to Ignorance

The fallacy of the appeal to ignorance occurs when advocates maintain that
something cannot be so because they, or the audience, have never heard of
it. Uninformed persons, for example, at one time declared the telephone to
be an impractical gadget because "Everyone knows you can't talk over
wires." Another example of the appeal to ignorance occurred in a debate on
guaranteed annual wages. The concept of cyclical fluctuations was important in many of these debates. One freshman debater, who had yet to take

his first economics course, had never heard of the term when he met it in an early season debate. Faced with an unknown concept he stoutly maintained, "Well, *I* never heard of— ah, uh— those— er— fluctuations, and *I* certainly don't think they influence our economy." The appeal to ignorance did not work in this instance—the judge *had* heard of cyclical fluctuations.

Unfortunately, the appeal to ignorance is sometimes successful with an uninformed audience. The defense against this fallacy is to provide the audience with the knowledge necessary to understand the argument. Unhappily, this is not always an easy task. Before the moon landings, it would have been almost impossible to refute the argument "Of course, you can't get to the moon, that's science fiction" before a popular audience without giving a lengthy technical explanation. In fact, the explanation might have had to be so lengthy and so technical as to be impossible to present within the available time.

N. Pseudo Questions

The fallacy of the pseudo question occurs when an advocate asks an unanswerable, "loaded," or ambiguous question; or a question based on a false assumption; or so many questions that an opponent cannot possibly answer them adequately within the available time. An example of this type of question is "Have you stopped cheating on examinations?"

Another example of this type of fallacy occurred when a negative speaker asked the affirmative fifteen questions. If the affirmative speaker had attempted to answer them in the ten minutes she had available, she would not have had time to present her case and would probably have lost the debate. Rather than attempting to answer them, she thanked her opponent for asking questions which went so directly to the core of the plan she intended to present and stated that the answers to all of the questions would be self-evident when she had completed her statement of the plan. Another advocate, confronted with the fifteen pseudo questions, used a touch of humor and replied, "My answers to the fifteen questions are seven 'yeses' and eight 'noes,' but not necessarily in that order. Now to get on with the debate . . ."

When it is readily apparent to those who render the decision that the questions are unreasonable, they may be dismissed lightly. In other cases, it is necessary to expose the questions as pseudo questions to indicate their unreasonableness, or at least to indicate that the person asking the questions has not demonstrated that they are relevant.

O. Appeal to Tradition

The fallacy of the appeal to tradition occurs when the advocate maintains that we should follow a certain policy because we have "always" done things that way. Thus a negative speaker, in a debate on the "comprehensive medical care for all citizens" proposition, argued against the affirmative's plan, saying it was unnecessary since physicians and hospitals had always provided free medical care for the indigent. The fact that something has been a long-standing tradition does not prove its merit. As Senator Sam Ervin once pointed out, murder and larceny have been practiced in all nations in all ages, but this fact does not make either murder or larceny meritorious.

P. Non Sequitur

So far we have avoided the Latin names of fallacies, but this one — which simply is a conclusion that does not follow from the premises or evidence on which it is based — is best known by its Latin designation. In the "medical care" debates, some affirmatives cited evidence showing numbers of people could not afford medical care and then argued that the government should provide free medical care for all citizens. In other debates, some negatives argued that the affirmative plan would be administered by a government bureau and would therefore be inefficient. Bureaucracy does have a bad reputation — but it does not follow that all government bureaus are inefficient.

Q. Post Hoc

This title is simply shorthand for the longer Latin phrase *post hoc ergo propter hoc* meaning "after the fact, therefore because of the fact." The fallacy lies in assuming a causal relationship where none is proven. American history provides one of the best-known illustrations of this fallacy. Every American President elected at twenty-year intervals since 1840 has died in office (Harrison, Lincoln, Garfield, McKinley, Harding, Roosevelt, and Kennedy). A remarkable coincidence, surely, but their election in a particular year was hardly the *cause* of their death.

Obviously there are many fallacies, and the possibility of their being introduced into arguments is almost unlimited. As advocates, we must be constantly on guard against these obstacles to clear thinking, not only in statements of others but in our own statements as well.

Exercises

1. Find the full text of a recent speech by a public figure. Compare this with excerpts of the speech printed in the newspapers or newsmagazines. Do you find a fallacy of omitted evidence? Remember, there is a great difference between an accurate condensation and the fallacy of omitted evidence.

2. Analyze some of the newspapers and newsmagazines published within the last month. Locate five fallacies in the editorial, opinion, or news sections of these publications; and locate five fallacies in the advertisements. Prepare a brief paper in which you state the fallacy as it appeared in its original form and explain why it is a fallacy.

3. Some of the following statements contain one or more fallacies. Prepare a list of the fallacies you discover in these statements:

a. Now Wags Dog Food contains 50 percent more protein! Get Wags Dog Food for your dog today!

b. Compulsory wage and price controls have worked successfully for years in Sweden; therefore, they will work in the United States.

c. Gun control laws are bad; that's how Hitler came into power in Germany.

d. Let's burn down the building to show our opposition to violence.

e. *Q:* What will be the cost of this plan during its first five years of operation?

A: Our country owes a debt of gratitude to the farmer. The farmer represents the American Way of Life. Farmers are good men. They live close to the soil. They have not come under the influence of socialist union bosses or Eastern internationalists.

f. Why is it that the Democratic Party always leads this country into war and the Republican Party always leads us into depression?

4. Prepare a five-minute speech in which you support or oppose a proposition of policy. Although most of your speech shall be developed in accordance with sound principles of argumentation and debate, include three carefully concealed fallacies. Present the speech before the class and invite your classmates to see if they can discover the fallacies. Prepare an outline for your speech, indicating the fallacies, and hand it to your instructor before you present the speech.

5. Prepare a five-minute speech in which you support or oppose a proposition of policy. Make sure there are no fallacies in your speech. As soon as you have presented your speech to the class, your instructor will designate another member of the class to deliver a five-minute refutation of your arguments, exposing any fallacies he or she may discover.

Chapter 11

Building the Brief

In previous chapters we have considered ways of discovering and testing evidence and argument. A collection of evidence and argument, however, is of little value until it is prepared in a definite pattern and organized into a logical form. Frequently, advocates find it desirable to organize their evidence and argument into the form of a brief. The brief may be regarded as a resource paper or a storehouse of materials from which they draw in building their case.

Opinion is divided as to the value of the brief, and there are wide differences in its use in argumentation. Some authorities maintain that the traditional brief is essential to effective argumentation and place great emphasis on its construction. Other equally distinguished authorities do not make use of the traditional brief at all.

Unquestionably, it is desirable to have a well-organized storehouse of evidence and argument at hand. Some find the brief the best way of organizing these materials; others organize the source materials more informally. Some advocates achieve the objectives of the brief by using a comprehensive filing system in which all available evidence and argument are catalogued under appropriate headings. Sometimes several attorneys working together on a case, a group of politicians supporting a particular piece of legislation, or members of a debating team adopt this system and establish a central file to which all cooperating advocates contribute evidence and argument. This system has the advantage of flexibility, and it can easily be kept up to date. However, it has some problems of administration, and it may lack something of the logical rigor of the formal brief.

Unquestionably, advocates should develop an organized and comprehensive system that will allow them to marshal effectively all of the relevant evidence and argument on a given proposition. Some advocates may achieve this objective informally as they build their case; others will prefer one of the three types of briefs considered in this chapter.

I. The Traditional Brief

The traditional brief consists of all the evidence and argument necessary to advance *one* specific way of supporting *one* side of a proposition. Thus advocates using the traditional brief select the one position they believe to be best and construct a brief to support that position. This type of brief is widely used in the courts, where requirements of legal procedure compel opposing attorneys to give each other advance notice of the position they intend to take. For instance, in most jurisdictions defense attorneys cannot claim that their clients are innocent of the crime of murder by reason of insanity without giving advance notice of their position to the prosecuting attorneys. Outside the courtroom, of course, opposing advocates seldom give each other formal notice of the approach they plan to take.

A. Organization

The organization of the brief as presented here applies specifically to the traditional brief. The general considerations are listed in the *inset*. In addition, let us consider the three main parts—Introduction, Body, and Conclusion—in more detail.

General Considerations

☐ The brief consists of three parts: *Introduction, Body,* and *Conclusion.*

☐ The principal statements of the brief are in the form of *complete sentences.* Subordinate statements may be in the form of phrases if their meaning is clear in this form and if this practice is followed consistently. Notations of sources of evidence may be in the form of standardized abbreviations.

☐ The language of the brief is impersonal and factual.

☐ The brief follows the conventional system of outlining and symbolization.

    I.
       A.
          1.
             a.
               (1)
                  (a)

☐ Each heading or subheading should include only one concept.

☐ The brief should be headed by a short title and a full statement of the proposition of debate. These headings should appear either on a separate page or immediately above the introduction. Since they are not actually a part of the brief, they are not indicated by symbols. For instance:

Power of the Presidency

Resolved: That the power of the Presidency should be significantly curtailed.

1. The Introduction This part of the brief should contain as much of the following material as is necessary to enable a reasonably well-informed layman to follow the development of the brief:

Immediate considerations (A brief statement of the factors which are immediately responsible for consideration of the proposition at this time.)

Relevant background (Such material about the history and origin of the problem as may be necessary to set it in its proper context.)

Definition of terms (A definition of the important words and phrases in the proposition and such other special words and phrases as will recur in the brief.)

Stipulations (Matters which, although necessary to an understanding of the proposition, need not and will not be supported by evidence and argument in the brief.) These include:

Matters offered for judicial notice (Those matters so widely accepted that proof of them is unnecessary.)

Admissions (Those matters which, although damaging to the position of one side, are so well established as to be impossible to refute.)

Exclusions (Those matters which, although related to the problem, are outside the scope of the proposition.)

Issues (A statement of all the potential issues.)

2. The Body The following considerations apply to the organization of the body of the brief:

Each main heading — represented by a roman numeral — states one major contention. Only one major contention is presented in each main heading.

Each main point is supported by subtopics, which present the evidence and argument to support the major contention.

The source of evidence is documented. A convenient method of keying evidence to the brief is considered on pages 162–163 under "A Sample Brief: Public Work for the Unemployed."

3. The Conclusion The conclusion of the brief is a short restatement of the issues.

B. Outline of a Brief

The *inset* (page 161) shows a typical traditional brief. Although only two points appear at most levels in the outline, the number of points — though always at least two — may vary according to the evidence and argument.

A condensed traditional brief is presented in the other *inset* (pages 162–163). In this brief each statement requiring evidence is supported by an evidence card. Each evidence card is numbered and that number is recorded at the appropriate places in the brief. A sample evidence card may be seen on page 70. The sequence numbers may be used to key the evidence cards to the

Outline: Typical Traditional Brief

Title (a short statement of the subject of the brief, usually stated in popular form)
The Proposition (an exact statement of the proposition)

Affirmative (or Negative) Brief

Introduction

  I. (Immediate considerations) This proposition is timely . . .
    A. _____
    B. _____

  II. (Relevant background) The history of this problem is important . . .
    A. _____
    B. _____

  III. (Definition of terms) The terms are defined as follows:
    A. _____
    B. _____

  IV. (Stipulations) The following matters are stipulated:
    A. (Judicial notice) It is well known that . . .
      1. _____
      2. _____
    B. (Admissions) It is recognized that . . .
    C. (Exclusions) This debate is not concerned with . . .

  V. (Issues) The issues of this debate are
    A. _____
    B. _____

Body

  I. (Statement of first issue — V.A. above) _____, for
    A. _____, for
      1. _____, and
      2. _____
    B. _____, for
      1. _____, for
        a. _____, for
          (1) _____, and
          (2) _____
        b. _____
      2. (Subsequent subpoints are developed in a similar manner.)
    C. _____

  II. (Subsequent major points are developed in a similar manner.)

Conclusion

  I. Therefore, as
    A. (Restate first issue) _____, and as
    B. (Restate second issue) _____, and as
We urge the adoption (or rejection) of (restatement of the proposition of debate).

Sample Brief: Public Work for the Unemployed

Resolved: That the federal government should establish a national program of public work for the unemployed.

Affirmative Brief

Introduction

I. This proposition is timely, for
   A. The Employment Act of 1946 commits the federal government "to promote maximum employment," (1) and
   B. President Kennedy has said unemployment is one of the most serious problems facing our country today, (2) and
   C. President Johnson has called for the passage of the Anti-Poverty Bill (3), and
   D. Congress recently passed several bills relating to this problem,
      1. The Manpower Development and Retraining Act (4)
      . . .
   E. Several bills relating to this problem are pending in Congress,
      1. The Youth Conservation Corps (9)
      . . .

II. The history of this problem is important, for
   A. Since 1946, we have been committed to a goal of maximum employment, and
   B. All of our efforts to reach that goal have failed.

III. The terms are defined as follows:
   (See Chapter 4, "Analyzing the Problem")

IV. Stipulations
   A. The following matters are offered by judicial notice: none.
   B. It is recognized that
      1. We have a high level of general prosperity in the country today.
      2. The Gross National Product is at a record level.
   C. This debate is not concerned with unemployment today; we are concerned with future deflationary unemployment.

V. The issues of this debate are*
   A. Recessions are inherent in our economy.
   B. In the depths of a recession we reach an intolerable level of deflationary unemployment.
   C. Deflationary unemployment results in direct, serious national and personal harm.
   D. Economic stabilization can only minimize unemployment.

* At this point the student may find it profitable to review "Discovering the Issues" in Chapter 4. He will note that issues A, B, C, and D are specifically related to the proposition and arise from the stock issue "Is there a *need* for a change in the status quo?" and the follow-up questions indicated in parentheses. These four issues are the *need issues* of this affirmative brief.

Issues E and F are the specific formulations of the stock issue "Will the *plan* proposed by the affirmative meet the need?" These two issues are the *plan issues* of this affirmative brief.

Issue G is simply a restatement of a stock issue "Will the plan proposed by the affirmative produce *advantages?*" These advantages, of course, must be spelled out in the development of this issue.

The number of issues required to establish *need, plan,* or *advantages* will, of course, vary with the subject matter of the proposition.

E. Public work can provide for effective economic stabilization.
F. The affirmative plan for public work will solve the problem of deflationary unemployment.
G. The affirmative plan will produce advantages.

Body

I. Recessions are inherent in our economy, for
   A. The Council of Economic Advisors pointed this out in their report to the President (14) and
   B. We have experienced four postwar recessions (15), (16), (17), (18) and
   C. Several economists say recessions are likely in the future (19), (20), (21), (22), (23), (24).

II. In the depths of a recession we reach an intolerable level of deflationary unemployment, for
   A. In October 1949, unemployment was 6.1% (25)
   . . .

III. Deflationary unemployment results in direct, serious national and personal harm, for
   A. The nation loses thirty to forty billion dollars from an unemployment rate of $1\frac{1}{2}\%$ above the frictional level. (31), (32), and
   B. Personal harm is seen in
      1. Loss of income (33), (34), (35) and
      2. Increase of debt, (36), (37), and
      3. Higher divorce rate among unemployed (38), and
      4. Higher suicide rate among unemployed (39), (40), and
      5. Higher crime rate among unemployed (41), (42), and
      6. Loss of status of unemployed father (43), (44), (45)
   . . .

IV. Economic stabilization can only minimize unemployment.
   . . .

V. Public work can provide for effective economic stabilization.
   . . .

VI. The affirmative plan for public work will solve the problem of deflationary unemployment.
   (A detailed statement of the plan, together with supporting evidence for various aspects of the plan must be provided.)
   . . .

VII. The affirmative plan will produce advantages.
   . . .

Conclusion

I. Therefore, as
   (The issues are restated at this point in the brief.)
We urge the adoption of a national program of public work for the unemployed.

brief. The statements presented in the sample brief are excerpts from a much longer brief.

II. The Full Brief

The full brief contains both affirmative and negative briefs. Prudent advocates will not limit themselves to a consideration of only one side of a proposition. In the State Department our diplomats seek to anticipate the plans of other nations. Similarly, businessmen and politicians constantly strive to predict the plans of their rivals.

In preparing the full brief, advocates must construct the best possible brief for the opposing side. They must be careful to avoid setting up a "straw man." The full brief is of little value if one side contains only the most obvious and most easily refuted arguments.

The organization of the full brief is similar to that of the traditional brief, with the affirmative brief presented first and followed by the negative brief. For any argument advanced in the affirmative or negative brief, there must be a counter argument, or an admission, in the other brief.

III. The Flexible Brief

The flexible brief is a full brief in which advocates seek to consider *all possible positions* that may be taken by either side in a debate. Although the case presented must be logically consistent, the full brief allows for consideration of potentially important but logically inconsistent positions and to make provision for them. The flexible brief also includes refutation of possible opposition arguments.

The full brief contains all of the available evidence and argument on a given proposition. In the flexible brief, logically inconsistent statements are introduced by qualifying phrases, which indicate that the advocate is aware of their inconsistency with other statements but has a special reason for including them. For instance, in order to consider all the evidence and argument on a given proposition, it may be necessary to include, in the negative brief, statements denying the need for a change in the status quo as well as arguments for a counter plan. Obviously, the negative cannot advance both arguments in its case, but all relevant arguments should be considered when building the brief. These two inconsistent arguments would be indicated in the brief in the following form:

(If the negative denies the need for a change in the status quo, it will advance the following arguments.)

There is no need for .... , for

A. _____ , and

B. _____

(If the negative advances a counter plan, it will present the following arguments for a change in the status quo.)

There is a need for .... , for

A. _____ , and

B. _____

(If the negative advances a counter plan, it will present the following plan.)

The need, as stated by the negative, is best solved by . . .

In the same manner, both the negative and affirmative briefs provide for refutation of possible arguments by the opposition. For instance, an affirmative brief might contain a section such as the following:

(If the negative maintains that the affirmative plan is not enforceable, the affirmative will present the following arguments.)

The plan is enforceable for,

A. _____ , and

B. _____

Building the flexible brief encourages advocates to think carefully about possibilities they might not otherwise develop. Once it is constructed, advocates will choose from among the various possible positions the one they will actually present. Because they have considered the various possible positions their opponents may take, they will be better prepared to meet and refute the arguments as the debate develops. In each of his four successful Presidential campaigns, Franklin D. Roosevelt outlined a plan of attack, or brief, that his Republican opponent might use. Some political observers maintain that Roosevelt's briefs were stronger than the ones actually used by his opponents. In any event, this advance analysis of the possible attacks his opponents might make helped Roosevelt to reply swiftly and effectively to their arguments as the campaign developed.

IV. Limitations of a Brief

The brief is a storehouse of materials. It is *not* the case the advocate will actually present. The special requirements of the case will be considered in the following chapters. Neither is the brief an outline of the argumentative speech. Its formal organization makes it useful as a resource paper, but it would produce far too "wooden" a style for a speech. The presentation of the case and factors of speech delivery will be considered in Chapter 19.

Exercises

1. As a term paper, prepare a brief on a proposition of policy. Your instructor will designate the type of brief (traditional, full, or flexible) to be used for this paper. Within a week of the time this paper is assigned, secure your instructor's approval of the proposition you plan to brief and submit a short paper in which you show your planned development of one main heading and demonstrate your knowledge of the principles of briefing.

2. As a term project, prepare a brief on a proposition of policy in the form of a card file. Your instructor will designate the type of brief (traditional, full, or flexible) to be used for this project. Include both evidence and argument in your file. Use index cards to indicate main headings. Within a week of the time this project is assigned, secure your instructor's approval of the proposition you plan to brief and submit a set of cards showing your planned development of one main heading in which you demonstrate your knowledge of the principles of briefing and an efficient system of organizing the file cards.

3. Prepare a traditional brief on a proposition of policy. Use the format illustrated in the sample brief (pages 162–163). Be sure to key your evidence cards carefully to the brief. Your instructor will designate a minimum number of evidence cards to be used.

4. With the approval of your instructor, several members of the class may join in the preparation of one brief in the form provided in exercises 1, 2, or 3.

Chapter 12

Requirements of the Case

The case is an outline of the issues and supporting materials selected and arranged for presentation in a specific situation; it is the *modus operandi* the debater plans to use in a given debate. The brief, as has been indicated earlier, is a storehouse from which the advocates draw materials for use in the particular situation. On most propositions, the well-drawn flexible brief allows the advocates to select any of several positions that they will take when they debate the proposition. The case, then, is the operational plan drafted by the speaker or speakers on one side of a proposition for the purpose of coordinating and presenting the reasoning and evidence with maximum effectiveness.

When several advocates on one side of a proposition seek to coordinate their efforts in securing a decision, the drafting of a case becomes a team function. Almost all debates conducted in parliamentary situations, almost all major courtroom debates, and almost all educational debates are team functions.

If the advocates on a given side of a proposition fail to coordinate their efforts and to agree upon a case, they reduce their effectiveness and leave themselves open to attack by their opposition, who will be quick to point out inconsistencies in their position. Even in so vast an undertaking as a national political campaign, which involves literally thousands of advocates on each side, an effort is made to provide a highly specialized form of case in the statement of the party platform. The party leaders hope that members of the party will subscribe to this platform, or case, and use it as the basis for their campaign speeches. In practice, of course, there are numerous deviations by campaign speakers; and, if these deviations are serious enough, they may affect the final outcome of the campaign.

The two debaters in an intercollegiate debate—just as a block of senators in Congress or a battery of lawyers before the Supreme Court or the party spokesmen in a Presidential campaign—will draft their case giving careful consideration to the various requirements of the case.

I. Requirement to Present a Prima Facie Case

The affirmative must present a *prima facie case*—one that in itself provides good and sufficient reason for adopting the proposition. Moreover, it must be both structurally and qualitatively strong enough to be logically self-sufficient. It must convince a reasonable and prudent person and stand on its own merits until or unless it is refuted. It may be helpful to review "The Prima Facie Case" in Chapter 3 and "Building the Affirmative Case" in Chapter 13 in seeking to establish a prima facie case.

This requirement is unique to the affirmative. The following requirements apply with equal force to both the affirmative and negative.

II. Requirement to Prove Inherency

The advocate must prove that the essentials of his case are inherent. This requirement may take the form of structural or attitudinal inherency.

A. Structural Inherency

This form of inherency may be important to both the affirmative and negative. For example, if an affirmative points to a certain need as a reason for adopting the proposition, it must prove that the need is inherent in the status quo; it must prove that the need could not be eliminated by repairs or that the need merely coexists with the status quo and could be eliminated without adopting the proposition.

In debating the proposition "Resolved: That the federal government should guarantee a minimum annual cash income to all citizens," some affirmative teams argued that poor people needed cash to obtain food, medical care, and housing. They then proposed a "cash income" plan to meet this need. Some negative teams meeting this case were quick to point out that these problems did not constitute an inherent need for a "cash income." The need for food was being met by food stamps — and if more food stamps were needed, they could be supplied through repairs in the status quo; the need for medical care was being met through Medicare and other welfare programs — and if more medical care was needed, it could be provided through repairs in those programs; the need for housing was being met through various public housing programs — and if more housing was needed, those programs could be expanded.

A structurally inherent need is one so fixed, so imbedded, so firmly a part of the status quo that it cannot be solved by modifications, adjustments, or repairs. There must be a basic, fundamental, structural change in the status quo to solve the need. Some affirmative teams debating the "energy" proposition were able to establish that the status quo could not meet the nation's energy needs. As these debates took place during the Arab oil embargo, this need issue was usually easy to establish and the main clash of the debate focused on the plan arguments.

The affirmative will claim that certain advantages will flow from its plan. Here, too, it must establish inherency; the affirmative must prove that the advantages are inherent in its plan, that they are *caused* by the plan and can be obtained *only* by the plan. If the advantages can be obtained without the plan, or by means other than the plan, the negative will argue that there is no reason to adopt the plan to obtain the advantages. There may be other advantages that come along with the plan without actually being inherent in the plan — the affirmative may claim these as "bonuses" or "plus factors" for their plan. The negative, however, will point out that these are incidental to, rather than inherent in, the plan and, if they are significant, may find ways to provide them without adopting the plan. Affirmative teams debating the "tax sharing" proposition were usually able to establish that the federal income tax was inherently more efficient than any other system of tax collection in the status quo or that the negative could propose as an alternative.

The negative must demonstrate inherency in its case. For example, the negative often argues that the affirmative's plan produced disadvantages. The negative must prove that a disadvantage it charges to the affirmative's plan is in fact inherent in that plan. In debating the "tax sharing" proposition, some negative teams offered the plan objection "The affirmative's plan will deprive the federal government of an important fiscal tool in combatting economic fluctuations." In their analysis they pointed out that, by giving the states a specific share of the income tax revenues, the federal government would lose the ability to curtail expenditures in time of inflation or increase them in time of recession as almost all that remained in the federal budget after tax sharing would be fixed expenditures (i.e., defense, social security, agricultural subsidies, veteran's benefits, etc.) that could not readily be changed to meet economic fluctuations. Some affirmatives, depending on the specific provisions of their plan, were able to demonstrate that this objection was not inherent in their plan. If their plan involved "only" two billion dollars, they would argue that there were many other areas where the government could increase or decrease expenditures by many billions of dollars to meet a temporary economic problem without impinging on fixed expenditures.

In arguing inherency, the negative may sometimes use the phrase *not propositional* and contend that the advantages claimed by the affirmative are not *unique* to the proposition, that they can be obtained without the proposition. In debating the "tax sharing" proposition, some affirmative teams pointed to the need for more funds for schools, proposed "tax sharing" with the requirement that the states spend the funds on schools, and then claimed the advantage of meeting the need of schools for more funds. A negative meeting this case argued that the advantage was "not propositional," that the advantage came from giving the schools more money, and that the affirmative did not show any advantage in providing that money through tax sharing. The negative continued to demonstrate that there were other ways in which more funds could be provided for schools, thus the advantage could be obtained without adopting the proposition which called for tax sharing. Had the affirmative been able to establish that tax sharing was the most advantageous method of supplying the money, they then would have been able to establish the advantage of "more money through tax sharing" as inherent in adopting the proposition.

B. Attitudinal Inherency

This form of inherency may be important to both the affirmative and negative. Classic examples of attitudinal inherency as a need argument are found in the fields of civil rights and equal rights. Some believe that all citizens should be treated equally. A barrier to such treatment was perceived in the attitude of some whites who inherently refused to allow blacks to attend certain schools, eat at certain restaurants, and so on. This attitude was so strong that it could not be changed. Thus, equal rights advocates saw this attitude as a need for equal rights legislation. They recognized that they could not change the attitude, so they resorted to the coercion of law to change the behavior of persons with a certain attitude. In the same way, some women felt that many employers had an inherent attitude that always caused them to pay women less than men for the same work. They felt the attitude could not be changed and, therefore, constituted an inherent need for legislation, which would use the coercive power of law to change employers' behavior.

Another example of attitudinal inherency is found toward the use of automobile seat belts. It is a proven fact that using seat belts saves lives. One might have expected that once this fact was proved the public, in the interest of saving their own lives, would rush to buy and use seat belts. As we know, this did not happen. Various safety councils mounted massive propaganda campaigns to persuade people to use seat belts. Yet few were persuaded. Finally, the federal government decided there was an inherent barrier in peoples' attitudes about using seat belts, and laws were enacted requiring manufacturers to install seat belts in all cars and to equip them in such a way that the car would not start or that buzzers would sound if the seat belts were not fastened.

Attitudinal inherency may also be argued by the negative to demonstrate that a plan will not work. In debating the "energy" proposition, some affirmative teams proposed that an independent federal commission be appointed to control the oil industry and expected that this commission would significantly change the way the oil companies operated. Some negative teams meeting this case argued it would not work because of attitudinal inherency. They argued the only people with sufficient expertise to serve on the commission would be oil company executives. Although they might serve for a few years on the commission as a public service, they could not be expected to stay long at the lower-paying government jobs. After that, they would be rehired by the oil companies. Thus, the negative argued, such persons were inherently sympathetic to oil-company policies and would be unlikely to make any rulings unfavorable to the oil companies.

The Eighteenth Amendment to the Constitution provided a classic example of attitudinal inherency blocking the workability of a plan. The amendment prohibited the manufacture, sale, or transportation of intoxicating liquors. In many jurisdictions, however, the attitude of the jurors was such that they did not believe there was anything wrong with manufacturing, selling, or transporting intoxicating liquors. Consequently, regardless of the evidence, they refused to bring in a guilty verdict.

III. Requirements of Significance

The advocates must prove that the essentials of their case are significant. If the affirmative claims there is a need to change the status quo, it must show the need to be significant; its plan must provide a significant change, and it must provide significant advantages. If only one or two advantages survive the negative's attack, they must be sufficiently significant in themselves to justify adopting the resolution. If the affirmative offers independent advantages and claims any one of them is sufficient to justify adopting the resolution, then each advantage must in fact be of substantial significance. The negative will often argue that an insignificant need does not justify the cost (as measured in dollars or perhaps in just the inconvenience of change) of adopting the plan or that an insignificant advantage is outweighed by the serious disadvantages they find inherent in the affirmative's plan. Thus significance is usually measured by comparison and contrast—that is, "This advantage is outweighed by this disadvantage." A well-conceived affirmative plan will produce some inherent advantages; and if the affirmative argues its case well, it may force the negative to admit this. Any plan, no matter how well conceived, may produce some disadvantages; and if the negative argues its case well, it may force the affirmative to admit this. Thus the issue becomes "Do the advantages *on balance* outweigh the disadvantages?" If the advantages are not significant and the disadvantages are significant, the negative should win this issue. On the other hand, if the advantages are significant and the disadvantages are not significant, the affirmative should win the issue. If both the advantages and disadvantages are significant—a very real possibility in a good debate—then the decision on this issue should go to the side demonstrating that *on balance* the weight of advantage or disadvantage rests with the side that claims it. There are disadvantages in wearing eyeglasses, for example. Yet most people who wear them have decided that, on balance, these disadvantages are outweighed by the advantages gained.

One cigarette company urged people to buy its products on the ground that it was "a silly millimeter longer"; a breakfast food company touted its product as being "just a little bit better." Facetious or trivial advantages may serve as the basis for decision in minor matters. On major matters, however, the reasonable and prudent person requires that significance be established. Significance, of course, must be established *in context*, that is, within the framework of the problem being debated. In debating "wage and price controls" the affirmative's advantage was narrowed at the end of the debate to the claim that its "standby" controls could go into operation one month earlier than the negative's. Was that one month advantage significant? The answer would turn on the ability of the teams to prove how much harm — or how little harm — to the economy would occur within the context of the situation they were describing. In debating the proposition "Resolved: That the federal government should adopt a program of population stabilization for the United States," some affirmatives produced a plan that would limit the population growth by one percent. Are x-million fewer people significant? The significance can be established only within the context of the proposition.

Prudent advocates will seek to establish the greatest significance that the evidence and argument will permit, recognizing that their opponents will seek to minimize their claims.

IV. Requirements Imposed by the Characteristics of Decision Renderers

Since the advocates naturally want to win the decision, they must consider carefully the person or persons who will render the decision and adapt their case accordingly. For instance, in debating the proposition "Resolved: That the nonagricultural industries of the United States should guarantee their employees an annual wage" before an audience composed of labor union members, the affirmative would do well to stress the benefits that would accrue to union members. Before an audience of industrial executives, however, the affirmative would do well to place a greater emphasis on the benefits that would accrue to industry from sustained purchasing power. If the decision is to be rendered by a critic judge or a panel of judges, the debaters should adapt their case to these key individuals. In most intercollegiate debates, the decision is rendered by a single judge who scrupulously seeks to render the decision solely on the basis of which team did the better debating. Such judges, however, often do have certain preferences about debate practices and the experienced debater learns of these preferences and adapts to them. For example: "Judge A doesn't like 'squirrel' cases," "Judge B doesn't like 'spread' cases," "Judge C won't listen to any arguments in overtime," "Judge D puts heavy emphasis on good delivery," and so on.

The debater should be aware that, in substantive debates, the judge or judges are often influenced by the reactions of the nonvoting audience. In his messages to Congress, for example, the President may deliberately use the audience to influence those who render the decision. Supposedly such messages are addressed to the Congress, which will render a decision on the message by voting for or against the legislation the President proposes. In fact, however, the President frequently seeks to "go over the heads" of Congress and to present his case to the people in the hope that they will bring pressure to bear on Congress and influence the members to vote as the President wishes. President Franklin D. Roosevelt was particularly expert at this type of presentation; he revived the custom of delivering Presidential messages to Congress in person and broadcasting them to the nation at the same time. Roosevelt was usually far more concerned with the national audience listening to him on the radio than he was with the Congressional audience before him. This practice of "going over the heads" of the immediate audience that renders the formal decision and appealing to the nonvoting audience is by no means new, nor was it unique with Roosevelt. We know that legislators are not altogether uninfluenced by demonstrations in the gallery and that juries are not impervious to the reactions of the spectators in the courtroom. National political conventions perhaps afford the ultimate example of this indirect means of influencing the judges, in this case the voting delegates. In these conventions, very expensive, carefully rehearsed, and professionally staged "spontaneous" demonstrations follow each nomination speech.

Most frequently, as students or citizens, we will seek to influence a single individual or a small group of individuals. In such cases, we should seek to learn as much as possible about the key individual and adapt our case to this individual. Although the key individual will be the focal point of our presentation, the desirability of securing a favorable response from the nonvoting audience should not be overlooked, since this response may influence the person who renders the decision. In a certain large corporation, the purchasing manager had the sole authority to determine the make of automobile that would be purchased for the salesmen. After ordering a fleet of B cars, he confided to a friend, "A cars are really better, but the salesmen wanted B. There wasn't a great deal of difference between the two, so I let the salesmen have the one they wanted." Apparently, the advocates for B cars did the better job of influencing the nonvoting audience.

V. Requirements Imposed by the Occasion

Argument does not take place in a vacuum, but in a specific context of time and place and with a certain relationship to events that precede and follow the argumentative speech or writing.

The college debater will find that the tournament situation calls for certain social amenities, graceful references to the opposing team and to the host college, a certain air of poised informality and conversational style. The final round of a tournament, conducted in the presence of distinguished guests, requires a greater degree of formality. An international debate requires well-chosen references to international relationships and to the visitors' nation and customs.

The necessity of adapting to the occasion applies to all advocates. Speakers on the highest governmental level face this same requirement. A dramatic example of the occasion's influencing the debate may be seen in America's entry into World Wars I and II. On April 2, 1917, President Wilson, in a lengthy speech reviewing the events of the previous several months, asked Congress for a declaration of war. The proposal was debated for several days and did not become law until April 6. On December 8, 1941, President Roosevelt, rejecting the advice of some of his Cabinet that he review the whole history of American-Japanese relations, gave a brief speech dealing only with the events of the previous day and asked Congress for a declaration of war. His proposal became law within one hour after he had finished speaking. The difference in the approach used by the two Presidents showed an awareness of the different situations in 1917 and 1941. The advocate, whether he is a college debater or a President, must be aware of the occasion and make appropriate adjustment to it.

VI. Requirements of Clarity and Relevancy

It is self-evident that the debate case must be clear, interesting, and relevant. The available time in a debate is always limited. In an intercollegiate debate, strict time limitations are imposed; and in other debates, such factors as limitations of radio or television time, an agreed upon time of adjournment, or simply practical considerations of sustained audience attention and interest place a limit on the time available to the advocates. Well-prepared debaters, therefore, always have at their disposal more material than they can possibly use in the time available. From the materials available to them, the advocates must select for use those items of evidence or illustration that will be most clear, most interesting, and most relevant to their purpose. Debaters speaking on the proposition "Resolved: That law enforcement agencies in the United States should be given greater freedom in the investigation and prosecution of crime" before a Massachusetts audience would certainly want to include references to the widespread criminal activity exposed by a Massachusetts crime commission at the very time this proposition was debated. Well-prepared debates will have several items of evidence available to support each issue of their case. Many of these items may have approximately equal value in fulfilling the logical requirements of their position; but they will select only those that will make their presentation most clear and interesting to the specific audience and that are clearly relevant to their overall purpose. A good rule for advocates is to make certain that everything included in their case is specifically relevant to their purpose and to exclude, ruthlessly, all materials that are not relevant. Here it should be noted that the social amenities of the debate and certain other factors of persuasion may not be relevant to the logical proof of the case; but they are relevant to the debater's purpose, which is to secure a decision.

The sequence in which the issues and materials of the case are presented is of great importance to the debater. Although the brief is drafted in logical form, the debater may find it advantageous to arrange materials in a fashion that will achieve maximum effect, even if this means a violation of logical organization.

VII. Requirements Imposed by the Probable Case of the Opposition

The advocates' task is not to overcome all possible opposition to their case; rather, it is to overcome the specific case presented by their opponents within the context of a given debate. In order to do this, the debaters must, in advance of the debate, make the best possible estimate of the position that will be taken by their opponents. The advocates can gain a real understanding of the problem only when they have thoroughly analyzed both sides of the proposition.

Salesmen, lawyers, generals, diplomats, and others devote a considerable portion of their time to estimating the probable moves of their opponents and to planning their own actions so as to anticipate and defeat the opposition. Advocates are well advised to study carefully the probable moves of their opponents and to be prepared to meet them. Many teachers of argumentation, from classical times to the present, have encouraged students to debate on both sides of the proposition selected for educational debate. Many contemporary intercollegiate debate tournaments are structured to provide the student such an opportunity. This procedure gives the student an opportunity to acquire knowledge of both sides of the proposition and of the requirements of both affirmative and negative cases. Few teachers of argumentation are interested in training propagandists for or against a given proposition. They are interested, however, in using a proposition as an educational tool, by means of which they may teach the theory and practice of argumentation. A student would not, of course, be asked to advocate publicly a position contrary to his or her convictions, and such a problem rarely arises in educational debating. National educational debate propositions usually deal with matters on which the average student has an open mind. After a number of debates on both sides of the proposition, the student is better able to formulate a considered judgment based on an intelligent analysis of the problem.

VIII. Requirements of Consistency

If the two advocates in an educational debate allow themselves to present contradictory or inconsistent arguments, the effect is almost certain to be defeat. The same consideration applies outside educational debate. During the third year of World War II, when the Allies and especially Britain had sustained almost uninterrupted disaster, a Motion of Censure was moved in the British Parliament. The effect of the motion, if carried, would be to put Churchill out of office. The supporters of the motion destroyed their position almost as soon as the debate began. As a member of Parliament pointed out immediately after the seconding speech:

. . . the mover has proposed a Vote of Censure on the ground that the Prime Minister has interfered unduly in the direction of the war; whereas the seconder seems to be seconding because the Prime Minister has not sufficiently interfered in the direction of the war.

As Churchill noted, "This point was apparent to the House . . . the debate was ruptured from its start."[1]

IX. Requirements of Flexibility during the Debate

As advocates, although we make the best possible estimate of the case of our opposition, we should remember that we can only estimate what position our opponent may take; we can never be certain in advance. If we draw up our case on rigid lines, we may find ourselves unable to adapt to the case actually presented by our opponent, and we may be handicapped seriously by the inflexibility of our own position. We would do well to follow the example of Winston Churchill, who carefully estimated the probable course of the debate in Parliament and often went into the House with seven or eight different, carefully prepared speeches. Once he learned the precise position his opponents took, he would select the most appropriate of his several prepared speeches.

The advocate's case should be sufficiently flexible to allow for adaptation during the debate itself. If several advocates join together to build a case, they should decide in advance what position they will take if the opposition presents a given course of argument, and they should be able to make a smooth transition to a different and previously prepared position. In educational debate, such adaptation typically occurs in the affirmative case at the start of the second affirmative speech. At this point, as at many others during

[1] For a more detailed consideration of the issues of this debate and Churchill's strategy, see: Winston S. Churchill, *The Hinge of Fate* (Boston: Houghton Mifflin Co., 1950), Book One, Chap. 23, "The Vote of Censure."

the debate, there is a high premium on flexibility. While the attacks must be anticipated, their exact form cannot be known until the first negative presents them. Then the second affirmative must move swiftly, smoothly, and consistently to refute the attacks made by the negative and must extend the issues introduced by his or her colleague. The prudent advocates are those who—in addition to making a careful estimate of the probable case of their opponents and preparing to meet that case—have also considered carefully every possible position that their opponents may take and have thoroughly prepared both their defense and attack for each of these positions. There is an answer for almost every argument that can be introduced into the typical debate dealing with probabilities. If we are taken by surprise by our opponent's argument, our answer must be impromptu and often it will be weak and ineffective. If, on the other hand, our opponent's argument has been anticipated, with the answer planned carefully in advance and held in reserve for just such an argument, we are much more likely to be effective.

In a debate, the clash seldom ends with our advancing a line of argument and our opponent's meeting that argument with an answer. We must assume that our opponent is well prepared and has counter argument ready for each of the major contentions of the debate. Therefore, we must prepare an answer not only for each of the probable arguments of our opponent but also for each counter argument that this opponent is likely to advance in support of his or her original contentions. In this way, we can prepare our arguments in depth and not only be ready to meet our opponent on the first level of argument—the initial clash of argument and counter argument—but also have additional evidence and argument at our disposal that we can use to reinforce our initial position through as many exchanges as may be necessary to sustain our position. This preparation is reflected in the debate card file, which should contain the evidence and argument we plan to use initially, as well as the supplementary materials we hold in reserve, should the occasion arise to draw upon them.

Exercises

1. Consider the requirement to prove inherency in a debate on the current national intercollegiate proposition:

a. Are there inherent needs in the status quo for adopting the proposition?

b. Are the advantages claimed for the plan inherently caused by the plan?

c. Can the advantages be obtained *only* by the plan?

d. Are the disadvantages the negative claims will be caused by the plan inherent in the plan?

2. Consider the requirement for proving significance in a debate on the current national intercollegiate proposition:

a. If the affirmative claims there is a need to change the status quo, is this need significant?

b. Is the plan a significant change in the status quo?

c. Are the advantages significant?

d. Are they *on balance* significant when contrasted with the likely disadvantages a negative will claim?

e. Are the disadvantages significant?

f. Are the disadvantages significant *on balance* when contrasted with the likely advantages an affirmative will claim?

3. Consider a plan currently being debated in Congress, in your state legislature, or by the governing body of your college. Apply the questions on inherency listed under exercise 1. Apply the questions on significance listed under exercise 2.

4. What are the requirements that might be inherent in the attitudes, interests, and intellectual capabilities of each of the following if they were asked to judge a debate on the current national intercollegiate debate proposition?

a. A professor of argumentation

b. A labor union official

c. The president of a local Chamber of Commerce

d. The members of a local Parent-Teacher Association

e. The members of a local Rotary Club

f. The students at a high school assembly program

g. A member of Congress

Chapter 13

Building the Affirmative Case

Every affirmative case must be a *prima facie case* — that is, it must in and of itself establish good and sufficient reason for adopting the proposition unless it is successfully refuted or weakened. As we have seen earlier, the presumption is in favor of the status quo, and conditions will continue as they are until good and sufficient reason is given for a change.

There are two basic types of cases available to the affirmative — the needs analysis and the comparative advantages analysis. The decision about which approach to use will depend upon the nature of the proposition and the advocate's analysis of the status quo.

I. Objectives of the Affirmative Case

A policy debate is usually in the area of probability and time limitations do not permit the introduction of all possible evidence and argument. The affirmative, therefore, is not required to prove absolutely that its need arguments establish the status quo as totally undesirable, that its plan will solve completely all of the needs, or that all of the advantages claimed will inevitably flow from the adoption of the plan. Such a degree of certainty is seldom attainable in human affairs. Rather, the affirmative must establish the highest possible degree of probability that these things will come about. For example, in debating the proposition "Resolved: That law enforcement agencies in the United States should be given greater freedom in the investigation and prosecution of crime," it was impossible for the affirmative teams to prove *absolutely* that such a policy would reduce crime. Nonetheless, many affirmative teams were able to establish a reasonably high degree of probability that such would be the result.

As advocates begin to build the affirmative case, they should keep in mind the two basic positions available to them — the needs analysis and the comparative advantages analysis. As they become familiar with the opportunities and limitations of these two basic positions, they will be in a position to choose the one best suited for their particular situation.

II. Needs Analysis Affirmative

The advocates select the needs analysis after study of the problem leads them to the conclusion that there is an inherent need in the status quo that can best be solved by adopting a plan of the type required or permitted by the proposition and that adopting this plan will solve the needs and thus provide advantages.

The essential elements of the needs analysis affirmative are shown here:

The *need* portion of the case consists of arguments to establish the need for changing the status quo because of its inherent disadvantages or weaknesses. The need presented by the affirmative *must* establish the foundation for the type of change required or permitted by the proposition and for the specific plan presented by the affirmative. For instance, an argument contending that unemployment is a nationwide problem and causes great harm to many people is not sufficient to establish a need for a national program of public work for the unemployed. Such an argument, if successfully established, would show a need for a change in the status quo (the current policies on unemployment), but it would not in itself be sufficient to show a need for a national program of public work. In order to establish a need for such a program, it would be necessary to indict the status quo and demonstrate that the private sector of the economy could not create more jobs, that state and local governments could not create more jobs, that retraining programs could not qualify the unemployed for existing unfilled jobs, and that fiscal and monetary policies could not create more jobs. The *plan* portion of the affirmative case consists of the proposed plan to meet the need that has been set forth. The debate resolution is a brief statement of the nature of the plan; the case contains a policy development of this plan. The *advantages* portion of the affirmative case consists of arguments designed to demonstrate that the plan will meet the need and produce benefits or improvements.

Logically, the affirmative case must be developed in this order: (1) presentation of the need; (2) presentation of a plan to meet the need; and (3) development of the advantages that will result from the acceptance of the plan. Depending upon the nature of the proposition and the circumstances prevailing at the time of the debate, it may be the objective of the affirmative to develop a present need or a future need.

In developing a *present need,* the affirmative argues that conditions *right now* require us to adopt the proposition. The present-need argument was used by many who debated the "right-to-work" proposition. They argued, in effect, "Right now, *today,* people are being forced to contribute to corrupt unions; right now, *today,* people are being forced to contribute to political activities they oppose. These evils are inherent in the status quo, the lack of 'right-to-work' laws—therefore, we must have 'right-to-work' laws."

In developing a *future need*, the affirmative argues that the status quo is inherently incapable of solving a problem that will, or may, come in the foreseeable future and that we must adopt the proposition to prepare to meet the future problem. The future-need argument was used by many who debated the "national program of public work for the unemployed" proposition. They argued, in effect, "Recessions are inherent in our economy. We *will* have a recession at some time in the foreseeable *future*. The status quo is inherently incapable of preventing a recession and the widespread and harmful unemployment that will come with it. Therefore, we must begin now to make plans for a national program of public work for the unemployed that we will put into effect when the recession strikes."

A. Types of Cases

Although other variations are possible, the needs analysis affirmative case usually may be classified in one of the following categories: (1) the classical affirmative; (2) the modified affirmative; (3) the moral-issue affirmative. The particular case an affirmative uses in a given situation will, of course, depend upon the resolution under debate, the available evidence and argument, the probable case of the opposition, the attitudes, interests, and intellectual capabilities of the audience, and the occasion.

1. Classical Needs Analysis Affirmative The classical needs analysis affirmative case maintains that the status quo is entirely unsatisfactory and that the only solution is the plan called for in the resolution. Advocates favoring an international agreement to prohibit the further development of nuclear weapons sometimes used such a case. These advocates maintained that the status quo—the absence of any agreement banning nuclear weapons development—caused grave dangers which could be remedied only by the plan they proposed.

2. Modified Needs Analysis Affirmative The modified needs analysis affirmative case maintains that, although the status quo has certain advantages, they are outweighed by certain inherent disadvantages or weaknesses and that the best solution is the plan called for in the resolution. Such a case was used by the proponents of a compulsory health-insurance program. These proponents admitted that voluntary insurance plans provided excellent service in some areas but maintained that the status quo worked great hardships on many citizens.

3. Moral-Issue Needs Analysis Affirmative The moral-issue needs analysis affirmative case maintains that, although the status quo is pragmatically satisfactory, it produces certain injustices that make the adoption of the plan called for in the resolution morally necessary. In debating the proposition "Resolved: That the United States should adopt a system of universal military service," some affirmative teams adopted this type of case. When confronted with evidence that the United States had won major wars without universal military service, they found it difficult to maintain that the status quo (no universal military service) was inadequate. Rather, they presented as a need the argument that the status quo permitted inequality of sacrifice in time of war and maintained that it was morally necessary for the burdens of war, as nearly as possible, to be borne equally by all.

B. Integrating the Case

In order to build a prima facie case, the affirmative must carefully integrate its position. Need, plan, and advantages must be so developed that they dovetail perfectly. The need must be sufficiently great to justify a change in the status quo; yet, at the same time, it must not be so great as to make it impossible for the plan to solve the need. The need and the plan must com-

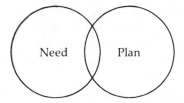

plement each other perfectly, and every point of need stated by the affirmative must be provided for in the plan advocated. Advantages, the third element of the affirmative case, are derived by demonstrating that the plan solves the alleged need and perhaps produces additional desirable conditions not present in the status quo. Thus, need, plan, and advantages must all be perfectly integrated into the whole structure of the affirmative case.

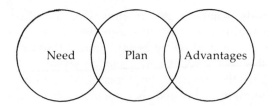

The plan is seen as the connecting link. It solves the problems raised by the presentation of the need and produces the advantages that the affirmative maintains will follow the adoption of the resolution. The affirmative's plan must be developed in sufficient detail to demonstrate that it can meet the alleged needs and that it can produce the alleged advantages. The affirmative is often confronted with the question of how much detail should be given in the presentation of the plan. Obviously, minute details of administrative operation of the plan cannot be given in the available time; but the affirmative does have an obligation to present the policy outline and the general administrative operation of its plan. The affirmative also must show the practicability of its plan. The affirmative is not required to demonstrate that its plan will be adopted; but it does have the responsibility of demonstrating that its plan, if adopted, would be workable. As we have seen earlier (Chapter 4, "The Meaning of 'Should' in Propositions of Policy"), the affirmative may fiat the *enactment* of its plan. It may not, however, fiat the *workability* of its plan if workability becomes an issue of the debate. If the plan calls for an increase in personal income taxes and a reduction of property taxes, it is pointless for the negative to raise the workability issue — the status quo has effective means of enforcing tax collections. In some cases, however, workability may become an all important issue. In debates on "comprehensive medical care for all citizens," one affirmative plan called for annual physical examinations of all citizens. The affirmative sought to slough their responsibility by saying this provision of their plan would be "enforced by all necessary means." The negative established that millions of citizens — through fear, ignorance, or apathy — would not volunteer for such examinations and argued that the affirmative must provide an effective enforcement mechanism or lose its claimed advantage. The inexperienced affirmative debater, in a moment of excess, responded that this provision of the plan would be enforced by "drawing and quartering." The next negative speaker argued that the method of enforcement provided by the affirmative — drawing and quartering — was not only counterproductive to health, but was so repugnant to contemporary standards of law enforcement as to constitute grounds for rejecting the proposition. The judge agreed; drawing and quartering may have worked in the Middle Ages, but it was an unworkable plan provision for contemporary America.

The affirmative may fiat reasonable provisions for their plan. For instance, they may stipulate that their administrative body be bipartisan or nonpartisan; they may stipulate geographic representation; they may provide that members of the body be lawyers, physicians, or accountants or meet various professional standards. Indeed, they may stipulate anything for which there is a reasonable warrant or relevant analogy.

The affirmative may *not*, however, fiat unreasonable provisions for their plan. For instance, in a debate on consumer protection the affirmative may not fiat that their administrative body will be headed by Ralph Nader; in a debate on crime control they may not fiat that the members of their administrative body will be incorruptible;[1] if they designate a Congressional com-

---

[1] Of course, one may attempt to provide for desirable qualities in appointees. The mayor of Cleveland recently appointed a special committee of clergymen — promptly dubbed "The God Squad" by the press — to investigate crime. The mayor's supporters hailed the appointments on the ground that the clergymen would be incorruptible; his opponents scoffed that clergymen led sheltered lives and did not know enough about crime to investigate it.

mittee to investigate the CIA they may not fiat that all of the members will be left-wing Democrats. In short, the affirmative plan is subject to normal political processes and its members are subject to normal human frailties. The affirmative may not appoint "Jesus Christ Superstar" to their administrative body and stipulate that miracles will be passed to overcome attitudinal inherency and any other problems that block the status quo from functioning in a state of perfection.

In debating the proposition "Resolved: That the federal government should grant annually a specific percentage of its income tax revenue to the state governments," the affirmative was not obliged to specify how much money would be given to each state, but it was obliged to present a policy by means of which such amounts could be determined.

Naturally, the importance of the plan in a debate on a proposition of policy will vary with the subject matter and with the attitude of those who render the decision. In many debates on the "energy" proposition the plan was all-important. If the affirmative advocates could produce a satisfactory plan, they had a very good chance of winning. If the negative could demonstrate that the plan was unworkable or produced significant disadvantages, they had an excellent chance of winning. In many debates on the proposition "Resolved: That the federal government should guarantee a minimum annual cash income to all citizens," the plan portion of the debate was of lesser importance. Since it is obviously *possible* for the federal government to make such a guarantee, most of the arguments on this proposition often centered on the *need* for the federal government to make such a guarantee and on the advantages (or disadvantages) that would result from the adoption of the proposition. In debates on "right-to-work" laws, some decision renderers were predisposed to agree with the affirmative if only it could produce a workable plan, while other decision renderers were interested not so much in the plan as in the need for such legislation.

The advantages portion of the affirmative case must be developed in sufficient detail to demonstrate that the plan meets the need and corrects the deficiencies and weaknesses that the affirmative has found in the status quo. Frequently, the affirmative maintains that its plan not only will eliminate these deficiencies and weaknesses but also will produce additional advantages not obtainable under the status quo. In developing this portion of its case, the affirmative must be careful to connect the advantages with the plan; it must demonstrate that the plan will cause the advantages and that the advantages will not result from other factors outside the scope of the plan. In debating the proposition "Resolved: That the federal government should guarantee an opportunity for higher education to all qualified high school graduates," some affirmative teams maintained that the USSR was educating more scientists than we were and that, if this resolution were adopted, we would educate more scientists and catch up with Soviet education. (At the time this proposition was debated, the Soviet space program was substantially ahead of the American program.) Negative speakers, however, were quick to point out that the status quo had a number of excellent federal scholarship programs for scientists – if we needed more scientists, we merely had to expand existing programs. The negative speakers continued their attack by pointing out that the affirmative's plan did not guarantee that *any* of the students helped under the proposition would study science. Thus, the negative – by demonstrating that one advantage claimed by the affirmative could be provided by minor repairs in the status quo (expanded science scholarships) and that another advantage claimed by the affirmative (more scientists) could not really be guaranteed – reduced the effectiveness of the affirmative's case.

III. Comparative Advantages Analysis Affirmative

The advocates select the comparative advantages analysis after study of the problem leads them to the conclusion that there is a better way of attaining the goals of the status quo. They accept the goals of the status quo, present a plan of the type required or permitted by the proposition, and argue that their plan will produce comparative advantages.

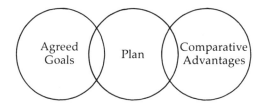

The comparative advantages case has always existed as an option for the affirmative. During the 1940s and 1950s – when it was termed the "improvements affirmative" – it was used occasionally but did not achieve great popularity. By the mid 1960s it was widely used, and by the 1970s it was probably the most widely used affirmative analysis by varsity debaters on the national circuit. Its increased use in substantive debate roughly paralleled its use in educational debate.

A. Origin of the Theory

As is true with so much in the field of argumentation, we can trace the origin of the theory of comparative advantages at least as far back as Aristotle. In the discussion of his "universal topoi," Aristotle pointed out:

Obviously, then, the speaker will need propositions regarding magnitude and smallness, and the greater and the less, considered generally and also in *comparing* cases –

for example in arguing which is the greater or less good, the greater or lesser act of injustice; and similarly with the other terms.[2]

A little further on, in his discussion of the aims of rhetoric, Aristotle told us:

Now the aim of one who gives council is utility; for men deliberate, not about the ends to be attained, but about the means of attaining them . . .[3]

Given Aristotle's definition of the word "ends" as he uses it in this context, we would probably agree with him. In contemporary practice, how-ever, we often debate about "ends" as well as "means." To avoid confusion, we will substitute the term "agreed goals" and say that, when people have agreed goals, they do not debate about the goals but about the means of attaining them.

Still further on in his *Rhetoric*, Aristotle set before us the basic concept of the comparative advantages case:

But when two courses are possible, it often happens that people, while granting that both are expedient [that each has its advantages], yet dispute as to which of them is the more expedient.[4]

This gives us the foundation of the comparative advantages analysis.[5] The affirmative grants that the status quo has certain advantages, but it maintains that its plan is comparatively advantageous. The affirmative argues that its proposal can do *more* for us or can reach our agreed goal more quickly, more efficiently, more fairly, or in some way that is more beneficial to us.

B. Origin of the Term

The term "comparative advantages" — as applied to the concept we are con-sidering — originated in 1817 with David Ricardo, who developed the theory as an economic concept along with John Stuart Mill and other English fol-lowers of Adam Smith.

In his treatise Ricardo pointed out that England could make cloth very efficiently and could produce wine, although only at considerable cost and

---

[2] Aristotle, *Rhetoric*, I, 3 (italics added).

[3] *Ibid*. I, 6.

[4] *Ibid*. I, 7 (the bracketed words appear in the Cooper translation).

[5] Subsequent to Aristotle's *Rhetoric* no less than twenty-three representative rhetoricians, covering a span of twenty centuries from the fourth century B.C. to the seventeenth century A.D. list expediency or advantages as a stock issue. See: Raymond E. Nadeau, "Hermogenes on 'Stock Issues' in Deliberative Speaking," *Speech Monographs*, Vol. 25 (March 1958), pp. 59–66. For a thoughtful contemporary view, see: Bernard L. Brock, "The Comparative Advantages Case," *The Speech Teacher*, Vol. 16 (March 1967), pp. 118–123.

even then of poor quality. On the other hand, Portugal produced superb wine very easily and could make cloth only with great inefficiency.

There were, of course, certain advantages to each country in producing both its own wine and cloth — important advantages as viewed by early nineteenth-century merchants. Ricardo, however, argued that there were greater advantages — that it was *comparatively advantageous* — for each country to specialize in that commodity it produced most efficiently and to trade for the other commodity that another nation produced more efficiently.

Ricardo's example was a simple one. It was a clear case of efficiency contrasted with inefficiency. What if all the efficiency were on one side? Modern economists argue the case this way:

One country may be *absolutely more efficient* in the production of every good than is the other country; the other country has an absolute disadvantage in the production of every good. But so long as there are differences in the *relative* efficiencies of producing different goods in the two countries, we can be sure that even the poor country has a *comparative advantage* in the production of those commodities in which it is relatively more efficient; this same poor country will have a *comparative disadvantage* in those other commodities in which its inefficiency is more than average.[6]

The theory is the same as when Aristotle set it out. A specific label — comparative advantages — has been added. An important concept has been brought into sharper focus — the comparative advantages case often may involve a trading off of advantages. The affirmative may be forced to give up a clear, inherent advantage of the status quo in order to gain a greater comparative advantage inherent in its plan.

Modern economists have developed forms of analysis that permit them to express this concept mathematically. Futurists, working in "think tanks" with computers, have developed a closely related set of theories and procedures known as "linear programming." While a number of articles on this subject have appeared in economics, business, and mathematical journals, the field does not lend itself to immediate utilization by the student debater concerned with policy propositions.

C. Essential Features

There are four essential features to the comparative advantages case. They are (1) identify the goals of the status quo, (2) integrate the plan with the goals, (3) provide inherent, significant advantages, and (4) prove these are comparative advantages.

First, the affirmative must identify and accept the specific goals and assumptions of the status quo that are relevant to the proposition. The affirmative must isolate the "agreed goals" or "ends" that both the affirmative and negative wish to achieve.

---

[6] Paul A. Samuelson, *Economics,* 9th ed. (New York: McGraw-Hill Book Co., 1973), p. 669.

Thus the need issue does not become an issue of the debate as it does when the need–plan–advantages analysis is used. If the affirmative has correctly analyzed the problem, and if it has correctly identified the goals and assumptions of the status quo, the negative will, in effect, concede the need issue. The negative cannot deny the need to reach the agreed goals in a way that will do more for us, or enable us to reach our agreed goals more quickly, more efficiently, more fairly, or in some way that is more beneficial to us. Rather, the negative will argue that the proposal of the affirmative should be rejected because of inherent defects and disadvantages. If, however, the affirmative has not identified the goals of the status quo correctly, the negative may be able to develop arguments proving that the goals are incompletely identified or that there are other goals which are equally or more important.

In debating the proposition "Resolved: That law enforcement agencies in the United States should be given greater freedom in the investigation and prosecution of crime," some affirmatives stated that one of the most urgent goals of society was to reduce crime. The negatives simply could not deny this — it would be pointless for them to attempt to debate this as a need issue. Some affirmatives, after stating this goal, then presented a plan to legalize wiretapping and argued that the advantage would be increased convictions and ultimately a reduction in crime. Negatives, meeting this type of case, often clashed with the plan and argued that wiretapping, when it was legal, had not been particularly effective in increasing convictions. They then sought — by setting out the disadvantage of invasion of privacy and all the abuses potentially existing in wiretapping — to counter the now minimized advantage of a possible slight increase in convictions. These disadvantages, they argued, outweighed any possible advantage flowing from the affirmative's plan.

Note that the affirmative must identify and accept the *specific* goals and assumptions of the status quo that are relevant to the proposition. In the "law enforcement" example just cited, the affirmative was correct in stating that "reducing crime" is a goal of American society. In a debate on an international disarmament treaty, the affirmative would have to find certain agreed goals that were common to America, the USSR, and other nations that might be parties to the treaty. In a debate in a business organization, "increased profits" would probably be the agreed goal of the board of directors. In a similar fashion, advocates must discover the agreed goals of the relevant group — their debate team, their business organization, American society, or the United Nations.

The goals just stated are phrased in general terms. For the purposes of debate, they must be specific. It is *not* the goal of American society to "reduce crime *by any means.*" No reputable business seeks "increased profits *by any means.*" Thus the plan to "reduce crime" must do so by socially acceptable methods. The plan to "increase profits" must be legal, ethical, and consistent with the other public and business responsibilities of the company.

While a general statement of the goal is often sufficient for the affirmative's opening statement of its rationale, the specific qualifications and limitations of the goal must be provided for in the plan. Many debates in which the "wiretap" case was used turned on the point of which was the more important goal of society — convicting some more criminals or assuring privacy for more citizens.

Second, the affirmative must present a plan that is perfectly integrated with the goals and assumptions it has specified. Note that this is an exact parallel of the need–plan–advantages analysis. In that case, the plan must solve the needs; in the comparative advantages case, the plan must satisfy the specified goals and assumptions. If the affirmative wishes to challenge the goals and assumptions of the status quo, it should move to a needs analysis and seek to establish a need for this change.

Third, the plan must produce advantages. Two considerations are involved here: (a) The advantages must be inherent in the plan. If the advantages can be achieved without the plan, or through some agency other than the plan, then there is no reason to adopt the plan. (b) The advantages must be significant. The reason for this has been suggested in the "wiretapping" case already considered under the first essential and to be considered further under the fourth essential feature.

Fourth, the affirmative must prove that these are comparative advantages. Two considerations are involved here: (a) The advantages must be better than any advantage that could be gained under the status quo. They must be better than any advantage produced by the status quo and better than any advantage that may *coexist* with status quo policies and agencies but that would be *excluded* by the affirmative's plan. (b) The advantages must outweigh the disadvantages. The negative is almost certain to stress the disadvantages of the plan, and the affirmative must be prepared to defend its plan.

The affirmative's proposal almost invariably will involve the loss of certain advantages gained under the status quo; and this loss is obviously a disadvantage of the affirmative's plan. The affirmative must be able to prove a net gain — that is, the advantage gained must be more valuable than the advantage lost.

The affirmative's proposal will almost invariably create some significant problems. Clearly, it is in the negative's interest to discover and present the strongest possible set of plan objections and to point out the inherent disadvantages of the plan. The affirmative will, of course, seek to refute or minimize these objections. Realistically, however, there will be some disadvantages that are irrefutable. Here again the affirmative must be able to prove a net gain — that is, the advantages of the affirmative plan, even when handicapped and discounted by its inherent disadvantages, must outweigh, be more valuable, be better, be comparatively advantageous to the status quo and to the status quo as it might be repaired by the negative.

Thus the affirmative is usually well advised to build its case to provide the most significant advantages it can reasonably claim. In debating the proposition "Resolved: That the federal government should grant annually a specific percentage of its income tax revenue to the state governments," an affirmative concluded the last rebuttal with the plaintive plea that its case was "just a little bit better" than the status quo and therefore merited the decision. As that debate drew to a close, it was apparent that the affirmative's plan did produce a taxing system that was "just a little bit" more progressive than the status quo and a method of tax collection that was "just a little bit" more efficient. While the slogan "just a little bit better" may serve as the basis for choosing a breakfast food, it is a very slender—although in certain circumstances a reasonable—basis on which to claim victory in a hard fought debate. In this case, the negative had established disadvantages and objections—loss of a fiscal tool to control the economy, the affirmative's inability to defend its distribution formula, the affirmative's failure to provide for "pass through," and the affirmative's inability to guarantee that the funds would reach those areas specified as its goals—that outweighed the "little bit" claimed by the affirmative.

D. Variations of the Case

Two contemporary variations of the comparative advantages case are (1) the criteria case and (2) the alternative justification case.

1. Criteria Case This variation is sometimes used when the advocate finds it desirable to provide a sharp focus on a specific aspect of the goals. In this case, the advocates establish their criteria for selecting the most advantageous plan to reach the agreed goals and maintain that their plan best satisfies the criteria. In debating "tax sharing," one affirmative maintained that the goal of the status quo was to achieve the most effective utilization of public funds. As criteria to judge plans to achieve this goal, this team stated that taxes should be collected by the most efficient agency and that tax revenue should be spent by the most efficient agency. They then presented a plan to abolish all state and local taxes, raise the income tax rate to produce the corresponding amount of revenue, and have all taxes collected in the form of income taxes through the Internal Revenue Service—the agency they claimed was the most efficient tax collector. An amount equal to current state and local revenues would be turned over to state and local governments—the agencies they claimed were most efficient in spending tax revenue for state and local needs.

2. Alternative Justification Case This variation is an ancient technique useful with broad propositions, in which the affirmative offers a multiplicity of *independent* reasons for adopting the resolution. For example, the attorneys of the House Judiciary Committee initially submitted twenty-nine articles of impeachment against President Nixon. In educational debate, the affirmative offers multiple minicases — for instance, on the "greater freedom in the investigation and prosecution of crime" proposition, one affirmative argued these minicases:

Legalize "no knock" searches to decrease drug traffic, and/or:

Legalize "stop and frisk" searches to decrease street crime, and/or:

Broaden "no bail" detention of previously convicted suspects to protect the public from recidivists.

This affirmative maintained that any one of the three self-contained cases was in itself good and sufficient reason for adopting the proposition and argued that unless the negative defeated all three of them the decision should be awarded to the affirmative. The advocate, in developing this type of case, must be very careful to ensure that the minicases are in fact independent and that the advantages they produce are significant. This approach may be developed either as a comparative advantage or as a needs analysis case.

There are two important constraints the student debater must consider before selecting this approach: (1) The time constraints of educational debate may make it impossible for the debater to establish multiple prima facie minicases. The famous impeachment trial of Warren Hastings, in which the prosecution argued alternative justifications, opened in Westminister Hall on February 13, 1788, and lasted over seven years. (2) Many judges believe that the integrity of the proposition constrains the affirmative to the advocacy of *one* policy change. They would thus view the minicases as *parts* of a whole and consider the disadvantages of any part as applying to the entirety of the resolution.

E. Integrating the Case

As with the needs analysis case, the comparative advantages case must be carefully integrated in order to establish a prima facie case. The agreed goals, the plan, and the comparative advantages must be so developed as to dovetail perfectly.

The agreed goals must be identified. As the advocate rarely accepts all of the goals of the status quo, we must identify the specific goals of the status

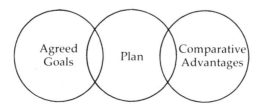

quo that are relevant to the proposition. The plan must be perfectly tailored to the agreed goals and must be presented in sufficient detail to demonstrate how it differs from the status quo and how it will produce the comparative advantages. The comparative advantages must be inherent in the plan; they must be significant; they must be better than any advantage that exists because of the status quo or that could be obtained through any repairs proposed by the negative; and they must be better than any advantages that may coexist with the status quo policies under consideration.

F. Some Examples

We have already considered some examples of comparative advantages cases. Although, as we have seen, the theory is ancient, its widespread utilization is relatively recent. Thus a few more examples may be helpful.

To return to the business example: A business executive might attend a company board meeting and announce, "I have a plan that will increase our profits by 15 percent." In the typical business organization no one will ask, "But do we need more profits?" Profits are the agreed goal of most business organizations. It is also an agreed assumption that the board should constantly strive to improve the company's profit position—the company is committed to making more profits as quickly as possible within the limitations previously cited. Thus, the need issue is never debated. Probably the only issue debated at such a board meeting would be "Will the plan really work?" The opposition might develop such arguments as "it involves automation, and the union will strike," or "it will increase pollution and we're committed *not* to increase pollution from our plants," or "if we adopt this plan we'll have to close down the Widget Division and that's exchanging a proven profit maker for a risky speculation," and similar arguments designed to show that the plan will not actually produce profits or that it would in some way endanger the company's future profit position or create socially unacceptable problems.

As another example, an insurance salesperson recently called on a professor to try to sell him a tax-sheltered annuity. He did not waste time arguing that the professor needed to make investments to provide for future income; the professor had conceded the need issue when he gave the salesperson an appointment. The meeting actually turned out to be a debate in which the salesperson sought to establish that his proposal was comparatively advantageous to other investment opportunities available to the professor.

Or consider the case of the young couple who decide to buy a new car. In this case, they have decided they want—or need—a new car. The problem they present to the salesperson is one that requires a comparative advantage analysis. There is no need issue to be argued—they have conceded it. The problem before the salesperson is to convince the couple that a product, or deal, is comparatively advantageous to competitive products or deals.

An actual example of the comparative advantages case in the field of politics may be found in the first campaign by Edward M. Kennedy for a seat in the United States Senate. He ran on the slogan, "He can do *more* for Massachusetts." The effective use of the comparative advantage analysis — as expressed in this slogan — allowed Kennedy to focus much of the campaign about the issue of which candidate would have the greater success in securing federal grants and federal projects for Massachusetts, which candidate would have the greater success in bringing to Massachusetts the jobs which would result from these grants and projects. His opponent did not care to raise the issue of whether or not Massachusetts *needed* federal monies and the resultant jobs. No need issue was argued in the campaign — both contenders agreed that one of a senator's major goals was to obtain federal monies for his state. (We may wonder whether this *should* be one of the major goals of a senator. However, we must recognize facts — this is the way many senators campaign, and this is the basis on which many citizens decide their votes.)

As we saw earlier, the comparative advantages analysis was relatively little used in the 1940s and 1950s and came into popularity in the mid-1960s. Thus, it may be significant to consider the economic history of those years. In the 1940s and 1950s we were under the sharp economic limitations imposed by recovery from the depression, World War II, and the Korean war. At that time, a person usually had to establish an urgent need for a new policy to be adopted — particularly if that new policy involved new taxes or new expenditures. Many accepted the philosophy of Viscount Falkland: "When it is not necessary to change, it is necessary not to change." By the mid-1960s we were well into the longest period of prosperity of our history — characterized as "the affluent society." In many situations, problems had only to be identified for us to do something about them; in many situations, society had arrived at agreed goals about problems.

President Kennedy, in a speech to the 1962 graduating class at Yale, offered this reason for the current popularity of the comparative advantages analysis:

Calhoun in 1804 and Taft in 1878 graduated into a world very different from ours of today. They and their contemporaries spent entire careers stretching over forty years in grappling with a few dramatic issues on which the nation was sharply and emotionally divided, issues that occupied the attention of a generation at a time: the National Bank, the disposal of the public lands, nullification or union, freedom or slavery, gold or silver. Today these old sweeping issues very largely have disappeared. The central domestic issues of our time are more subtle and less simple. *They relate not to basic clashes of philosophy or ideology but to ways and means of reaching common goals* — to research for sophisticated solutions to complex and obstinate issues.[7]

---

[7] John F. Kennedy, "Some Modern Economic Myths," Commencement Address at Yale University, June 1962 (italics added).

The comparative advantages analysis is not appropriate for all of the issues of our times. The needs analysis is best suited to many situations. The advocate, after thorough study of the problem, must select the most effective type of analysis taking into consideration the proposition, the status quo, the available evidence and argument, the attitudes, interests, and intellectual capabilities of the audience and the occasion.

IV. Building for Optimum Capability

Obviously, since the affirmative has the burden of proof, it must take the offensive and mount a strong attack and aggressively advance its case. Much of what we have considered thus far has to do with the affirmative's offensive position. It must be remembered, however, that debate does not take place in a vacuum and that an able negative will mount strong attacks against the affirmative. Therefore, the affirmative must build its case and deploy its evidence so as *to achieve the optimum balance of offensive and defensive capabilities.*

In building their case, the advocates must anticipate the probable areas of negative attack. In so doing, they frequently can adjust their case so as to avoid or blunt many negative attacks before they can be made. In developing cases on the "comprehensive medical care for all citizens" proposition, many affirmative advocates first considered adopting the widely publicized Kennedy proposal as their plan. As they studied possible negative attacks, they discovered that the $70-billion annual cost of the Kennedy proposal provided the negative with a myriad of plan attacks. After considering the difficulty of answering the potential attacks, many affirmative teams rejected the Kennedy proposal and opted for another plan. Some chose the Burleson Plan, favored by the Health Insurance Association of America, which cost "only" $4-billion annually. The same negative attacks still applied, but it was much easier to defend a $4-billion expenditure than a $70-billion expenditure.

On the same proposition, some affirmative advocates thought it would be a good idea to provide annual physical examinations for all citizens as a plank in their plan. At first they discovered a good deal of evidence recommending such examinations. Later they discovered evidence—which they were sure their opponents would also find—indicating that such examinations for the whole population were counterproductive when subjected to cost–benefit analysis. (The argument went that it would take so much time to give over 200 million physical examinations a year that physicians would not have time to do anything else.) Thus some affirmatives eliminated what had initially seemed to be a desirable plank for their plan and provided instead for multiphasic testing for the population. This method would check for many, but not all, diseases and, as the tests would be administered by physicians' aides and analyzed by computers, were of low cost both in dollars and physicians' time.

While it is defensively sound to tailor the plan to avoid the strongest negative attacks, advocates are *cautioned* that they still must provide a plan that will produce *significant* advantages. Obviously, it is easier to answer the cost attacks on a $1-billion plan than on a $70-billion plan. Given the context of the proposition, however, does the $1-billion plan produce significant advantages? The task of the affirmative advocates is to build a plan that achieves the optimum balance of offensive and defensive capabilities.

Advocates also have the task of providing the most effective deployment of their evidence. In debating the "minimum annual cash income for all citizens" proposition, many negative teams were prepared to agree that poor people needed more medical care, more food, better housing, and so on, but argued that this need could better be met through Medicaid, food stamps, government housing programs, and so on. They would then be prepared to argue that giving cash to poor people would not solve the need by introducing evidence that "poor people spend their cash on beer and potato chips rather than on nourishing food or medical care or better housing." Some affirmative teams had evidence directly countering this which showed that "poor people spend their money as wisely as middle income people." The problem before the affirmative was when was it best to use this evidence. Should they introduce it in the first affirmative speech before the negative could make their argument, or should they hold it back for refutation after the negative advanced their argument? There is no universal answer to this sort of question — the advocates must weigh their decision carefully in the context of the proposition and the probable strategy of the opposition. In one specific case, a good affirmative team chose to use the evidence, stated as briefly as possible, in the first affirmative speech. They found that this forced their negative opponents either to drop the argument or to go into such a lengthy analysis of the counter evidence that they were forced to slough other issues. Thus, as measured by decisions won, this affirmative team made the correct strategic decision about the deployment of their evidence. There is a risk in such anticipatory refutation, however. If the advocates use valuable time in anticipating arguments that are never made and that are not essential to their case, they may find that they lose time that could better be used in advancing their case. The task of the affirmative advocates is to deploy their evidence so as to achieve optimum balance of offensive and defensive capabilities.

V. Outlines of Typical Affirmative Cases

The outlines — in the *inset* on pages 196–199 — demonstrate typical affirmative cases on propositions of policy. These outlines — which have been used

Comparative Advantages Analysis: Contemporary Format

First Affirmative Constructive Speech

I. Introduction
   A. Amenities: recognize chair, judge, audience, occasion, briefly express pleasure at taking part in this debate if the occasion is a formal one — otherwise begin with B.
   B. State the affirmative's rationale. (One debater began by saying "Because we agree with the President's Commission on Law Enforcement and the Administration of Justice, which begins its definitive publication, *The Challenge of Crime in a Free Society*, with these sobering words, 'There is much crime in America, more than ever is reported, far more than ever is solved, far too much for the health of the Nation . . . ,' the affirmative today is resolved . . .")
   C. State the proposition exactly. (The debater quoted in B concluded his sentence by stating the proposition, ". . . That law enforcement agencies in the United States should be given greater freedom in the investigation and prosecution of crime.")
   D. Define the terms of the proposition, or indicate that the terms will be operationally defined by the plan.
   E. Tell what the affirmative will do in this debate and what you will do in your speech.
      1. _____
      2. _____
      . . .

II. Body
   A. Present the affirmative plan clearly, concisely, and persuasively. (If the plan is any more complicated than "Amend the Constitution to lower the voting age to eighteen," the advocate must provide a carefully developed series of "planks" that will make this plan clear and easy to comprehend.)
   B. Prove the first advantage that will be achieved by the plan.
      1. Prove the advantage cannot be achieved by the status quo.
      2. Prove the advantage cannot be achieved without the plan.
      3. Prove the advantage is inherent in the plan.
      4. Prove the advantage is significant.
   C. Prove the second advantage in the same way.
   D. Prove the third advantage in the same way.
   E. Prove any remaining advantages in the same way.
   F. (Depending on the type of case you are using, demonstrate that any one advantage — or the advantages taken as a whole — justify adopting the resolution.)

(It must be remembered that this is the core of the advocate's case. In the actual delivery of the case, the advocate will spend most of the time developing the body of the speech. Each issue should be carefully organized with a coherent substructure.)

III. Conclusion
   A. Summarize the affirmative case.
      1. Recapitulate the plan.
      2. Restate the advantages.
   B. Conclude your speech with a strong persuasive appeal for the adoption of the resolution.

Second Affirmative Constructive Speech

I. Introduction
   A. Amenities: recognize chair, judge, audience, occasion, briefly express pleasure at taking part in this debate if the occasion is a formal one—otherwise begin with B.
   B. Answer any plan questions asked by the first negative speaker.

II. Body
   A. Defend propositionality, if necessary.*
   B. Defend goals if necessary.
   C. Defend inherency, if necessary.
   D. Prove advantages cannot be achieved without adopting the resolution, if necessary.
   E. Prove the advantages are inherent in the plan, if necessary.
   F. Prove the advantages are significant, if necessary.
   G. Prove the plan will achieve the advantages, if necessary.
   H. Review the affirmative case issue by issue in the order presented by the first affirmative.
      1. Briefly summarize any issue not attacked by the negative.
      2. Refute those issues attacked by the negative and extend the affirmative case by providing additional evidence and argument to support your case.

III. Conclusion
   A. Summarize the affirmative case.
      1. Recapitulate the plan.
      2. Restate the advantages.
   B. Summarize your refutation of the negative's attack.
   C. Conclude your speech with a strong persuasive appeal for the adoption of the resolution.
   (If the negative has offered a counter plan: (1) defend and advance the affirmative case, (2) attack the counter plan, using the organization of a first negative constructive speech, and (3) prove the affirmative plan is better.)

First Affirmative Rebuttal

I. Introduction: Tell what issues you will deal with in this speech.

II. Body
   A. Refute the second negative's attacks.
      1. Prove workability, if necessary.
      2. Disprove or minimize significance of disadvantages, if necessary.
      3. Prove plan will achieve advantages, if necessary.
      4. Contrast now disproved or minimized disadvantages and prove, if possible, that on balance the advantages outweigh the disadvantages.

* See Chapter 14 for a discussion of this and other types of Negative refutation.

B. Refute the first negative rebuttal.
   1. Reestablish the affirmative case by refuting the negative attacks.
   2. Extend your case by introducing further evidence and analysis to support your case.*

III. Conclusion
   A. Summarize your rebuttal of the negative's attack.
   B. Prove that the affirmative case stands intact.
   C. Conclude with an effective persuasive appeal for the adoption of the resolution.

Second Affirmative Rebuttal

I. Introduction
   A. Indicate those issues of the debate with which the negative has not contended, or on which it has shifted ground.
   B. Point out the main issues of the debate that remain in contention. If the negative has raised a number of objections, organize these objections under a few main issues.

II. Body
   A. Using the same method of proving your issues as in your constructive speech, reestablish those issues that the negative has sought to refute and that have not already been reestablished by your colleague by summarizing the previous evidence and argument and by introducing further evidence to substantiate arguments previously presented.
   B. Make a running summary of the entire debate, dealing with each issue in the order set forth in the first affirmative constructive speech. Show how each issue has been established in spite of the negative's contentions. Summarize your answer to each negative argument. Concentrate on the major issues still in contention, focus on the proofs underlying the negative's issues, and demonstrate that they are inadequate to support the negative's issues.

III. Conclusion
   A. Summarize the entire debate.
   B. Demonstrate the desirability of the affirmative's position as contrasted with that of the negative.
   C. Conclude with the strongest possible persuasive appeal for the adoption of the resolution.

* New evidence may be introduced at any point in the debate. New lines of argument may not, however, be introduced in the rebuttal speeches of educational debates. Rules of procedure regulate the introduction of new evidence into courtroom debates.

Needs Analysis: Contemporary Format

First Affirmative Constructive Speech

The needs, plan and advantages are presented in this speech.

Second Affirmative Constructive Speech

The first negative's attacks are refuted in this speech. Needs and advantages are extended with additional evidence and argument.

First Affirmative Rebuttal

This speech follows the same outline as the comparative advantages format.

Second Affirmative Rebuttal

This speech follows the same outline as the comparative advantages format.

Needs Analysis: Conventional Format

First Affirmative Constructive Speech

The needs are presented in this speech.

Second Affirmative Constructive Speech

The plan and advantages are presented in this speech and the first negative's attack on the need issues is refuted.

First Affirmative Rebuttal Speech

The second negative's attack on plan and advantages is refuted. The first negative rebuttal attack on need is refuted. The entire affirmative case is reviewed and extended.

Second Affirmative Rebuttal Speech

This speech follows the same outline as the comparative advantages format.

for a number of years by debating teams as starting points in the construction of affirmative cases—are specifically designed for educational debate, the type of argumentative situation in which the student will have the greatest opportunity to learn the principles of argumentation. The concepts of case organization presented here may be adapted to any type of argumentative situation, with appropriate adjustments for the audience, the occasion, and the opposition.

The final draft of a case should be the product of extensive rewriting and editing and should reflect the advocate's maximum skill in speech composition. It must be so written that when the speech is presented the advocate can achieve his maximum effectiveness in delivery. The student may find it helpful to review Chapter 18 ("Presenting the Case: Speech Composition") and Chapter 19 ("Presenting the Case: Delivery") when building an affirmative or negative case.

The first outline is of a comparative advantage affirmative case in the contemporary format; the second is of a needs analysis case in the contemporary format; and the third is of a needs analysis in the conventional format. The first outline is presented in some detail; the second and third are presented in briefer form, to illustrate the structure that may be readily adapted from the first outline.

These case outlines and the various types of cases discussed previously are stated in general terms. It is the task of the advocate to adapt these generalized concepts to the specific details of the particular resolution under consideration, making effective adjustment to all the requirements of drafting the case.

For many years almost all intercollegiate debates have been conducted on propositions of policy, since such propositions provide the best opportunity for attaining maximum educational value from debating. It should be noted, however, that propositions of fact and value are frequently subjects of substantive debates. All that has been said about the affirmative case in a proposition of policy applies to debates on propositions of fact and value as well. The issues, of course, will be different, and the plan and advantages may be omitted from the case. The debater who knows the principles of preparing a case on a proposition of policy will surely be able to make an easy transition to the preparation of a case on a proposition of fact or value.

A common debate on a proposition of fact takes place in our law courts when the resolution is, in effect, "Resolved: That John Doe committed burglary." Since the crime of burglary is defined specifically in most jurisdictions, the issues of the debate are consequently defined by law. Typically, the issues in such a debate will be as follows:

I. John Doe forcibly entered into the dwelling house of another person.

II. John Doe made this entry at night.

III. John Doe made this entry with intent to commit a felony therein.

To obtain a conviction, the affirmative (the District Attorney) must prove all of these issues. If the negative (the defense attorney) can refute any one of these issues, John Doe cannot be convicted of burglary, although he may be convicted of a lesser charge.

In a debate on a proposition of value, the issues are drawn from moral precepts or critical standards rather than from statute law. For example, in the proposition "Resolved: That preemptive war is justifiable," the issues are the considerations of moral law that the affirmative seeks to establish as applicable to this resolution.

The case outline is frequently a team undertaking, drafted by the advocates on a given side of the resolution for the purpose of coordinating their efforts and presenting their evidence and argument to maximum advantage within the context of a given situation.

When the situation permits, beginning debaters usually choose the needs analysis conventional format. The second affirmative speaker often feels more secure if a portion of his or her constructive speech—the plan and advantages—may be preplanned. As they gain in experience, the affirmative speakers may find it advantageous to use the needs analysis contemporary format, thus freeing the second constructive speaker to devote his or her entire time to refutation of the first negative's attacks and to reinforcing the affirmative case. Beginning debaters often find that they can develop a comparative advantages case more successfully after they have had some experience with needs analysis cases.

In substantive debates the advocates will make similar decisions, basing their choice of case not only on the nature of the proposition and their analysis of the status quo but also on the evidence and argument available to them and on their experience with various types of cases.

Exercises

1. Attend an intercollegiate debate and prepare an outline of the affirmative case. Attach to this outline a written critique (500 words) of the affirmative case, in which you evaluate the organization and development of the case.

2. Prepare an outline and a written critique (500 words) of an affirmative case on a contemporary problem as presented in a recent speech. For the texts of speeches, consult *Vital Speeches, Representative American Speeches,* the *New York Times,* or *U.S. News & World Report.*

3. Prepare an affirmative case outline on a proposition of policy, value, or fact to be handed to your instructor. In preparing this and other exercises you may, with the consent of your instructor, draw on materials you have prepared in connection with earlier chapters.

4. Working with another member of the class, prepare an affirmative case outline on a proposition of policy, value, or fact for delivery in class. Hand a copy of the case

outline to your instructor. If time permits, invite the class to discuss the case after you have presented it orally.

5. Conduct a class discussion in which you consider the following question: Which type of case analysis is the more effective for general use with the current national debate proposition—a needs analysis or a comparative advantages case?

6. Can an effective counter plan be developed for use with the current national debate proposition? If the answer is *yes*, develop blocks of argument to defeat potential counter plans.

7. Arrange with other members of the class to present a classroom debate on a proposition of policy. After the debate, conduct a thorough critique with special emphasis on the affirmative.

8. Select a bill currently being debated in Congress. Study the arguments used by the affirmative speakers supporting the bill. What type of case are they using?

Chapter 14

Building the Negative Case

The negative case generally requires considerable flexibility in planning. A careful analysis of the proposition will probably enable the negative to determine the issues most likely to be advanced by the affirmative. Until the debate is actually underway, however, the negative team will not know precisely what type of case the affirmative is using; they will not know what weight the affirmative will attach to each issue, nor exactly what evidence and argument will be used by the affirmative in developing its issues. This uncertainty places a high premium on the negative's ability to adapt to the affirmative's case as it is presented.

I. Objectives of the Negative Case

As has been indicated earlier, the burden of proof rests upon the affirmative. In theory, the negative need not even speak until the affirmative has presented a prima facie case. The prudent advocate will recognize, however, that popular audiences sometimes assume that "silence means consent" and may accept a proposition on the basis of less than a prima facie case. Therefore, the advocate must be prepared to reply to any affirmative case, even though it does not meet all the logical requirements of a prima facie case. In the courtroom, the defense may move that a case be dismissed on the ground that the prosecution or plaintiff has not presented a prima facie case. This procedure, however, is not generally available outside the courtroom.

While the burden of proof rests on the affirmative, the negative has the *burden of rebuttal*—that is, the negative must refute the issues of the affirmative, or the affirmative will prevail. The *burden of the negative*, then, is the burden of rebuttal that the negative must seek to shift to the affirmative.

There are *two basic types* of cases available to the negative—*refutation* or *counter plan*. In the diagrams in the following discussion of these two types of cases, the affirmative case is represented by the three interlocking circles on the left of the page, while the negative refutation is represented on the right of the page.

II. Refutation Negative Case

The refutation case may be used against either the needs analysis or the comparative advantages affirmative case. The advocates select the refutation negative position after study of the problem and analysis of the affirmative case lead them to the conclusion that the affirmative can best be refuted by carrying one or more of the issues considered in this section. The specific development of this case and the particular issues the negative uses in any given situation will, of course, depend upon the resolution under debate, the available evidence and arguments, the actual case of the opposition, the attitudes, interests, and intellectual capabilities of the audience, and the dynamics of occasion.

It must be emphasized that each refutation negative case is custom built and adapted to the specific affirmative case it must oppose. The negative selects among its arsenal of potential issues and develops those best suited for use in a particular situation. While carrying one issue—workability, for instance—could win for the negative, the prudent advocate recognizes that the able affirmative has anticipated and is prepared for all possible attacks. Thus, as the negative can rarely be sure of winning an issue until the debate is over, it usually finds that the wisest course is to attack all vulnerable areas of the affirmative case, concentrating its major attacks on the most vulnerable areas—for instance, not only attacking workability but also providing minor repairs and proving that disadvantages outweigh advantages.

Affirmative Case   Negative Refutation

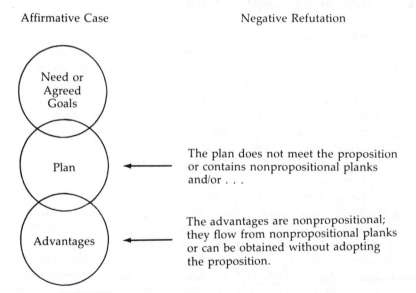

Need or Agreed Goals

Plan ← The plan does not meet the proposition or contains nonpropositional planks and/or . . .

Advantages ← The advantages are nonpropositional; they flow from nonpropositional planks or can be obtained without adopting the proposition.

A. Attack Propositionality

When advocates argue that a matter is not propositional or not "topical," they maintain that it is not related to, or does not directly stem from, the proposition being debated. In the law courts, an attorney may object to evidence, a question, or an argument on the ground that it is not relevant to the case before the court. If the judge sustains objection, the matter is excluded. In parliamentary debate, the chair should rule "out of order" any remarks or proposed amendments that are not germane to the business before the house. (The stringency with which this rule is enforced varies—for example, the U.S. Senate does not require that a senator's remarks be germane.) In educational debate, propositionality may be the basis, or part of the basis, for the decision. In less formal situations, reasonable persons tend to dismiss irrelevant arguments. Attacks on propositionality are usually directed against the plan or one or more of the advantages.

1. Of the Plan The proposition "Resolved: That the federal government should grant annually a specific percentage of its income tax revenue to the state governments" provides an interesting example. This proposition mandated four specific things for the affirmative's plan: (1) an annual grant, (2) a specific percentage of the revenue, (3) funds coming from federal income tax revenue, and (4) funds distributed by the federal government to the state governments. If any one of these items were missing, the negative would have grounds for arguing "not propositional." In debating the "energy" proposition, some affirmative teams argued a "gun control" case; their plan banned the sale of hand guns on the ground that the "energy" in the cartridges killed people, and they claimed the advantage of fewer deaths. Some negative teams meeting this case were able to establish that the plan was not propositional by pointing out that the plan controlled guns —not energy. The sale of cartridges was still permitted under the affirmative's plan and streetwise criminals would readily acquire homemade "zip" guns.

The affirmative may add some nonpropositional provisions to its plan to provide for a reasonable implementation of its proposal. For example, in debating the "revenue sharing" proposition, some teams provided that the funds could not be used for (1) matching federal funds for federal categorical grant programs or (2) highway construction.

2. Of the Advantages The advantages must flow from the adoption of the resolution as operationally defined by a plan congruous with the resolution. If the negative can prove an advantage is nonpropositional, that advantage should be rejected as a reason for adopting the resolution.

If the advantages come from a nonpropositional provision of the plan, the affirmative is in trouble. On the "revenue sharing" proposition, some affirmative teams required the states to give the funds to the public schools and claimed the advantage of better education.

Negatives meeting this case were usually able to prove that the provision was nonpropositional and that the advantage of better education came from giving the money to the schools and not from any of the four items mandated in the resolution. They also demonstrated that the advantage was "not unique" to the resolution. The same advantage could be achieved by having the federal government give money (and not necessarily income tax revenue) directly to the schools.

As we have just seen, the advantage of "better education" was non-propositional. As we have also seen, reasonable nonpropositional planks may be added to the plan to provide for its reasonable implementation. Any advantage that comes from a nonpropositional plank of the plan is in itself nonpropositional. For example, the provision that no revenue sharing funds be used for highway construction was a reasonable nonpropositional constraint. If, however, the affirmative claimed as an advantage that it would reduce waste in highway construction, such an advantage would be clearly nonpropositional—it stemmed from adopting a nonpropositional plank of the plan. Of course, it would also be "not unique," in that any waste in highway construction could be eliminated by legislation other than revenue sharing.

B. Attack Goals

In attacking the goals of a comparative advantage case, the negative may seek to demonstrate that (1) the goals are incompletely identified or (2) there are other equally or more important goals.

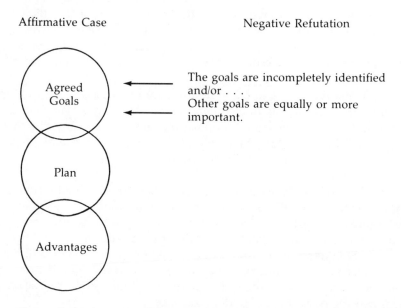

1. **Goals Incompletely Identified** If the affirmative has incompletely identified the goals of the status quo, the negative should point this out and identify the goals fully within the context of its rationale. In a debate on the "greater freedom in the investigation and prosecution of crime" proposition, one affirmative speaker stated that the goal of society was "to reduce crime." A negative debater responded:

Reducing crime is an incomplete statement of the goal of American society. We all want to reduce crime, but the negative today stands with the great legal scholar Blackstone who warned, "It is better that ten guilty persons escape than one innocent suffer." This is why we say the affirmative's goal is incompletely identified. The real goal of society is to reduce crime while preserving due process and other essential Constitutional rights.

2. Other Goals Important In a debate on the "tax sharing" proposition, an affirmative team maintained that the agreed goals of the status quo were to attain a more efficient system of tax collection and a more progressive system of taxation. A negative team meeting this case argued that a more important goal of the status quo was to maintain the American system of federalism. They were unable to refute the affirmative's claim that their plan would produce the advantages of "more efficient collection" and "more progressive taxes." However, they were able to minimize these advantages by demonstrating that repairs in the status quo could produce almost as much efficiency in tax collection and almost as progressive a system of taxation. They then developed their argument that the affirmative's plan destroyed the federal system by making the states dependent on the federal government for their revenues, thus reducing the states to *de facto* departments of a central government. They then cited the disadvantages they claimed were inherent in a system of central government. In weighing the now minimized advantages against the disadvantages, the negative advocates claimed that, on balance, there was a net disadvantage to the affirmative's plan.

C. Attack Need

The objective of the negative here is to demonstrate that the affirmative has not proved the existence of a need or to prove that there is no need.

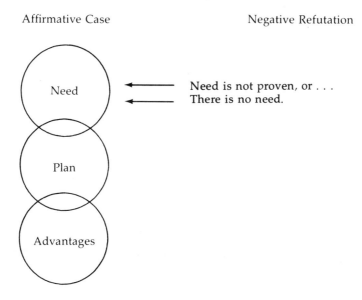

Affirmative Case   Negative Refutation

Need   Need is not proven, or . . .
There is no need.

Plan

Advantages

1. Need Not Proven In debates on the proposition "Resolved: That the United States should enact a compulsory fair employment practices law," some affirmative speakers advanced as a major need issue the contention that there is widespread discrimination against blacks in employment practices. In support, they offered evidence to show that the average black receives a lower average wage than the average white worker. Negative advocates, using the attack on the need negative case, were quick to point out that the affirmative had not established that discrimination was the cause of the lower average wage received by blacks. In this case, negative speakers would introduce counter evidence and argument to show that the average black lived in the South where all workers received a lower average wage, that the average black had a lower level of educational attainment, and that these factors were the cause of the lower average wage. Thus the negative maintained that the affirmative's issue, even if true, did not prove the existence of discrimination or a need for the law called for in the resolution, because the affirmative had failed to demonstrate that the lower average wages of blacks were caused by discrimination and not by other factors.

This very argument, once actually used by student debaters, was later recognized in federal practice. At one time the federal government required contractors to sign a "no discrimination in hiring" agreement. Later, recognizing the difficulty of proving discrimination, the federal government shifted the burden of proof and required contractors to sign an agreement to undertake "an affirmative program to hire workers from minority groups."

2. No Existing Need In debating the "energy" proposition, some affirmatives called for the federal government to ban any further construction of nuclear energy plants to generate electricity. They pointed out that the status quo was committed to the construction of such plants and argued, as their need issue, the claim that when we had a hundred or more such plants there would be an intolerable risk of radiation leakage or explosion. Many negatives argued that no need existed or would exist. They maintained that nuclear power plants were perfectly safe and that there was no possibility of any leakage or explosion. They cited evidence stating that there had never been any fatality caused by a civilian nuclear power plant and extended their argument by citing the elaborate safety precautions already in existence. Debates on this issue provided excellent examples of the clash of evidence. There was excellent evidence available to both sides, and the clash was inevitably won by the team that could provide the most recent evidence from the best qualified authorities, who could be quoted most directly to the point under dispute.

D. Attack Inherency

As inherency has been considered earlier (Chapter 12, "Requirement to Prove Inherency"), we will treat it only briefly here. Two types of inherency arguments are often used by negative teams: (1) there is no inherent barrier in the status quo blocking the achievement of the advantage, and (2) the advantages are not inherent in the plan.

Affirmative Case   Negative Refutation

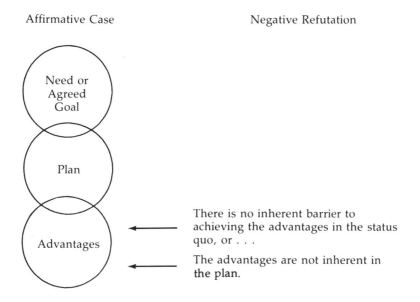

There is no inherent barrier to achieving the advantages in the status quo, or . . .

The advantages are not inherent in the plan.

1. Of the Status Quo Barrier The negative seeks to prove that there is no justification for adopting the resolution, since the advantages claimed by the affirmative can be achieved without the plan. In debating the "energy" proposition, some affirmatives proposed a plan whereby the government would require all electric generating plants to use coal as their only fuel and to generate electricity by the magnetohydrodynamic (MHD) process. They argued that this method used cheap and plentiful coal and was far more efficient than the status quo methods of producing electricity. As an advantage they claimed that the oil now used by the electric plants—and which was in critically short supply—would be made available to industries that could not substitute coal as a source of their energy. Some negatives meeting this type of case responded by pointing out that the affirmative had cited no reason why the electric industry would not adopt the MHD process of its own volition. Using a conditional argument, they maintained—since coal was both abundant and cheap—that, if the process really was more efficient, then it would obviously be more profitable for the electric companies to adopt MHD and that they would do so promptly, and there was no justification for the plan. Some affirmatives had difficulty in responding to this argument until they found evidence which enabled them to argue that the very high initial cost of MHD equipment was an inherent barrier to its being adopted by electric companies. The cost was so high that many years would pass before the companies realized any profit from the changeover. Thus, they argued, the only way to obtain the advantages of MHD was to adopt the resolution and use federal control to require the electric companies to do it.

2. Of the Advantages A good beginning point is to study carefully the affirmative's plan to discern whether there are any nonpropositional planks. Any advantages that flow from such provisions are clearly nonpropositional. In addition, the negative must be alert to the possibility of a noninherent advantage being claimed from a properly propositional plan. In debating the "energy" proposition, some affirmatives called for the federal government to spend $10-billion on research on solar and geothermal sources and to mandate the use of these sources to supply the nation's electricity needs within ten years. The negative quickly pointed out that success is *not inherent* in research. Thus the affirmative could not guarantee that solar and geothermal sources could meet our electricity needs in ten years or indeed ever. After all, they noted, we have spent billions of dollars over many years on cancer research without finding a cure for cancer. And alchemists devoted centuries of research to the problem of the transmutation of the base metals into gold.

E. Provide Repairs or Modifications

Two types of repair or modification arguments may be used by the negative: (1) to solve needs and (2) to provide advantages. The repairs or modifications should be relatively few and relatively minor; they must be consistent with the status quo; there should be ample precedent for such actions; and they must be capable of being put into effect without making any structural change in the status quo.

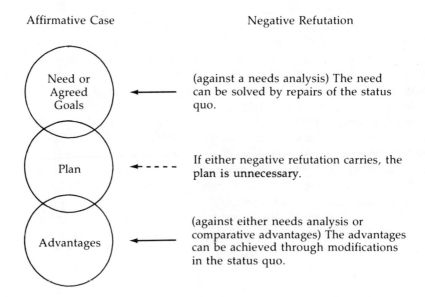

Affirmative Case   Negative Refutation

Need or Agreed Goals — (against a needs analysis) The need can be solved by repairs of the status quo.

Plan — If either negative refutation carries, the plan is unnecessary.

Advantages — (against either needs analysis or comparative advantages) The advantages can be achieved through modifications in the status quo.

1. To Solve Needs This type of argument is used when the negative is forced to admit certain shortcomings in the status quo but believes they can be repaired by status quo mechanisms. Usually the negative first seeks to minimize the need issues (see "Attack Significance," page 217) and then presents its repairs. For example, in debates on the proposition "Resolved: That law enforcement agencies in the United States should be given greater freedom in the investigation and prosecution of crime," some negative teams argued that the laws already on the books were entirely adequate to deal with crime; all that was needed were more funds to provide for better enforcement. They maintained that more funds would provide more "hardware," that is, more computers, walkie talkies, mobile communication centers; more funds would enable them to upgrade the police forces by paying higher salaries to attract and retain more able men and to provide in-service training; more funds would provide more prosecutors and more judges, thus assuring prompt trials; more money would provide more effective rehabilitation programs in prisons; and more money would provide more parole officers to supervise the prisoners once they were released. This combination of repairs — while maintaining the status quo laws — would significantly reduce crime, they argued.

In debates on the "comprehensive medical care" proposition, many negative teams made effective use of repairs. If the affirmative limited their need analysis to the claim that "poor people can't afford medical care," the negative quickly offered repairs to extend Medicare, Medicaid, free clinics, the free care provisions of the Hill-Burton Act, and many other programs. The negative noted that all of these programs existed in the status quo, that they provided ample precedent for the government to provide free medical care for poor people, and that no structural change in any program was required.

2. To Achieve Advantages This type of argument is used when the negative believes that the advantage claimed by the affirmative can be achieved without adopting the resolution — that the advantage is "not unique" to the proposition — but by merely making some modifications in the status quo. The debater might choose to make a conditional argument and show the advantage *could* be provided by modifications without advocating that the advantage actually be achieved. If the advantage could be achieved without adopting the resolution, then it is not a justification for adopting the resolution.

In debating the "energy" proposition, some affirmatives introduced a plan to ban the use of coal in producing electricity and mandated the use of nuclear power plants. One of the advantages they claimed was "cleaner air." A negative team meeting this case argued the status quo was already working to provide cleaner air, and if we wanted still cleaner air, all we had to do was modify the standards of the Air Quality Act, since ample technology existed to make this practical. Thus, by merely making a minor modification in the status quo, we could achieve the advantage of cleaner air without adopting the affirmative's plan and suffering all the inherent disadvantages of nuclear power plants which the negative would seek to prove in the "disadvantages" portion of their case.

The negative, of course, must exercise discretion in making modifications or repairs. A multiplicity of repairs or modifications might open the way for the affirmative to argue that the negative has admitted the need or advantage of so many repairs or modifications that we should "go all the way" and adopt the resolution.

F. Attack Solvency

Typically, the negative will seek to minimize the need (see "Attack Significance," page 217) and later prove that the plan will not work (see "Attack Workability," page 213).

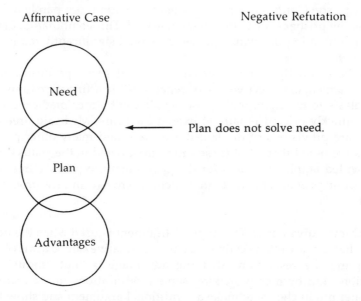

In developing the "plan does not solve need" argument, the negative concentrates on attempting to prove that the plan—even if it works exactly as the affirmative wants it to—will not solve the need. For example, in debates on the "guaranteed annual wage for nonagricultural workers" proposition, some affirmatives argued, as their need issue, that the purchasing power of unemployed persons must be maintained; they cited evidence that millions of persons were unemployed annually and then presented a plan that would provide a guaranteed annual wage for employees with one year's seniority. Negatives meeting this case argued that it did not provide solvency because millions of the unemployed cited in the affirmative's need were agricultural workers, who were not covered in the plan (indeed they were excluded by the resolution), and then introduced evidence to show that most unemployed persons had less than one year's seniority prior to their discharge and hence would not receive the guaranteed annual wage provided for in the plan. The plan would work for the relatively few unemployed persons with one year's seniority, but not for the millions cited by the affirmative in their need issue.

In a debate on the "energy" proposition, an affirmative established as its need that "dependence on foreign oil sources is undesirable" and proposed as its plan immediate authorization of the Alaskan pipeline (Congress had not then enacted the enabling legislation). The negative argued that the Alaskan pipeline would provide only a fraction of the amount of oil imports and, therefore, would not solve the problem. They extended their argument with evidence showing that the demand for oil was steadily increasing and that even with the affirmative's plan our dependence on foreign oil imports would increase both in number of gallons and as a percentage of total United States oil consumption even with the Alaskan pipeline operating at full capacity. This affirmative lost badly. In a later tournament, they changed their plan to provide oil from Alaska *and* a variety of other domestic sources.

G. Attack Workability

The negative's objective here is to block adoption of the resolution by proving that the plan proposed by the affirmative is unworkable. To do this, the negative should present a series of concisely stated, closely reasoned arguments. In preparing for this, as with other negative issues, the advocates often develop a series of "blocks" against potential affirmative plans. When

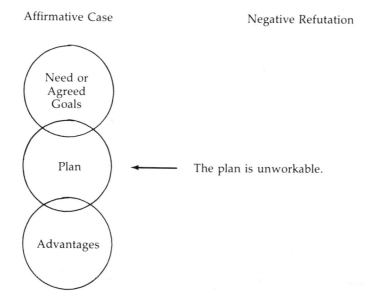

Affirmative Case   Negative Refutation

Need or Agreed Goals

Plan   ←——— The plan is unworkable.

Advantages

they hear the plan the affirmative is actually presenting, they pull the appropriate blocks from their file and adapt them to the specific plan presented by the affirmative.

Debating the "energy" proposition, one affirmative team cited the energy shortage as their need and proposed to solve the need by a plan that called for the federal government to require electric plants to phase out the use of oil and coal and to build solar, geothermal, and nuclear plants to produce electricity. Well-prepared negatives usually had blocks of arguments prepared for each of these energy sources. One negative argued against this plan by introducing evidence to establish:

1. Solar energy is unworkable because (1) it has never been proven in commercial use; (2) its potential is geographically limited by cloud cover; (3) the fuel cell method is prohibitively expensive — it would increase the cost of electricity one thousand times; and (4) the reflector method is prohibitive in land cost — it would require an area equal to the size of 21 states to solve the affirmative's needs.

2. Nuclear energy is unworkable because (1) the long time lag before reactors can be built — all present nuclear plants are two to seven years behind schedule and future plants will be delayed even more because of lengthy law suits and hearings where the dangers to life and environment will be argued; and (2) there is now a shortage of uranium necessary to operate the present plants — there just will not be enough uranium to operate the number of plants proposed by the affirmative.

3. Geothermal is unworkable because (1) there are very few potential sources of commercially useful size; (2) these are located in earthquake prone areas, where drilling for the hot water might in itself cause earthquakes, or in areas remote from any population to use the electricity they might produce; and (3) there is a shortage of copper which makes it commercially impractical to transmit electric power over great distances.

The negative concluded their workability argument by demonstrating that all three of the energy sources proposed by the affirmative could not solve their need.

H. Prove Plan Will Not Achieve Claimed Advantages

In developing this argument, the advocate concentrates on attempting to prove that the plan — even if it works exactly as the affirmative wants it to — will not achieve the advantages claimed by the affirmative.

In debating the "comprehensive medical care" proposition, one affirmative, in its plan, provided free medical care for all citizens and claimed as one of its advantages "better medical care for the poor." The negative argued the plan could not achieve this advantage because (1) there are few physicians in the rural and ghetto areas where most poor people live; (2) the poor lack the money to pay for transportation to travel to the areas where the physicians practice; (3) many of the poor are ignorant of the value of early medical

Affirmative Case   Negative Refutation

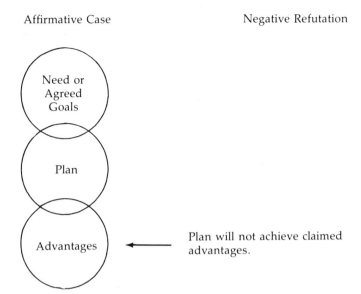

Plan will not achieve claimed
advantages.

care and will not seek it; (4) many of the poor are afraid of medical care and
will not seek it until their condition is critical; and (5) many of the working
poor cannot afford to take time off to seek medical care until their condition
is critical.

In debating the "law enforcement" proposition, some affirmatives proposed as their plan that wiretapping be legalized for state and local police
forces and claimed as their advantage that there would be more convictions
of criminals as wiretaps would produce direct evidence of crimes. Negatives
meeting this case argued the plan would not achieve the advantage as criminals would assume their phones were tapped and take counter measures.
They argued the criminals would (1) reduce the use of the phone, (2) use
scrambler phones, (3) use electronic devices to discover untapped phones
and use those phones, (4) use randomly chosen public phones, (5) use frequently changed codes, (6) use frequently changed argot, and (7) use frag-
mentary references and identification.

I. Prove Disadvantages

The negative's objective here is to block the adoption of the resolution by
proving the plan proposed by the affirmative will produce disadvantages
and that these disadvantages outweigh any possible advantage the plan may
achieve. To do this, the negative should present a series of concisely stated,
closely reasoned arguments. In preparing for this, as with workability and
other negative attacks, the advocate develops a series of "blocks" against
potential affirmative plans and adapts them to the specific plan presented by
the affirmative.

Affirmative Case   Negative Refutation

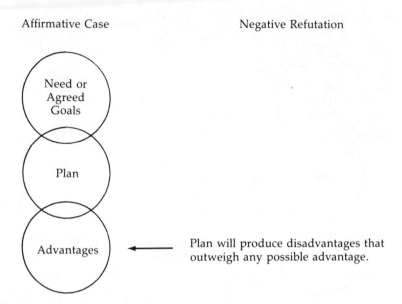

Plan will produce disadvantages that
outweigh any possible advantage.

In debating the "energy" proposition one affirmative, having established
as its need that strip mining damaged the environment, provided a plan
that banned all strip mining and claimed the advantage of a better environment. A negative meeting this case argued that banning strip mining
(which it called surface mining) would produce the following disadvantages:
(1) cause a shortage of copper (most copper came from surface mines);
(2) cause a shortage of iron (most iron came from surface mines); (3) exacerbate the oil shortage (as oil would be used as a partial replacement for
surface-mined coal); (4) increase the cost of electricity (as scarce oil and more
expensive deep-mined coal would be used to replace surface-mined coal);
(5) increase inflation (as a result of 1, 2, 3, and 4); (6) increase unemployment
(as a result of 1, 2, 3, 4 and 5); (7) increase black lung disease (as more people
would work in deep mines under the affirmative's plan); (8) increase the
number of mine accidents (working in deep mines is inherently more dangerous than working in surface mines); (9) cause dependence on unreliable
foreign sources for coal (as present deep mines could not meet the demand
for coal and, as it takes several years to get new mines into production, we
would have to import coal; foreign sources might embargo coal, as the Arabs
embargoed oil); (10) exacerbate the balance of payments problem (as dollars
would flow out of the country to buy coal).

The negative then concluded this portion of their case by arguing that
these disadvantages far outweighed whatever aesthetic advantages might
be gained by viewing a landscape untouched by surface mining as contrasted
with a landscape reclaimed after surface mining.

Of course, the negative must *prove* the disadvantages. As we saw earlier
on page 37, "Whoever introduces an issue or contention into the debate has
a burden of proof."

J. Attack Significance

The negative objective in attacking significance is to prove that the needs or advantages of the affirmative are not sufficiently significant to justify adopting the resolution.

Affirmative Case   Negative Refutation

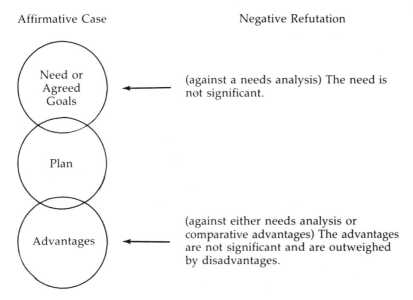

(against a needs analysis) The need is not significant.

(against either needs analysis or comparative advantages) The advantages are not significant and are outweighed by disadvantages.

1. Of Need In debating the "information gathering" proposition, some affirmatives cited the activity of army intelligence agents in photographing demonstrators at antiwar rallies. They claimed this activity had a "chilling effect" on some citizens and discouraged them from exercising their Constitutional rights. They claimed this "chilling effect" was a "harm" that constituted a need for a ban on this type of governmental information gathering. Some negatives meeting this case attacked the significance of the need by pointing out that hundreds of thousands of persons attended this particular rally; obviously, they had not been "chilled." They argued that the negative had failed to quantify the "chilling effect"; they had failed to show that anyone had stayed away from the rally because he was "chilled." They maintained "no quantification, no significance." (Of course, an extreme civil libertarian would argue that even if only one person is discouraged from exercising his Constitutional rights, this situation constitutes a need to change the law.) They extended the argument conditionally; maybe some people were "chilled" but came to the rally anyway — thus, no harm. Or, they continued, maybe some of those photographed were subversives who intended to use the cover of the rally to plan bombings, assassinations, and kidnappings. If they were "chilled" from plotting these activities, it was not a harm, but rather an advantage. At the very least there had to be a number of pickpockets and pursesnatchers in a crowd of this size. If they were "chilled" from plying their trade, so much the better.

Sometimes the negative can establish that there is no significance to the affirmative's need. More often they will establish a lack of significance "on balance." Thus this negative concluded its argument by saying:

The unproven possibility may exist that a few innocent souls were "chilled" and didn't attend the rally to exercise their Constitutional rights. But consider the facts on balance. There are actual and potential criminals at large. These will cause great harm to society if unchecked. To protect society, the government must gather information on criminals. In the process it necessarily gathers information on some innocent people too. That's inherent in the process and it causes no harm. It's better that a few Casper Milquetoasts stay home than that criminals should be shielded from police observation.

2. Of Advantage In debates on the "energy" proposition, some affirmatives presented a plan providing for a ban on offshore drilling for oil and claimed the advantage of protecting the environment by (1) preventing unsightly oil rigs, (2) protecting fish life, and (3) preventing ecological damage from possible oil leakage. Some negative teams meeting this argued the advantages were not significant as (1) the oil rigs would be miles offshore so no one could see them from the shore, (2) oil rigs provided a feeding ground for the fish, thus the fish population actually increased in this area, and (3) oil leakage was rare and even in those few instances where it occurred the wildlife population grew back to normal in two years. They concluded their argument by maintaining that the affirmative provided no significant advantage, since offshore wells did no harm to the environment and in any event the need for oil clearly outweighed the insignificant environmental considerations presented by the affirmative.

K. Use Conditional Refutation

As we have seen earlier (in Chapter 12 on "Requirements of Consistency"), the advocate must develop consistent arguments; and the arguments must be consistent with one another and with the arguments of his or her colleague. Clearly, the debater cannot say, "There is no need, besides the need is insignificant, and furthermore minor repairs can solve this significant need." He may, however—*provided he makes his position very clear*—offer conditional refutation. He must *not* present his argument in such a fashion that the audience "ought to be able to figure out" it is conditional; rather, he *must* present it with such clarity that the audience *will inevitably* recognize it as conditional.

Some examples of conditional refutation were provided earlier in this section. Under "Attack Significance," note that the debater argued: (1) "chilling" not proved; (2) *if* a few were "chilled," they came to the rally anyway—thus no harm; (3) *if* criminals were "chilled"—good; (4) *if* a few innocents were "chilled," that was not significant and, in any event, it was necessary to protect society. Under "Provide Repairs," note that debaters may show that a claimed advantage *could* come from something other than the proposition without advocating that the advantage actually be obtained. (They might later want to attack the advantage as not significant or as being actually disadvantageous.) Or, instead of providing repairs, the advocates might point out that repairs *could* be provided to solve a need or achieve an advantage and thus there is no justification for adopting the resolution.

III. Counter Plan Negative Case

The advocates select the counter plan negative position after their study of the problem and analysis of the affirmative case have led them to the conclusion that the affirmative has defined the needs or goals of the status quo incorrectly. The negative—maintaining that there is a different need or goal but that the affirmative plan is incapable of solving or attaining it—then proposes an entirely different plan, basically inconsistent with the plan called for in the resolution as the solution to the problem.

A. Developing the Counter Plan

This case is difficult in that the negative, in redefining the needs or goals, may appear for a time to be conceding the debate. The negative also has the exacting task of presenting a plan that is inconsistent with the resolution and of demonstrating that this plan is at least as good a solution to the problem (as redefined by the negative) as is the affirmative's proposal. If the negative's counter plan is as good as the affirmative's plan, the affirmative has failed to carry its burden of proof, and the decision in an educational debate must be awarded to the negative.[1] Usually the negative will seek an "overkill" and try to demonstrate the superiority of its position, thus providing a wider margin of victory.

It should be emphasized that the negative's counter plan must be inconsistent with the proposition; otherwise, the affirmative will be able to adapt the negative's proposals to its own plan and thus prevail. The principal clash in a debate in which the counter plan negative case is used comes in the efforts to demonstrate the superiority of a given plan. It should be noted that, in using a case of this type, the negative does not merely accept but redefines the needs or goals as presented by the affirmative; furthermore, the plan of the negative not only must be inconsistent with the plan of the affirmative—it must also be integrated perfectly with the needs or goals as redefined by the negative.

In debates on the proposition "Resolved: That the United States should

[1] See Chapter 3, "Presumption and Burden of Proof."

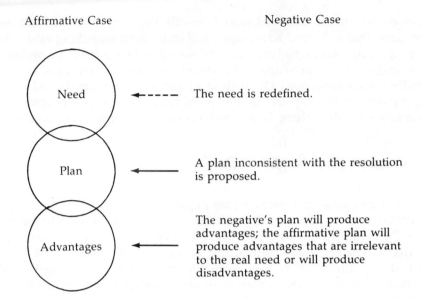

Affirmative Case   Negative Case

Need ◄ - - - - The need is redefined.

Plan ◄────── A plan inconsistent with the resolution is proposed.

Advantages ◄────── The negative's plan will produce advantages; the affirmative plan will produce advantages that are irrelevant to the real need or will produce disadvantages.

adopt a system of universal military service," the principal need issue of some affirmatives was that in future wars the United States would require more manpower for military service. To meet this need, these affirmative teams introduced a system of universal military service. Negatives using a counter plan case redefined the need and maintained that the primary need of the United States in a future war would be for greater firepower. The counter plan introduced to meet this need provided for a reduction in size of the Army, an increase in size of the Air Force, and concentration of additional funds on the development of nuclear weapons and long-range missiles. Since both programs required the expenditure of vast sums of money, only one of the programs could be adopted; hence, they were mutually exclusive. It is interesting to note that one proposal offered as a counter plan in an educational debate was subsequently adopted as government policy.

The counter plan negative may be used against some comparative advantages analysis affirmatives. In debating the "tax sharing" proposition, some affirmative teams stated that the goals of the status quo were to provide more funds for schools and welfare agencies. As most schools and welfare agencies are funded by state governments or their subdivisions, they claimed "tax sharing" as the best plan.

A negative team meeting this type of affirmative analysis redefined the goals of the status quo and maintained that the primary goals were to provide more funds for schools and welfare agencies located in areas where people were in the greatest need. These areas, they demonstrated, were in the inner cities. They claimed the schools were relatively well provided for and that there were few welfare recipients in the affluent suburbs. The

Affirmative Case   Negative Case

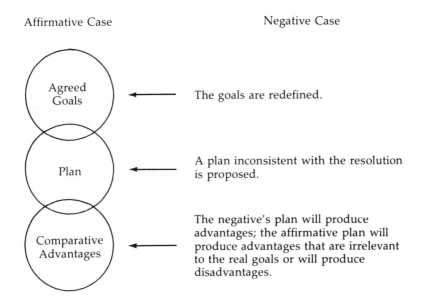

The goals are redefined.

A plan inconsistent with the resolution is proposed.

The negative's plan will produce advantages; the affirmative plan will produce advantages that are irrelevant to the real goals or will produce disadvantages.

counter plan introduced to meet the redefined goals provided that all federal funds available for these purposes should be given through grants-in-aid programs specifically directed to the inner cities. As grants-in-aid programs provided for payment by the federal government directly to local agencies without reference to the state governments, the plan was inconsistent with the proposition. At the time this proposition was debated, the federal government gave *some* grants-in-aid to *some* schools (e.g., in "impacted areas") and for *some* welfare purposes (e.g., experimental "maintenance of income"). However, as the negative's plan called for aid to *all* schools and *all* nonfederal welfare programs in *all* inner cities, it was a new policy going far beyond the scope of a repairs case. Since both plans called for the use of "all available federal funds," only one of the plans could be adopted—they were mutually exclusive. The negative claimed its plan was more advantageous as it concentrated funds in the area of greatest need, while the affirmative plan would, under certain distribution formulas, give more money per capita to the wealthiest sections of the states.

This type of case appeals to advocates who feel that the affirmative has defined the problem inaccurately and has presented a plan ill suited to the real needs or goals of the status quo. The potential use of the counter plan as a negative case further demonstrates that debate is not a bipolar situation, with the participants exclusively oriented for or against a given proposition, but a far more flexible situation that permits a multisided examination of the problem. Since the negative has the option of presenting a plan that it feels is better suited to the problem, an almost infinite range of possible solutions may thereby be introduced into the debate.

B. Integrating the Counter Plan

The advocates using the counter plan negative case must take special care to integrate their positions. While the counter plan case should be planned long in advance, the decision to use it in a given debate is usually best made only after the first affirmative presentation. Since the counter plan must be perfectly adapted to the specific affirmative case under attack, this frequently requires a good deal of during-the-debate coordination by the negative speakers. Not only must they integrate their counter plan with the needs or goals as they have redefined them; they must also carefully integrate their indictment of the affirmative plan to ensure that one speaker's plan attacks on the affirmative cannot be applied with equal force to the counter plan.

C. Conditional and Hypothetical Counter Plans

The conditional counter plan is a variation of the conditional refutation considered earlier. In developing this type of case the negative argues: (1) the status quo can solve the problem; and (2) *if* the status quo can't solve the problem, the negative counter plan can. There are two important constraints the student debater must consider before selecting this approach. First, the time constraints of educational debate may make it impossible to adequately develop *both* the defense of the status quo and the counter plan. Second, as we have seen earlier, conditional arguments must be presented with great clarity. This requirement for clarity, when combined with the difficult in itself counter plan, makes for a doubly complex problem for the debater.

The hypothetical counter plan was developed as a response to the alternative justification affirmative. One debater argued it this way:

We would suggest a hypothetical counter plan. That is, at the end of the debate, if the affirmative doesn't carry all three advantages, adopt whatever ones they do carry and use the rest of the money to fund things like tax rebates, pollution control, et cetera. That, we suggest, would be a superior policy system unless they can carry all three advantages, which is the resolution.[2]

Student debaters are cautioned that many judges reject this approach, holding that the counter plan must be a fully developed policy and requiring the negative to argue its case in depth.

IV. Outlines of Typical Negative Cases

The outlines—pages 223–227—of typical negative cases on propositions of policy have been used for a number of years by debating teams as the

[2] "Final Debate," *Journal of the American Forensic Association*, Vol. 10 (Summer 1973), p. 21.

Against Comparative Advantages Analysis: Contemporary Format

First Negative Constructive Speech

I. Introduction
   A. Amenities: recognize chair, judge, audience, occasion; briefly express pleasure at taking part in this debate if the occasion is a formal one—otherwise begin with B.
   B. Ask any questions the second negative may have about the plan.
   C. Briefly state the negative's rationale in this debate. (In a debate on the "federal aid for higher education" proposition, for example, a first negative speaker began by saying "The negative today will maintain that the historically successful combination of private, local, and state financing is meeting, and will continue to meet, the needs of all qualified high school graduates.")
   D. If you disagree with the affirmative's definitions, prove that the negative's definitions are the only valid interpretations.
   E. Tell what the negative will do in this debate and what you will do in your speech.
      1. _____
      2. _____
      3. _____
      4. _____
      5. _____

II. Body
   A. Attack propositionality, if vulnerable.
   B. Attack goals, if vulnerable.
   C. Attack inherency, if vulnerable.
   D. Provide modifications, if possible.
   E. Attack significance of claimed advantages, if possible.
   F. If a counter plan is used, the counter plan and its advantages are presented in this speech.

(Although in these sample outlines the body of the speech takes only about as much space as the introduction and conclusion, it must be remembered that this is the core of the advocate's case. In the actual delivery of the case, the advocate will spend most of the time developing this portion of his or her speech. Each issue should be carefully organized with a coherent substructure. Move down the affirmative's case structure line by line; clash not only with each issue, but get into the substructure and refute the affirmative's supporting arguments with counter evidence and counter arguments.)

III. Conclusion
   A. Summarize the negative's attack on the affirmative's case.
      1. Recapitulate each issue succinctly.
      2. Tell the audience what these issues prove.
      3. Show how this supports your case.
   B. Tell what your colleague will prove and show how this will strengthen your case.
   C. Conclude your speech with a strong persuasive appeal for the rejection of the resolution.

Second Negative Constructive Speech

I. Introduction
   A. Amenities: recognize chair, judge, audience, occasion; briefly express pleasure at taking part in this debate if the occasion is a formal one—otherwise begin with B.
   B. Tell what you will do in your speech.

II. Body
   A. Attack propositionality of plan, if vulnerable.
   B. Attack workability of plan, if possible.
   C. Prove plan will not achieve advantages, if possible.
   D. Prove plan will produce disadvantages, if possible.
   E. Contrast the now minimized advantages with the disadvantages and prove, if possible, the disadvantages outweigh the advantages.
   F. If a counter plan has been presented, contrast this with the affirmative's plan and demonstrate that the problem, as redefined by the negative, can be solved by the negative's counter plan and that this represents *at least as good* a solution to the problem as does the affirmative's plan. If possible, demonstrate that the counter plan is a *better* solution to the problem.

III. Conclusion
   A. Summarize the issues you have presented.
   B. Conclude with a strong persuasive appeal for the rejection of the resolution.

First Negative Rebuttal

I. Introduction—tell what issues you will deal with in this speech.

II. Body
   A. Focus on the second affirmative's response to your constructive speech.
      1. Reestablish the negative position by refuting the affirmative's responses.
      2. Extend your case by introducing further evidence and analysis to support the attacks made in your constructive speech.
   B. Focus on the weakest element of the affirmative case. (Again, it should be noted that the advocate will spend the greatest portion of time on the body of the speech.)

III. Conclusion
   A. Summarize your rebuttal of the affirmative's case.
   B. Show the advantages of the negative's position.
   C. Conclude with an effective persuasive appeal for the rejection of the resolution.

(These two consecutive negative speeches represent the negative's greatest opportunity to advance its case. If the negative is going to win, it usually must be ahead at the conclusion of this speech. Note the division of labor between these two speeches. The second negative constructive focuses entirely on the plan; the first negative rebuttalist focuses exclusively on the remainder of the affirmative case.)

Second Negative Rebuttal

I. Introduction
   A. Indicate those issues of the debate with which the affirmative has not contended or on which it has shifted ground.
   B. Point out the main issues of the debate that remain in contention.

II. Body
   A. Demonstrate that the first affirmative rebuttalist's answers to your constructive speech were unsatisfactory; use further evidence and argument to reenforce your attacks.
   B. Demonstrate that the first affirmative rebuttalist's answer to the first negative rebuttal was unsatisfactory; use further evidence and argument to reenforce your position.
   C. Make a running summary of the entire debate, dealing with each issue in the order it was set forth in the debate. Demonstrate how the negative has destroyed the affirmative case by its refutation of all or certain affirmative issues, or by presenting a counter plan. Focus on the main issues that will establish the negative case. Demonstrate that the position of the affirmative is untenable in face of the negative case.

III. Conclusion
   A. Summarize the entire negative case.
   B. Summarize the entire debate.
   C. Show the advantages of the negative's position as contrasted with that of the affirmative.
   D. Conclude with the strongest possible persuasive appeal for the rejection of the resolution.

starting point in the construction of negative cases. These outlines, like the affirmative outlines in the previous chapter, are specifically designed for educational debate. However, students may apply the principles of case construction they learn in educational debate to any type of argumentative situation by making proper allowance for those who render the decision, the occasion, and the opposition.

The first outline is for use against a comparative advantages affirmative case in the contemporary format; the second is for use against a needs analysis affirmative case using the contemporary format; and the third is for use against a needs analysis affirmative case using the conventional format. The first outline is presented in some detail; the second and third are presented in briefer form to illustrate the structural differences. The other principles of organization may be readily adapted from the first outline.

These case outlines and the various negative options discussed previously are stated in general terms. It is the task of the advocates to adapt these generalized concepts to the specific details of the particular affirmative case they meet, making effective adjustment to all of the requirements of drafting

Against Needs Analysis: Contemporary Format

First Negative Constructive Speech

Ask any questions the second negative may have about the plan.

Present the negative's rationale.

The major portion of the speech is spent in refuting the needs and attacking the advantages.

Attack propositionality, goals, and inherency and provide repairs, as appropriate.

If a counter plan is used, the counter plan and its advantages are presented in this speech.

Second Negative Constructive Speech

The major portion of this speech is spent in attacking the plan.

Extend on your colleague's attack on the advantages.

Extend on your colleague's attack on the needs.

Contrast the now minimized advantages with the disadvantages and prove, if possible, that on balance the disadvantages outweigh the advantages.

If a counter plan is presented, contrast this with the affirmative's plan and demonstrate that the counter plan is as good a solution to the problem — or preferably that it is a better solution.

First Negative Rebuttal

Demonstrate that the affirmative response to your first constructive speech was unsatisfactory.

Extend your case with further evidence and argument.

Focus on the weakest element of the affirmative case.

Second Negative Rebuttal

Demonstrate that the first affirmative rebuttalist's answers to your constructive speech were unsatisfactory; use further evidence and argument to reinforce your attacks.

Demonstrate that the first affirmative rebuttalist's answers to the first negative rebuttal were unsatisfactory; use further evidence and argument to extend your position.

Make a running summary of the entire debate.

Against Needs Analysis: Conventional Format

First Negative Constructive Speech

Present the negative's rationale.

Focus on the need issues, provide an in-depth attack.

Attack propositionality, inherency, and significance, as appropriate.

The provision of repairs is limited by the fact that the plan has not yet been presented.

Second Negative Constructive Speech

The major portion of this speech is spent in attacking plan and advantages and in developing disadvantages.

Extend on your colleague's attack on the needs.

Provide repairs as appropriate; extend on your colleague's repairs as appropriate.

Contrast the now minimized needs and advantages with the disadvantages and prove, if possible, that on balance the disadvantages outweigh the advantages.

If the negative is using a counter plan, present the counter plan and its advantages. Demonstrate that the need as redefined by the negative can be solved by the counter plan and that this represents at least as good a solution to the problem — or preferably that it is a better solution.

First Negative Rebuttal

Focus on the need issues; demonstrate that the affirmative response to your first constructive speech was unsatisfactory.

Extend your case with further evidence and argument.

Focus on the weakest element of the affirmative case.

Second Negative Rebuttal

Demonstrate that the first affirmative rebuttalist's answers to your constructive speech were unsatisfactory; use further evidence and argument to reinforce your attacks.

Demonstrate that the first affirmative rebuttalist's answers to the first negative rebuttal were unsatisfactory; use further evidence and argument to extend your position.

Make a running summary of the entire debate.

the case. Not all of the negative refutation issues are equally applicable to all propositions or to all affirmative cases. The advocates must choose the negative issues best suited to the specific resolution and the specific affirmative case under consideration.

Refutation cases and counter plans do not apply equally to all resolutions or affirmative cases. For example, when the proposition "Resolved: That the United States should extend diplomatic recognition to the communist government of China" was debated during the Eisenhower years, debaters found it impossible to construct an effective counter plan. In theory, of course, they could have argued that the United States should declare war on China but, as such a proposal was contrary to traditional American opposition to preemptive war, it was rejected as an ineffective position.

Advocates should not rule out either type of case, however, nor any of the potential refutation issues too early in their planning, lest they overlook important aspects of the proposition; and prudent advocates will keep their options open and will construct all possible negative cases before selecting the one case they will actually use in debate.

The negative, in directing its refutation, must be careful to focus its counter argument at the core of the affirmative case and not at the periphery. Just as the affirmative is required to establish the highest degree of probability possible in support of its case rather than prove absolutely all of its contentions, so too the negative is not expected to disprove absolutely the affirmative issues it refutes. Rather, it must raise such a degree of doubt as to make a reasonable and prudent person unwilling to accept them. In those cases where the negative seeks to establish issues in support of its own position, the same requirement of the highest possible degree of probability applies.

This chapter has been concerned primarily with the negative case on resolutions of policy; all that has been said, however, can be applied to propositions of value or propositions of fact. Although the issues will be different and the plan and advantages may be omitted from the affirmative case, the negative will continue to have the responsibility of refuting the issues introduced by the affirmative or of raising other issues that will make the affirmative position untenable.

Exercises

1. Attend an intercollegiate debate and prepare an outline of the negative case. Attach to this outline a written (500-word) critique of the negative case in which you evaluate the organization and development of the case.

2. Prepare an outline and a written critique (500 words) of a negative case on a contemporary problem as presented in a recent speech. For the texts of speeches, consult *Vital Speeches, Representative American Speeches,* the *New York Times,* or *U.S. News & World Report.*

3. Prepare negative refutation blocks for each of the applicable issues for a proposition of policy, value, or fact to be handed to your instructor. In preparing for this and other exercises you may, with the permission of your instructor, draw upon materials you have prepared in connection with earlier chapters.

4. Using the current national debate proposition, prepare negative refutation blocks for each of the applicable issues.

5. After completing exercise 4, conduct a class discussion in which you consider the following questions: Which negative refutation issues are most effective for general use with the current national debate proposition? Which are least likely to be effective?

6. Can an effective counter plan be developed for use with the current national debate proposition? If your answer is *yes*, draw up such a counter plan.

7. Arrange with other members of the class to present a classroom debate on a proposition of policy. After the debate, conduct a thorough critique of the debate with special emphasis on the negative.

8. Select a bill currently being debated in Congress. Study the arguments being used by the negative speakers against the bill. What refutation issues are they using?

Chapter 15

Refutation

Debate does not take place in a vacuum—but in the presence of opposition. The debater is always confronted with the necessity of overcoming objections that are raised by the opponent. The process of overcoming these objections is known as *refutation*. Strictly interpreted, this term means to overcome opposing evidence and reasoning by proving that it is false or erroneous. The term *rebuttal*, strictly interpreted, means to overcome opposing evidence and reasoning by introducing other evidence and reasoning that will destroy its effect. In practice, the terms refutation and rebuttal are used interchangeably, except that the second speech by each advocate in an educational debate is designated as the rebuttal speech.

In educational debate, advocates are required to refute only the specific arguments advanced by their opponents. In substantive debate, advocates face the necessity of refuting any evidence and reasoning that may influence the decision renderers.

I. Shifting Burden of Rebuttal

As the preceding chapters on cases indicated, the burden of proof always remains with the affirmative, whereas the burden of rebuttal is initially the negative's. This burden of rebuttal shifts back and forth between the opponents in the course of the debate and is finally placed on one side or the other. The side that bears the burden of rebuttal at the conclusion of the debate is the loser. In the typical intercollegiate debate, the first affirmative speaker usually establishes his case sufficiently well to place the burden of refutation on the negative. It is the task of the first negative speaker to shift that burden back to the affirmative. The second affirmative speaker, by rebuilding and reinforcing the case, seeks to shift the burden to the negative again. At this point in the debate, the negative presents its second constructive speech and its first rebuttal. In these two speeches the negative seeks to shift the burden of rebuttal back to the affirmative. Obviously, these consecutive presentations provide the negative with its maximum opportunity to shift the burden decisively. In each of the remaining rebuttal speeches, the advocates seek to carry their share of rebuttal and to shift the burden to their opponents. The affirmative's last opportunity comes in the final speech of the debate, wherein the second affirmative speaker has the opportunity to review the entire debate and to demonstrate that the negative has not carried its burden of rebuttal.[1]

II. Purpose and Place of Refutation

The process of refutation must be included in every speech of the debate. Obviously, the first affirmative speech, as it opens the debate, cannot include direct refutation since no opposition has preceded it. Even this speech, however, may well include a certain amount of anticipatory refutation, although care should be taken that such anticipatory refutation is directed to issues that the negative must inevitably support, and not against "straw men" that the affirmative hopes the negative will advance. (See the *inset* for a list of processes of refutation.)

In general advocates should refute an important issue early rather than allow it to stand unchallenged for any length of time. Possible exceptions to this might occur when advocates ignore an issue for the moment while waiting for the opposition to commit itself further on the issue. Sometimes advocates will attempt to foster this process deliberately by advancing a limited refutation, encouraging the opponents to pursue further a given line of argument that will fully commit them to a position the advocates will

---

The Processes of Refutation

☐ Overthrowing the opposition's evidence by demonstrating that it is invalid, erroneous, or irrelevant.

☐ Overthrowing the opposition's evidence by introducing other evidence that contradicts it, casts doubt on it, minimizes its effect, or shows that it fails to meet the tests of evidence.

☐ Overthrowing the opposition's reasoning by demonstrating that it is faulty.

☐ Overthrowing the opposition's reasoning by introducing other reasoning that turns it to the opposition's disadvantage, contradicts it, casts doubt on it, minimizes its effect, or shows that it fails to meet the tests of reasoning.

☐ Rebuilding evidence by introducing new and additional evidence to further substantiate it.

☐ Rebuilding reasoning by introducing new and additional reasoning to further substantiate it.

☐ Presenting exploratory refutation — preliminary refutation offered for the purpose of probing the opponents' position and designed to clarify the opponents' position or to force them to take a more definite position.

---

[1] See Chapter 21 for an outline of the speaking sequence and time allotments used in intercollegiate debating.

refute later. Thus the advocates are able to bring into the debate arguments their opponents might wish to avoid. For example, in debates on the proposition "Resolved: That the nonagricultural industries of the United States should guarantee their employees an annual wage," some affirmative advocates argued that significant numbers of persons were unemployed at the time this proposition was being debated. In using exploratory refutation, some negative advocates advanced a deliberately weak refutation — introducing evidence that some unemployed persons had built up substantial savings during the years they had worked — and drew the conclusion that some workers did not need a guarantee of annual wages. Some affirmative advocates responded to this refutation by answering that the vast majority of unemployed persons did not have substantial savings, since low-seniority workers were the first to be laid off and many of them had worked only a few months prior to their unemployment. Once the negative advocates had obtained such an admission from the affirmative as a result of their exploratory refutation, they were able, later in the debate, to focus on their main line of refutation. They then argued that, since the wage guarantees proposed by the affirmative required at least a year's seniority before becoming effective, the proposed plan did not meet the need of the low-seniority workers, who — according to the affirmative — made up the largest group of unemployed.

III. Preparation for Refutation

As advocates, we should prepare our refutation with the same care that we prepare other portions of our case. Effective refutation is seldom the result of improvisation, but comes from careful analysis and preparation.

We must be thoroughly familiar with all evidence and reasoning related to the proposition under debate. Our knowledge of the subject should never be confined to our own case or to the case we expect the opponent to use; rather, it should include all possible aspects of the resolution. We should make certain that our research on the subject has been sufficiently detailed so that we will not be taken by surprise by new evidence or reasoning introduced by the opposition. We should recognize that on most propositions the evidence is seldom complete; new evidence, or new interpretations of evidence, may appear frequently. Thus, we should never assume that our research is complete but should continue it until the very moment of the debate.

One college debating team won a major tournament, in part, because they used more recent evidence than the opposition. During the tournament the President sent his budget message to Congress. This message contained some new information relating to the economic proposition debated in the tournament. One team redrafted their case overnight to include the new information. When this team met other teams who had not studied the President's message, they found that the opposing speakers were at a serious disadvantage when they attempted to refute new evidence with which they were not familiar.

The advocates should have a broad perspective in the preparation of their refutation. They should never limit themselves to one point of view or to one philosophy. They should seek to analyze carefully both sides and should consider fully all possible positions that may be taken on the proposition. As they prepare their refutation, they might well follow the example of Allen Drury's fictional senator as he prepared for a crucial debate: "First, by a conscious effort that he had found effective many times before, he deliberately drained his mind, as much as was humanly possible, of every preconception, every emotion, every prejudice, every thought that filled it on the subject heretofore."[2]

Student debaters will find that one of the best means of improving their refutation is to debate on both sides of the proposition. In this manner they will gain a wider perspective and avoid the danger of seeing only one side. The advocate in nonacademic debates drafts the strongest possible cases that the opponent might use and prepares refutation for each of these cases. The advocate should consider not only the evidence the opponent may use but also the lines of argument that may be introduced and the philosophical position that may form the basis of the opposition's case.

In planning answers to the possible cases advanced by an opponent, the advocate should give careful consideration to the phrasing of any refutation. If the advocate's thinking has proceeded merely to the stage "If the opposition quotes Mr. A, I will quote Mr. B," the refutation is likely to be verbose, uncertain, and lacking in specificity. Rather, the advocate should plan the phrasing of the refutation, making sure that the words are well chosen, sharp, and specific, and that the reasoning is cogent.

IV. Arranging Material for Refutation

Until the debate is actually under way, the advocates cannot be certain what position their opponents will take; they must therefore have a broad and deep store of materials from which to draw refutation, and these materials must be so arranged that they are readily available.

One effective way of doing this is to prepare a refutation block for each possible argument or piece of evidence the opposition may use and to record that reasoning or evidence in an easy-to-retrieve form. At the start of the season, one negative debater prepared a block for use against possible

---

[2] Allen Drury, *Advise and Consent* (Garden City, N.Y.: Doubleday & Co., 1959) p. 273.

funding provisions affirmative teams might use on the "comprehensive medical care" proposition (see the sample card in the *inset*).

In his card file, this advocate had evidence cards keyed to the retrieval numbers on his sheet. As he heard the specific funding provisions of the affirmative plan, he would pull the appropriate disadvantage cards and adapt them to the specific plan before him. As the season went on and he learned of more possible funding provisions, he provided for them as well as increasing the depth of his attacks on the provisions he was already familiar with.

Sample Refutation Block

```
                          DISADVANTAGES

1000.1    FUNDING DISADVANTAGES

1000.11   MORE EXPENSIVE--Medicare and Medicaid cost 3 to 4
          times as much as government planners expected

1000.12   DEFICIT SPENDING--accelerate inflation

1000.13   INCOME TAX INCREASE--unstable collections

1000.14   RAISING TAXES--discourage both work and investment

1000.15   RAISING CORPORATE TAXES
          1000.151   worsen international competitive situation
          1000.152   burden all income levels
          1000.153   cause employers to release marginal
                     employees

1000.16   CLOSE TAX LOOPHOLES--produce only $1-billion revenue

1000.17   END OIL DEPLETION ALLOWANCE--increase cost of gas,
          oil, and natural gas

1000.18   REDUCE CAPITAL DEPRECIATION--hinder long-term
          economic growth and employment opportunities

1000.19   TAX MUNICIPAL BONDS--harm economic growth

1000.20   CUT DEFENSE SPENDING--cause unemployment
```

The construction of detailed blocks and card files are the marks of conscientious student debaters. As advocates, we are well advised to prepare refutation with similar thoroughness, using any method of recording material that is convenient and readily accessible. As we gain in knowledge and experience our dependence on mechanics will be reduced. At the start, however, specific, detailed preparation is essential.

V. Selection of Evidence and Reasoning

Just as our refutation file should contain more material than can be used in any one debate, our opponents' speeches will probably contain more evidence and reasoning than we can possibly refute in the allotted time. The problem before us, then, is one of selection. The fundamental concept underlying refutation is that we must seek to refute the *case* of our opponent. To do so, we must have an accurate picture of that case as it is presented. A useful method of analyzing the opposition's case and of preparing refutation may be seen in the representation of a debater's flow sheet (*see inset*).

This is a representation of a flow sheet kept by a second negative speaker before she spoke. As a matter of convenience many debaters record the "case" arguments on one side of the flow sheet and the plan arguments on the other side or on a separate sheet. (Of course, the plan is an essential part of the case in a debate on a policy proposition, but recording it separately not only provides more space but also helps the debater to focus more sharply on the different issues of the debate and to achieve greater clarity in his or

The Flow Sheet

1 A	1 N	2 A	2 N	
xxx		xxx		
xxx	xxx	xxx		
xxx	xxx	xxx		
xxx	xxx	xxx		

"Case" Side

1 A	1 N	2 A	2 N	
xxx			xxx	
xxx			xxx	
xxx				
	xxx	xxx		
	xxx	xxx		

Plan Side

her arguments.) This particular second negative has noted that the first affirmative speaker presented a rationale for his case, a plan consisting of three planks and three advantages. (The rationale and the advantages are recorded on the "case" side, the planks of the plan are recorded on the plan side.) She has prepared two plan questions that her colleague asked in the first negative speech. Her colleague then went on to argue that the first advantage can be achieved by minor repairs, that the second advantage is not significant, and that the third advantage is not inherent in the plan. She kept brief notes on her colleague's arguments so that she would know what issues her colleague dealt with and how he handled them. During his speech, she was pulling evidence and blocks of argument from her file and adapting them to the affirmative plan. Next, the second affirmative speaker noted that the negative did not respond to the affirmative's rationale and then proceeded to clash with each argument advanced by the first negative and to extend the affirmative's advantages arguments. During this speech, the second negative speaker noted answers to the plan questions and adapted her arguments accordingly. She decided the main thrust of her speech would be devoted to attacking the workability of the plan and to demonstrating that it would produce disadvantages.

The use of a flow sheet allows advocates to keep a record of the debate as it develops—to record the flow of argument—and helps them to select the issues they must attack or defend.

With a little practice the advocate will develop his or her own system of abbreviations, which will allow the recording of a great deal of information in concise form. Debaters often use $8\frac{1}{2}$" $\times$ 14" legal pads or even larger art pads for their flow sheets.

As advocates study their opponents' case, they must select the issues they wish to refute. In selecting those issues, they will be guided by three criteria:

1. To refute those issues that are basic to the opponents' case.

2. To refute those contentions on which the opponents have spent a significant portion of time or have claimed as major issues.

3. After dealing with the real (1 above) or apparent (2 above) issues, to select those contentions remaining in the opponents' case that they can refute most effectively.

VI. Securing Evidence and Reasoning

If we feel that the opposition has avoided an issue, or has not made its position clear on some significant matter, we may ask questions to bring that issue into the debate or to clarify the matter in doubt. In these circumstances, our purpose in asking questions is to elicit a response on which refutation may be based. Questions asked merely for casual information have no value in the debate. In asking questions, we must be careful to establish that the question is relevant and that it deals with a significant matter. For example, in debating the proposition "Resolved: That the federal government should subsidize the higher education of superior students," a negative speaker, who felt that the affirmative plan omitted an important detail, asked this question:

We would like to ask the affirmative to explain to you what method they propose to use in locating the superior student. We find that responsible educators have expressed serious doubts as to the ability of existing tests to predict future scholastic success. Therefore, unless the affirmative can demonstrate to you that they have an effective method of locating the superior student we must conclude that their plan is impracticable.

VII. Organization of Refutation

A. Basic Organization

The basic organization of refutation involves five clearly defined stages for the advocate:

1. Identify the argument you are attacking or defending clearly and concisely.
2. State your position succinctly.
3. Introduce evidence and argument to support your position.
4. Summarize your evidence and argument.
5. Demonstrate the impact of this refutation in weakening your opponent's case or in strengthening your own case.

This final stage is perhaps the most critical and is the one most frequently overlooked by the beginning advocate. Much of the effect of refutation is lost unless we relate it clearly to the case of the opposition or to our own case.

B. General Considerations

In addition to the basic organization of refutation, we should be aware of these general considerations of refutation:

1. Begin refutation early. It is usually to our advantage to begin refutation early — both early in our speech and early in the debate. The purpose of beginning refutation early in the speech is to offset immediately the effect of some of the opponents' arguments. This does not mean, however, that the first portion of the speech should be reserved for refutation and the balance of the speech devoted to a constructive presentation. Rather, the skilled debater will interweave refutation and constructive materials throughout the entire speech. It is usually not desirable to allow a major contention to go unrefuted for too long a time in the debate. Usually an argument should be refuted in the next available speech. Thus a plan attack made in the second negative speech must be answered in the first affirmative rebuttal. If the affirmative waits until the final rebuttal to answer this argument, the judge may weigh the answer lightly, saying "Well, yes, they did finally get around to it, but it was so late that the negative had no chance to reply."

2. Conclude with constructive material. Usually it is desirable for us to conclude a speech with constructive material designed to advance our own case. Thus, after giving the listeners reasons for rejecting the opponents' position, we give them positive reasons for concurring with our position.

3. Incorporate refutation into the case. Although we are usually well advised to open a speech with refutation, refutation is by no means confined to the first part of the speech. Since the well-planned case is prepared to meet many of the objections of the opposition, we will often find it advisable to incorporate refutation *into* our case. For example, in debating the proposition "Resolved: That the federal government should grant annually a specific percentage of its income tax revenue to the state governments," some negative teams objected to the adoption of the resolution on the ground that it would place an additional burden on the taxpayer. In refuting this objection, some affirmative teams made use of *built in* refutation by pointing out that the gross national product was rising (as, indeed, it was at the time this proposition was debated); thus incomes would rise and more revenue would be derived from the same tax rate.

4. Evaluate the amount of refutation. Advocates often ask, "How much refutation is necessary?" Unfortunately, no definitive answer is available, since the answer varies from one occasion to another and is found only in the mind of the judge or the audience. We should observe the judge or audience closely during the course of our speeches and should watch for both overt and inconspicuous signs of agreement or disagreement when presenting refutation, in order to adapt to our audience more effectively. As a minimum, we should develop our refutation through the five basic stages of refutation. Our goal is to introduce enough refutation to satisfy a reasonable and prudent man. We should avoid the too brief statement of refutation, such as "The recent Brookings Institution study disproves this contention." Such a statement may suggest a line of refutation to the advocates; but until this line of refutation is actually developed within the context of the debate, it is of little value.

5. Use the opposition's organization. Frequently, it is advisable to build refutation around the organization established by the opposing speakers.

In such a case, the advocates follow the outline of the opposition's case and seek to refute each issue and supporting contention of that case in the order of presentation used by the opposition. The cumulative summary method is particularly useful in this type of situation, since it affords a high degree of adaptability and provides for direct clashes on a number of issues. This method should be used with caution, however, since the opposition has undoubtedly organized the case in the manner most advantageous to its position, and in using that organization the advocates are meeting their opposition "on their own ground."

6. Reorganize the opposition's case. Frequently, the organization of the opposition case is not readily adaptable to refutation in the form in which it has been presented. In such cases, the advocates may reorganize the opposition's case into a more convenient form. In so doing, they must make clear to the judge or audience that their reorganization is reasonable and that their refutation is directed to the opponents' case and not against a "straw man." Such a method may become necessary, for example, when the opposition has used a "shotgun refutation." This type of refutation — actually a series of questions or objections — is sometimes used by negative teams. In reorganizing this type of negative case, one affirmative speaker introduced his refutation in this way:

The negative has raised nine objections to the plan of the affirmative. We find that the first four questions (here he briefly identified them) relate to the cost of the affirmative plan and that the remaining questions (here he briefly identified them) relate to the workability of our plan. First, let us consider what the plan would cost, and second, let us consider how this plan will actually work.

7. Make use of contingency plans. Advocates will find it desirable to prepare contingency plans — that is, blocks of evidence and argument prepared in advance to raise against issues they believe will be fundamental in meeting the opposing case. Prudent advocates, in fact, will have a number of contingency plans available. In the course of the debate, they will determine which contingency plans are applicable to the case presented by the opponents; then, of course, they must adapt the contingency plan to the specific argument used by the opposition.

For example, in debates on a national program of public work for the unemployed, the negative could safely assume that the affirmative would have to argue that unemployment is harmful. A negative team prepared contingency plans to meet affirmative arguments on "frictional unemployment," "cyclical unemployment," "long-term unemployment," and so on. In their contingency plan on "long-term unemployment" (unemployment of fifteen weeks or more), they assembled evidence to establish that (a) a large percentage of the long-term unemployed were women seeking a second job to finance a fur coat or a trip to Bermuda, (b) a large percentage were elderly persons with retirement income, (c) a large percentage were teenagers seeking part-time jobs, and (d) only a very small percentage were heads of families. Recently, one good college team had a contingency plan of twenty-three objections prepared for possible affirmative plans. After the actual affirmative plan was presented, the negative was usually able to select several objections which it could apply to the *specific* plan used by its opponents.

VIII. Methods of Refutation

A. Evidence

Evidence is refuted by applying the tests of evidence and demonstrating that the evidence advanced by the opposition fails to meet these tests. (See the tests of evidence considered in Chapter 7.) Counter refutation against attacks on one's own evidence consists of demonstrating that the opposition has applied the tests of evidence incorrectly.

B. Reasoning

Reasoning is refuted by applying the tests of reasoning and demonstrating that the reasoning advanced by the opposition fails to meet these tests. (See the tests of reasoning considered in Chapter 8.) Counter refutation against attacks on one's own reasoning consists of demonstrating that the opposition has applied the tests of reasoning incorrectly.

C. Fallacies

Fallacies are refuted by exposing the arguments of the opposition as fallacious. (Fallacies, and methods of refuting fallacies, are considered in Chapter 10.) Counter refutation against attacks on one's own arguments as fallacies consists of demonstrating that the arguments are in fact valid.

D. The Dilemma

This type of refutation consists of establishing that an opponent's argument logically leads to only two possible positions, both of which are unsatisfactory. The two possible positions are referred to as the "horns of the dilemma." The advocate using this method maintains that, since there are only two possible positions and since both are unsatisfactory, the issue must be rejected. In using the dilemma, the advocate must be careful to follow this method:

1. State the dilemma clearly.
2. Demonstrate that there are only two possibilities.
3. Demonstrate that both possibilities are undesirable.

Methods of refutation similar to the dilemma are the trilemma, wherein three possibilities are presented; the tetralemma, wherein four possibilities are presented; and the polyemma, wherein many possibilities are presented. In using each of these latter methods, the advocate must be careful to follow this method:

1. State the possibilities clearly.
2. Demonstrate that these include all the possibilities.
3. Demonstrate that all the possibilities are undesirable.

The use of the dilemma is one of the oldest of rhetorical methods, with the classical example attributed to Corax and Tisias. In the fifth century B.C., Corax, a famous teacher of rhetoric, sought to collect a fee from his pupil Tisias. In the course of the trial in the Sicilian court, Corax maintained, "If Tisias wins this case he must pay me, for his victory will prove I have taught him well. If Tisias loses this case he must pay me, for the court will so order it." Tisias, however, had apparently learned about the dilemma from his professor. He sought to refute the dilemma by introducing a counter dilemma, maintaining "If Corax wins this case I should not pay him, for my defeat will prove that his teaching was worthless. If Corax loses this case I will not pay, as the court will rule that there is no debt." Legend has it that the judge, entering into the spirit of the occasion, threw the case out of court, saying "Bad crow, bad egg."

The use of the dilemma is by no means limited to ancient times. Recently a cigarette company built its advertising campaign about this theme: "Winston tastes good like a cigarette should." "That statement is grammatically incorrect; one should say *'as* a cigarette should.'" "Whatta ya want — good grammar or good taste?"

The *counter refutation* against the dilemma may take several forms:

1. Introduce a counter dilemma.
2. Demonstrate that there is an alternative not included in the dilemma.
3. Demonstrate that one of the alternatives of the dilemma does not represent an unsatisfactory position.

E. Reductio ad Absurdum

This method of refutation consists of extending the opposition argument to its logical conclusion and demonstrating the absurdity of that conclusion.

For example, in debating the proposition "Resolved: That the United States should favor the policy of self-determination for subject peoples throughout the world," a negative speaker argued that the United States should not favor self-determination for subject peoples, because subject peoples lacked successful experience in democratic government. An affirmative speaker in replying to this argument used the method of *reductio ad absurdum* and pointed out that, if this principle were accepted, then no one should go near the water until he had successful experience in swimming. The objective of speakers using the method of *reductio ad absurdum* is to locate the general principle underlying their opponents' reasoning and to demonstrate the absurdity of that principle. The method of *reductio ad absurdum* should be used in a brief statement and in reference to some example within the experience of the audience. The touch of humor and ridicule that often accompanies the use of this method sometimes allows it to make a lasting impression in the mind of the judge or audience.

The *counter refutation* against *reductio ad absurdum* may follow one of these methods:

1. Demonstrate that the general principle attacked is actually not the general principle involved.

2. Demonstrate that, although the general principle attacked may be correct, quantitative or qualitative differences between the matters compared render the attack invalid.

For example, a negative speaker replied to the method of *reductio ad absurdum* in the example above by pointing out that if a man went into deep water without knowing how to swim, he could only lose his own life, whereas if a nation sought to govern itself without successful experience in democratic government, it might endanger the whole free world.

F. Residues

The method of residues consists of dividing a matter into two or more parts that include all the possible parts of the matter, then demonstrating that all but one of these parts is unsatisfactory and that the one remaining part is satisfactory. In debating the proposition "Resolved: That the use of nuclear weapons should be prohibited by international agreement," a debater using the method of residues organized his argument as follows:

1. Unrestricted use of nuclear weapons is unsatisfactory.

2. Limited use of nuclear weapons is unsatisfactory.

3. Therefore, the use of nuclear weapons must be prohibited.

Although the elimination of all but one alternative creates a strong presumption in favor of that alternative, prudent advocates will not stop with mere statement. They will continue their argument by demonstrating the advantages and benefits that will accrue from the acceptance of this alternative.

Unlike the method of the dilemma, the method of residues seeks to demonstrate that one of the alternatives is satisfactory. In using the method or residues, the advocate must be careful to include these steps:

1. State the possibilities clearly.
2. Demonstrate that these include all the possibilities.
3. Demonstrate that each of the possibilities but one is unsatisfactory.
4. Demonstrate that the one remaining possibility is satisfactory.

The *counter refutation* against the method of residues may follow one of these patterns:

1. Demonstrate that there is an alternative not included in the residues.
2. Demonstrate that one of the alternatives does not represent an unsatisfactory position.

For example, in the debate on the use of nuclear weapons, a debater introduced counter refutation against the method of residues cited above by introducing another alternative: that the use of nuclear weapons should be reserved to the United Nations. In this debate he demonstrated that this represented a more satisfactory alternative than the prohibition of the use of nuclear weapons and thus refuted the use of the method of residues.

G. Exposing Inconsistencies

In using this method of refutation, advocates carefully follow their opponents' arguments, watching for possible inconsistencies in their case. If and when they locate an inconsistency, they expose this to the judge and audience, usually to the considerable disadvantage of their opponents. In debating the proposition "Resolved: That the federal government should abolish agricultural price supports," an affirmative speaker found an inconsistency in the negative case and called it to the attention of the judge and audience by stating:

The negative has taken an inconsistent position on the effects of abolishing agricultural price supports. The first negative speaker has told you that abolishing agricultural price supports will work a great hardship on the farmer and will drive him from his farm. The second negative speaker has told you that abolishing agricultural price supports won't reduce farm surpluses because the farmer will stay on his farm and will continue to produce surpluses even if price supports are abolished. Obviously both negative speakers cannot be correct. The affirmative submits that both conclusions are wrong. Abolishing agricultural price supports will not work a great hardship on the farmer and it will reduce farm surpluses.

H. Exposing Irrelevant Arguments

In using this method of refutation, the advocates demonstrate that the opposition's arguments are irrelevant to the proof of its case. The advocates are not particularly concerned with the validity of the opposition's arguments in this connection; they merely seek to show that valid or not, they are not relevant to the case. For example, in debating the proposition "Resolved: That the federal government should guarantee an opportunity for higher education to all qualified high school graduates," a negative speaker exposed the irrelevancy of an affirmative argument by stating

The affirmative has told you that each year 60,000 to 100,000 qualified high school graduates do not go on to college. Yet at no time did that affirmative team introduce any evidence to show that those students were motivated to go to college. The affirmative did not introduce any evidence to show that those students ever applied for admission to college. The affirmative did not show that any of those students tried to get a scholarship and were denied one. The affirmative did not show that any of those students tried to get a loan and were denied one. The affirmative did not show that any of those students tried to get a part-time job to work their way through college—and could not get such a job. Therefore, we submit that any evidence about numbers of qualified high school graduates not going to college is irrelevant, unless that affirmative can go back and show you convincing evidence that those graduates were first motivated to go to college and secondly that existing forms of private and state aid couldn't help them.

I. Adopting Opposing Arguments

In using this method of refutation, the advocates turn the tables on the opposing team and use their own arguments against them. The opportunity to turn the tables usually comes only when a speaker has not fully thought through the implications of an argument. As debaters, we should be alert for such openings in our opponents' arguments and should be prepared to turn their arguments and evidence to our own advantage. For example, in debating the proposition "Resolved: That the federal government should adopt a program of compulsory wage and price controls," a negative speaker argued that such controls would not work because, when voluntary guidelines had been tried earlier, they failed when labor and management refused to abide by them. In turning the tables, this negative speaker stated:

The negative is absolutely right when it said guidelines didn't work. And why didn't they? Because they were *voluntary*. Voluntary guidelines simply won't work. That's why the affirmative today is calling for a program of *compulsory* wage and price controls. We'll put all the muscle of the federal government behind our program. Instead of saying "Please don't raise your prices," we'll say "If you raise your prices, we'll hit you with a penalty that will hurt." The negative is right; voluntary methods didn't work—our compulsory program will work.

J. Continuing Summary

The use of the continuing summary is a method of making refutation more effective. Instead of refuting a part of our opponents' case and then letting the matter drop, we should use the continuing summary method to summarize their refutation as we go along, briefly reminding the judge or audience of each part of the opposition's case that has been previously refuted as we introduce still further refutation. Thus we create a greater cumulative impact in the minds of a judge or audience and place a more decisive burden of counter refutation upon the opposing team.

Exercises

1. Arrange to have a debate presented in class. Follow the debate carefully, making a detailed flow sheet. At the conclusion of the debate, conduct a class discussion in which you seek to determine at what points the burden of rebuttal shifted from one side to the other.

2. Attend an intercollegiate debate. Prepare a written report (500 words) in which you evaluate the effectiveness of the refutation of each team.

3. Study the debate in Appendix B. How would you evaluate the effectiveness of the refutation of each side? How many examples can you find of the methods of refutation?

4. Arrange a series of direct-clash debates in class as an exemplification of refutation methods. Divide the class into groups of five or six. Let each group select one issue of the current national debate proposition. The first affirmative speaker will have five minutes to support that issue; each subsequent speaker, alternating negative and affirmative, will have three minutes in which to deliver refutation or counter refutation.

5. Prepare in written form your refutation of an editorial appearing in a recent issue of a daily newspaper. Hand the editorial and your refutation to the instructor.

6. Write a "letter to the editor" of your local newspaper in which you refute an editorial, an opinion expressed in a column, or another letter to the editor. If your letter is well written, brief, and signed with your name and address, there is a good possibility the paper may publish it.

Chapter 16

The Advocate as a Person

The audience's opinion of the advocate as a person has a great influence on whether or not it will accept his or her arguments. Long ago Aristotle pointed out:

The character of the speaker is a cause of persuasion when the speech is so uttered as to make him worthy of belief; for as a rule we trust men of probity more, and more quickly, about things in general, while on points outside the realm of exact knowledge, where opinion is divided, we trust them absolutely. This trust, however, should be created by the speech itself, and not left to depend upon an antecedent impression that the speaker is this or that kind of man.[1]

This ancient theory is confirmed by contemporary communication studies,[2] and its truth may be observed by a study of present-day speeches of students, average speakers, or world leaders. *Ethos*—or credibility, or image—is important in all argumentation, written or spoken. We are more likely to agree with the point of view expressed in a book if we think that the author is a credible person. Our agreement or disagreement with an editorial is likely to be influenced by whether or not we like the newspaper in which it appears. Our willingness to accept a news item as an accurate report may be influenced in the same way by our opinion of the newspaper.

In the speaking situation, *ethos* is defined as *the character of the speaker as perceived by the audience*. Outside the speaking situation *ethos* is defined as *the character of a person, group, or institution as perceived by the public*. Note that this definition does not consider the *actual* character of the person—often a difficult or impossible quality to measure. Rather it considers the character as *perceived* by the audience or the public—an easier quality to measure.

An example is furnished by Adolph Hitler, today regarded as a man of

---

[1] Aristotle, *Rhetoric*, I, 2.

[2] See, for example: Carl I. Hovland, Irving J. Janis, and Harold H. Kelly, *Communication and Persuasion* (New Haven: Yale University Press, 1953); Kenneth Andersen, *Persuasion: Theory and Practice* (Boston: Allyn & Bacon, 1971); James C. McCroskey, Carl E. Larson, and Mark L. Knapp, *An Introduction to Interpersonal Communication* (Englewood Cliffs, N.J.: Prentice-Hall, 1971); James C. McCroskey, *An Introduction to Rhetorical Communication*, 2nd ed. (Englewood Cliffs, N.J.: Prentice-Hall, 1972); Kenneth Andersen and Theodore Clevenger, Jr., "A Summary of Experimental Research in Ethos," *Speech Monographs* (June 1963) pp. 59–78; Jack L. Whitehead, Jr., "Factors of Source Credibility," *Quarterly Journal of Speech* (February 1968) pp. 59–63; and Kim Giffin, "The Contribution of Studies of Source Credibility to a Theory of Interpersonal Trust in the Communication Process," *Psychological Bulletin* (August 1967) pp. 104–120.

evil character. In the 1930s and 1940s he may well have been a man of evil character, but millions of Germans *perceived* him as a man of good character and thus responded favorably to him.

Since the advocate most often deals with "points outside the realm of exact knowledge," the character of the speaker, or writer, as seen by the audience is of enormous importance. Indeed, the advocate has no choice whether or not ethos will influence the audience. The audience, consciously or not, will form an opinion about the speaker as a person; and this opinion will have an important influence on its decision to accept or reject arguments. The only course open to the advocate, then, is to do those things that will build credibility in the eyes of an audience.

Much can be done before the speech begins. The civic leader with a reputation for sound thinking on community problems has an advantage over an unknown newcomer to the community; the attorney with a reputation for winning cases has an advantage over an attorney with a less impressive record; and the student debater who has won two or three major tournaments has an advantage over the debater who has not acquired a reputation. Entertainers, politicians, businessmen, and almost all national leaders of public opinion maintain staffs of public relations advisors and spend vast amounts of money to build favorable impressions. Political candidates have found it advantageous to spend vast sums of money on television commercials that allow them to present a totally controlled picture of themselves. Thus they hope to present an "image," or ethos, that will have the desired effect on the voters. In 1968, Richard Nixon made extensive use of television commercials and of panel shows produced by his staff.[3] However, the speaker must *create ethos within the speech* itself and not depend upon prior reputation or publicity. Thus an examination of the speeches of world leaders such as Franklin Roosevelt, Winston Churchill, Charles de Gaulle, and others who brought enormous prestige into the speech situation will reveal that within the speech itself they were careful to devote considerable attention to the building of ethos.

We are not concerned here with the special means of building ethos available only to those with large staffs and generous budgets at their disposal. Rather, we will consider those methods available to most speakers, including student debaters, and yet, at the same time, methods that world leaders also use in their speeches.

I. Components of Ethos

The classical components of ethos are competence, integrity, and intention. To these three, contemporary scholars have added the component of dynamism. The members of the audience will decide, consciously or uncon-

---

[3] See: Joe McGinniss, *The Selling of the President 1968* (New York: Trident Press, 1969).

sciously, whether or not they believe the speaker has these qualities, and they will determine the extent to which they believe these qualities, or their opposites, are present in the speaker. The task of the speaker is to make the audience believe that he or she has these qualities in good measure. The audience often does not consider these factors in isolation — usually it is impact of the total amalgam that establishes the speaker's credibility.

A. Competence

In evaluating the speaker's competence, the audience will assign degree values to the answers to such questions as "Is the speaker knowledgeable on the subject at hand?" "Is the speaker in a position to have relevant information?" "Is the speaker wise, intelligent, reliable, authoritative, expert, qualified, and logical?"

B. Integrity

In evaluating this component, the audience will assign degree values to the answers to such questions as "Is the speaker trustworthy, reliable, safe, honest, decent, and virtuous?"

C. Intention

In evaluating this component, the audience will assign degree values to the answers to such questions as "What are the speaker's intentions toward us?" "Does the speaker have our best interests at heart?" "Is the speaker objective, impartial, openminded, kind, and friendly?" or "Is the speaker trying to manipulate us?"

D. Dynamism

In evaluating the speaker's dynamism, the audience will assign degree values to the answers to such questions as "Is the speaker confident, aggressive, emphatic, forceful, and possessed of a flair for showmanship?" This component is an intensifier. If the speaker is perceived favorably in one or more of the other three components, the favorable effect will be intensified. If the speaker is perceived unfavorably, then the unfavorable effect will be intensified. Unlike the other three components, an excess of dynamism may be perceived negatively. If the speaker "comes on too strong" we may reject the approach.

If we perceive a speaker as intelligent, untrustworthy, manipulative, *and* dynamic, we may feel that we have good reason to fear a dangerous demagogue.

A low perception of dynamism may offset desirable qualities. During the 1970 Presidential campaign, some of George McGovern's supporters saw him as "decent" and "sincere" but after listening to his monotone delivery said, "This guy's better than Seconal—no charisma, no pizzazz, no passion, boring, can't pull votes, a loser."[4]

Among modern Presidents, Franklin D. Roosevelt and John F. Kennedy were the most successful in projecting all four components to their contemporary audiences.

As a first step in building ethos in the eyes of an audience, the advocate should strive to develop these desirable qualities. This is only a first step, however, since these qualities cannot influence the *argumentative* situation unless the advocate makes the choices necessary to reveal them to the audience.

II. Factors Contributing to Ethos

The audience's determination of the speaker's ethos is not based on any one factor of ethos but rather on an interlocking of all of these factors. These factors, taken together, influence the audience's decision about the competence, integrity, intention and dynamism of the speaker and thus determine its evaluation of a person's ethos. Different factors will have varying degrees of importance with various audiences, and we must analyze each audience and make the choices appropriate to it. In matters related to the following factors, we must make a choice. Our success will be determined to a significant degree by our ability to make those choices that will raise our ethos in the eyes of our audience.

We begin to raise or lower our ethos from the moment the audience first becomes aware of our existence. This moment often comes when we first step onto the stage or are seated at the speaker's table; as intercollegiate debaters, it usually comes when we arrive on the campus of the host college for a tournament. Although there may be a considerable lapse of time between this moment and the time the speech is actually presented, we have started to lodge initial impressions in the minds of at least a part of our audience.

A. Preparation

There is no substitute for thorough preparation. Yet, it is not sufficient that we be prepared; we must reveal this fact to the audience. Although the audience would be quickly bored with the details of our preparation, we must so present our arguments that it will become apparent to the audience

---

[4] Shirley MacLaine, *You Can Get There From Here* (New York: W. W. Norton & Co., 1975), p. 48.

that we have studied the problem with care, that we have selected our material thoughtfully, and that we are well versed in all matters relevant to the problem. It is obvious that presidents and prime ministers have vast staffs and the almost unlimited resources of governmental agencies at their disposal to furnish material for their speeches. Yet, an examination of their speeches will reveal that they take pains to assure their audiences they have studied this matter personally and that they are using the most recent and best available evidence. If heads of governments find it important to reveal their preparation to the audience, it is even more important that student advocates emphasize their preparation. Well-chosen, concise references to the background and history of the problem, knowledgeable handling of all phases of the problem, clear and confident reference to source material, and the ability to distinguish readily between major and minor evidence and arguments all help speakers to reveal their preparation. Advocates should give evidence of their preparation not only within the speech itself but in their conduct before and during the speech. The quiet and efficient arrangement of card files and other reference material before the speech and businesslike use of them during the speech suggest thorough preparation.

B. Seriousness

Audiences are more likely to believe speakers who take their subject seriously than those who treat it facetiously. This specifically does not mean that speakers should take *themselves* too seriously; audiences resent the "stuffed shirt." When Gerald R. Ford became President at a traumatic moment in American history, he remarked, "Remember, I'm a Ford, not a Lincoln," giving an impression that he did not view himself with pretensions. At the same time, speakers should treat the subject, the audience, and the occasion with appropriate seriousness. Many successful political speakers interject humor into some of their speeches, but they are careful to avoid the reputation of being humorists. Lincoln, Franklin Roosevelt, and Churchill used humor to make telling points in some of their wartime speeches, but they were careful not to create the impression that they were treating the war or any of the major political problems with a lack of seriousness. Adlai Stevenson interjected some delightful humor into his political speeches. (Some of his supporters felt that he did so much of this that he acquired a reputation as a humorist and that this was a handicap in his Presidential campaigns.)

Intercollegiate debaters should be careful to present to the audience serious concern with the problem under debate and serious appreciation of the educational opportunities in the debate situation. They should use humor with restraint and interject it into the debate situation only when it can make their point more effectively than it could be made in any other way.

C. Sincerity

The speaker should convey the impression to an audience that he or she is honest in thought and deed, and free from hypocrisy and dissimulation. Lincoln, Theodore and Franklin Roosevelt, Eisenhower, and Kennedy were particularly effective in projecting this quality. Calvin Coolidge, Herbert Hoover, and Thomas E. Dewey seem to have been less successful in externalizing this quality. Some contemporary political commentators saw them as "cold," "aloof," or "distant." Richard Nixon was often considered insincere. During the 1972 campaign, his opponents gave wide circulation to a particularly unflattering photograph of Nixon bearing the caption "Would you buy a used car from this man?" The speaker must be careful to avoid actions or words that will lead the audience to suspect any insincerity.

Skillful speakers can sometimes simulate the factors of ethos and thus create a false impression in the mind of the audience, and in so doing may secure acceptance for their arguments. If, however, the audience detects falseness or dishonesty, speakers are confronted with an almost insuperable barrier to gaining the confidence of the audience. The wisest course to follow is that of cultivating both the factors of ethos and the ability to project these qualities to an audience.

In the 1972 Presidential campaign, McGovern's sincerity was seen as one of his strongest qualities by his supporters. Belief in this quality plummeted when McGovern, who had first announced he was "1,000 per cent behind" his vice-presidential running mate, Senator Eagleton, dropped him from the ticket a week later.

D. Confidence

As speakers, we should exude an air of quiet assurance. We should always appear to be in command of ourselves and the situation around us. The best way to do this, of course, is to be thoroughly prepared for all eventualities. The unexpected, however, has a way of happening. The speaker who becomes unnerved by some unexpected refutation adds to the effectiveness of that refutation; the speaker who retains his or her composure minimizes the effect of the unexpected. Although we should be confident, we should never appear to be arrogant. Audiences seem to delight in cutting the arrogant speaker "down to size." In 1974 it was widely predicted that Governor Gilligan would win re-election in Ohio. Some observers felt that a major factor in his razor-thin defeat by Governor Rhodes was that many voters perceived Gilligan as "too confident" and "arrogant." Successful politicians master the difficult problem of appearing confident and yet not too confident.

In a recent major intercollegiate tournament, the affirmative team, in the opinion of competent observers, won a critical debate. The judge, unfortunately, was a substitute inexperienced in educational debate. As the judge reviewed his notes before filling out the ballot, one of the affirmative speakers slouched in his chair in an air of utter dejection upon remembering that he had failed to use an important piece of evidence. The negative team promptly thanked their opponents for an interesting debate, thanked the judge for his attention, packed up their reference material briskly, and left the room with an air of quiet satisfaction. The inexperienced judge later confessed, "It was a close debate; the affirmative team acted as though they had lost, the negative team acted as though they had won, so I voted for the negative." This example appears to be a clear case of the judge "reading" and responding to the nonverbal communication of the debaters. (See also: the section on "Analysis of the Key Individual during the Speech" in Chapter 17 and the section on "Nonverbal Communication" in Chapter 19.)

E. Poise

Audiences tend to be more willing to believe a speaker who is poised, who is at ease in the speech and in the social situation that surrounds the speech, and who has a sensitive awareness of the social amenities appropriate to the occasion. Franklin D. Roosevelt and John F. Kennedy, for instance, seemed to be equally at ease amid the stuffy ceremony of receiving a foreign monarch or an informal chat with an unknown farmer, or while speaking at a formal college commencement or at a boisterous political rally. Congressmen, educators, attorneys, and businessmen who can conduct themselves with savvy in the social affairs that surround many argumentation situations are often able to carry the ethos they establish into the argument itself. College debaters who, throughout a tournament, conduct themselves as mature students whose primary purpose is to benefit from important educational opportunities, gain an enormous advantage in ethos over novices who conduct themselves as exuberant sophomores who are more interested in socializing than debating.

Poise within the speaking situation itself is revealed by the speaker's entrance into the auditorium or room where the speech is to be given. The experienced speaker greets other speakers with quiet cordiality, arranges notes and reference material with calm efficiency, and listens with polite attention to other speakers without revealing any reaction to their arguments. When the time comes to speak, he or she approaches the lectern with a calm, sure step, and, after a brief, cordial statement of appreciation to the hosts and expression of pleasure at being there and meeting the other speakers, devotes the time to building rapport with those who render the decision and to presenting arguments. The amenities of an intercollegiate debate suggest that after the debate speakers thank their opponents for an interesting debate, possibly engage in some polite conversation with the judge *after* he or she has completed the ballot, repack their notes in an unobtrusive manner, and withdraw. Only the greenest freshman would attempt to prolong the arguments after the conclusion of the debate or would presume to question the judge about a critique or decision.

F. Friendship

Because it is easier to believe our friends than it is to believe those who are not, advocates should show themselves to be friendly to those who render the decision. At the same time, advocates should manifest friendship toward those who constitute the audience and show friendship, or at least courtesy, toward opponents. Thus advocates should show the same deference to those who render the decision that an attorney shows to the judge and jury, that a politician shows to an undecided legislator, or that a salesman shows to a prospective customer. Our society expects a display of friendship and respect for judge and audience. Thus the rules of Congress and various legislative bodies set certain minimum standards below which the advocate may not sink without censure. Debaters may tear the opponents' arguments to shreds but may never, in word or action, suggest any attitude toward the opponents as persons but one of politeness. Outside the realm of educational debate, there are a few cases when this does not apply. The attorney may seek to destroy the credibility of a hostile witness by showing him or her to be a disreputable person; the prosecutor seeking a harsh penalty must usually portray the accused as a loathsome person. However, even in such relatively rare and highly specialized cases, the attorney is expected to treat opposing counsel with courtesy. Perhaps the classic example of courtesy to one's opponents is to be found in Britain's declaration of war against Japan on December 8, 1941. Churchill sent a note couched in correct diplomatic phraseology to the Japanese Ambassador. Although some objected to the courtly wording and traditional expressions of honor and esteem, the Prime Minister brushed these objections aside. Even though he was planning to destroy his nation's enemies, he saw no reason for not being polite while informing them of his intention. Advocates are seldom required to kill their opponents, so it costs them even less to be polite. It may well pay dividends in credibility.

G. Common Ground

It is easier to believe a speaker who shares many things in common with us than a speaker who does not. Dwight Eisenhower had spent much of his adult life outside the United States or in the specialized atmosphere of army command schools, or as a Supreme Commander of the armed forces; Kennedy's family's fortune was numbered in hundreds of millions of dollars. The specialized lives of these men meant that they had little in common with the average voter. Their ability to win Presidential elections and the great influence they exerted while in office, however, stemmed largely from their ability to identify themselves with the interests of the average voter. As advocates, we must be careful to establish ourselves on common ground with our audience without falling into the fallacy of popular appeal. We must demonstrate that we share many interests and beliefs with our audience, and we must seek to demonstrate that the position we uphold in the debate coincides with the interests of the audience.

Speakers may often establish common ground by showing that they are aware of the identity of the audience and the problems that confront them. An examination of the speeches of any Presidential candidate will reveal that the candidate almost always seeks to associate himself with the people in the audiences or the city in which he is speaking. Typical of campaign oratory was one of Eisenhower's speeches in Florida.

Next, I want to pay my personal tribute to Florida. Here is a place I like to visit. I regret sincerely that my visit today can touch only two of your cities, and that only briefly. Had I the opportunity to go through your cities and streets, not only here and in Miami but throughout all the other towns of Florida, I would deem it a very great honor.[5]

Such statements in political speeches may seem trite and hackneyed, since the candidate must express similar sentiments about so many cities. The almost invariable use of such statements, however, suggests that candidates have found them to be important in building ethos with the audience. When these statements are presented with freshness, vigor, and sincerity, they probably do have the desired effect.

While Eisenhower's speeches furnish us with typical examples of the use of the common-ground approach, the speeches of Franklin Roosevelt provide masterful examples of the more sophisticated use of this method. Roosevelt used the common-ground approach with a great degree of success in his "fireside chats." His speeches abound with "we," "you and I know," "you and I believe." He so structured many of his speeches as to picture the listener and himself sitting side-by-side, facing a common problem together. In his "fireside chat" of May 26, 1940, for example, he said, "Let us sit down together again, you and I, to consider the pressing problems that confront us." As Roosevelt's opponents discovered, once advocates can establish the idea that they and those who render the decision are comfortably seated together facing a common opponent, that common opponent is going to have a rather difficult time gaining the belief of the audience. At the same time, the speaker should avoid claiming too much common ground. The gallery of the Pennsylvania legislature roared with laughter when State Representative Blaine C. Hocker overclaimed common ground by remarking in debate, "I'm not talking as a Republican; I'm speaking as a human being."

[5] From Eisenhower's speech of October 29, 1956, delivered at the Jacksonville airport.

H. Moderation

Since audiences generally find it easier to believe the reasonable, temperate man than the impassioned zealot, most speakers will usually find it advantageous to display moderation. Their gestures should be moderate. They should avoid both the "wooden" absence of gesture and movement and the declamatory gestures favored in William Jennings Bryan's day. Contemporary taste favors easy but restrained gesture and movement. In their choice of words, speakers should avoid both overuse of idiom and colloquialism and the flights of "purple prose" of a Webster of the 1800s. Contemporary usage favors the conversational style.

The abrasive style and nonnegotiable demands of dissonant dissenters have turned off some who might have been convinced by a more moderate and reasoned approach. While such tactics have a short-term publicity value, they are usually counterproductive in the long run. A thoughtful observer, former Senator Margaret Chase Smith, once warned: ". . . the excess of dissent on the extreme left can result in repression of dissent. For repression is preferable to anarchy and nihilism to most Americans."[6]

In presenting our arguments, we will usually find that understatement is often more effective than overstatement. Such statements as "the affirmative has absolutely proved," "we categorically deny the claim of the negative," or "the negative must prove beyond a shadow of a doubt" are hallmarks of the novice. Experienced advocates advance their arguments in more moderate terms and make it easy for the audience to agree with them.

I. Firmness

Some of the complexity of the problem of developing ethos may be perceived in the situation that as speakers, while giving evidence of some of the milder qualities such as moderation, we must also give evidence of firmness. On those issues that are vital to our case we must take a vigorous stand and display a crisp, decisive, businesslike attitude. We should evidence the courage of our convictions. Audiences seem to respond favorably to a certain combativeness in some speakers. When Franklin Roosevelt lashed out at "economic royalists," when Churchill snarled at Hitler and Mussolini, when Harry S Truman "gave them hell" on his whistle-stop campaign of 1948, and when the usually genial Eisenhower showed a flash of temper, the public responded enthusiastically. It should be noted that these speakers did not sustain their combative mood long. Although they established themselves in the public eye as tough and uncompromising on certain matters, they also took care to demonstrate their reasonableness and moderation on many other matters.

[6] Speech in the Senate, June 1, 1970.

J. Dress

There is much to the old saw that "clothes make the man." One's style of dress can be chosen to go a long way toward evoking a conditioned response from anyone one meets. A Manhattan "wardrobe engineer" has had considerable success in teaching dress habits that enable salesmen to sell more insurance, trial lawyers to win more cases, and executives to exert more authority. In one experiment an actor, posing as a trainee in a large corporation, was instructed to ask 100 secretaries to retrieve some information from their files. When dressed in "lower-middle-class" style, he was able to get only 24 percent of the secretaries to go to their files for him; when he dressed in "upper-middle-class" style, 84 percent of the secretaries did his bidding.[7]

Studies in communication theory confirm this. Eisenberg and Smith point out: "To the wearer clothes represent an effort to control the reactions of others, and to the observer they are a means by which the individual can be socially classified."[8]

Frightening proof of the success of this factor is found in the history of the Boston Strangler. Despite the fact that a strangler was known to be at large and women were constantly warned against admitting strangers to their apartments, women continued to admit the Strangler, who dressed for his crimes in innocuous green workman's clothes.

Experienced advocates are careful to select their dress to produce a desired reaction in their audience. An interesting example of the debate affecting the advocates' dress occurred during the televised hearings of the House Judiciary Committee on the impeachment of President Nixon. During the closed sessions reporters often described the members' clothing as "rumpled" or "casual." When they moved to the televised hearings, the members underwent a notable change as they all appeared in rather conservative clothing as a part of their effort to impress the viewers with the seriousness and weight of their arguments.

Thus debaters should dress in a manner that will enhance their credibility and project an image of serious, able advocates attuned to the formality of the occasion. College seniors are usually aware of this point—note their appearance as they go for job interviews.

K. The Speaker's Associates

The speaker's associates often have a significant effect on the audience's perception of ethos. If the speaker is associated with persons we like, per-

---

[7] See: *Time* Vol. 100, No. 10 (Sept. 4, 1972) p. 67.

[8] Abne M. Eisenberg and Ralph R. Smith, Jr., *Nonverbal Communication* (Indianapolis: Bobbs-Merrill Co., 1971), p. 107.

sons we admire or persons we respect, we are predisposed to react favorably to the speaker. On the other hand, if the speaker is associated with persons we dislike, persons we disdain or persons we hate or fear, we are predisposed to react unfavorably to the speaker.

Pragmatic proof of the importance of the speaker's associates is found in any major political campaign. A standard ploy for most candidates is to surround themselves with popular figures from politics, sports, the arts, and the widest possible range of ethnic backgrounds. In the 1972 Presidential campaign, Lorne Greene of TV's "Bonanza" rode in convertibles with Hubert Humphrey; Carroll O'Connor, TV's "Archie Bunker" did spot commercials for John Lindsay; Red Skeleton told jokes for Richard Nixon; and Shirley MacLaine was the star attraction at many of George McGovern's fund-raising parties.[9] Obviously the candidates hoped that by associating with popular celebrities they would convert the celebrities' fans into voters for themselves.

An examination of almost any campaign — for public or campus office — will usually reveal that the candidates seek to identify themselves with popular associates and to identify opponents with unpopular associates. The influence of associates is not limited to celebrities and throngs of campaign workers; it also applies even when the speaker has only one identifiable associate. Thus student debaters often insist that their debate partners present an appearance that will favorably impress the judge or audience.

It must be noted that association with popular figures is not a guarantee of success. Franklin Roosevelt and Dwight Eisenhower were men of towering ethos when they campaigned for the Presidency, and many Congressional candidates sought to ride on their coattails. Roosevelt always carried enough candidates on his coattails to win control of both Houses for his party. Despite his nine million vote plurality in 1956, however, Eisenhower was unable to carry enough candidates with him to win control of either House for his party.

Exercises

1. Examine the text of a recent speech by the President of the United States. What factors of ethos did the President use?

2. Bring to class the text of a speech delivered by a public figure within the last month in which you think the speaker was particularly effective in developing the factors of ethos.

3. Prepare a five-minute speech for presentation in class in which you present the affirmative (or negative) of a significant contemporary proposition. In this speech develop the factors that will tend to build your ethos in the eyes of the audience. Hand your instructor an outline of the speech; in the margin of the outline indicate

[9] See: Shirley MacLaine, *You Can Get There from Here* (New York: W. W. Norton & Co., 1975), pp. 54–55.

the points in your speech designed to develop the factors of ethos and label the factors of ethos you intend to develop at that point.

4. Your instructor may find it advisable to lead a class discussion evaluating the speeches in exercise 3. Contribute to the discussion by offering suggestions as to how the speaker could have further developed factors of ethos.

Chapter 17

The Role of Motivation

As advocates, we quickly discover that the use of logic alone is often insufficient to gain our objectives of securing the decision of others. Frequently, we find it necessary to use various forms of motivation, as well as logical argument, to secure decisions. The role of motivation has been recognized for centuries.

Quintilian pointed out: "Proof may induce the judges to regard our case as superior, but an appeal to the emotions will do more—it will make them wish our case to be better—and what they wish they will believe."[1] This ancient dictum has wide application in contemporary society. If jurors pity the defendant, they are more likely to believe the arguments of the defense attorney. If voters identify with a certain candidate, they are more likely to believe the campaign statements of that candidate. No sane person, of course, uncritically assumes that the things he or she wishes are fact. There is, however, an important relationship between wishes and beliefs in those areas where decisive proofs are not available. For instance, so far it has been impossible to establish decisive proof that one popular brand of soap, cigarettes, or automobile is clearly superior to rival brands. Thus, in the absence of logical proofs to support the claims of one company against those of its rivals, the sale of many products is largely dependent upon motivational appeals.

In learning to sell to our subconscious, another area the merchandisers began to explore carefully was that involving our secret miseries and self-doubts. They concluded that the sale of billions of dollars worth of products hinged to a large extent upon successfully manipulating or coping with our guilt feelings, fears, anxieties, hostilities, loneliness feelings, inner tensions.[2]

The use of motivation in political affairs is as old as politics itself. Political campaigns today are increasingly conducted with the specific and calculated intent of bringing maximum motivational pressures to bear on the electorate. Candidates are making increasing use of public relations and advertising firms that apply the techniques learned in the business world to the political scene. The Kennedys, Rockefeller, Johnson, Nixon, and all recent major political candidates have made extensive use of private pollsters to keep them informed on the trends of public opinion.

---

[1] Quintilian, *De Institutione Oratoria,* VI, 2.
[2] Vance Packard, *The Hidden Persuaders* (New York: David McKay Co. 1957), p. 57.

Advocates who would succeed in winning a decision from others must know and be able to apply various types of motivation in order to achieve their objective. The degree to which an appeal to the emotions influences a decision is often difficult to determine. When asked why they reached a certain decision, people tend to rationalize and respond by giving a seemingly logical reason whether or not this was the real reason for their decision. In many cases, of course, the real reason may be unknown to the person.

An appeal to the emotions is often felt to have little effect on the outcome of an educational debate, since the qualified judge places special emphasis on logical argument. Yet emotional appeals may be the deciding factor in determining our purchase of a brand of cigarettes, or soap, or automobile, or even in our vote in a Presidential election. Although the effect of a specific motivational appeal in a particular situation is elusive, we must recognize that motivational appeals often have an enormous impact on the audience and that the use of motivational appeals by advocates is necessary.

I. Ethics of Motivation

Because motivational appeals are such a powerful instrument of persuasion, their use raises an ethical problem. Some think that the individual who uses motivational appeals is synonymous with the demagogue manipulating the mob in the manner of Hitler or Mussolini, or the cynical huckster exploiting the gullible consumer. With such an image in mind, they deplore the use of motivational appeals. But this view oversimplifies the problem, since motivational appeals are essential to worthwhile causes. In the 1940s, while Hitler was using motivational appeals to inflame the German masses for world conquest, Churchill was using motivational appeals to steel the British will to resist.

The study of persuasion through the use of motivational appeals is comparable to the study of any other art or science. Just as one who has studied chemistry may use that knowledge to produce poisons or life-saving medicines, so one who has studied motivational appeals may use this knowledge for good or evil purposes. The responsible advocate will be guided in his use of motivational appeals by the ethical standards considered earlier.[3]

Both ethical considerations and intelligent self-interest dictate that the advocate present valid arguments. The speaker who uses invalid arguments, intentionally or not, runs grave risk of exposure by competent opposition. Once even a portion of a speaker's arguments is exposed as invalid, he or she comes under a severe handicap and may find it almost impossible to secure a favorable decision.

There is no dichotomy between motivation and valid argument. The effective speech blends both. We are never confronted with a choice between

---

[3] See Chapter 2 ("Ethical Standards for Debate"), p. 27.

using motivational appeals *or* valid argument; our task is to use both. And we may conclude that the use of motivation is necessary and its use raises no ethical problem, as long as the basic premises and supporting contentions of the speech are based on sound argument.

II. Analysis of Motivation

The problem before the advocate is to dovetail the decision he favors with the prevailing beliefs of those who render the decision. This task may be accomplished by application of the following:

1. *Discover what those who render the decision prefer, want, or believe.* To do this, we must perform a careful analysis of those who render the decision. This may involve an analysis of millions, in the case of a Presidential campaign, or the analysis of a few key individuals with the power to render a critical decision.

2. *Establish reasonable proof that the proposal will give them what they prefer, want, or believe.* To do this, we must bring carefully marshalled argument to bear to establish the credibility of our proposal.

3. *Establish reasonable proof that the proposal is practical and relatively easy.* There is no reason for those who render the decision to adopt the proposal unless it is practical, and we must present cogently reasoned argument. Further, we must demonstrate that the proposal is relatively easy to implement. The key word here is *relatively;* the proposal must be shown to be either an easy thing to do or easier than the consequences of not adopting the proposal.

Many scholars have worked long and hard at classifying human needs. One contemporary psychologist, Maslow, whose work has received much attention in the field of communication theory, lists five general categories of human needs:[4]

Physiological Needs: These are the basic needs of man — oxygen, food, water, shelter, sex and elimination of wastes. Until these needs have been fulfilled, man cannot consider other needs.

Safety Needs: Once the physiological needs are met, the need for safety becomes the next most important. We want to be secure in our persons, our homes, our jobs, our country, our environment. A change in environment often produces at least temporary insecurity — the college student typically experiences insecurity during the beginning of the freshman year or at the start of a summer or semester abroad.

Belonging Needs: Once the security needs are reasonably satisfied, the love, affection and belonging needs are likely to emerge. Most people want to associate with and be approved and accepted by others — friends, a companion or spouse, family, classmates, fellow workers, groups of people with whom we tend to identify. While the number of groups — and the types of groups — people join will vary enormously, most people experience the need to belong to some group.

[4] Abraham H. Maslow, *Motivation and Personality*, 2nd ed. (New York: Harper & Row, 1970.)

Esteem Needs: Once the belonging need is reasonably satisfied, Maslow predicts the esteem needs surface. We want (1) strength, achievement, competence, confidence, independence and freedom and (2) reputation, prestige, status, dominance, recognition and appreciation.

Self-Actualization Need: Once we have reasonably fulfilled the previous needs, the need for self-actualization may often come to the fore. This is the need to grow and to live up to our potential — to achieve self-fulfillment or self-realization — to become everything one is capable of becoming.

Note that the needs are arranged in a hierarchy. If a person urgently and simultaneously needs oxygen, security, and esteem, there is no choice but to seek oxygen first. Note, too, that the needs will change as time and surrounding situations change. The need for self-actualization may take the form of making the high school basketball team, becoming a star debater in college, gaining admission to a prestigious graduate school, becoming a writer, a painter, or an inventor.

This formulation is of basic needs stated in broad terms and presented by Maslow as applying to human beings in general.

Audiences: Preferences, Wants, and Beliefs

Democracy Most of us believe in democracy, and there is a growing belief in participatory democracy. Although there are some obvious exceptions, most of us believe in our political system and tend to regard other political systems as inferior or hostile. This belief in a political system is distinct from approval or disapproval of specific individuals or problems. Thus the Supreme Court, as an institution, is usually above criticism, but specific decisions or various justices may come under sharp attack.

The Individual Our society tends to place great value on the individual. In general, we believe that individuals should be free from most restraints and that many opportunities should be made available to them. We also believe that individuals are capable of solving, and should be expected to solve, many problems on their own initiative.

Conformity At the same time, most people believe that the individual should conform to certain norms, such as dressing and acting in conformity with the standards of their peer group. Many institutions in our society are designed to aid or pressure the individual to conform to certain norms. As observers of the campus scene know, students are particularly susceptible to pressure to conform to current styles of dress — witness shifts from minis to maxis to midis, from faded jeans to French jeans, from boots to "earth" shoes.

Helpfulness Most people believe in helping others, and many will go out of their way to help a stranger. The vast outpourings of wealth on organized philanthropies are unprecedented in human history. Many examples of generous and spontaneous aid to individuals or large groups stricken by disaster or tragedy are easily found.

The list here (*see inset*) is designed for contemporary American society and more specifically limited to the preferences, wants and beliefs likely to be operative in audiences in a debate situation where there is a desire to reach a rational decision on the problem at hand. (If there is an urgent need for oxygen there is no time for debate. We either know what to do and do it — as a submarine crew or miners — or we act quickly on instinct and are either lucky or dead.)

It is the task of the advocate to discover the preferences, wants, or beliefs of the particular audience that will render the decision. Our listing is an eclectic compilation drawn from a variety of psychological, sociological, communication theory, and rhetorical sources.

In considering the beliefs of our listeners, we must always keep in mind that human beings are complex. Their beliefs are not always static, they frequently are transient. What is of great importance today may be of less importance tomorrow. Early psychologists often listed self-preservation as the strongest of human motivations, and at times it is. History, however, is replete with examples of heroes and martyrs who placed other values be-

---

Competition A belief in competition is deeply ingrained in our society. Although some prefer to drop out or stop out, most people favor the competitive system in economic, political, and social affairs. Our political system is based on competition between candidates and parties, much of our legislation is designed to require economic competition, and even community projects are often based on competition among teams of fund raisers. Many share Vince Lombardi's credo: "Winning isn't everything. It's the only thing."

Power and Influence Most of us want to have some power and influence over others, and we tend to respond favorably to those things that will give us power and influence. Many groups are organized precisely for this purpose — for example, civil rights groups, agricultural workers, consumer groups, and others. They feel that only by acquiring power, can they change the system. [Many believe it is not how you play the game, but whether you win or lose. They believe it is better to win than to lose; they admire a winner. A winner in almost any area gains prestige that may be transferred to other areas. Many alumni are impatient with a football coach who builds character but does not win games; many citizens are impatient with a Secretary of State who does not force foreign nations to comply with our wishes.]

Submission At the same time, many of us want to avoid the responsibility of making decisions and to avoid any kind of controversy. Thus we often submit to the decisions of others. The old military custom of passing the buck and avoiding the responsibility of making a decision is not unknown in business, industry, or education. Although there is a tendency to go along with the decisions that have been made, there is a growing resistance to all types of authority and an increased emphasis on individual freedom.

fore self-preservation, and hardly a week goes by without the press recording some incident of heroism wherein a person has risked or sacrificed his life to save others. And human beings are not always consistent. They may hold apparently mutually exclusive beliefs at almost the same time. A number of conflicting wants may influence the college student who has to choose between goofing off and devoting a few extra hours to working on an important term paper. Perhaps most important of all, people are not machines. We can turn on the ignition of our automobile and be reasonably confident that the motor will start. We cannot with the same degree of confidence apply motivational techniques to an audience and expect a predetermined response.

The list is merely suggestive—no definitive list exists. Using this as a starting point, the advocate should develop a list of the particular beliefs most influential upon the specific audience he seeks to influence at the moment he addresses them. Furthermore, such a list should be arranged in rank order of the priority each belief has for the audience. (Methods of audience analysis are considered later in this chapter.)

Today there are many who march to the beat of a different drum. Some

---

Audiences: Preferences, Wants, and Beliefs (cont'd)

Ambition While there are some who reject ambition, most people remain eager to improve their lot in life. They want to get more out of life than their parents did, and they want their children to have a better life than they have. Most people still approve of working hard and getting ahead.

Leisure At the same time, we are placing an increasing value on leisure. Many students are ambitious to make good grades—but do not want to appear to be grinds. Some labor leaders are pressing for a four-day week, in the belief that their members will find more leisure an even more attractive issue than more money. Home appliances, ready-mixed foods, and countless gadgets are sold on the basis that they make it possible to cut down house work. Camping and sports equipment companies are enjoying an unprecedented boom as their products help millions to enjoy their leisure.

Newness Many people believe that something new is better than something old. This week's hit lyric is assumed to be better than last week's. A new or different way of doing something is often assumed to be better than the old, familiar way. Many graduating seniors seek a job with a new, small firm rather than an old, established one, in the belief their work will be more exciting or offer more opportunities.

Security At the same time, most of us want security. We favor proposals that will render us, our families, our group, or our nation safe from the unknown, the dangerous, or the undesirable. Many believe that security is to be found in the old and familiar—thus many graduating seniors seek a job with an "old, established" firm rather than with a new one. A certain way of doing things is often assumed to be good simply because things have "always" been done that way.

turn off, drop out, or stop out of the mainstream while others are actively hostile to society. Some who seek to do their own thing find themselves under enormous pressure to conform to their peer group. Their lifestyle often makes them unlikely participants in any process of rational decision making. Those who want to communicate with them need to undertake a very careful analysis of the audience or individual. The listing applies to the majority of audiences. A different listing would have to be developed for the special cases of deviant audiences.

It should be noted that in any given situation a complex of motivational forces, rather than a single force, is usually influential. What makes high school students decide to go to college? Perhaps they are motivated by a belief that a college education will help them make more money (economic success). It is unlikely, however, that this motivational factor alone is decisive. They may want to go to college because that is what their friends are going to do (conformity), they may not want to let high school rivals get ahead of them (competition), they may want prestige in the community (social acceptance and public recognition), they may want to postpone going

---

Optimism Despite some notable exceptions, conditions generally have improved rather steadily in our society. Perhaps this is the basis for our widespread belief in optimism. Most of us—including protesters—believe that things will improve in the future.

Economic Success Most of us measure success in economic terms, and accumulation of wealth is often equated with success. Many students will readily state that they are going to law school, or medical school, or are following a certain course of studies because they hope it will enable them to make more money than they might expect to make in some other line of endeavor.

Science Things scientific, or those things that appear to be scientific, enjoy prestige in our society. Most people like things to work effectively. "Scientific" tests are offered as proof for many things—see almost any television commercial. Scientists are often prestige figures, and their words often carry weight outside their area of special competency.

Social Acceptance and Public Recognition Most want to be accepted socially. Most like to be treated with deference and respect, to win the signs of public recognition. Some college students go to great lengths to win membership on a team or an honor society. After college, men and women often spend vast amounts of energy or money to win the signs of public recognition.

Pleasure Many of us believe that pleasure is a desirable goal. We devote a lot of time and money to pleasure, and our expenditures are generally viewed with approval. Many goods and services are sold simply because they will give pleasure, not for any utilitarian function.

to work (leisure), they may want to do something different (newness), they may be motivated by a desire to serve their fellow humans (helpfulness).

As advocates, we must also be aware that in any given situation there may be motivational factors working against the decision we seek. A speaker at a freshmen orientation program might use a variety of appeals to motivate the freshmen to concentrate on their studies. Other factors working against the speaker's purpose—factors that the speaker would have to overcome—might include the freshmen's desire to join various student organizations (social acceptance and public recognition), a desire to emulate their class-mates (conformity), a desire to take part in the fun of college life (pleasure), and various other conflicting desires.

If the audience is homogeneous, we will probably obtain best results by the intensive application of a very few carefully selected appeals; if the audience is heterogeneous, we will have to use a larger number of appeals. In deciding which appeals to use, we should try to discover the beliefs *actually* dominant in our audience's thinking, not the beliefs we wish they held. When he was Secretary of State, John Foster Dulles was quoted (perhaps inaccurately) as having told the Arabs and the Israelis that they should "settle their differences in a spirit of Christian charity." Whether or not we share, or even approve of a belief, is totally irrelevant. We cannot intelligently attempt to influence an audience until we know the beliefs of our audience.

In addition to discerning the preferences, wants, and beliefs prevalent in the audience, the advocate must also determine the *attitude* of the audience about these factors. The desire for economic success might highly motivate some students to undertake the arduous studies necessary to become a physician. The desire for economic success, however, would probably be completely ineffective in motivating the same students to become professional gamblers or bank robbers. Although they might desire economic success very much, their attitude would control their susceptibility to this motivation. Still other medical students might reject economic success and be motivated by a desire to practice in the ghetto.

III. Analysis of the Audience

In order to discover the preferences, wants, and beliefs of the audience, and to secure the other information necessary to prepare an effective speech, we must know as much as possible about our audience. The questions in the *inset* (pages 268–269) suggest information that speakers need to know about an audience. Most of these questions are relevant for most advocates on most propositions. Special considerations may make some of them unnecessary or may make necessary the addition of other questions. If we are to speak before a familiar campus group where we already have a good idea of who will be in the audience, the answers will come quickly and easily. If, as is often the case, we are to speak before an unfamiliar audience, we must turn to the sources of information about the audience and undertake research that will equip us to answer the questions effectively.

A. Sources of Advance Information about the Audience

We are usually fortunate in that there is usually a wealth of information available about an audience. Our task is to make maximum effective use of this information.

1. Public Sources of Information Public opinion polls, newsmagazines, and newspaper articles and editorials report public opinion on both national and local matters. Speeches and books report or comment upon public opinion, attitudes, beliefs, and desires on a wide range of subjects. These sources of information have to be studied critically, however. Some of the reporting will be superficial; some will represent the wishful thinking of the reporter; some will be keenly analytical. These various sources, if studied carefully, will give us useful information from which we can draw conclusions about an audience. If we are speaking to a group of college students, we can find without too much difficulty a number of recent articles commenting on the current generation of college students. Similar articles could be found about labor union members, suburban housewives, or any other special group that might make up the majority of the advocate's audience.

In addition to the widely circulated publications, there are also the special publications particular to the group or area from which the majority of the audience will be drawn. Civic, social, religious, professional, and labor organizations usually have newspapers or magazines devoted to matters of special interest to them. The small town and the major residential areas within large cities usually have weekly newspapers featuring matters of local interest. A careful study of these will provide a number of useful clues about an audience.

2. Private Sources of Information Advocates can often answer many of the questions about an audience from *their own personal knowledge.* As a college debater, if you were invited to address the freshman class of your college during Freshman Orientation Week for the purpose of urging them to try out for the debating team, you would probably not have to undertake any extensive research to find out about your audience. From your day-to-day contacts with students, from your own memories of what interested you as a freshman, you would probably be able to develop a fairly accurate statement of the attitudes of your audience. A member of one college's chapter of Phi Beta Kappa could probably make a fairly accurate preliminary audience analysis of the members of Phi Beta Kappa on another college campus.

Although it is necessary to guard against attaching undue weight to a stereotype, experienced speakers nonetheless have been able to formulate useful generalizations that allow them to make helpful preliminary audience analyses of such groups as the P.T.A., Rotary, Hillel, NAACP, and many other organizations.

We may also gain further information about the audience from *our own associates*. Someone invited you to address the audience, or you persuaded someone to arrange for you to appear. Thus you have a contact with a member of the "in group," a person who knows a number of the people in the audience and has enough influence with them to choose the speaker. This person, or it may be a group, is an excellent source of information. William Kunstler, controversial activist and attorney for the Chicago Seven and the Wounded Knee Two, who was active on the lecture circuit after his

---

What the Advocate Needs to Know about the Audience

Audience Attitude toward the Speaker

1. What is the probable audience attitude toward the speaker as a person?

2. What is the probable audience attitude toward the organization the speaker represents or is identified with?

3. What is the probable audience attitude toward the point of view the speaker represents?

4. What is the probable audience attitude toward the proposition the speaker is supporting (or opposing)?

The Occasion

1. Why have these people assembled as an audience?

2. What will precede the advocate's speech?

3. What will follow the advocate's speech?

4. Are there any customs, ceremonies, or traditions that relate to the occasion?

5. Who else will speak on this occasion?

6. What will the other speakers probably say?

7. What leaders of the group or distinguished guests will be present?

8. How will their presence influence the audience's decision?

9. How much time is available?

10. What is the physical condition of the room in which the advocate will speak?

famous trials, found that even the ride from the airport to campus was a useful source of information:[5]

I also try to understand what controversies are in existence in the community so I can relate them to a local issue if it is humanly possible; if there is someone fighting for tenure, if it's a school; or if there is a dispute over ROTC, or over coed dorms, or "grass" or what have you. I try to find that out on the road from the airport to the school or to the place where I am to speak. I am usually just burning with questions, and I listen a great deal to what they tell me. Then I utilize it.

Even if we have no direct contacts within an audience, we are likely to have associates who are representative of the audience or familiar with the attitudes of the audience.

Experienced advocates often try out a speech or a certain treatment of key issues on selected representative audiences before they present the

[5] Beatrice K. Reynolds, "An Interview with William M. Kunstler: Rebel Rhetor," *Today's Speech* (Fall 1974), p. 43.

The Audience

1. Is the audience homogeneous or heterogeneous?

2. Does one age group predominate in the audience?

3. What is the probable size of the audience?

4. Does the audience consist predominantly or exclusively of members of one sex?

5. What is the educational attainment level of the majority of the audience?

6. Are there significant numbers of any one occupational group in the audience?

7. Are there significant numbers of any one ethnic group in the audience?

8. What common interests do members of the audience share?

9. To what groups or organizations do significant numbers of the audience belong?

The Audience and the Advocate's Purpose

1. Will the audience know the speaker's purpose in advance?

2. What does the audience know about the subject area relating to the speaker's purpose?

3. What experience has the audience had with proposals similar to those of the advocate?

4. How would the audience be affected by the advocate's proposal?

5. What beliefs, prejudices, or predispositions does the audience have that relate to the speaker's purpose?

speech or critical arguments to the audience that will actually make the decision. The very favorable audience response to Churchill's "we shall never surrender" statement in his Dunkirk speech came as no surprise to the Prime Minister. He had used this approach a week earlier in a private meeting with a group of twenty-five experienced politicians and members of Parliament and had won an ovation from them. William Jennings Bryan's Democratic Presidential nomination following his famous "Cross of Gold" speech came as a surprise to many, but not to Bryan and his associates. He had used every means at his disposal to get a chance to speak at the convention and had planned the speech carefully. Most of the arguments advanced in that speech had been tested in scores of previous speeches. The concluding sentence that gave the speech its title had been used a few times previously, and Bryan, recognizing its electric effect on other audiences, had saved it for the proper moment. Prudence dictates that we must analyze our audience carefully and that whenever possible we should test our speech with a representative audience, however small, before delivering the speech to the audience that will actually render the decision.

If our analysis of the audience leads us to conclude that the audience is hostile, we are confronted with a special circumstance that requires special adaptation (*see inset*). Fortunately, such audiences are relatively rare—most

---

Suggestions for Dealing with the Hostile Audience

1. Discover why the audience members are hostile.
   a. They may be opposed to the speaker's position on the proposition. (The speaker is on the "wrong" side of the abortion issue, the busing issue, or whatever.)
   b. They may be opposed to the speaker as a person for two reasons: (1) Because of the kind of person the speaker is. (The speaker may be a police officer, a capitalist, or whatever.) (2) Because of the ideas the speaker holds. (The speaker is perceived as not only wanting to present the "wrong" side of a controversial issue, but as actually believing in it.)
2. Develop strategies for dealing with the hostile audience.
   (The great technique in dealing with the hostile audience is ethos—see Chapter 16).
   a. Prove that experts, authorities, famous people, people the audience respects—do not share the audience's views on the particular issue at hand. (You may wish to review the section on expert evidence in Chapter 6.)
   b. Enhance your own credibility.
3. Develop general approaches to the hostile audience.
   a. Develop common ground with the audience (see Chapter 16).
   b. Achieve an affirmative response: Present a series of facts, assertions, or questions to which the audience will *inevitably* say "yes." Keep the statements brief and unrelated to the subject of the debate. (The hope here is that, if the audience is made to say "yes" often enough, some of the hostility will evaporate.)

audiences that attend a debate are prepared to hear both sides. Sometimes, however, the audience, or a vocal part of it, is so hostile to one position that the dissidents may try to disrupt the debate even though this means denying an opportunity for the refutation of the point of view they object to.

B. Analysis of the Audience during the Speech

Besides audience analysis *before* a speech, we should also analyze our audience *during* the presentation, since the audience will react in various ways to the speech—and these reactions will give us useful clues. Such obvious demonstrations as applause, cheers, cries of approval or disapproval are readily interpreted. Bodily action of the audience, also, can usually be easily interpreted. If the speaker has the audience literally sitting on the edge of their chairs or observes them slumped lethargically, he or she can usually draw reliable conclusions about their attention. The silent attention of the audience or a murmur of conversation will provide the advocate with useful clues. If the members of the audience focus their eyes on the speaker, this says one thing; if their gaze shifts about the room or to other members of the audience, this says something else. Some experienced speakers can

---

    c. Use the circuitous approach: Begin by dealing with interesting, attention-getting matters specifically adapted to the audience but irrelevant to the purpose of the debate—then make a transition to your real subject. (Difficult to do given the time constraints of a debate, but sometimes necessary.)

    d. Use the inductive approach: Start with a series of specific examples which prove your point—but don't state the conclusion. If the examples are well chosen, the audience will draw the desired conclusion, but you will have escaped the onus of stating it.

    e. Use candor plus an appeal for fairness: Lay all your cards on the table—recognize that the audience is hostile and immediately make an appeal for fairness and equal time. Some political speakers have had notable success with this technique in dealing with hecklers.

    f. Counter dominance: Here the speaker uses sheer dynamism to overwhelm the hostile audience. The opposition is beaten down and the audience is turned around. (Examples of this technique abound in fiction. On the late night movie, the sheriff rides into town just in time to send the lynch mob home with a few stern words. Well-documented examples from history are rare. This technique is mentioned for the record, but *is not recommended*.)

Note that techniques a, b, c, and d may be used in combination. Technique e should be used alone, and technique f is probably found only in the realm of fiction.

successfully interpret the facial expressions of the audience. William Kunstler said:

> I do feel the vibes very strongly. I never could in the beginning, but now I really have a sense of how the audience is feeling. I can tell when they're hanging on every word. I can tell when they're hostile. I can tell when they really dig what you're saying.[6]

The truly effective speaker is highly skilled at picking up the vibes provided by the audience, interpreting them, and adapting to them to establish rapport with the audience.

IV. Analysis of the Key Individual

In many situations we do not have the problem of convincing all members of an audience; rather, we are concerned with winning a decision from a key individual or from a very small group of individuals who have the power of decision in a particular situation. A President may allow his cabinet to vote on various matters debated at a cabinet meeting, but as Lincoln pointed out, only one vote, the President's, matters. Truman expressed the same idea when he pointed to his desk and said, "The buck stops here." In many governmental, business, and other organizations, decisions may be avoided, postponed, referred, or the "buck passed" to others until they reach a key individual who can or must make the decision. The salesperson must frequently convince a single purchasing agent to make a sale to a particular company. The college student quickly learns that within various clubs, and even in the official business of the college, there are frequently key individuals who have the power of decision on various matters. The intercollegiate debater may on occasion address very large audiences, but the decision is usually rendered by a single judge or by a panel of three judges. One of the great advantages of intercollegiate debating is that students usually have many opportunities to speak in the small audience situation and the opportunity to adapt arguments to a key individual. By analyzing the judge in an educational debate and adapting the case to him or her, students have an opportunity to gain experience in an argumentative situation closely paralleling many situations they will face in the future when directing arguments to a key individual. Although the student speakers may hope that after graduation they will frequently speak in Madison Square Garden or over television networks they will, in fact, address the majority of their arguments to small audiences or to key individuals. Even the President, who usually can command a larger national audience than

[6] Reynolds, *op cit.* p. 45.

any other individual, addresses vast audiences far less frequently than he argues with small groups of key congressmen who can decide the fate of legislation.

Many of the questions we must answer about the key individual are substantially the same as those we must answer about the audience. In preparing a list of questions about the key individual, the advocate may begin by reviewing "What the Advocate Needs to Know about the Audience" (pages 268–269) and substituting the words "key individual" where applicable.

A. Sources of Advance Information about the Key Individual

1. Public Sources of Information There are extensive public sources of information about key individuals. Key individuals of general public interest are extensively reported in the press. There are special publications designed expressly for the purpose of furnishing the advocate with information about key individuals. The publishers of the various *Who's Who* books emphasize the value of their works to sales personnel and others in their advertising. *Poor's Register of Directors and Executives* lists the leading officers, directors, technical personnel, traffic managers, and purchasing agents of thousands of leading companies together with case histories of thousands of top executives with their home addresses, educational background, year and place of birth, and interlocking connections. The National Debate Tournament publishes a *Booklet of Judges*, which attempts to compile information about judges and their philosophies. A careful study of the sources suggested in Chapter 5 ("Exploring the Problem") will also provide answers to many of these questions.

2. Private Sources of Information We can often answer many of the questions about the key individual from *our own experience.* Lawyers often visit court, when they have no cases there, to study a jury similar to one that will hear their case, to study attorneys who may someday be their opponents, and to study judges who may someday preside when they try cases. As students, you have probably had many opportunities to study your instructors before approaching them with a plea for permission to turn in your term papers late. In many cases, advocates have at least some opportunity to study the key individual prior to the presentation of a case.

In addition, *our associates* are often an excellent source of information about the key individual, and we can get this information through informal conversation or by means of an organized effort. One of the important functions of governmental intelligence agencies is to maintain elaborate files on key individuals in both hostile and friendly nations. When President Roosevelt died in office, the British embassy immediately cabled Prime

Minister Churchill a most detailed analysis of the new key individual in Washington—President Truman. We may also assume that following Richard Nixon's resignation every embassy in Washington sent an analysis of President Ford to their governments. Governments are not the only organizations to recognize the importance of such information. Attorneys often make a careful study of the presiding judge. Major fund-raising agencies maintain particularly elaborate dossiers on known or potential givers of large sums. Debating teams sometimes maintain files about debate judges, carefully recording their opinions about the proposition, sources of evidence, their preferences for types of debate cases, and their prejudices for styles of delivery.

Much of the information about the key individuals may be gathered informally. The sales manager will usually give the new sales representative a few words of advice about the best approach to use with a certain purchasing agent. In college, upper classmembers may pass on advice about professors to freshmen. Some of the reports may be grossly inaccurate; others, highly analytical. The advocate must weigh them carefully.

B. Analysis of the Key Individual during the Speech

The analysis of the key individual is both easier and more difficult than the analysis of the audience. It is more difficult, in that it is usually inappropriate for the key individual to give such overt signs as applause or cheers. Often the key individual, such as the judge in the courtroom or the judge at an educational debate, will deliberately try to conceal any sign of approval or disapproval as the arguments are developed. At the same time, it is usually easier, because we do not have to give our attention to many individuals, but only to one or to a very small group. When directing our whole presentation to the president of the bank, to the credit manager of the corporation, to the judge in the jury-waived trial, or to the judge in the educational debate, we have a better opportunity to study the subtle signs of agreement or disagreement, of attention or inattention, and thus have a better opportunity to adapt our motivation and argument than we do when we must consider the whole audience.

There is evidence that debaters can "read" nonverbal stimuli and interpret it correctly. Sayer found, in one research study, that debaters in general evaluated the judges' nonverbal stimuli and predicted their decisions with 66.5 percent accuracy, while "better" debaters (defined as those with 5–3 or better records) were 80.7 percent accurate.[7] While we do not know precisely what the nonverbal stimuli were—Sayer postulates they may have been eye contact, facial expression, and bodily movement and posture—nor how the debaters interpreted them, it is apparent that debaters, operating on

[7] See: James Edward Sayer, "Debaters' Perception of Nonverbal Stimuli," *Western Speech*, Vol. 38 (Winter 1974), pp. 2–6.

an intuitive basis, have considerable success in analyzing the key individual during the debate.[8]

The problem becomes more complex when an audience is present along with the key individual, such as the spectators at a court trial. In such a situation, we must give priority to those who render the decision—but must never neglect the nondeciding audience. Indeed, we must make specific efforts to secure responses from them, for they may exert a favorable influence upon those who render the decision.

Exercises

1. Bring to class six advertisements from magazines published within the past week in which you find motivational appeals used. Identify the appeals used. Identify the audience to which the appeal is directed. Do you consider the appeal effective for this audience? Why?

2. Bring to class the text of a speech, delivered within the past few months by a public figure, in which you find motivational appeals used. Identify the appeals used. Identify the audience the speaker addressed. Do you consider the appeal effective for this audience? Why?

3. Draw up a list of the preferences, wants, and beliefs of your classmates that would be relevant to a debate on the current national intercollegiate debate proposition.

4. Prepare a three-minute speech for presentation in class in which you support or oppose a proposition of policy. Include some motivational appeals that you feel would be effective upon your classmates in relation to this proposition. Prepare an outline of the speech for your instructor. In the margin of the outline identify the motivational appeals you plan to use.

5. Assume you are the affirmative (or negative—specify which) in a debate on the current national intercollegiate debate proposition. Prepare a written set of answers to the questions listed under "What the Advocate Needs to Know about the Audience" in terms of: (a) your class, (b) a selected campus organization, (c) a community service organization (Kiwanis, Rotary, Lions), (d) a local consumer organization, (e) a local political organization. Compare your answers with those of other members of your class.

6. Assume the same debate situation as in exercise 5. Prepare a written set of answers to the questions suggested under "the key individual" as applicable to: (a) your college president, (b) the mayor of the city where your college is located, (c) one of the deans of your college, (d) your parents, (e) the member of Congress from your district.

[8] See the section on "Nonverbal Communication" in Chapter 19.

Chapter 18

Presenting the Case: Composition

The case, as indicated in earlier chapters, is the operational plan drafted by the advocates on one side of a proposition for the purpose of coordinating their reasoning and evidence and presenting their position with maximum effectiveness. The case outline incorporates some elements of speech composition and is an important starting point. It is not a speech, however, nor an editorial nor a book. It is the blueprint from which the advocates will develop their actual debate speeches. Although the case can serve with equal effectiveness as the basis for a written document, our concern here is with the *presentation* of the case. In presenting their case orally, the advocates are concerned with composing speeches that will gain the attention of the audience, hold interest, make it impossible for the listeners to fail to understand their arguments, and make it easy to agree with their case.

I. Written and Oral Style

There are significant differences between written and oral style. Wichelns pointed this out when he said:

All the literary critics unite in the attempt to interpret the permanent value that they find in the work under consideration. That permanent value is not precisely indicated by the term beauty, but the two strands of aesthetic excellence and permanence are clearly found. . . .

If now we turn to rhetorical criticism . . . we find that its point of view is patently single. It is not concerned with permanence, nor yet with beauty. It is concerned with effect. It regards the speech as a communication to a specific audience, and holds its business to be the analysis and appreciation of the orator's methods of imparting his ideas to his hearers.[1]

Writers can usually work at a more leisurely pace than speakers. They may often write and rewrite their arguments; they may polish and repolish style. They must consider enduring aesthetic standards and think of an

---

[1] Herbert A. Wichelns, "The Literary Criticism of Oratory," in *Studies in Rhetoric and Public Speaking In Honor of James Albert Winans,* by Pupils and Colleagues (New York: The Century Co., 1925), pp. 208 ff.

"audience" that will read their arguments months or years afterwards. A writer's "audience" may also proceed at leisure. Readers may stop to ponder a point, consult a reference work, or reread a passage.

Speakers, on the other hand, usually work under stricter time limitations. If they do not reply promptly to their opponents' argument, their opportunity to reply may be forever lost. While writers may hope that readers will reread their words, speakers have only one opportunity to reach their listeners. Their arguments must be instantly intelligible to the audience. If listeners miss an argument, its value is lost unless the speaker repeats it. Most important, the speaker is concerned with a very specific audience on a very specific occasion. Morely pointed out:

The statesman who makes or dominates a crisis, who has to rouse and mold the mind of senate or nation, has something else to think about than the production of literary masterpieces. The great political speech, which for that matter is a sort of drama, is not made by passages for elegant extract or anthologies, but by personality, movement, climax, spectacle, and the action of the time.[2]

Although, as speakers, we are not concerned with the production of literary masterpieces, we are concerned with the production of masterful oral arguments. Our concern with style is neither more nor less than that of the writer; it is different. Activist Kunstler cites this example: "I've listened to Justice [William] Douglas speak—I've shared a platform with him several times—and he is a terrible speaker. And yet he can write the most beautiful opinions. So I guess it's a different thing."[3] The writer must strive for a style that will have permanence; the speaker must strive for a style that will be appropriate to the moment.

II. A Philosophy of Style

There is no one style of speech that is suitable to all speakers and to all time. The style of Webster was magnificent for his times, but today it would be considered too formal, too florid. Style also bears the stamp of the individual. The styles of Roosevelt and Churchill were both great, yet they were different. No knowledgeable student of speech would be likely to mistake one of Roosevelt's conversational "fireside chats" for one of Churchill's more formal "orations." The student will readily recognize the differences in Kennedy's crisp "ivy league" style, Johnson's folksy "Texas" style, Humphrey's exuberant style, Wallace's "slugging" style, and Ford's flat Midwestern style.

[2] John Morely, *Life of William Ewart Gladstone* (New York: St. Martin's Press, 1903), Vol. II, pp. 589–590.

[3] Beatrice K. Reynolds, "An Interview with William M. Kunstler: Rebel Rhetor," *Today's Speech* (Fall 1974), p. 45.

The "fireside chat" developed by Roosevelt and revived by Ford is well suited to the requirements of radio and television speaking and to the taste of contemporary American audiences. We should not seek to emulate the style of a great speaker; rather, we should seek to discover the style best suited to us and to our audiences, and develop that style to a high point, modified by the occasion and the audience. An attorney, for instance, would use one style of speaking when addressing a rural jury and quite a different style when pleading before the Supreme Court; yet in both cases he or she would have the same purpose: to win an acquittal for his client. As another example, an advocate with a purpose of winning support for intercollegiate athletics would find it advisable to use one style of speaking in addressing a football rally and quite a different style in addressing a chapter of the American Association of University Professors. Even substantially similar audiences will expect important differences in style on different occasions. The style of speech appropriate for the stag banquet of the senior class would be quite different from the style appropriate to a commencement address.

III. Factors of Style in Speech Composition

The factors of style considered here reflect the tastes of contemporary audiences. These general principles must be modified as special considerations enter the situation. A speech at a football rally, for example, would probably require very short sentences, informal even flamboyant vocabulary, violent partisanship, and overall brevity. A speech before a group of educators, on the other hand, would probably require somewhat longer sentences, more dignified vocabulary, more formal structure, more restrained partisanship, and a more lengthy overall development.

A. Conciseness

Short sentences and succinct phrases are preferred by contemporary audiences in contrast to the full, flowing prose popular in the last century. Today speakers should seek a concise expression of their ideas. Conciseness involves not only the succinct expression of ideas, but also applies to the overall length of the speech. One- or two-hour speeches were quite the usual thing in the day of Webster, Clay, or Calhoun. Perhaps the expense of radio and television time has helped to set the pattern of a half hour as the usual maximum for a speaker today, and the average speech is often briefer.

Time is precious to us as advocates. Those portions of our speeches that are under complete control (e.g., the first affirmative, sometimes the plan objections, etc.) should be the product of extensive rewriting and editing until each issue is stated with maximum conciseness and clarity and phrased for maximum impact on the judge or audience. Each piece of evidence should be presented with a cogent lead-in and edited to eliminate all extraneous words (while preserving with scrupulous honesty the author's intent). Note, for example, the opening of the first affirmative speech cited in the sample affirmative outline on page 196. The speaker stated the affirmative's rationale, aligned a high prestige source with his case (the President's Commission was unquestionably the best and most recent source of evidence on the proposition at the time this speech was presented), and stated the proposition in one 78-word sentence that took approximately 30 seconds to deliver. A less skilled speaker would have devoted two or three less cogent sentences to the introduction, another sentence to the proposition, and perhaps consumed two minutes or more of precious time before getting into the case structure.

B. Clarity

Clarity is of overwhelming importance to us as advocates. A perfectly sound case, a case superior to the opposing case, may be defeated if the audience fails to see the connection between our arguments or if the listeners do not get the point of our evidence. Our objective is to present our case with such great clarity that it is impossible for the average member of the audience *not* to understand the case. Carefully planned organization, well-chosen examples, and precise language will help us achieve clarity.

C. Appropriateness of Vocabulary

Our vocabulary must be appropriate for the audience and the occasion. Experienced lecturer William Kunstler reports his method of adapting his vocabulary to his audience:[4]

For example, if I speak to an undergraduate audience I use a far different approach than when I am talking to the Junior Chamber of Commerce in Minnatonka, Minnesota, or a bar association, or a group of older people.

The difference, I think, is that in talking to the young people I consciously try to use language, that while not being condescending, is at least in the genre to which they are accustomed. And I try to bring into the talk some relationship to the language of an undergraduate without sacrificing any content and without sacrificing any rhetorical artistry that you can utilize and without, I hope condescension, because I think that condescension is probably the worst sin any speaker can commit.

The task of the advocate is to present often complex messages in readily comprehensible language geared to the genre of the decision renderers and with rhetorical artistry that will have a favorable impact. Student debaters should note that their approach is often the exact opposite of Kunstler's.

---

[4] *Ibid.,* p. 37.

They should consciously try to use the language and genre to which their often older audiences are accustomed.

D. Simplicity of Structure

The overall structure of the speech must be simple. Our objective is to make it easy for those who render the decision to follow our case. We should seek simplicity, too, in the structure of our sentences and passages. The complex or compound sentence, replete with subordinate clauses and studded with commas and semicolons, may, on careful reading, serve to express an idea with considerable precision. Our listeners, however, cannot see the punctuation in our notes, nor do they have a chance to reread a difficult sentence. Simple sentences are more desirable for speakers.

E. Concreteness

Specific rather than vague or general words or phrases will increase the impact of our ideas. We should seek the word or phrase that will convey the exact shade of meaning we intend. The use of specific detail will often heighten interest and add an air of authenticity to the speaker's words. When Franklin Roosevelt urged Congress to declare war on Japan, he gave them specific details of Japan's attack:

Yesterday the Japanese government also launched an attack against Malaya.
Last night Japanese forces attacked Hong Kong.
Last night Japanese forces attacked Guam.
Last night Japanese forces attacked the Philippine Islands.
Last night Japanese forces attacked Wake Island.
This morning the Japanese attacked Midway Island.

Roosevelt's masterful use of specific, concrete details of Japan's attack had a tremendous impact on Congress and the public.

Sometimes the speaker must use unfamiliar words or phrases. These can be made more specific by careful definition.[5]

F. Imagery

If we can paint a vivid picture in the minds of our audience, we enhance our opportunity of persuading them. A deftly phrased image will have an immediate impact on listeners and may linger in their memory to influence future as well as immediate decisions.

[5] See Chapter 4, "Analyzing the Problem," for methods of defining terms.

In a debate on the proposition "Resolved: That executive control of United States foreign policy should be significantly curtailed," a first affirmative speaker began by saying:

"All the people who lined the streets began to cry, 'Just look at the Emperor's new clothes. How beautiful they are!' Then suddenly a little child piped up, 'But the Emperor has no clothes on. He has no clothes on at all.'" In 1947 the United States created the Central Intelligence Agency and donned the cloak of secrecy to pursue communism. Experience has proven the cloak we donned was nothing more than the Emperor's new clothes, hiding far less than we have long pretended and exposing America to peril.

A new phrase—"iron curtain"—entered the world's vocabulary when Winston Churchill proclaimed, "From Stettin in the Baltic to Trieste in the Adriatic an iron curtain has descended across the Continent."[6]

G. Connotation

Our concern with the selection of words and phrases is not limited to the choice of words within the vocabulary of our audience. We are also concerned with the problem of choosing words and phrases with a sensitive awareness of their emotional connotations. Consider the following examples of phrases that present a concept in a "good" and a "bad" light.

Unemployed persons over age sixty-five receive money from the federal government. Is this "Social Security" or a "dole for the indigent unemployables"? Billions of dollars are spent to provide medical care for the aged and poor. Are these programs "Medicare" and "Medicaid" or "bureaucratic bungling" and a "rip off of the taxpayer by organized medicine and the drug industry"? United fund organizations collect monies for various groups. Is this "voluntary giving" or an "organized shakedown"? Are men employed to secure favorable press notices about their clients "public relations counselors" or "hucksters"? Each of these designations involves an element of slanting. But decisions are often influenced by just such slanted phrases. The use of the words "Social Security," "Medicare," and "Medicaid" were important factors in securing the enactment of the programs now known by those names. Joseph Conrad said, "Give me the right word and the right accent and I will move the world."[7]

[6] Actually Senator Arthur H. Vandenberg had used this phrase four months earlier; but it is Churchill's speech that the world remembers. It is fitting that we identify the phrase with Churchill. Although he was not the first to use the phrase publicly, he was apparently its originator. Some months before the Vandenberg speech, Churchill used the phrase in a then secret telegram to President Truman—a message about which Churchill later said, "Of all the public documents I have written on this issue I would rather be judged by this." Truman used to circulate some of these messages among a small circle of Senate leaders.

[7] Joseph Conrad, *A Personal Record* (Garden City, N.Y.: Doubleday & Co., 1923), p. xvi.

H. Climax

The development of climax is an important consideration in both written and speech composition. The advocate's speech typically contains a series of issues. Each of these should be built up to a climax, and the speech as a whole should build toward a final major climax. We will often find it advantageous to place a strong climax very near the beginning of our speech to capture audience attention. Our final climax may frequently be in the form of an effective summary of our major arguments combined with a strong persuasive appeal. If we use an anticlimactic order, beginning with our strongest arguments and tapering off with our least effective arguments, we will diminish the force of our case and will leave a weak impression with those who render the decision. We have three problems relating to climax: (1) we must open with an attention-getting climax; (2) we must end at a high point leaving a strong, lasting impression with our audience; and (3) we must offset the climax of a previous speech by our opponents.

IV. Rhetorical Factors in Speech Composition

The rhetorical factors of *coherence, unity,* and *emphasis* aid the advocate in composing an effective, well-organized speech. The outlines of typical debate cases presented in Chapters 13 and 14 incorporate some of the factors of speech composition—and it may be desirable to reread those chapters in connection with this section.

A. Coherence

The speech must be arranged so effectively that it will be instantly intelligible to those who render the decision. The intelligibility of a speech depends in large part on coherent organization. Often beginning advocates have a cluster of evidence and reasoning that seems convincing to them but has no effect on those who render the decision. The same evidence and reasoning rearranged by skilled advocates may win a decision. The difference here is that the skilled advocates have learned to arrange or order their materials carefully and to blend them together with effective transitions into a coherent whole.

1. Order The materials of the speech must be presented in a carefully determined order designed to have maximum effect on those who render the decision. The issues of the proposition must be presented in an effective sequence. The supporting materials for each issue must be so arranged as to lend maximum support to the issues. Often, as advocates, we may first think of presenting our arguments in logical order. In many situations, logical order is the most effective arrangement. In other situations, however, we may find it desirable to arrange our arguments in a psychological order adapted to our audience.

Other arrangements that are effective in certain situations include the problem-solution order, the "this-or-nothing" order, the topical order, and the chronological order. Sometimes the use of one arrangement for the overall speech, and another for the development of certain supporting arguments, is effective. In debating the "energy" proposition, one debater used a combination of methods in his first affirmative speech. The organization of the debate case was *problem-solution:* the problem was identified and a solution proposed. Other types of organization were used in the development of the issues. Following is an excerpt from the outline of his speech:

I. Today's energy crisis is not a matter of just a few years but of decades.
(Under this heading the debater used *chronological* order to show how the crisis had come about and why it would project into the future.)

II. Alternative sources of energy are impractical.
(Under this heading the debater used the *this-or-nothing* order, as he considered and dismissed various alternative sources, concluding that coal was not an alternative as both coal and uranium were needed.)

III. Nuclear power is safe.
(Under this heading the debater used *chronological* order reviewing the history of civilian nuclear power from its start to the present and claimed an unparalleled safety record.)

IV. There is no reasonable alternative to nuclear power.
(Under this heading the debater again used the *this-or-nothing* order to argue that there would be an energy famine unless the affirmative plan were adopted.)

Even though we may use a variety of methods, our objective is always to so order and arrange our materials as to achieve coherence.

2. Transition Transitions may be regarded as bridges between the various parts of the speech. It is not sufficient to have a well-ordered series of arguments to provide coherence. We must also connect the parts of our argument in a way that makes it easy to follow the development of the total case. In many cases, a transition may be only a word or a phrase. In a closely reasoned argument, however, an effective transition often includes three parts: (a) a terse summary of the preceding arguments; (b) a brief forecast of the next argument; (c) a concise demonstration of the relationship between the two arguments.

The debater whose outline was cited above used the following transition in developing his fourth issue:

Remember our analysis: One, the energy crisis will last for decades. Two, alternative sources are impractical and three, nuclear power is safe. With this in mind consider the statement signed by 31 scientists — including 10 Nobel Prize winners — appearing in the *New York Times* on the 16th of this month: "On any scale the benefits of a clean, inexpensive, and inexhaustible domestic fuel far outweigh the possible risks. We can see no reasonable alternative to an increased use of nuclear power to satisfy our energy needs." And that's our fourth issue: There is no reasonable alternative to nuclear power.

Well-planned transitions make it easier for the audience to see the relationship of various parts of the argument and to link the parts of the speech together into an effective whole.

B. Unity

We should have one clear, definite, and specific objective for a speech. Once we have established this objective clearly in our mind, we may proceed to composing a speech designed to attain that objective. The effective speech has unity of purpose and mood.

1. Unity of Purpose Unity of purpose requires that the speaker have one and only one specific purpose for his speech. The rhetorical purpose of the advocate is to prove, or to disprove, the proposition of debate.

It is well to recognize that the advocate may have a nonrhetorical purpose in addition to the rhetorical purpose. In such cases, the nonrhetorical purpose is the *real* purpose of the speech, and the rhetorical purpose becomes the *apparent* purpose of the speech. This distinction between real and apparent purposes is sometimes found in political debates. There is some evidence to suggest that some legislators who urged the addition of civil rights amendments to federal housing or school aid bills were not really supporting civil rights, but were using this as a device to achieve their real purpose of defeating the housing or school bills. The discerning student of argumentation will readily find examples suggestive of this type in a number of debates on contemporary affairs. The word "suggestive" is used here since we cannot always establish a person's real motives. Understandably, advocates with real purposes that differ from their apparent purposes make an effort to conceal this difference. Some sales talks, for example, are cleverly designed to convince the consumer that a low-priced appliance is no good and that a fantastically overpriced "de luxe" model is really a much better buy. The salesperson's real purpose, of course, is to sell the overpriced appliance, and the apparent purpose is merely a "come on." Although we may deplore the fact that the real and apparent purposes of the speaker are not always the same, we must recognize that such a situation sometimes exists.

Once we determine the purpose of our speech, we then proceed to the composition of a speech designed to achieve that purpose. As we compose our speech, we must make certain that everything that goes into the speech — evidence, reasoning, ethical appeals, motivational appeals — contributes to the purpose of the speech. Anything that does not contribute to the attainment of the purpose—no matter how interesting, amusing, or informative it may be—must be ruthlessly excluded from the speech.

An example from educational debating will serve to illustrate this point. One student, who had many of the qualifications of an excellent debater, consistently lost debates on the "energy" proposition mentioned earlier. A senior physics major, he was particularly well informed on nuclear power reactors. His response to negative workability attacks were brilliantly informative speeches on nuclear reactors. In fact, one judge commented that the student had delivered one of the best informative speeches the judge had ever heard on the operation of nuclear reactors. The student's problem was that he presented so much information on workability that—although he clearly carried that issue—he failed to respond to the disadvantages attacks. When he restructured his response-to-workability blocks, deleted the fascinating, informative, but irrelevant material and retained only the critical refutation, he then had time to get to other major arguments and enjoyed much more success in winning decisions.

2. Unity of Mood Unity of mood requires that we sustain a certain mood, emotional feeling, or "tone" appropriate to our purpose, audience, and occasion. Our materials should be in perfect unity with the mood we have chosen for our speech. Evidence and reasoning that may meet the logical requirements of the proposition but not the mood requirements should be replaced by materials that will meet both requirements.

A debater favoring a program of national compulsory health insurance decided she would seek to establish a mood of pity. To support her argument about the cost of medical care, she offered a series of examples of long-term illness. One ill-chosen example shattered the mood she sought to sustain:

One young girl, just the age of many in this audience, spent seven long, lonely, tragically wasted years in the cold isolation of a TB hospital. One man in the prime of life, the age of many of your parents, spent five years in the living hell of bone cancer suffering the most terrible pain known to man. One dear old lady, the age of some of your grandparents, spent fifteen years in a mental institution knitting a 27-foot-long scarf.

The audience of high school youngsters were still chuckling about the old lady and her 27-foot-long scarf while the debater completed her arguments showing the high cost of long-term hospitalization.

C. Emphasis

Not all parts of a speech are of equal importance—some are indispensable to our case, others are of lesser importance. Our problem is to emphasize the more important parts of our speech. Emphasis makes it easier for the audience to grasp and retain the ideas we must get across if we are to prove our case. Emphasis may be achieved by position, by time, and by repetition.

1. Position Emphasis may be achieved by the position given to an idea. The *beginning* and the *ending* provide greater emphasis than does the middle. This principle applies to the speech as a whole, to an argument within the speech, and even to a sentence.

Consider the following excerpts taken from speeches in debates on "right-to-work" laws. The speeches come from two different debates, but the same issue is involved. Note the difference in emphasis:

They just don't work. That's the simple fundamental fact about "right-to-work" laws—they just don't work. Let's look at the record. Let's go right down the list of states with "right-to-work" laws. In every case we'll see they just don't work.

Let us consider the feasibility of the proposal advanced by the affirmative. Let us examine the facts in those states where this plan has been tried. We will find that such legislation does not work effectively to produce any significant change in labor-management relationships. There are now seventeen states that have legislation of this type. As we review the evidence from these states we find . . .

Both speakers maintained that "right-to-work" laws do not work. The first speaker emphasized this claim by giving it both first and last position; the second speaker buried it in the middle of his passage.

2. Time Time is of the essence in argument—and we must spend our time wisely. The greater part of our time must be devoted to the important arguments. We never have sufficient time to cover all possible arguments, or to refute fully all of the contentions of our opponent. Therefore, we must single out the important matters and emphasize them by the amount of time we give them.

3. Repetition Repetition and redundance are often viewed with disapproval in writing, and the author is given stern injunctions to avoid them. For the speaker, however, judicious repetition is essential. Repetition aids both clarity and emphasis. If listeners miss a critical word or phrase that is uttered only once, the speaker's case may never be clear to them. Listeners cannot turn back the page to reread something they missed the first time. We must compensate for the probable inattention among some members of our audience by reiterating critical material. The old slogan "Tell them what you're going to tell them, tell it to them, and tell them what you've told them" has considerable merit. We cannot use italics, capital letters, or boldface type, but we can use repetition. Repetition may be achieved by repeating the same idea in the same words or by restating an idea several times in slightly different ways.

During his 1964 campaign for the Vice Presidency Senator Humphrey used repetition skillfully. In attacking the voting record of the Republican standardbearer, he said, "Most Democratic senators and most Republican senators voted for the civil rights bill — *but not Senator Goldwater.*" As he continued to list bills opposed by the Republican candidate, the crowds took up the theme and chanted the concluding phrase, "... *but not Senator Goldwater,*" along with Humphrey.

Student debaters rarely have throngs of admirers to chant their punch lines along with them, so they must provide their own repetition. A first affirmative speaker arguing the "curtail executive control of foreign policy" proposition repeated his major claims, saying:

Our first contention: Discovery of covert operations undermines American objectives; discovery undermines American objectives. . . .

Our second contention: The only way to prevent discovery is to end all operations; the only way to prevent discovery is to end all operations.

The repetition is intended to lodge the argument firmly in the minds of the judge and audience and to ensure that the judge will record the speaker's exact phrasing of this argument on a flow sheet. Such overt repetition is accepted by many judges, who recognize the pressures a speaker is under in a tournament. A more subtle method of repetition is required for general usage.

V. Methods of Dramatization

When dealing with certain types of audiences, we may find it necessary or advantageous to dramatize our ideas. If the audience is a believing audience, favorably disposed to our point of view, it will be desirable to deepen and intensify their beliefs to move them to accept our position. Dramatization is also important with apathetic audiences, audiences that really do not care about the matter before them. The problem is to wake up such audiences — to demonstrate that the matter before them really is important. Dramatization is dangerous with hostile audiences, audiences frankly opposed to our point of view. Here, dramatization will serve only to intensify the hostility and objections of the listeners. Dramatization is of lesser value with truly neutral audiences, audiences that are frankly reserving their decisions until the facts are in — they want evidence and solid reasoning. However, since we are frequently confronted with believing or apathetic audiences, it is well for us to consider methods of dramatization.

A. Use of the Fable

The fable may be defined as a story in which nonhumans — usually animals — act and behave in the manner of humans. The use of the fable is one of the oldest but still one of the most effective methods of dramatization. Aesop used it centuries ago to score telling points. In his "Speech on the British Constitution," John Stuart Mill used a fable he considered "worth a thousand syllogisms." Edmund Burke used a fable in his "Reflections on the Revolution in France." More recently, one of the most biting indictments of communism appears in George Orwell's *The Animal Farm*. On the surface, this is a story about some animals that dispossessed a farmer and a vile group of pigs that enslaved the other animals under the slogan "All animals are equal, but some are more equal than others." It soon becomes apparent, however, that this is not really a story about animals. The farmer is quickly identified as the Czar of Russia, one pig is readily identified as Trotsky, another as Lenin, another as Stalin. Had Orwell written a scholarly tome entitled *The Evils of Communism,* a few hundred copies of the book might have been sold, and a few thousand persons might have read it. However, he chose to use the form of a fable, a form readily understood by the popular audience. In this form, he reached scores of thousands through the hardback edition of his book, countless additional thousands through the paperback editions, and probably millions through the full-length motion-picture cartoon version of his book. Juleus has suggested the following rules for creating fables:

1. Phrase your moral or idea to be illustrated simply and pointedly.

2. Select your characters—animal, mineral, or vegetable. Remember this is to be a study in contrasts: human frailties opposed to strengths, right versus wrong, wisdom against ignorance.

3. Give your characters the qualities of man. Make them speak.

4. Give virtue, wisdom, truth, and right their rewards.

5. Revise your fable carefully to cut out unnecessary verbiage. Strive for precision and conciseness.[8]

It must be remembered that the fable is subject to refutation. Before using a fable, we should consider the possibility that our opponents will seize upon an ill-considered fable and turn it to their own purposes.

B. Audience Participation

The involvement of members of the audience in the speaking situation is an effective way of securing their participation. Evangelists carefully structure their revival meetings for this purpose. Members of the audience are invited to sing together, to stand together, to raise their hands together, to come forward together. The well-known evangelist Billy Graham regularly employed a staff of hundreds to encourage the audience to participate in the carefully structured situation. Most of us do not have the financial resources

---

[8] Nels Juleus, "The Fabulous 'For Instance,'" *Today's Speech,* Vol. 7 (April 1959), pp. 5–6. Reprinted by permission of Nels Juleus and *Today's Speech.*

to maintain an elaborate staff, but we can secure audience participation through inviting the audience to respond either overtly to our questions or silently in answer to our rhetorical questions. Our questions should be so chosen that the audience response *must* be favorable to our purpose. Examples:

In a debate on the "medical care" proposition before a Kiwanis Club, one debater asked her audience, "How many have hospital insurance?" Every hand in the room went up. Then she asked, "How many have insurance that will cover catastrophic illness where the bills might run up to $20,000 or $30,000 a year?" She paused as almost every hand in the room went down. "That's what we are going to be talking about today. Catastrophic illness. Illness that will drive 100,000 families into bankruptcy this year."

In a debate on the "energy" proposition before a Junior Chamber of Commerce during the Arab oil embargo, one debater asked his audience, "How many had trouble getting gas this week?" Almost every hand in the room went up. "How many had to change their plans or cancel a trip because of the gas shortage?" Again, almost every hand went up. "And did you notice the price went up?" A chorus of "Yeses." "Well, those are the problems we're going to talk about today. And things are going to get a lot worse unless the affirmative's plan is adopted promptly. Here's what we propose . . ."

C. Massing of Detail

The massing of detail, the heaping of one factual situation on top of another, the use of observable, human-interest details can create a dramatic impact. Robert G. Ingersoll used this technique in his speech on Napoleon; Edward R. Murrow used it in his wartime broadcasts from London. John Kennedy used this method to some extent in his debates with Richard Nixon and later in many of his Presidential press conferences. Intercollegiate debaters often use this method as they cite fact after fact to demonstrate the need for their plan. Debaters on the "right-to-work" proposition were able to achieve this effect as they cited the testimony before Senator McClellan's committee to establish corruption and violence in union activities.

D. Use of Telling Detail

The use of the telling detail, the minute but essential detail, demonstrates to the audience that the advocate has covered the ground thoroughly and adds an air of authenticity. Such telling detail may be derived from a careful study of the problem or from personal observation. Skilled trial lawyers in malpractice suits have honed this technique to a fine art to gain million-dollar-plus settlements or judgments. Instead of blandly stating that their clients had been injured, the trial attorneys provided telling details:

Following a faulty decompression laminectomy, a dentist was left totally paralyzed, unable even to control his bowel and bladder functions. The jury awarded the plaintiff $1,685,000.

During the course of a minor operation someone forgot to attach a suction device to a breathing tube. As a result a young college student suffered major brain damage and was left a quadriplegic who has double vision and cannot hold a pencil or speak. Two physicians and two hospitals settled out of court for $1,065,000.

Because of a faulty reading of an infant's bilirubin level, treatment was delayed for hours and the infant suffered irreversible brain damage. A teenager at the time suit was brought, he was still blind and deaf. His mental level was that of a three-month-old infant; and although he can move his arms and legs aimlessly, he cannot turn over. The court awarded his family $1,019,000.

As this is not a medical textbook, the "telling details" given here are only suggestive. The trial attorneys were unsparing in giving the juries all of the gruesome details. Those who wish to see the full development of this technique should consult the transcript of a malpractice trial.

E. Use of Narrative

The use of the narrative is often helpful in building a case. Sometimes a large portion of a speech can be cast in the form of a story which makes the point with telling effect — the parables of Christ are examples. Collegiate orators have delivered effective speeches advocating wider use of parole and rehabilitation for criminals by telling stories of conditions in prisons; a plea for better treatment of narcotic addicts was made more effective by a story picturing the sufferings of an addict. Since the narrative form often involves very few examples, care must be taken to establish that these examples are sufficiently representative to serve as a basis for generalization. The college orator telling the story of shocking conditions in one mental institution, for example, must assure the audience that the conditions are not unique but are typical of many institutions. The advocate, such as the college debater, who must work within tight time limits should give preference to the brief narrative and carefully weigh the amount of time used in narration against the other requirements of the case to achieve proper proportion. It must be remembered that the narrative, like the fable, is subject to refutation and must be chosen with care.

F. Use of Illustration, Example, or Short Narrative

Often the advocate will find it desirable to present an illustration or example in the form of a short narrative or to tell a series of short narratives to make a point. Martin Luther King, Jr., made use of this method in his "I Have A Dream" speech at the Lincoln Memorial. Perhaps the best-known speech making use of a series of short narratives is "Acres of Diamonds," and the story of the speech is fascinating. With this speech, Russell H. Conwell rose from obscurity to become one of the best-known speakers of his day. Over the years he delivered the speech thousands of times and became a millionaire from the fees he received for this one speech. He used some of the income from this speech to endow Temple University, and for many years the university acknowledged the role of this speech in its establishment by canceling all mail sent through the university postage meter with the words "Built on Acres of Diamonds." In this speech, Conwell emphasized his point by repeating it again and again, each time in the form of a different illustration or example presented as a short narrative.

G. Comparison

Comparison, simile, and metaphor are valuable aids to the speaker. In using *comparison,* the speaker implies that one thing is in the same general classification as another, that the two objects or concepts or persons being compared are more alike than different. Hank Aaron has been compared to Babe Ruth although they played in different eras. *Simile* is an imaginative comparison between things essentially unlike except in the particular aspect under consideration. Muhammad Ali boasted that he "floated like a butterfly and stung like a bee." *Metaphor* is an imaginative declaration that one thing is another. When Vince Lombardi played college football, sportswriters declared he was "a block of granite."

Comparisons are highly effective if they are fresh, original, and well chosen. The overused comparison is a cliché; hackneyed and uninteresting, it often detracts from the speaker's effectiveness. Such well-worn phrases as "heavy as lead," "cold as ice," or "hot as Hades" are "dry as dust." The particularly apt comparison quickly gains wide circulation and works effectively for the speaker until its impact is dulled by too frequent repetition. We should seek to phrase comparisons that express our ideas in a striking, different, yet appropriate manner.

H. Contrast

Contrast may be used to heighten and intensify an idea. Kennedy made frequent use of contrast in his speeches; his Inaugural Address abounded with contrasts phrased in parallel structure:

United, there is little we cannot do in a host of cooperative ventures. Divided, there is little we can do—for we dare not meet a powerful challenge at odds and split asunder.

Let us never negotiate out of fear. But let us never fear to negotiate.

Ask not what your country can do for you—ask what you can do for your country.

I. Combination of Methods

Often the speaker finds it desirable to use a combination of methods to achieve or intensify dramatization. Columnist Sylvia Porter used this method effectively when, at the dawning of the Decade of the Trillions, she said:

What does "trillion" mean to you? How can you grasp the magnitude of $1 followed by a string of 12 ZEROS? Let me try to show how.

If you stacked one trillion $1 bills on top of each other, the pile would go up 67,866 miles or more than a third of the way to the moon. (Visualize that alongside of the Apollo spaceship!)

If you laid one trillion $1 bills end to end, the string would stretch 97 million miles—more than 200 round trips to the moon or more than one one-way trip to the sun. (Can you visualize it?)

If you laid $1 trillion in $1,000 bills end to end, they would reach nearly four times around the earth (97,000 miles).

If you patched $1 trillion in $1 bills together on a single sheet, this sheet of money would cover the states of Rhode Island and Delaware—and you still would have some billions left over.

If you had $1 trillion in silver dollars, your hoard would weigh more than 29 million tons—equivalent to about 350 giant steamships.

With $1 trillion, you could buy every American family a home costing close to $20,000 or every American individual a round-the-world trip or 100 million students a four-year college education at $2,500 a year . . .[9]

VI. Audio Materials

The widespread availability of inexpensive tape recorders has increased the use of audio materials in many argumentative situations. Recordings of conversations, business meetings, and speeches are frequently introduced as evidence in courtrooms. Political speakers frequently make tape recordings of their own speeches, so that they may have evidence of their exact words in case they are misquoted by others. Audio materials are extensively used in business and in scientific research to record data. Whenever a rocket is shot into space, elaborate use is made of audio materials. If the rocket fails to function properly, the recording of the details of the countdown may help to locate the trouble. At large airports, recordings are frequently made of all radio communication between the control tower and pilots. These recordings may become evidence of the messages actually exchanged. But audio materials are not limited to transcriptions of speeches. In business and industry, for example, they may be used to record noise levels in offices, factories, airports, or other areas. Audio materials, like visual materials,

[9] Sylvia Porter, "Decade of Trillions is Dawning on U.S.," January 5, 1970. Publishers-Hall Syndicate. Reprinted by permission.

are subject to the control of the person preparing them. Consequently, the tests of evidence must be applied with care.

VII. Visual Materials

Visual materials may be used as a method of dramatization; they also may be used at any point in the speaking situation where they will serve to advance the advocate's case.[10] Visual aids are widely familiar; almost every classroom is equipped with at least a chalkboard for visual aid, and the armed services have developed elaborate training aids. Visual aids are by no means limited to teaching; they are frequently used by advocates. The attorney in the courtroom may introduce as an exhibit a murder weapon or a picture of the scene of an accident. A Cabinet officer, testifying before a Congressional committee on his department's budget, almost invariably will use a number of charts and diagrams to illustrate the needs of his office.

A. Types of Visual Materials

Consideration will be given here only to the types of visual materials that may be prepared or secured by the average speaker. Such visual aids as may be secured through the use of specially prepared motion pictures or television programs are beyond the resources of most speakers.

1. Symbolic Symbolic visual materials — including charts, diagrams, drawings, pictures, and similar representations — are perhaps the most widely used type. Student debaters frequently have occasion to make use of visual aids. In debates on guaranteed annual wages, it was often necessary to refer to the cyclical fluctuations in our economy. Arguments on this matter could usually be developed most effectively with the aid of a chart showing these fluctuations. In debates on federal aid for education, advocates sometimes found it advantageous to introduce graphs showing the difference in average state expenditure per student. In debates on foreign aid, some advocates found it desirable to use world maps to show the location of recipient nations.

2. Small-Scale Replicas The small-scale replica is a useful visual aid when it is impossible or impractical to bring the actual object under consideration into the room. Advocates of a new civic building may find it advisable to bring a model of the building before the voters. Advocates seeking a change of zoning laws to permit a new shopping center may find it advisable to bring a model of the shopping center to the hearing of the zoning board.

[10] See Chapters 6 and 7 for a consideration of visual materials as evidence.

Government officials appearing before Congressional committees may introduce a replica of a new type of airplane, ship, or missile.

3. The Actual Object When the actual object under consideration is small enough to be brought into the room, it may be an effective visual aid. A college debater who desired to maintain that a guaranteed annual wage would be inflationary illustrated the effect of inflation by tearing a piece of paper the size of a dollar bill in half. The sales representative who wants to sell an electric typewriter brings the machine to the office and invites the prospective buyer to witness a demonstration.

B. Use of Visual Materials

The use of visual aids is governed by a few simple considerations:

1. The visual aid must supplement the speech. The visual aid must aid the speaker, not compete for the attention of the audience. It is therefore desirable to keep the visual aid out of the sight of the audience until that point in the speech when we are ready to use it. It must be removed from sight when we finish using it. Once a visual aid has been introduced into an argument, it must be made available to the opposition. In intercollegiate debating, a visual aid (unless it is a sketch on a chalkboard, which is erased during the course of the speech) is left near the lectern, where it is readily accessible. It is undesirable to give visual aids to the audience during a speech, however. If the advocate distributes copies of a chart or pamphlet to the audience during a speech, some of the audience will inevitably read page five when the advocate wants them to read page seven, or they will strike up a conversation about the chart with the person next to them. If the speaker asks the audience to pass around an object and consider it, the resultant confusion and conversation will divert some attention from the speaker.

Visual materials introduced by an opponent must be dealt with quickly and effectively. In a debate on price and wage controls, an affirmative speaker maintained that such controls were necessary because of cyclical fluctuations in the economy and drew a diagram on the chalkboard showing the fluctuations in the economy since 1970. The negative speaker who followed this presentation opened his speech by saying:

The affirmative has introduced an interesting diagram into the debate. [The speaker picked up an eraser as he said this.] But these fluctuations occurred during the Vietnam conflict, and they have not shown you that we are going to have another Vietnam. [The speaker then erased this portion of the diagram.] This fluctuation came when the dollar was devalued, and they haven't demonstrated that we are going to have another devaluation. [The speaker erased this portion of the diagram as he spoke.] Now this fluctuation occurred when the Arabs embargoed oil, and they haven't proved that another embargo is likely, nor have they shown that the events which caused any of the other fluctuations are likely to recur. [The speaker finished erasing the diagram as he spoke.] Let's turn to a consideration of what actually did happen when controls were used in 1971 and 1973.

In another case, a college debater disposed of several carefully prepared charts, which had been left standing near the lectern by his opponent, by simply collecting them and placing them face down on a table, saying: "We'll return to a consideration of these charts later if time permits, but first I would like to review with you some of the other issues of this debate."

2. Visual materials must be visible. It should be obvious that the visual aid must be large enough and that the contrasts must be sharp enough to be seen easily by the audience. A visual aid clipped from a newspaper or newsmagazine may be very helpful to the advocate, but it is usually too small to be visible to the audience. Such aids may be rendered usable by an enlarged reproduction of their essential features.

3. Simple visual materials can be effective. We may often discover visual aids that are too small or contain too much extraneous material to be usable in themselves, or we may find it desirable to develop visual aids from data we have found. In such cases, we are faced with the necessity of making our own visual aids. Some advocates are discouraged at this point and feel that only a professional artist can produce a visual aid suitable for use in the speech situation. Such is not the case. The homemade visual aid, if it is done neatly with reasonable care and precision, can be highly effective. If a chalkboard is available, it may be used for a quick sketch that does not require much precision of detail. If the details are important, however, or if the visual aid requires much time in preparation, we should make the visual aid in advance of the speech situation, preparing it on poster board and using contrasting colors, rather than attempting to prepare it during the speech itself, thus interrupting the speech and losing the attention and interest of our audience.

4. The speaker must be familiar with the visual materials. We should be so thoroughly familiar with them that we can devote full attention to communicating a point effectively. If we are using pie graphs to indicate energy sources and energy consumption, for example, we should be able to indicate the wedge representing water power unhesitatingly at the appropriate moment and not have to interrupt our speech to search for it.

If the visual materials include any mechanism or moving parts, we should be thoroughly familiar with its operation and should check the equipment immediately before beginning the speech. The salesperson who is not quite sure how a pocket calculator operates to perform powers, reciprocals, and other functions would probably lose the sale.

In composing a speech, we should give careful consideration to the possible use of these materials. Carefully selected, well-prepared visual materials can often allow us to present complex matters more briefly than would be possible by an oral presentation alone, and they may make our case more effective.

Exercises

1. Prepare a five-minute speech in which you support or oppose a proposition of policy. Drawing on the factors of style considered in this chapter, compose the speech in a style best suited to your audience.

2. Refer to newspapers and magazines for the texts of recent argumentative speeches by national figures. Find examples of three of the following; illustrate your examples by quotations from the text of the speech.

a. Appropriate vocabulary	g. Fable
b. Imagery	h. Audience participation
c. Climax	i. Narrative
d. Coherence	j. Comparison
e. Unity	k. Telling detail
f. Emphasis	l. Contrast

3. Prepare a five-minute speech in which you support or oppose a proposition of policy. Drawing on the methods of dramatization considered in this chapter, dramatize one of the major arguments.

4. Prepare a five-minute speech in which you support or oppose a proposition of policy. Use visual aids to supplement your case.

5. What speaker, prominent on the public scene today, do you regard as being particularly effective in speech composition? Justify your choice by citing specific examples from his speeches.

Chapter 19

Presenting the Case: Delivery

Once we have composed our case, our next step is to deliver it. It is not enough to have a well-composed case — although that is essential. In order for the speech to achieve its impact, we must add effective delivery. The importance of delivery in oral communication has been stressed since the days of Aristotle, who pointed out: "Success in delivery is of the utmost importance to the effect of the speech."[1] Modern students of communication theory confirm this classical dictum. McCroskey examined a number of experimental studies and concluded: "Good delivery allows the rhetorically strong message to have its normal effect. Poor delivery tends to inhibit the effect of a verbal message."[2] Hopefully, we have composed a rhetorically strong message; now we must prepare to deliver that message in a way that will secure the desired decision from our audience.

I. Methods of Delivery

There are four methods of delivery available to the speaker: impromptu, extemporaneous, manuscript, and memorization.

A. Impromptu

We use the impromptu method of delivery when we make little or no preparation for the presentation of our thoughts. In fact, since the impromptu speech is made without specific preparation, we have no organized case and do not compose the speech in advance of delivery. If at this very moment we were asked to defend our views on United States foreign policy, our response would be impromptu. We could draw on our general knowledge of the subject, on such information as we happen to gather in our reading, and on such ideas as we may have formulated, but we would have to organize our ideas as we go along.

The one advantage of being familiar with the impromptu method is

---

[1] Aristotle, *Rhetoric*, III, 1.

[2] James C. McCroskey, *An Introduction to Rhetorical Communication* (Englewood Cliffs, N.J.: Prentice-Hall, 1968), p. 208.

that in some circumstances it is the only method available to the advocate. When news of an important development is received in the Senate during the day's session, for example, a senator might find it desirable to speak on this matter at once. A sales representative might meet a prospective customer unexpectedly and find that this is just the opportune moment to attempt to make a sale. The business executive, while attending a board of directors' meeting, might learn of a new problem for the first time and be called upon to participate in debate on the problem immediately. Each of them would probably have a good general background on the problem, but in these situations they would have had no opportunity to make specific preparations. Since the impromptu method is often the only available method, argumentation teachers sometimes require their students to present impromptu arguments, so they may have experience in organizing and presenting a case under impromptu conditions.

The best preparation for meeting the impromptu situation when it arises is experience in delivering prepared speeches. Actually, we may plan and organize the impromptu speech to a degree. We will have at least a few seconds in which to organize our thoughts, and, if we are experienced speakers, we can do much in a very short time. Some speakers have developed the faculty of thinking ahead and planning their future lines of argument while they are speaking on matters of lesser importance that do not require their full attention.

B. Extemporaneous

The extemporaneous speech is a prepared speech. In delivering the extemporaneous speech, we neither read from a manuscript nor memorize our entire speech. We may or may not make use of notes; we may or may not read short quotations as a part of our speech; and we may or may not memorize a few short passages of our speech.

The extemporaneous method provides almost all of the advantages found in other methods of delivery and very few disadvantages. Its greatest advantage lies in the fact that it is both prepared and flexible, allowing us to plan exactly what we wish to say and the way in which we wish to say it. Thus all of the advantages of building the case and speech composition may be brought to bear in the extemporaneous speech. In addition, because the speech is planned but not frozen, we can modify our presentation to adapt to the situation and to the statements of previous speakers. Since we can watch the audience closely during the speech, we can gauge the listeners' reaction and adapt the speech to their response.

The disadvantages of the extemporaneous method are few. The extemporaneous speech does admit a greater possibility of error than do the manuscript or memorized speeches, but careful planning and preparation can minimize this risk. When the time element is critical, as in a radio or television speech, the extemporaneous method may pose some problems for the beginning speaker. It is more difficult to control the time with this method than with the manuscript or memorized speech. Experienced speakers, however, develop an excellent sense of time, and the college debater has little difficulty in adjusting to the time limits prevailing in intercollegiate debate. The repeat guests on television talk shows are those who have learned to adapt to the strict time requirements while retaining the spontaneity of the extemporaneous method. Political candidates, who are faced with the necessity of making numerous speeches each day at the height of the campaign, usually develop "The Speech"—a block of material in which they can present their views extemporaneously in as little as five minutes or extend them to as much as twenty minutes as the occasion requires. Almost all debaters, be they students or senators, use the extemporaneous method of delivery. Only extemporaneous delivery provides for the carefully prepared on-the-spot adaptation and refutation so essential to effective debate.

The extemporaneous method most frequently makes use of note cards. Typically, they are 4 x 6 cards, which the speaker holds in his hand or places on a lectern. For television much larger cards are used, and they usually are placed "off camera."

C. Manuscript

In using the manuscript method, we prepare our speech carefully, write it out in full, and read it to our audience. The advantage of the manuscript is that it provides us with the maximum opportunity to say exactly what we want to say in exactly the way we want to say it. The presence of the manuscript will give us assurance that under the pressure of the debate, we will speak the words exactly as we have planned them. When minimizing the possibility of error is the prime consideration, the manuscript speech is generally used. In delivering a State of the Union Message or other major state addresses, all Presidents of the United States, even those who were brilliant extemporaneous speakers, have used the manuscript method. A "slip of the tongue" in such a situation would be too dangerous; it might lead to a domestic or international crisis.

The disadvantages of the manuscript method include the lack of flexibility and the difficulty of reading the manuscript effectively. Since the manuscript is prepared in advance of the occasion, it does not provide for adjustments to the situation, to previous speeches, or to audience reaction. Furthermore, the manuscript often becomes a barrier between the speaker and the audience when the speaker's objective is to establish rapport with the audience. Audiences would rather have the speaker *talk with* them than *read at* them. Skilled speakers, when they find it necessary to use a manuscript, often plan their delivery in such a way as to create the impression that they frequently depart from the manuscript.

Experienced debaters have found it worthwhile to master the art of effective delivery from a manuscript. As we practice the delivery of our speech, we should give careful consideration to the "Steps to Good Delivery" considered later in this chapter.

Those portions of the speech which are under the advocate's complete control — that is, where there is little or no need or opportunity for adaptation — must reflect his maximum skill in speech composition. The first affirmative speech, for example, provides the greatest opportunity for advocates to say precisely what they want to say in precisely the way they want to say it and to deliver their carefully chosen words with maximum effectiveness. The well-planned first affirmative speech is a masterpiece of composition and delivery. The issues, the contentions, the transitions, the analysis, the evidence[3] and the summaries should be polished to perfection so that they will be recorded on the judge's flowsheet — or lodged in the minds of the audience — precisely as the speaker wants them. The well-written and well-delivered first affirmative speech is a graceful, forceful, highly literate, lucid, cogent statement that should be a powerful factor in advancing the affirmative's case. There are many places in a debate where a well-planned manuscript may be adapted to the situation. Experienced debaters prepare "blocks" or "speech segments" for these situations, that is, short manuscripts, which by use of extemporaneous methods may be blended into their total speech. Negative debaters prepare blocks of plan attacks. The plan attacks, of course, must be adapted to the specific case of the affirmative. Frequently, however, it is possible to anticipate a considerable part of this portion of the negative's case. The negative speaker may select from a number of previously prepared blocks — choosing the one *directly* relating to the particular affirmative plan of the moment and carefully adapting it to the *specifics* of that plan. The debater is cautioned that judges and audiences do not like "canned arguments." The scripted plan attack will work effectively only if it is *adapted* to the exact plan used by the affirmative and only if it is presented so that it appears spontaneous.

D. Memorization

Memorization of the entire speech is little used by advocates today. This method is still required in many college oratory contests, because it furnishes an educational opportunity to emphasize considerations of speech composition and delivery. Outside of the contest situation, however, most advocates do not feel they can afford the time necessary to memorize a speech. The memorized speech is, in fact, a manuscript that has been memorized. It provides all of the advantages of the manuscript method, as well as the additional advantage that the manuscript is not present. Memorization also provides the maximum opportunity for polished presentation. With this ad-

---

[3] Again the admonition — evidence may be edited to eliminate extraneous material — but the advocate must scrupulously preserve the author's intent.

vantage, however, there is a potential disadvantage. Inexperienced advocates who memorize their speeches often appear stilted and artificial and lacking in apparent spontaneity. Further disadvantages of the memorized speech include the time necessary for complete memorization, the lack of flexibility also found in the manuscript speech, and a special hazard in the possibility that the advocate may forget a portion of his speech. Many speakers, however, *do* find it advantageous to memorize speech segments.

The answer to an obvious plan attack may be rambling and ineffective the first time debaters respond to it. After they have met the attack in essentially the same form several times, they may hone their answers to perfection and present them concisely and incisively. Prudent advocates preplan answers to recurring problems—and to problems they anticipate may arise.

A consideration of the advantages and the disadvantages of the four possible methods makes it apparent that in most situations the best method for most advocates is the extemporaneous method. In using the extemporaneous method, we frequently find it necessary to have at hand evidence cards that contain quotations or statements we wish to use in a very specific form. Often we find it advantageous to memorize brief passages of our speech. For example, we might wish to conclude a speech with a very carefully phrased summary. If we felt that reading this summary from a card would lessen its effect and yet we wished to be very precise in that statement, we might memorize our concluding sentences. And when our opponent introduces important unexpected matters into the debate, we must meet them with impromptu refutation.

II. Steps to Good Delivery

A. The Speech Outline

The speech outline is different from the brief or case outline. The brief is a carefully drafted logical document. Were it presented orally as a speech, the brief would be dry, dull, and uninteresting to the average listener. The case outline, as an operational plan that coordinates the evidence and reasoning of the speakers on a given side of the proposition, is more specifically adapted to the audience than the brief, but it is not a speech outline. The speech outline is a detailed plan of exactly what we intend to say, and it indicates the manner in which we intend to say it to a specific audience.

B. The Speaker's Notes

The speaker's notes are an adaptation of the case outline. Typically, our notes consist of a number of cards of convenient size, which contain an out-

```
┌─────────────────────────────────────────────────────────────────┐
│                                                                   │
│   OTHER BARRIERS TO RECEIVING COMPREHENSIVE MEDICAL CARE          │
│                                                                   │
│   A.  Ignorance rather than money is real barrier.               │
│       1.  Advisory Board for Public Policy quote                 │
│       2.  Newsweek quote                                          │
│       3.  Mueller quote                                           │
│   B.  Fear of physicians and hospitals is a barrier.             │
│       1.  Sen. Hansen, Hearings quote                            │
│       2.  Health Care Story quote                                │
│   C.  Shortage of physicians is a barrier.                       │
│       1.  Robbins quote                                           │
│       2.  U.S. News and World Report quote                       │
│       3.  Cray quote                                             │
│   D.  Maldistribution of physicians is a barrier.                │
│       1.  Nolan quote                                            │
│       2.  N.Y. Times quote                                        │
│       3.  Sen. Kennedy, Hearings quote                           │
│       4.  Times quote                                             │
│       5.  HEW quote                                              │
│                                                                   │
└─────────────────────────────────────────────────────────────────┘
```

line of our speech and are assembled together with the various evidence cards we plan to use.

Although the brief and case outline must carefully follow the principles of good outlining, there are no rules governing the form of the speaker's notes. The only consideration is that they serve effectively to remind us of both the major structure and the details of our case. (See the typical example of a speaker's notes—one of several "negative block" cards prepared by a second negative speaker for use in a debate on "comprehensive medical care.")

C. Preparation

Just as we must prepare by building our case and composing our speech, we must also prepare the delivery of our speech. Experienced advocates do not deliver a speech for the first time to those who render the decision. Rather, they deliver it a number of times, preferably to colleagues who will be able to give useful suggestions on improving the delivery. If we consider the problems of delivery for the first time as we address those who render the decision, our statement will be far less effective than if we have delivered our speech or block a number of times, anticipated the potential problems in delivery, and worked out the most effective way of presenting a position. The requirement of flexibility, of course, means that we will revise our speech up to the very moment of delivery. We should also anticipate probable arguments of our opponents and practice the way we will answer them should they be used.

President Ford spent a week working with his advisers and a 12-man production crew to prepare for one fireside chat. When a television commentator took a "cheap shot" and said it was "a rehearsed speech complete with props," one of the President's staff responded, "What would he like, an *un*rehearsed speech? What do they think this is, amateur night?"[4] Obviously, neither presidents nor debaters want to appear amateurish. The only way to avoid this is through thorough preparation.

III. Nonverbal Communication

We communicate with others not only through language — verbal behavior — but by means of nonverbal behavior as well. When we address an audience, we use not only verbal language but also vocal expression and body language. The meaning the audience perceives from our message comes not from our words alone, nor alone from vocal expression or body language. The message is perceived as an interrelation of all these factors. For example, such a simple verbal message as "Hi" can, with the addition of appropriate vocal expression and body language, be perceived to mean: "I love you," "Have I seen you somewhere before?" "Don't interrupt me now, I'm too busy to talk," or a wide variety of other meanings. Thus, it is our task, as advocates, to use the techniques of nonverbal communication to clarify and enhance our message. Nonverbal communications must be *consistent* with the verbal communications, however. Some thought Nixon was insincere and contrived in his TV appearances, maintaining that when he made a verbal statement, "It's great to be back here in California!" the nonverbal clue — the smile — came just a fraction of a second too late.

The importance of nonverbal communication is stressed by modern students of communication theory. Hance, Ralph, and Wiksell maintain, "The ideas and feelings that we want to express to our audience are determined as much by nonverbal behavior and by vocal signals as they are by the words we use."[5] Harrison has estimated that "in face-to-face communication no more than 35 percent of the social meaning is carried in the verbal messages."[6] Much of the remaining 65 percent of meaning comes from the delivery of nonverbal messages.

[4] John Weisman, "He Always Hits His Marks," *TV Guide* (May 31, 1975), p. 7.

[5] Kenneth G. Hance, David C. Ralph, and Milton J. Wiksell, *Principles of Speaking*, 3rd ed. (Belmont, Calif.: Wadsworth Publishing Co., 1975), p. 250.

[6] Randall Harrison, "Nonverbal Communication: Explorations into Time, Space, Action and Object," in James H. Campbell and Hal W. Hepler, *Dimensions in Communication*, 2nd ed. (Belmont, Calif.: Wadsworth Publishing Co., 1970), p. 285.

A. Vocal Expression

We communicate with our audience partly by means of vocal expression. The words we pronounce are intended to be heard by our listeners and to have meaning to them. Some considerations of vocal expression important to the advocate include:

1. Rate The rate at which we talk is important. We must speak slowly enough for the audience to follow us, but not so slowly that the audience will lose interest in our words. Beginning advocates sometimes try to pack too much evidence and reasoning into a short time; consequently, they are forced to deliver their speech at so rapid a rate that the audience cannot follow them without difficulty. Those who render the decision are not always willing to make the necessary effort to follow them, and they may thus defeat their own purposes. The solution to this problem is often found in careful speech composition. Rather than using three pieces of evidence, and delivering them at too rapid a rate for easy comprehension, it would be better to use one well-chosen piece of evidence, integrating it carefully into the case and helping to drive it home by use of an effective rate. We may do well to listen to good speakers both in audience situations and on radio and television, and note the rate they use; and we should adapt our own rate to suit the needs of our audience.

Experienced varsity debaters operating in tournament situations on the national circuit are under great pressure to pack as much evidence and argument as possible into the time limits. Their delivery may often exceed 200 words per minute. (The second affirmative speaker in Appendix B reached 245 wpm in the rebuttal.) Their opponents will strain to follow every word; the judge, usually an argumentation professor, understands the situation and often is willing to concentrate on the speech and record the arguments accurately on a flow sheet. The human mind is easily capable of absorbing far more than 200 words a minute, *provided the listener is willing to concentrate and provided the delivery is intelligible.* We are warned, however, that audiences of the general public are not willing to provide the same degree of concentration that is available in the tournament situation. Successful advocates are able to adapt their rate to the requirements of the judge and audience. Observe the delivery of television network anchormen — their rate is usually ideally suited to general public audiences.

2. Pitch Pitch refers to the tone level of the voice. Men generally have a deeper pitch than women and adults a deeper pitch than children. A pitch appropriate to the advocate's age and sex is an important consideration.

3. Intensity Intensity refers to the loudness or softness of the speaker's voice. As a minimum, our voice must be loud enough to be heard easily by everyone we want to reach. In some circumstances, this may require the use of a public address system. In such cases, we should address the microphone with normal conversational intensity and allow the electronic system to provide the needed amplification rather than shout into the microphone. At the same time we must guard against too much intensity. Beginning debaters sometimes make the mistake of addressing a small audience in a classroom with an intensity that would be appropriate for a large gathering in an auditorium. Our intensity should be such as to make it easy and pleasant for those who render the decision to hear us.

4. Flexibility We should be able to adapt our voice, as well as our arguments, to the situation. One type of delivery is appropriate at a football rally; quite another, in a small committee meeting.

We may use variation of rate, intensity, and pitch to add effectiveness to our delivery. For example, when we come to a particularly important concept in a speech, we might use a much slower rate, greater intensity, and a deeper pitch than we had previously used. When we come to a minor transition, we might provide contrast by increasing rate, lowering intensity, and raising pitch. These variations must be accomplished with subtlety, however. If the variation is too obvious, it calls attention to itself rather than to the argument the speaker wishes to emphasize. Listen to good speakers in audience situations or on radio or television. Their use of variation to increase effectiveness will not be apparent on the surface, but if we look for the use of variation, we will see how good speakers vary their delivery to achieve a desired effect.

5. Quality The quality of our voice is important—we want our voice to be such that people will find it easy and pleasant to listen to. Good quality results from the presence of good resonance and from the absence of undesirable noise elements in the voice. Undesirable qualities resulting from the improper production of tone are breathiness, nasality, huskiness, and throatiness. Other voice qualities, considered undesirable in most circumstances, include tones that are aspirate, guttural, falsetto, pectoral, metallic, or shrill. We should try to cultivate the presence of well-modulated, resonant tones. Under certain conditions (considered under "Expressional Patterns"), we will deliberately use unpleasant voice qualities to convey special meaning to our audience. With these special exceptions, which are confined to isolated words or brief passages, our overall quality should be such as to produce a pleasant reaction in the audience.

6. Fluency We should cultivate verbal fluency. Because beginning speakers are sometimes at a loss for words, they may vocalize pauses while they grope for the next word and fill their speech with "er," "ah," and "uh." A good knowledge of the subject, a well-developed case outline, a well-composed speech plan, and advance delivery of the speech will help the advocate to overcome these problems and acquire the necessary verbal fluency. Practice in impromptu speaking, too, helps us to develop verbal fluency.

7. Expressional Patterns Our concern with delivery is not limited to the production of clear, pleasant, readily intelligible speech. On many occasions we will use nuances of delivery to convey meaning. Skillful advocates use rate, pitch, intensity, quality, and inflection to create an expressional pattern giving special meaning and emphasis to certain words and phrases in their speeches. With a well-chosen expressional pattern, we can do much to clarify and communicate our meaning. No one who has ever heard protesters snarl "Pigs" could fail to comprehend their loathing of the police. Expressional patterns can be used to express friendly as well as unfriendly attitudes. Ed McMahon on TV's "Tonight Show" sets the stage with a warm and friendly "H-e-e-r-r-e's Johnny!"

B. Body Language

We communicate with our audience partly with verbal language, partly with vocal expression, and partly with body language. Just as audiences are influenced by the speaker they hear, so too are they influenced by the speaker they see. Radio speaking is, of course, an exception, but when the speaker appears before audiences, in person or on television, the audiences are influenced by what they see. Birdwhistell believes that we do most of our "talking" with our body movements. He maintains that we pour out information with our shrugs, our hands and body movements, our eyes, and our facial expressions and that these signals are often *more* reliable messages than the words we utter.[7] Some considerations of body language important to the advocate include:

1. Eye Contact We should maintain direct eye contact with members of the audience throughout our speech. Of course, we will have to refer to our notes or manuscript, but this should be done as briefly as possible. The *vast majority* of our time should be spent in looking *at* and talking *to* our audience. If there is a key individual in the audience—as a single judge for a debate—we may focus most of our attention on that key individual. We will, however, establish some eye contact with others in the audience. In a general audience situation, we should make sure that we establish eye contact with persons in all parts of the audience, thereby getting vital *feedback* from the audience.

2. Movement Our movement, when speaking, should be *purposeful.* Our movement should aid us in communicating with our audience. The way we approach the lectern, for example, is important. If we approach the lectern with a confident step and with quiet authority take possession of the rostrum, our ethos is enhanced. Our movements should be easy, economical, purpose-

---

[7] Ray L. Birdwhistell, *Introduction to Kinesics: An Annotation System for Analysis of Body Motion and Gesture* (Washington, D.C.: Foreign Service Institute, Department of State, 1952).

ful, yet apparently spontaneous. We should not remain in a fixed position behind the lectern, nor rooted to one spot on the rostrum as if we were wooden Indians. For example, we might move away from the lectern and move closer to our audience to emphasize a major issue; we might move from one side of the rostrum to the other as we make a transition from one issue to another.

Our movement should never be such as to compete with our case for the attention of the audience. The story, which just might be true, is told of a young prosecuting attorney who lost his first case in a burglary trial, although he had ample evidence of the guilt of the accused. The novice lawyer was so nervous that in presenting his evidence he continually paced to and fro before the jury. This pacing so attracted the attention of the jury that they concentrated on estimating how many steps he took in each direction and how many miles he walked in the course of the trial, rather than following the case he was attempting to present.

3. Gestures Our gestures should be purposeful, aiding our communication with the audience. There is a distinct preference today for the restrained gesture in contrast with the flamboyant breast-beating of another century. As with movement, the gesture should be easy, economical, purposeful, yet apparently spontaneous. When we use a three-fingered gesture as we say, for example, "There are three major issues . . . ," it should appear natural and spontaneous rather than calculated.

4. Facial Expression Our facial expression should be consistent with the attitude we are trying to express. One novice debater was so pleased to be participating in his first intercollegiate debate that he smiled happily as he said, "The energy crisis is going to produce the worst depression this country has ever seen." The incongruity of the speaker's pleasant smile did much to minimize the effect of his argument on this issue.

Experienced communicators such as Johnny Carson or William Buckley can convey a world of meaning by a tilt of an eyebrow, the toss of a head, the curl of a lip, or by a slight change of expression. And, of course, others are constantly trying to "read" our facial expressions. After an important conference, reporters often tell us that the President or the Secretary of State looked "pleased" or "tense," "confident" or "worried."

Speech delivery and composition involve many considerations. As in many other arts, the great art is to conceal the art. As advocates, our purpose is to win a decision. We use the arts of speech communication to help attain this objective. When the debate is over, we are not interested in having the audience applaud our clever word choice, or comment on the quality of our voice, or note our graceful gestures; rather, we want them to make the decision we have argued. The arts of speech communication must never attract attention to themselves, but must be blended into the total communicative effort to secure the decision of the audience.

Exercises

1. Read a transcript of a Presidential press conference. Can you identify the questions the President expected and for which he had prepared an extemporaneous reply, and those questions which he did not expect and to which he gave impromptu replies? Report your findings to the class and support your conclusions with quotations from the press conference.

2. Use the following method to gain some experience in impromptu speaking. At one class meeting, the instructor will announce a proposition of policy that will serve as the subject for impromptu speeches. At the next class meeting, the instructor will have a number of slips of paper, each containing a statement of an issue, line of argument, or piece of evidence important in this proposition. Draw one of these slips at random and support or refute the statement.

3. Use the following method to gain some experience in manuscript speaking: Prepare a three-minute speech in which you support or oppose a proposition of policy. Plan this speech so that the greater part of your time will be spent in reading quotations or carefully phrased statements from 4×6 cards or from a manuscript. (Some speakers find it convenient to arrange their cards or script in acetate jackets.) Plan your delivery so that you will handle your materials smoothly and communicate effectively with the audience while reading. The instructor and your classmates will criticize your delivery and offer suggestions for improvement.

4. Use the following method to gain some experience in the use of vocal expression. Arrange with your instructor to prepare a tape recording outside of class. In the recording present a three-minute speech in which you support or oppose a proposition of policy. Use the various considerations of vocal expression to make your delivery more effective. Play the recording in class. Your instructor and classmates will criticize your delivery and offer suggestions for improvement.

5. Use the following method to gain some experience in the use of body language. Arrange with your instructor to prepare a videotape recording outside of class. In the recording present a three-minute speech in which you support or oppose a proposition of policy. Use the various considerations of body language to make your delivery more effective. Play the videotape recording in class. Your instructor and classmates will criticize your delivery and offer suggestions for improvement.

6. Prepare a three-minute speech in which you support or oppose a proposition of policy. Use all of the considerations of speech delivery to present your case with maximum effectiveness. Your instructor and classmates will criticize your delivery and offer suggestions for improvement.

Chapter 20

Evaluating the Debate

We want to know "What was the vote?" "What was the verdict?" "Who won?" Members of Congress put their voting cards into the electronic slots, then the electronic scoreboards on the gallery walls light up, and we learn the fate of legislation. The judge in the courtroom asks the foreman of the jury to state the verdict, and we learn the outcome of the trial. In educational debate the judge rises to announce the decision, or in a tournament situation the teams gather to await the announcement of results. Everything we have considered thus far builds to the climatic moment—the decision.

How do we evaluate the debate? What is the basis for the decision? The decision should be based either on the proposition of debate or on the debate itself. In substantive debate, the decision should be rendered on the proposition itself; in educational debate, the decision should be based on the debate itself—that is the comparative merits of the opposing teams, not the merits of the proposition.

I. Evaluating the Substantive Debate

A. The Proper Basis for Evaluation

The decision on a substantive debate should answer the question "Which side is right?" To arrive at the answer, persons rendering decisions should do the following:

1. Apply their knowledge of argumentation to evaluate the evidence and reasoning advanced by the opposing advocates.
2. Take into consideration all relevant evidence and reasoning that was not introduced into the debate.

Having done this, they are in a position to answer the question "Which side is right?"

For example, in a Senate debate on the proposition "Resolved: That the defense budget should be reduced to ——," the affirmative advocates might have presented the better debate case; their evidence and reasoning might have been superior to that of the negative. Some senators, however, by virtue of their position on certain committees, might have had access to secret

309

information that led them to believe that a reduction in the defense budget would be contrary to the national interest. Because this information was secret they could not introduce it into the debate. Thus, although the affirmative had done the better job of debating, these senators might vote for the negative, which they believed to be right even though it had not proved its position in the debate.

B. Other Factors Influencing Evaluation

Other considerations sometimes enter into the evaluation of the substantive debate. Sometimes the decision is rendered to answer the question "Which side is in my best interest?" and sometimes it is based on matters entirely irrelevant to the debate.

It is not altogether unreasonable to suggest that legislators sometimes vote in a certain way in order to please their party leaders or special interest groups and thus secure patronage or certain favors. Legislators, of course, are not the only ones who sometimes render decisions based on the answer to the question "Which side is in my best interest?" For example, a businessman might vote against a proposed policy, which had been proved better than the status quo in a debate at a board of directors meeting, because it would be contrary to his personal financial interests. At a civic club meeting, some members might vote for a proposition that debate had demonstrated to be unwise because the social leaders of the community supported the plan. Also, it would probably not require extensive research on the part of students to find examples from campus politics of votes in student organizations that were not based on the merits of the proposition.

Decisions on substantive debates are further confused because decisions are sometimes based on matters entirely irrelevant to the proposition. For example, Dwight Eisenhower and John F. Kennedy had a charisma for millions of voters, while Lyndon Johnson and Richard Nixon, even when winning, did not arouse the same hero worship.

Although we must recognize that decisions on substantive debates are sometimes based on selfish motives or irrelevant factors, we must also recognize that debate is the best way of solving many of the problems of our society. Great debates have influenced the course of our history, and on many occasions those who rendered the decision rose above their personal interest when casting their votes. The responsibility of the advocates is to have sufficient knowledge of the principles of argumentation and debate that they may be able to demonstrate that their side is right. Aristotle summed up this responsibility when he wrote of the value of rhetoric:

Rhetoric is valuable first, because truth and justice are by nature stronger than their opposites; so that, when decisions are not made as they should be, the speakers with right on their side have only themselves to blame for the outcome.[1]

[1] Aristotle, *Rhetoric*, I, 1.

This principle of Aristotle's can apply only in a free society. In communist Russia, for instance, many persons with right on their side have been sent to concentration camps without any opportunity to convince any significant number of persons. Even in a free society, however, decisions on substantive debates are not always rendered on the merits of the proposition. Intelligent self-interest requires that we should be able to determine which side of a proposition is right when we are required to render a decision on a proposition of importance to us. To do this, we must have knowledge of the principles of argumentation and debate and be able to apply the proper basis of evaluation.

II. Evaluating Strategy

Evaluation of the strategy used by debaters sometimes poses a problem for the judge of both the substantive and the educational debate. The problem apparently arises from a tendency to consider strategy as something "bad." Actually, of course, strategy is inherent in all argumentative speeches and writings. In every argumentative speech or writing, the advocates must select materials; they must arrange materials; they must decide when and how to use these materials and how they will present them—this is strategy.

We have our Constitution partly because it is better than the Articles of Confederation that preceded it and partly because the advocates of that Constitution used more effective strategy than their opponents in the debates that preceded its adoption. Various federal aid for education bills were for years defeated in Congress partly because of the strategy of certain congressmen in adding antisegregation amendments to those bills. Many of our present laws and regulations, and the policies of many private organizations, are in force because their supporters used more effective strategy than their opponents. It is also quite probable that some very good laws and policies have been defeated because their supporters used inept strategy. Thus, in both substantive debate and in educational debate, a decision should never be rendered for or against a side because it has used strategy—both sides necessarily used strategy. The question should be "Was the total case sound?"

III. Evaluating the Educational Debate

A. Judged as an Educational Process

There are two contexts within which a debate may be judged: as a substantive debate in which the decision is rendered on the merits of the proposition or on other factors or as an educational process, with the decision rendered on the comparative merits of the opposing debaters. A decision based on the merits of the proposition, or on the other factors that sometimes influence the decision on a substantive debate, is not admissible in educational debate. Such a decision might have little or no reference to the merits of the debate itself. Because it represents the judge's opinion of the proposition, rather than his evaluation of the debaters, it has no value in an educational process. In order to contribute to the educational process of debate, the decision on an educational debate must be based on the *comparative merits of the opposing teams;* and it is the function of the judge to answer the question "Which team did the better debating?" Obviously, such a decision must be rendered entirely without reference to the judge's personal feelings about the merits of the proposition.

B. Judged by Educators Expert in Argumentation

Educators are defined within this context as individuals whose special knowledge of argumentation and debate qualify them as experts in this field. They are also well-informed on the subject matter of the proposition of debate. Only such persons are, competent to perform the function of a judge, since only they have the knowledge necessary to evaluate the educational process of debate and the ability to render an educationally valuable decision. The American Forensic Association emphasizes the importance of competent judging in its "Code of Contests in Oratory":

Contests should be judged only by persons competent in speech evaluation. Normally such competence will derive from speech education or from professional experience in public speaking. Judging short of this standard is indefensible. The contest becomes a sham if the occasion for judging is misconceived as an opening for honoring local dignitaries or exploiting their publicity value, or is simply misunderstood as an incidental aspect of the contest situation. Competent criticism should be the right of the participants.

IV. Functions of the Judge

Judges of educational debates have two functions: one, they must discern which team did the better debating; two, they must report their decisions in an educationally useful manner.

A. Discerning Which Team Did the Better Debating

Judges of educational debates must answer the question "Which team did the better debating?" as the basis for the decision.[2] To answer this question, they are guided by certain principles.

[2] There are two penalty situations for which a team might be given an automatic loss. One, considered later in this section, involves the use of evidence of doubtful credibility. The second is a forfeit (usually for being late for the scheduled starting time of a debate) as stipulated in the rules of a tournament.

1. They must apply their total knowledge of argumentation and debate. In debates, an almost infinite range of possible problems may become factors in judging. Therefore, they must be able to bring to bear a comprehensive knowledge of the principles of argumentation and debate to evaluate the problems and render the decision.

2. They must set aside their special knowledge of the subject for the duration of the debate. Although judges are usually expected to have only the knowledge of well-informed persons on the subject of the debate, often they have devoted much study to the subject and frequently acquire considerable special knowledge. This additional knowledge may produce certain attitudes, stereotypes, anticipations, or even occasional distortions in their thinking on the proposition. Their responsibility as judges requires that they set this knowledge aside for the duration of the debate and, in rendering the decision, consider only the evidence and reasoning that the students introduced into the debate. For example, one team may introduce some evidence found in an article by Mr. A. The judge may know that Mr. A's position is superficial and that it could easily be refuted by evidence found in a scholarly book written by Mr. B. However, the judge must set this knowledge aside for the duration of the debate. Unless and until the opposing team refutes the weak evidence drawn from Mr. A's article, that evidence must be accepted at its face value within the context of the debate. The subject-matter experts ordinarily do not make good judges for educational debates. Because of their very expertness in the field, they have usually formed considered judgments on the proposition, after long and careful study, and consequently find it exceedingly difficult to set this judgment aside for the duration of the debate.

Judges may properly draw on their special knowledge of the subject in critiques to suggest ways in which the debaters may improve their arguments. Here judges take cognizance of the strength or weakness of the subject-matter knowledge of the debaters and reflect their findings in the quality-rating points on the ballot. Should judges discover a deliberate misuse of evidence, they should impose an appropriate penalty. The American Forensic Association's "Standards" stipulates: "No team clearly guilty of using evidence of doubtful credibility in a debate should be awarded a decision, regardless of other circumstances."

3. They must base their decisions on the debate as it is presented. Judges, since they are experts on argumentation and debate, could undoubtedly refute easily some of the arguments advanced in the debate. They might know that one team could have taken a much stronger position than it took. However, they must never require the students to debate *them* rather than the opposing team. They must never ask, "Could I refute a particular argument?" but rather "Did the opposing team refute that argument?" They do not ask whether a team's position was weak or strong in relation to the ideal position, but whether the team's position was weaker or stronger than that of their opponents. For example, in debating the proposition "Resolved: That executive control of United States foreign policy should be significantly curtailed," an affirmative team took the position that the United States should adopt a foreign policy of isolation. In the opinion of one educator who was asked to judge this debate, a foreign policy of isolation would be folly for the United States. His opinion, however, was irrelevant to his function as a judge. The question was not "Is isolation good or bad for the United States?" but rather "Did the affirmative team support its case for curtailing of executive control of United States foreign policy within the context of the debate?"

In fact, since the debate must be judged within its own framework, almost any statement made or any position taken by either team stands until refuted—with the exception of the last affirmative speech, when the judge may take judicial notice of the validity of evidence or of the introduction of a new concept. If a team fails to ask the judge to take judicial notice of an obvious error or contradiction in their opponents' case, the judge must assume they have failed to detect the error and it must stand against them.

Judges, of course, take cognizance of the strengths and weaknesses in a debate case and refer to them in their critiques and reflect their findings in the quality-rating points on the ballot.

4. They must take comprehensive notes during the debate. Experienced educators who have judged thousands of debates are known for the care with which they take notes during a debate. All judges would do well to develop a comprehensive note-taking system, so that they can record all

---

The Flow Sheet

1 A	1 N	2 A	2 N	1 NR	1 AR	2 NR	2 AR
xxx		xxx		xxx	xxx		xxx
xxx	xxx	xxx			xxx		
xxx	xxx	xxx		xxx		xxx	xxx
xxx	xxx	xxx		xxx	xxx		

"Case" Side

1 A	1 N	2 A	2 N	1 NR	1 AR	2 NR	2 AR
xxx			xxx		xxx	xxx	
xxx			xxx		xxx	xxx	xxx
xxx							
	xxx	xxx					
	xxx	xxx					

Plan Side

of the significant developments during the debate in order to evaluate the debate effectively. Experienced educators judging educational debates find the flow sheet to be the most convenient method of taking comprehensive notes.

Judges using the flow-sheet method seek to record the development of each issue throughout the debate. This is essentially similar to the debater's flow sheet considered earlier in Chapter 15, but with one difference. The debater—on a flow sheet—may make notes to aid in planning future speeches; the judge, of course, will record the arguments only as they are actually presented by the debaters. A sheet or sheets of paper, usually $8\frac{1}{2}'' \times 14''$ or larger, will be used. The issues are recorded horizontally and the paper may be ruled vertically to indicate the various speeches.

In the diagram (*see inset*) the judge's notes on the development of each issue are indicated by "xxx." The arguments of the first affirmative speaker are recorded in the column headed "1 A" and his rebuttal arguments are recorded in the column headed "1 AR." Similar designations are used for the other speakers.

Although the methods suggested here are designed specifically for use in judging the educational debate, they may be readily adapted for use in rendering a decision on a substantive debate. Many trial judges and attorneys use a comparable method to follow a courtroom debate, and many business executives use a comparable "balance sheet" to aid them in weighing arguments in a debate on corporate policy. Whenever it is necessary to render a decision on an important debate, it is desirable to develop some system that will facilitate the process of analyzing and weighing the arguments.

B. Reporting the Decision in an Educationally Useful Manner

The decision, as part of the educational process of debate, must be reported in a manner that will contribute to the further educational attainment of the students. This may be done either through the medium of an oral critique or by the use of a carefully prepared ballot, or by a combination of these methods.

1. The Oral Critique If the oral critique is used, the judge is allowed a few minutes to review his notes before he is called upon to present his critique. The effective critique should do the following:

1. Review the progress of the debate.
2. Cite examples of effective application of the principles of argumentation and debate.
3. Offer suggestions for improvement.
4. Cite the factors most significant in determining the decision.
5. Announce the decision.

When the oral critique is used, adequate time should be allocated for its presentation.

2. The Ballot The ballot is the more common method of reporting decisions on educational debates today, because it is often desirable to secure a written or a lasting record of the decision. When a ballot is used, an oral critique may be presented as well; or the judge may be asked to prepare a written critique on those portions of the ballot that will be handed to the participating teams. The effective ballot should do the following:

1. Record the decision on the debate.
2. Record quality-rating points on important criteria for each debater.
3. Record the rank of each debater in the debate.
4. Provide place for a written critique addressed to each debater.
5. Provide for each team a record of the achievement of each of the participants in the debate.
6. Provide a permanent record of the debate.

A ballot that meets these requirements is shown on page 317. Form C (shown) and Form E are made available by the American Forensic Association and are currently the most widely used debate ballots in the country. Form E omits the boxes and is provided on larger paper ($8^1/_2 \times 14''$) to provide more space for comments and the basis for decision. Both are prepared in convenient triplicate no-carbon form. At the conclusion of the tournament, the top (white) sheet is usually given to the affirmative; the second (yellow) sheet to the negative team; and the third (pink) sheet is retained by the tournament director.

V. Some Criteria for Evaluating Debate

The judge must draw on his or her total knowledge of argumentation and debate in evaluating the clash of evidence and argument in a specific debate. Consequently, no short list can include *all* the factors that may enter into the decision in a particular debate. The following listing includes factors that are frequently important in the decision and will thus give debaters some insight into the judge's thinking.

A. Evaluating Analysis

Is the definition of terms reasonable? (Both judges and audiences are often impatient with a quibble over terms—they tend to favor the team that states

American Forensic Association Debate Ballot   ᶠᴼᴿᴹ **C**

Division_____ Round_____ Room_____ Date_____ Judge_____

Affirmative_____ Negative_____

Check the column on each item which, on the following scale, best describes your evaluation of the speaker's effectiveness:

| 1—poor | 2—fair | 3—average | 4—excellent | 5—superior |

1st Affirmative 1 2 3 4 5	2nd Affirmative 1 2 3 4 5		1st Negative 1 2 3 4 5	2nd Negative 1 2 3 4 5
		Analysis		
		Reasoning		
		Evidence		
		Organization		
		Refutation		
		Delivery		

Total_____   Total_____   Total_____   Total_____

Team Ratings: AFFIRMATIVE: poor   fair   average   excellent   superior
NEGATIVE: poor   fair   average   excellent   superior

Rank each debater in order of excellence (1st for best, 2nd for next best, etc.).

COMMENTS:
1st Aff. (name)_____Rank (   )

COMMENTS:
1st Neg. (name)_____Rank (   )

2nd Aff. (name)_____Rank (   )

2nd Neg. (name)_____Rank (   )

REASONS FOR DECISION

In my opinion, the better debating was done by the_____
(AFFIRMATIVE OR NEGATIVE)

_____   _____
JUDGE'S SIGNATURE   SCHOOL

a reasonable definition and gets on with the debate.) Are the issues presented really the major issues inherent in the proposition? Do the debaters clearly establish them as such? Which team does the better job of focusing on the major issues? Which team developed the better strategy?

B. Evaluating Reasoning

Does the reasoning of the debaters satisfy the tests of reasoning considered earlier? Do the debaters point out weaknesses in the reasoning of their opponents? Undoubtedly, both teams will introduce conflicting reasoning on many points. The judge must therefore apply the tests of reasoning to determine which team's reasoning has the greater weight.

C. Evaluating Evidence

Does the evidence used by the debaters satisfy the tests of evidence considered earlier? Do the debaters point out weaknesses in the evidence of their opponents? Undoubtedly, both teams will introduce conflicting evidence on many points. The judge must therefore apply the tests of evidence to determine which team's evidence has the greater weight.

D. Evaluating Organization

Which team organized its case better? Which provided for the better organization of issues? Of supporting contentions? Which provided the better transition from one argument to another? From one speech to another? Which case was clearer? Easier to follow?

E. Evaluating Refutation

Which team did the better job of attacking the case of their opponents? Did they "go for the jugular vein" — and refute the material essential to their opponents' case? Or did they waste time at the periphery of the debate and never close in on the major issues? Which team did the better job of "minimax"? (The term is borrowed from military planners and means "to minimize the maximum damage an enemy can do." A team must expect that some damage will be done to their case — how effective have they been in minimizing that damage?) How effective has the team been in rebuilding those portions of their case that came under attack?

F. Evaluating Delivery

Good delivery helps the debaters in all of the matters previously considered by making the presentation more effective. Poor delivery, of course, hurts the debaters on all of these matters by making the presentation less effective. Nevertheless, many educators find it desirable to draw on their knowledge of the factors considered earlier in Chapter 19, "Presenting the Case — Delivery," and make a separate evaluation of delivery.

G. Evaluating the Whole Debate

Finally, it is important to remember that judges do *not* evaluate individual items on a ballot, assign points, and add up the score to "find out who won." The ballot is an instrument that judges use to *report* decisions. They use the flow sheet to help bring their total knowledge of argumentation and debate to bear on the amalgam of evidence and reasoning presented in debates. They carefully weigh the evidence and reasoning presented; they critically evaluate the opposing cases; they weigh the value of refutation and counter refutation; they analyze the totality of the debate. Ultimately, they answer the question "Which team did the better debating?" and *then* report that decision on the ballot and assign points to report their evaluation of the quality of debating.

VI. Functions of the Ballot

A. Reflecting the Decision

Since decisions are based on judges' total knowledge of argumentation and debate, the ballot reflects rather than determines the decision. In making decisions, judges must draw on a far wider range of criteria than could possibly be included in any ballot. The six phases of argumentation and debate included on the ballot are important in all debates, but their specific importance in the ultimate decision may vary from one debate to another.

B. Reporting the Quality of the Debaters' Work

For educational purposes, debaters should know not only judges' decisions on debates, but also their evaluation of the quality of a debate in these six important phases. In assigning quality points, judges not only compare one team with another—of course, the side doing the better debating inevitably is awarded the higher total—but they also compare the work of the debaters with the standards they expect of superior debaters at a given level of maturity and experience.

C. Ranking the Debaters

Rank is a function of quality points. Therefore, the debater receiving the highest number of quality-rating points necessarily receives the rank of 1; the next highest, 2; the next highest, 3; and the lowest, 4. The recording of rank provides no information that cannot be directly derived from the quality points; but it is recorded as a separate item for the convenience of tournament directors, who must have this information immediately available should it be necessary to break ties in a tournament. A tie in a debate is, of course, a logical impossibility. If the judge discerns that the two teams merit exactly the same number of quality points, then the decision must be awarded to the negative.[3]

D. Serving as an Educational Tool

At the conclusion of the debate or tournament, the ballots are distributed to the participants. The ballots thus become available to the director of forensics as an important educational tool. After a tournament, debate directors often arrange conferences in which they review the judges' evaluations with each student. Although the quality of a student's work will vary from one debate to another and different judges may place a somewhat different emphasis on different aspects of argumentation, the reports of the student's work in a number of different debates as recorded by a number of different judges provide important insights into the student's ability and allow the director to plan a program of further study and training suited to the student's needs.

Although forensic directors ordinarily do not judge an intercollegiate debate involving a team from their own schools, they will judge many debates between their own students as they prepare for intercollegiate debates. The evaluations given at this time are often a most valuable part of the students' education. There is usually time for a much more detailed critique than is possible in other circumstances. Since the directors have seen the students debate many times, often over a period of several years, they have considerable knowledge about their students' abilities and limitations and more insight into a student's problems than a judge who sees the student only once.

VII. Special Ballots for Special Purposes

The ballot presented on page 317 may be used for most types of debate.[4] The exceptions are the English type of debate, which uses a division of the house, and Parliamentary debate, which may use any of the various methods of voting. In addition, direct-clash debating and audience-decision debating require special ballots.

---

[3] See Chapter 3, "Presumption and Burden of Proof."

[4] See Chapter 21, "Modern Procedures in Educational Debate: Types of Debate."

UNIVERSITY DEBATING TEAMS

Judging Form for Direct-Clash Debates

Classification_____ Round_____ Date_____ Judge_____

Aff. Team_____ vs. Neg. Team_____

No. of clashes won: Aff._____ Neg._____

Therefore, the winner of this debate was the_____
                                             (Aff. or Neg.)
Team from:_____ Signed:_____
          (Name of College)   (Judge)

FOR THE AFFIRMATIVE TEAM

Aff._____ vs. Neg._____ Judge_____

Clash 1 _____   _____
Clash 2 _____   _____
Clash 3 _____   _____
Clash 4 _____   _____
Clash 5 _____   _____

No. of clashes won: Aff._____ Neg._____
Decision won by: _____

FOR THE NEGATIVE TEAM

Aff._____ vs. Neg._____ Judge_____

Clash 1 _____   _____
Clash 2 _____   _____
Clash 3 _____   _____
Clash 4 _____   _____
Clash 5 _____   _____

No. of clashes won: Aff._____ Neg._____
Decision won by: _____

A. Ballot for Direct-Clash Debating

The decision in a direct-clash debate is awarded to the first team to win three clashes, and the case as a whole is not considered in these clashes. A special type of ballot is used (see page 321).

(see page 321)

```
                    UNIVERSITY DEBATING TEAMS

                 Audience Shift-of-Opinion Ballot
_____

INSTRUCTIONS TO THE AUDIENCE:

   The debaters will appreciate your interest and coopera-
tion if you will, both before and after the debate, indicate
on this ballot your personal opinion on the proposition of
debate.
   The proposition is:  "Resolved:  That (the proposition of
debate is stated here)."
_____

BEFORE THE DEBATE              AFTER THE DEBATE
FILL OUT THIS SIDE             FILL OUT THIS SIDE

(Check one)                    (Check one)

                               ____ I believe more strongly
                                    in the affirmative than
                                    I did.

____ I believe in the          ____ I believe in the
     affirmative of the             affirmative of the
     resolution.                    resolution.

____ I am undecided.           ____ I am undecided.

____ I believe in the          ____ I believe in the
     negative of the                negative of the
     resolution.                    resolution.

                               ____ I believe more strongly
                                    in the negative than
                                    I did.
```

B. Ballot for Audience Decision

Since lay audiences obviously lack the qualifications necessary to evaluate the debate as an educational process, their decision has value only when the merits of the proposition are being considered or when certain data are being collected for research purposes. An audience-decision ballot is sometimes used as a device to heighten audience interest. In such cases, a shift-of-opinion ballot may be used. The ballot shown here (page 322), a modification of the Woodward Ballot,[5] provides a means of compensating for the lack of understanding of the principles of argumentation and debate found among most audiences. Members of the audience are simply asked to state their beliefs about the proposition before and after hearing the debate, and the decision is based on the shift of audience opinion. At the conclusion of the debate, the ballots are collected and tabulated as those recording a shift to the affirmative, those reporting no change, and those reporting a shift to the negative. The team that has effected the greater shift of opinion is determined by an inspection of the tabulation. The results obtained by this method may be regarded as interesting, but not necessarily significant. Carefully controlled tests of statistical reliability are necessary to guard against chance variables. These controls, or the use of other experimental methods, require more elaborate statistical procedures than are practical for the average educational debate.

In presenting debates before popular audiences, the student gains valuable experience in addressing large groups and has an opportunity to analyze and adapt to the popular audience. Audience-judges challenge the student to win a popular response, whereas educator-judges challenge the student to win a critical response. It is educationally necessary that students should have their work evaluated by persons who know more about argumentation and debate than they do—the educators—rather than by persons who know less about argumentation and debate than they do—the popular audience. It is inherent in our tradition of liberal education that students should seek the highest rather than the lowest common denominator.

Exercises

1. Arrange for a debate to be presented in class. During the debate, members of the class will take comprehensive notes on the debate. Following the debate, they will complete the ballot presented on page 317. After the ballots are completed, hold a class discussion in which the decisions of the members of the class are considered and any differences in their decisions and quality ratings are analyzed.

2. Arrange for a debate to be presented in class. Have the class use the shift-of-opinion ballot presented on page 322.

[5] See: Howard S. Woodward, "Measurement and Analysis of Audience Opinion," *Quarterly Journal of Speech*, Vol. 14 (February 1928), pp. 94–111.

3. Attend an intercollegiate debate and prepare a ballot similar to the one on page 317, recording your decision on the debate. If possible, secure a copy of the ballot used by the judge for that debate. Write a brief paper in which you report your decision and that of the judge. What factors most influenced your decision? If your decision differs from that of the judge, what factors do you think account for the difference?

Chapter 21

Modern Procedures:
Educational Debate Formats

Although debating is as old as civilization itself, the procedures of debating have evolved and changed considerably over the centuries. Educational debating today, while retaining the essential values of debating in ancient times, has adapted its form to contemporary requirements. The various formats of modern educational debate provide a useful parallel to contemporary substantive debates and, at the same time, a format consistent with modern educational requirements. To gain the full benefit of educational debate, the student should be cognizant of its various formats.

I. Formats of Debate

The various formats of educational debate have certain common elements: (1) both sides must have an equal number of speakers; (2) both sides must have an equal amount of time; (3) the affirmative must speak first and last. Educational debate today makes use almost exclusively of the two-man team; the three-man team so popular at the turn of the century is now a museum piece.

The National Developmental Conference on Forensics, held in 1974, recommended: "More frequent use of alternative events and formats in forensics should be encouraged." We will consider first the standard format and then ten alternative formats.

A. Standard

The standard format is overwhelmingly the most widely used type of debate in the United States today. The organization of this format is as follows:

First Affirmative	Ten minutes
First Negative	Ten minutes
Second Affirmative	Ten minutes
Second Negative	Ten minutes
First Negative Rebuttal	Five minutes
First Affirmative Rebuttal	Five minutes

| Second Negative Rebuttal | Five minutes |
| Second Affirmative Rebuttal | Five minutes |

B. Cross Examination

Moot-court debating, the educational form of judicial debate, makes use of cross examination as a part of the training of law students. Such debates are conducted under the rules of legal procedure. Forms of cross-examination debating developed for wider educational application include the Oregon Plan and its various modifications.[1]

The following version, adopted for use at the National Debate Tournament, provides an opportunity for each of the four debaters to participate as both questioner and respondent.

First Affirmative Constructive	Ten minutes
Cross examination of First Affirmative	Three minutes
First Negative Constructive	Ten minutes
Cross examination of First Negative	Three minutes
Second Affirmative Constructive	Ten minutes
Cross examination of the Second Affirmative	Three minutes
Second Negative Constructive	Ten minutes
Cross examination of the Second Negative	Three minutes
First Negative Rebuttal	Five minutes
First Affirmative Rebuttal	Five minutes
Second Negative Rebuttal	Five minutes
Second Affirmative Rebuttal	Five minutes

Edward Bennett Williams, once called "the country's hottest criminal lawyer," gave this tough but practical advice on the most difficult of trial techniques, cross examination:

It is . . . the art of putting a bridle on a witness who has been called to do you harm, and of controlling him so well that he helps you. You must think of him as a man with a knife in his hand who is out to stab you, and you must feel your way with him as if you were in a dark room together. You must move with him, roll with him. You must never explore or experiment during cross examination. *You must never ask a question if you do not already know the answer.* If you do know it and the witness refuses to say what you know, you can slaughter him. Otherwise he may slaughter you. Never attack a point that is unassailable. And if you hit a telling point, try

[1] J. S. Gray, "The Oregon Plan of Debating," *Quarterly Journal of Speech Education,* Vol. 12 (April 1926), pp. 175–180.

not to let the witness know it. Keep quiet and go on. The time to dramatize it to the jury is during your closing argument.[2]

All of the considerations of argumentation and debate apply to cross-examination debate. In addition, there are 'certain considerations arising from the form of this debate:

1. The questioner should try to elicit responses that will lead to admissions, contradictions, or other advantages that he or she may use effectively later in constructive speeches or rebuttal.

2. The questions should focus primarily on arguments developed in the speech of the respondent. However, questions about arguments in a previous speech by the respondent's colleague, or any matter relevant to the proposition, are admissible.

3. The questioner and the respondent should treat each other with courtesy. Sarcasm, "browbeating," or obvious evasion boomerang to the discredit of the one using them.

4. Both the questioner and the respondent should bear in mind that they are not conducting a private conversation but are asking questions and giving responses designed to have an effect upon the judge and audience. To facilitate communication with the audience, both speakers stand and face the audience during the question period.

5. Once the questioning has begun, neither the questioner nor the respondent may consult a colleague.

There are also additional considerations for questioners:

1. Questioners must always have clear purposes for their questions. The purposes need not always be immediately apparent to the respondents or the audience, but each question must be carefully designed to help the questioners achieve a definite objective.

2. Before the debate, the questioners should prepare for cross examination by drafting a series of questions on each of the probable issues of the debate. During the debate, they should follow their opponents' arguments carefully and adapt questions to the specific case advanced by the opponents.

3. Questioners should try to elicit brief responses (although they may not require a "yes" or "no" answer). They may not cut off a reasonable qualification, but they may cut off a verbose response with a statement such as "Thank you, that gives us enough information" or "That's fine, thank you, that makes your position clear."

4. The questioners should not comment on the responses. The time to do this is in later constructive or summary speeches, when the significance of the responses must be tied into the case as a whole.

---

[2] *Life* Magazine, June 22, 1959, p. 116. Used by permission of Edward Bennett Williams and *Life*. (Italics added.)

5. The questions should be brief and easily understandable. Unduly long or ambiguous questions, or questions containing negatives, may confuse the opponent, but they may also confuse those who render the decision. The question "Do you not agree that it is not undesirable to have the Supreme Court removed from the political pressures and lobbying that influence Congress?" is a poor one. A respondent would certainly ask for a clarification of this question, and the resultant waste of time would reduce the number of questions that could be asked.

6. Questioners may briefly set the stage for a question: "You are no doubt familiar with Justice Holmes' statement . . ."

7. Questioners should never ask a question unless they already know the answer. One questioner gave his opponent an excellent opportunity when he asked, "You claimed that the Supreme Court has made unwise decisions. Can you cite any examples of such decisions?" The respondent advanced his own case by replying "I certainly can. The decisions on the income tax laws and the child labor laws delayed needed social reform for years. And further . . ."

8. Questioners should not attempt to attack unassailable points. Some of the points of the respondents' case will probably be so well established as to be irrefutable. An unsuccessful attack on them will merely make their strength more obvious to those who render the decision. Questioners should focus their attack on those points they can carry.

9. Questioners may sometimes find it desirable to use a summary question to conclude a series of questions: "Then, since you have admitted that the Supreme Court correctly interpreted the Constitution in this case and that Congress was wrong, do you still maintain that Congress should be given the power to reverse the Supreme Court?" Respondents would no doubt answer this question in a way favorable to their cases. The questioners hope, however, that those who render the decision might answer in a different way in their own minds.

Finally, there are considerations for respondents:

1. Respondents must bear in mind that each question is designed to destroy their cases or to advance the cases of opponents. Consequently, they must be constantly on guard.

2. Respondents must answer any reasonable questions.

3. Respondents may refuse to answer ambiguous or "loaded" questions. Questions of the "Have you stopped cheating on examinations?" variety may be rejected by demonstrating that the question is ambiguous or "loaded" and by requesting a more reasonable rephrasing of the questions.

4. Respondents may qualify their responses. The "Yes, but . . ." qualification is weak. It is better to state the qualifications first and then give a direct response. To illustrate: Q.—"Do you believe that all branches of the government should be responsive to the will of the people?" A.—"I believe that the Supreme Court is responsive to the long-term will of the people by protecting their Constitutional rights. With this important Constitutional safeguard, I would say that government should be responsive to the will of the people."

5. Respondents should promptly admit not knowing the answer to a question. For example: Q.—"Do you admit that the Court reversed itself in the Jones vs. Opelika case?" A.—"I'm sorry, I'm not familiar with that case."

6. Respondents should not attempt to defend an indefensible point. It is better to yield a point immediately than to allow questioners to wring admissions from them in a series of questions that will only fix the point more firmly in the minds of those who render the decision.

C. Direct Clash

In direct-clash debating, the focus is on the issues and the judge takes an active role in the conduct of the debate. Forms of direct-clash debating include the Paget Plan and its various modifications.[3] The following version is designed for two-man teams:

Definition and Analysis:

First Affirmative defines terms and outlines the basic position of the affirmative team, stating the issues the affirmative wishes to debate.	Five minutes
First Negative accepts or rejects affirmative analysis, states the basic position of the negative, and accepts or rejects the issues proposed by the affirmative. The negative, of course, may propose additional issues it wishes to debate. If the negative wishes to propose a counter plan, it must present it as an issue at this time.	Five minutes

The judge may rule on the issues at this time.

First Clash:

Second Affirmative presents a single issue which he believes vital to the affirmative case.	Four minutes
Second Negative refutes preceding speech.	Three minutes
First Affirmative reestablishes his colleague's argument.	Three minutes
First Negative concludes refutation.	Three minutes

At the end of this clash the judge records on the ballot the side that has won the clash and announces the decision.

Second Clash:

Second Negative presents a single issue.	Four minutes
Second Affirmative refutes.	Three minutes
First Negative reestablishes.	Three minutes
First Affirmative concludes refutation.	Three minutes

The judge records and announces the decision.

[3] E. H. Paget, "Rules for the Direct-Clash Plan," *Quarterly Journal of Speech,* Vol. 23 (October 1937), pp. 431–433.

Third Clash:

This clash follows the same pattern as the others.

The First Affirmative initiates the issue.

The judge records and announces the decision. If an additional clash is needed, then—

Fourth Clash:

This clash follows the same pattern as the others.

The First Negative initiates the issue.

The judge records and announces the decision. If an additional clash is needed, then—

Fifth Clash:

This clash follows the same pattern as the others.

The Second Affirmative initiates the issue.

The judge records and announces the decision. The clashes on each issue are limited strictly to the issue. The entire debate case may not be considered in the clashes.

After the definition and analysis phase judges may, if they find it in the interests of good educational debate to do so, play an active role in the conduct of the debate. If the definition of terms and statement of basic positions have been clear and cogent, the judges may allow the debate to proceed without further direction. If, however, they find a significant disagreement over terms, they may rule that the first clash deal with this problem. If the statement of the basic positions of the teams has not been clear, the judges may state the issues inherent in the analysis and determine the order in which they shall be debated. If, in any of the clashes, a speaker evades the point, answers so inadequately as to make the team's position untenable, or answers so well that the opposition cannot maintain its position, the judges may stop the clash at this point.

The debate continues until one team has won three clashes; thus there may be three, four, or five clashes in a direct-clash debate.

D. Heckling

This format emulates legislative debate in that the speaker may be interrupted for a question.

First Affirmative   Ten minutes
Heckling by First Negative
First Negative   Ten minutes
Heckling by Second Affirmative

Second Affirmative	Ten minutes
Heckling by Second Negative	
Second Negative	Ten minutes
Heckling by First Affirmative	
First Negative Rebuttal	Five minutes
Heckling by First Affirmative	
First Affirmative Rebuttal	Five minutes
Heckling by Second Negative	
Second Negative Rebuttal	Five minutes
Heckling by Second Affirmative	
Second Affirmative Rebuttal	Five minutes
Heckling by First Negative	

In order to interrupt a speaker, the heckler must rise and ask, "Will the speaker yield for a question?" The speaker must yield. The question must be short and must be related to the subject of the speaker's remarks. The heckler may interrupt the speaker four times during a constructive speech, at any time after the third minute of a speech and prior to the eighth minute of the speech; and the heckler may interrupt twice during the rebuttal speech, at any time after the first minute of the speech and prior to the fourth minute of the speech. As in the cross-examination debate, the questions should be designed to elicit information that the hecklers will later use to advance their own case or to refute the opponents' case. The judge will penalize the hecklers if they ask unduly long or irrelevant questions. This debate format requires very careful timing, and the timekeeper is usually instructed to announce at the proper intervals: "Heckling may begin," or "Heckling must cease."

E. Lincoln-Douglas

This format is simply a two-man debate, named in honor of two famous debaters who used this form. Although its use is very limited in intercollegiate debate, it is often used for training purposes in the argumentation classroom. This format continues to be used in political circles. The famous Kennedy-Nixon debates marked the first time in American history that Presidential candidates met in debate in the tradition of Lincoln and Douglas. The City Club of Cleveland regularly arranges such debates between candidates for major public offices in Cleveland and Ohio.

One organization of this format is as follows:

Affirmative	Ten minutes
Negative	Fifteen minutes
Affirmative	Five minutes

The Lincoln-Douglas format may be combined with the cross-examination format, as was done in the Bicentennial Youth Debates.

The organization of the combined formats is as follows:

Affirmative constructive	Eight minutes
Cross examination by negative	Three minutes
Negative constructive	Ten minutes
Cross examination by affirmative	Three minutes
Affirmative rebuttal	Four minutes
Negative rebuttal	Six minutes
Affirmative rebuttal	Four minutes

The time limits suggested here are often used in the classroom. In political debate, the time limits are usually tailored to radio or television requirements.

F. Debate-Forum

This format is simply one of the previously discussed formats, most frequently the standard, followed by a forum period during which time members of the audience are invited to address questions to the debaters. Usually a faculty member serves as chairman of the debate and conducts the forum period. In the debate-forum, the speeches are often shortened. Con-

---

Customary Arrangements

A through G are conducted in approximately the same manner. Formats H through K require certain special arrangements (see the discussion of each type).

☐ The physical arrangements customarily include a chair and a table placed at the rear center of the platform for the chairman, a lectern placed at the front center of the platform for the use of the speakers, and a table and two chairs placed at each side of the platform for the debaters. Customarily, the affirmative is seated at the chairman's right. The timekeeper is usually seated in the first row of the audience and is provided with a set of time cards (usually twelve 3 × 4 cards of light cardboard held together by a metal binding and bearing the markings: 10, 9, 8, 7, 6, 5, 4, 3, 2, 1, $\frac{1}{2}$, STOP) and a stop watch. The judge or judges are seated at convenient places in the audience and are provided with ballots on which to record their decisions and flow sheets on which to take notes during the debate. If the chairs in the room are not designed to provide space for writing, clipboards should also be provided.

☐ The chairman announces the proposition of debate and introduces the speakers to the audience. He or she may make such other introductory remarks if appropriate,

structive speeches may be only six minutes long and rebuttal speeches only three minutes long. Thus it is possible to present the debate and a twenty-minute forum period within an hour's time.

Considerable tact is sometimes required on the part of the chairman, who must prevent a few questioners from monopolizing the forum period, discourage speeches disguised as questions from the floor, and restate verbose or ambiguous questions in meaningful form — and, of course, restate inaudible questions from the floor so that they may be heard by the entire audience. In general, the chairman sets the tone of the meeting and must keep the situation firmly in hand so that the program will move forward purposefully.

G. Off Topic

Off-topic debates are debates on a proposition other than the current national intercollegiate debate proposition. They may be single debates presented before an audience, or they may be tournament debates. (See Chapter 22 — "Types of Tournaments.")

H. Appellate

This format emulates the legal debate of the appellate courts.[4] The organization of the appellate debate is as follows:

[4] This type of debate was developed by J. Garber Drushal of the College of Wooster. It was first presented at a symposium of the Northeast Ohio Debate Conference. Used by permission of J. Garber Drushal.

---

but the remarks should be brief and should not express any opinion on the proposition under debate.

☐ The timekeeper holds the cards so that they are constantly visible to the speaker, adjusting the cards each minute (each thirty seconds for the last two cards) to show the speaking time remaining.

☐ At the conclusion of the debate, the timekeeper collects the ballots from the judges and hands them to the chairman, who announces the decision. If a critic judge is used rather than a panel of judges, the chairman may by prearrangement invite the judge to give a critique and announce the decision. If an audience-decision ballot is used, the timekeeper and one or two assistants should collect the ballots at the conclusion of the debate. If there is a forum period, the ballots may be tabulated during this time and the result announced at the conclusion of the questions.

☐ In a tournament, since a number of debates are conducted simultaneously, the timekeeper often also serves as chairman. In many tournaments, decisions are not announced at the conclusion of individual debates but are published at the conclusion of the tournament.

First Affirmative	Fifteen minutes
First Negative	Fifteen minutes
Second Affirmative	Twelve minutes
Second Negative	Twelve minutes
Negative Rebuttal	Five minutes
Affirmative Rebuttal	Five minutes

Two special features of this format are the use of the brief and the active participation of the judges as cross examiners.

Prior to the debate, the members of each team prepare a four-page typewritten brief. At a time mutually agreed upon, usually one or two weeks in advance of the debate, copies of the brief are sent to the opposing team and to the judges. Additional copies are duplicated and are distributed to the audience at the time of the debate. Each brief contains the major arguments of the team. Arguments not presented in the briefs may not be introduced into the oral presentation. Each major argument must be supported by a citation of evidence sufficiently specific to permit ready reference. The oral presentation, however, is not limited to evidence cited in the brief. The brief also contains a definition of terms, with sources cited. The oral presentation need not cover all of the arguments in the brief, since the written material is before the judges and the audience. In their oral presentation, the speakers present constructive argument to advance their own case and refutation against the oral and written arguments of their opponents.

There are three judges, one of whom serves as chief judge and chairman of the proceedings. The judges may question the debaters at any time except during the first and last two minutes of the constructive speeches. There are no questions during the rebuttal speeches. In their questions, the judges should attempt to clarify points made by the speakers, explore the relationship between evidence and contentions, inquire about the usefulness of evidence and the validity of reasoning, and, if necessary, determine the authenticity of evidence. The judges should not comment upon the replies of the debaters nor engage in colloquy with them. If the members of one team decide to omit one or more of the written arguments from their oral presentation, this omission should not count against them. An unchallenged argument is to be evaluated on the basis of the written presentation. If an argument is challenged, the clash of argument is to be evaluated as in other types of debate.

The decision is based on both the brief and the oral presentation. The decision is announced by the chief judge, who uses from six to ten minutes for an explanatory opinion. The other judges may use five minutes each to present a concurrence or dissent.

I. Parliamentary

Parliamentary debate is a specialized format involving the use of special procedures. This format is considered separately in Chapter 23. The English format, which is considered next, may be regarded as a modified format of parliamentary debate. Actually, it is a modification of a format of educational debate used at British universities and is a modification of the format used in the British House of Commons.

J. English

The regular visits of British teams to this country have led to some interest in English style of debate. The following rules, which represent a modification of the regular British procedure, were designed to bring the debate within suitable time limits.[5]

1. The President calls the House to order and announces the motion for debate.

2. Ten-minute speech by a previously designated speaker moving the adoption of the motion.

3. Ten-minute speech by a previously designated speaker opposing the motion.

4. Seven-minute speech by a previously designated speaker seconding the adoption of the motion.

5. Seven-minute speech by a previously designated speaker opposing the motion.

6. At this point the floor is open to any member of the House who desires to speak. The time limit on these speeches is five minutes. No member may speak more than once. Members favoring the motion and those opposing it speak alternately. The President indicates the side entitled to the floor by announcing "I will now recognize a speaker for the motion" or "I will now recognize a speaker opposed to the motion."

7. Any speaker except the one who opens the debate may be interrupted by any member of the House at any time. Such interruptions take one of two forms: (a) If the rules have been infringed, a member is entitled to rise and point this out to the President, at the same time describing the infringement which he believes has taken place; (b) The second type of interruption permitted is a direct request for information addressed to the speaker who has the floor. To make this sort of interruption a member must first rise to his feet in such a manner as to attract discreetly the attention of the President. The speaker, if he wishes to be interrupted, will sit down. If he does not sit down, and ignores the member who desires to interrupt, the latter must resume his seat. An interruption on a point of information must be made in the form of a question and is addressed to the speaker through the President. The interrupter may not himself impart information to the House; he may only seek to elicit information from the speaker. The President will rule the speaker out of order if his interruption does not constitute a genuine request for information.

[5] Douglas Ehninger, "Outline of Procedure for the English-Style of Debate," *The Gavel*, Vol. 30 (March 1948), pp. 51–53. Reprinted by permission of Douglas Ehninger and Delta Sigma Rho.

8. The debate on the motion proceeds in the fashion outlined for one hour and thirty minutes, at which time the speaker who originally moved the adoption of the resolution presents a five-minute speech answering the arguments which have been presented against it and summarizing the discussion. Immediately following this speech there is a division of the House. Abstentions are indicated by informing the tellers. The numbers having been added up, the President announces the result from the Chair.

9. Members favoring the motion sit facing those who oppose it, the former ranging themselves on the President's right, the latter on his left.

10. The speeches are clocked by a timekeeper. Members must bring their remarks to a close upon receiving his signal.

11. Members may speak on any phase of the subject they desire. The President will, however, rule out of order any member who attempts to introduce material which is obviously not germane to the discussion.

K. Forensic Progression

The forensic progression provides an opportunity for the student to participate in several different types of forensic situations. The organization of the forensic progression is as follows:

1. The problem area of the forensic progression is announced in advance of the tournament. If the event is held in the early season, the area of the national intercollegiate debate proposition is usually used; if the event is held later in the season, a problem area other then the current national proposition is usually chosen.

2. Each college may enter two or four participants.

3. The students are assigned in groups of eight for Rounds I, II, and III.

4. In Round I each student gives an informative speech on the problem area.

5. In Round II the students participate in group discussion, examining the problem and attempting to discover some possible solutions.

6. In Round III each student gives a persuasive speech in which he or she advocates one particular solution to the problem.

7. If a problem area other than the national debate proposition has been used, the directors, who have served as judges during Rounds I, II, and III, meet and formulate a debate proposition reflecting the analysis of the participants they have observed in the previous rounds.

8. The students are assigned to positions for split-team debates. (For a consideration of the method of split-team debating see Chapter 22.)

9. After a reasonable interval to allow the students to prepare, the tournament may proceed to any desired number of rounds of debate—usually six or eight.

II. The Audience

The 1974 National Developmental Conference on Forensics recommended:

Audience debating should be promoted through public appearances on the national proposition and on issues of local concern, as well as through tournaments, or rounds within tournaments, based on the audience vote model.

Directors of forensics regularly provide opportunities for their students to speak before a variety of audiences. Since a number of debates are conducted simultaneously in a tournament, the audience for any one debate is usually small. The debaters thus have an opportunity to adjust to a limited audience and can gain experience in directing arguments to the key individual (in this case the judge) in that audience. In the final round of a tournament, which is usually well attended, the debaters have an opportunity to address an audience well versed in argumentation; and they now seek to influence several key individuals, since three or more experts usually serve as the panel of judges for the final round of a tournament.

In addition to the audiences found in tournaments, general public audiences may be found on the campus and in the community. Sizable campus audiences are usually obtained for debates with traditional rival institutions. Since, however, audiences that may be obtained on any one campus are usually limited in size, debates are sometimes presented before various community audiences. Schools, church groups, and civic and social organizations are often interested in securing debates for their programs. Community audiences may be used for tournament as well as individual debates. The "Debate Days in Detroit" tournament presented by Wayne State University schedules the debates of that tournament before various civic and school audiences. In this way, audiences totaling 10,000 to 15,000 can observe tournament debates.[6] Local commercial radio and television stations, as well as educational radio and television stations, may be interested in carrying well-planned debates adapted to their special needs, thus offering further opportunities to obtain experience in various types of communication situations.

The tournament situation makes provision for both the novice and the experienced debater. In fairness to both the student and the audience, the director of forensics usually assigns only the more proficient debaters to appear before campus and community audiences. Debates conducted before such groups require that the debaters undertake a careful audience analysis and make specific preparation in terms of the audience. Factors of audience analysis and adaptation are considered in Chapter 17.

Although it is hoped that debates presented before public audiences will

[6] John K. Boaz and George Ziegelmueller, "An Audience Debate Tournament," *Speech Teacher*, Vol. 13 (November 1964), pp. 271–276.

be both interesting and profitable for the audience, they should never be regarded as entertainment. Debates presented before public audiences should be regarded as an opportunity to educate the student about audience analysis and to educate the audience about debate. The listeners, of course, may attend a debate for a variety of reasons. Some may want to gain more information about the subject of the debate; some may hope to use the debate process to help them arrive at a decision on the proposition. These reasons, however, are subordinate to the educational reasons for presenting the debate.

One way of informing the audience of the purposes of educational debate is illustrated by Robert P. Newman, of the University of Pittsburgh, who included this statement on a printed debate program:

The speakers in this series are not authorities on the topics debated, though they have read about and discussed them a great deal. Neither are they practicing attorneys, though the techniques they use and the principles they follow are similar. Nor are they members of Congress, with power to act upon the questions debated. They are students engaged in an educational activity which we hope will provide them with techniques of dealing intelligently with public issues.

Most important, the debaters you will hear do not have the final answers to the questions they are discussing. If such answers existed, the topics would not be debatable. Democracy presupposes that decision on such matters will be reached by discussion, argument, and compromise; and not solely by reference to experts nor by following the dictates of a "leader." The topics being debated in this series we regard as being genuinely two-sided. The debaters will not settle them, nor should they be expected to.

When critic judges are used in the public audience debate situation, they can make a significant contribution to the audience's knowledge about debate by explaining the factors leading to a decision in a manner that will be interesting and informative to the audience as well as profitable for the debaters.

III. Adapting the Debate to Communications Media

The use of public address systems, radio, or television enables debaters to reach larger audiences and poses the problem of adapting the debate to the special requirements of the media to be utilized. The public address system requires only a simple adjustment; radio and television require a more complex adjustment and afford the opportunity to develop a type of debate specifically designed for the medium and for the specific broadcast situation (*see inset, pages 340–341*).

Speakers sometimes must use radio or television at the same time that they are addressing an audience assembled before them. It is difficult to adapt a style of debate or a style of speaking to two such different audience situations. Although some superior speakers are able to reach both audiences effectively, it is usually preferable to concentrate on one audience. For debaters, the problem is simple. They must direct their principal attention to the audience that will render the decision. Most political speakers consider radio or television audiences more important, because they include a greater number of voters who will render the decision with their ballots. Franklin Roosevelt was one of the first political speakers to make this decision. As early as 1928, he began to design some of his major political addresses primarily for the benefit of his radio audience and the press, rather than for the delegates and audience in the convention auditorium.

Present-day speakers sometimes have the problem of three audiences: the audience physically present before them, the radio audience, and the television audience. In such a situation, most speakers give priority to the television audience. Although speakers must decide which audience will receive principal attention, they should avoid any obvious neglect of the other audiences and should seek, insofar as possible, to include all audiences in the presentation.

In both radio and television debates, time is of great importance, and this factor places a premium on extemporaneous speeches, which allow speakers to condense or extend remarks as the situation may demand.

In television debates, two cameras are usually used; often one camera is turned on a participant other than the speaker to allow the audience to see various reactions to the speech. Speakers should direct their remarks to the "live" camera—the one with a small red light burning near the lenses—unless the program format calls for addressing remarks to the moderator or to some other participant. If a monitor—a television set showing the program going out over the air—is in sight, the speakers should ignore it.

In general, television debates require more planning than radio debates, because the medium is more complex and the special problems of camera placement, sets, lighting, and the need for rehearsal time influence the format to be used. In planning the format of the television debate, it should be remembered that television is a *visual* medium; and the debate format should be selected and its presentation planned with this factor in mind.

Debaters should plan to arrive at the studio well ahead of broadcast or recording time to allow the producer or director to make the necessary arrangements: check for voice balance, adjust lighting, plan camera arrangements, and so on. For a radio debate, speakers should make a point of getting acquainted with the various signals that will be given from the control room as cues at different points during the program. For the television debate, speakers should make a point of acquainting themselves with the various signals the floor man will give from time to time during the debate, and they should prepare themselves to present their speeches in a conversational manner amid the apparent chaos of the movement of cameras and technicians during the broadcast.

Suggestions for Adapting to Media

Public Address System

☐ Avoid the use of a public address system unless it is clearly needed for the speakers to be heard in the auditorium.

☐ If possible, test the public address system before the audience arrives.

☐ Before beginning a speech, adjust the microphone to a convenient height and place it in a convenient location—so that it is sufficiently close to you but does not obstruct your access to the lectern or your view of the audience.

☐ Allow the public address system to amplify your voice; do not shout into the microphone.

☐ Remain close to the microphone during your talk, adjusting your movements and gestures to the microphone and avoid moving "off mike."

Radio

☐ Adapt your style as if you were speaking to two, three, or four persons, seated in their living rooms.

☐ Since you cannot ordinarily use visual aids in a radio speech, you must depend upon vivid and precise words to paint the desired pictures in the minds of your audience.

☐ If you use a manuscript (for plan or negative blocks) remember you must simplify complex arguments and present them in a conversational manner.

☐ The format of radio debates must be adjusted to the time available. Sometimes only half-hour or fifteen-minute time segments are allotted for the debate. In such situations, the speeches should be short, and there should be a frequent change of speakers. Sometimes a program format may evolve wherein the moderator addresses questions, based on the principal issues of the debate, to members of each team alternately, and they respond with a one- or two-minute answer; in other cases a modification of cross-examination debate may be used. The best format for radio debate is usually worked out in consultation between a director of forensics who knows the problems of debate and a radio producer who knows the problems of radio.

Television

☐ Keep in mind the same considerations of style that apply to radio in your television debates.

☐ You may use visual aids in television, and their use is often effective. Visual aids must be prepared in consultation with the television program director, so that they meet the special requirements of television and so that necessary arrangements are made to get them "on camera" at the proper time.

☐ Movements, gestures, or facial expressions can be seen by the audience and have value in communicating to the television audience. Movement must be within previously defined limits—the speaker must not move "off camera." Gestures and facial expression as well as movement should be restrained, since the camera will frequently take a tight head "shot" of the speaker.

☐ Dress is important in the televised debate. In addition to the considerations cited in Chapter 16, certain special considerations relate to television. Women should avoid large, bright pieces of jewelry and noisy bracelets. Everyone should avoid clothing with sharply contrasting colors or "busy" patterns. Both men and women may need makeup for color television; this special makeup is usually applied by a studio makeup artist. If you wear eyeglasses only occasionally, remove them to simplify the problem of light reflection. If you wear eyeglasses constantly, however, you should wear them during the telecast, since you will probably feel more comfortable, and you will avoid the tendency to squint.

☐ Keep the use of a manuscript to an absolute minimum. Most program directors strongly prefer that the speaker use the extemporaneous manner of speaking with a minimum of notes.

☐ The style of television debates must be adjusted to the time available and to the special problems of the medium. The sketches indicate floor plans used in various television debates. (M designates the program moderator; L, the lectern; D, a debater; J, a judge; and A, an audience member who appears on camera.)

Plan I: The moderator and debaters are seated at an L-shaped table.

Plan II: The moderator is seated apart from the debaters' table and the debaters speak from the lectern.

Plan III: The judges and a number of audience members are seated on raised chairs in "jury box" style. (Two lecterns are provided so that the debaters may stand facing one another during cross examination.)

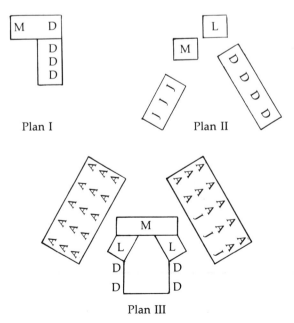

Plan I

Plan II

Plan III

Exercises

1. Plan and conduct a standard format debate in class. It may be necessary to modify the time limits to meet available class time.

2. Plan and conduct in class debates using some of the alternative formats considered in this chapter.

3. Listen to a radio debate. Prepare a written report (300 words) evaluating the effectiveness of the program format.

4. Watch a television debate. Prepare a written report (300 words) evaluating the effectiveness of the program format.

5. If audiotape-recording equipment is available, plan and record a debate using a format suitable for radio. Play the recording for the class. Conduct a discussion in which the class is invited to evaluate the effectiveness of the recording (a) as a debate and (b) as a format for radio debate.

6. If videotape-recording equipment is available, plan and record a debate using a format suitable for television. Play the recording for the class. Conduct a discussion in which the class is invited to evaluate the effectiveness of the recording (a) as a debate and (b) as a format for television debate.

Chapter 22

Modern Procedures:
The Tournament

In seeking the full realization of the values inherent in educational debate, we have developed certain procedures and practices designed to provide maximum educational opportunity through orderly administration of large numbers of debates. One of the most distinctive features of modern procedures is the tournament. Today more than twice as many students participate in tournament debates as in nontournament debates, and the average student participates in more than ten times as many tournament debates as nontournament debates. Since such a large part of contemporary educational debate is conducted through the medium of the tournament, we need information on the various forms of tournaments and plans of administration so that we may better understand their purpose.

I. The Tournament

The tournament is a method that provides broad educational opportunities by bringing together teams from a number of schools for a number of debates within a short space of time. A tournament may make use of almost any debate format, although the standard format is used far more frequently than any other. A tournament is divided into rounds—that is, groups of debates that take place simultaneously. Each team participates in several rounds of debate and thus has the opportunity to debate several times during a tournament. Often tournaments are held on a Thursday, Friday, and Saturday and provide for eight rounds followed by octa-final elimination rounds. Considerable variation in the structure of the tournament is possible, however, and a tournament may be limited to three rounds of debate in a single afternoon (as are the training tournaments conducted by the Greater Boston Forensic Association), or it may extend over several days (as do the tournaments of the Southern or Western Speech Communication Associations).

The carefully planned debate tournament, designed to achieve the highest educational standards and operated to provide maximum efficiency under the administration of an educator well trained in argumentation, is one of the great educational debate techniques. Originally developed in the 1920s as a device to provide an increased number of debates at a lower unit cost, the tournament has become the dominant factor in educational debating. It continues to provide an increased number of debates at low unit cost and has obvious administrative advantages over the home-and-home, triangle, and tour forms of debating that it has largely replaced; however, its great popularity has resulted from its educational values.

Through the tournament medium, it is possible to assemble selected students from a score or more schools for eight or more hours of debating—which might be regarded as the equivalent of comprehensive examinations in argumentation and debate—in a single weekend. In the tournament, students have an opportunity—all too rare in education—to have their work evaluated by educators from a number of institutions. At the same time, debate directors have an opportunity to study the results of a dozen different methods of teaching and thus are able to enrich their teaching. Since most debating teams attend a number of tournaments in the course of a year, this valuable process is repeated on many occasions. Few other forms of education provide students with so many challenges to do their best: immediate incentives in the form of decisions and awards, as well as long-term incentives in the form of growth and development. Today the debater—in his undergraduate life, as after graduation—competes with opponents from all parts of the nation. For many years the debate tournament was uniquely American. In recent years, however, British universities and the British government, through the British Broadcasting System, have also conducted them. Canadian teams regularly participate in American debate tournaments, and some Canadian universities conduct their own tournaments. Most tournaments recognize outstanding achievement by presenting a trophy to the winning college, and often other awards are presented on the basis of the quality of the debating as well as on the basis of wins and losses.[1]

II. Types of Tournaments

Although a number of variations in the types of tournaments are possible, most tournaments may be classified into one or more of the following types:

A. Novice or Varsity

Novice tournaments are designed for students new to debating, usually first-year debaters. Varsity tournaments are for students experienced in debating, usually those students with more than one year's experience or above-average achievement. The purpose of this distinction is to provide approximately equal competition.

[1] See page 317 for a ballot which may be used to record wins and losses, as well as quality points.

B. Team or Unit

Team tournaments are designed for teams (i.e., two debaters) that are prepared to debate on *both sides* of the proposition. Such tournaments provide maximum educational opportunity, since the students present both affirmative and negative cases. These tournaments are usually reserved for the more experienced varsity debaters. There are an even number of preliminary rounds in such a tournament, since all teams must debate an equal number of times on the affirmative and negative side. If a team tournament is also an elimination tournament, it may be necessary for a team to debate more often on one side than the other in the elimination rounds. *Unit tournaments* are designed for units—that is, four debaters, two of whom function as an affirmative team and two of whom function as a negative team *throughout* the tournament. Such tournaments provide an opportunity for intensive experience *on one side* of the proposition and are used for both novice and varsity debaters. Unlike the team tournament, the unit tournament does not require an even number of preliminary rounds.

C. Elimination or Nonelimination

The elimination tournament—which brings together in a final round the two teams, or teams of the two units, with the greatest achievement—is designed to provide additional educational opportunities and the incentive of further competition for those teams that demonstrate superior achievement. Most elimination tournaments have a number of nonelimination rounds in which all teams participate. Nonelimination tournaments are designed to provide an equal number of debates for all teams or units in the tournament.

D. Sweepstakes

The sweepstakes tournament is designed to encourage the student and the participating colleges to enter debate *and* various other forensic events that are conducted as a part of the tournament. Achievement in debate and each of the other forensic events is weighted by sweepstakes points, and an award is presented to the school attaining the highest number of sweepstakes points; other awards are often presented to high-ranking schools as well. The method of administering a sweepstakes tournament may be seen in the regulations of the Eastern Forensic Association:

1. A college must enter at least two events in order to be considered for the sweepstakes trophy.

2. The trophy will be awarded to the college that has the greatest number of sweepstakes points computed on the following system:

a. For each win in debate—4 points (thus a maximum of 48 points for any college in a six-round unit tournament).

b. Points in persuasive speaking and extemporaneous speaking will be awarded for each of three rounds. In each section the best speaker (low total rank of the two judges—ties broken by percentage points) will receive three points; the next highest speaker will receive two points; and the next highest will receive one point. (Thus a maximum of 18 points may be won in each event by any one college that enters two speakers in each event.)

E. Split Team

The split-team tournament pairs students from different colleges as teams. Each participating college enters four students designated as first affirmative, second affirmative, first negative, and second negative speakers. The schedule for the first round of the tournament might provide that the first affirmative from college A would be teamed with the second affirmative from college B to debate the first negative from college C and the second negative from college D. The two students on each team are allowed approximately three-quarters of an hour in which to coordinate their evidence and reasoning and to plan their case. In the succeeding rounds of the tournament, other combinations are provided so that each participant has a new colleague in each debate. The purpose of this type of tournament is to provide students with the experience of selecting and organizing a case within a very short time and of coordinating their arguments with those of colleagues they may not have met before.

F. Off Topic

In the off-topic tournament, the students debate a proposition other than the current national intercollegiate debate proposition. The off-topic proposition is usually announced when the tournament invitation is issued a few weeks before the event takes place. If the tournament is a two-day event, sometimes a different off-topic proposition is used each day. If there are elimination rounds, the teams are paired in the manner considered later in this chapter. A coin is then tossed, and the winner may choose which of the two off-topic propositions will be debated and the loser has the choice of sides. Off-topic tournaments may be scheduled as single events or as a division of a regular tournament.

G. Multitype

Although the great majority of tournaments use the standard debate format, a tournament may, of course, use any format. The multitype tournament includes more than one format within the framework of a single tournament.

For example, a multitype tournament might include a round of standard debate, a round of cross-examination debate, a round of direct-clash debate, and a round of heckling debate. The purpose of this kind of tournament is to provide the student with experience in several debate formats within a short space of time.

H. Other Types

In addition to those already listed, other types of tournaments include: freshmen only, freshman and sophomores, or junior (the term is used here to indicate less experienced debaters of any class), and championship (the term is used here to indicate experienced debaters with winning records regardless of class).

Some tournaments are operated with various divisions (i.e., a novice division and a varsity division). Such tournaments are, in effect, multiple tournaments conducted simultaneously.

Other classifications of tournaments include open, limited, and invitational. An open tournament is one for which the host will accept registrations from all interested colleges up to the limit of available facilities. A limited tournament is one in which participation is in some way limited, usually to members of an organization—e.g., to members of the Eastern Forensic Association or to chapters of Delta Sigma Rho–Tau Kappa Alpha. As the nomenclature for types of tournaments is not thoroughly standardized, the tournament host should carefully and clearly "define terms" in the tournament invitation, and the director of forensics should study the invitation carefully before assigning students to a particular tournament.

III. Tournament Schematics

The tournament schematic is a schedule indicating the operational procedure of the tournament. The principle underlying the tournament schematic is that it provides for the orderly and objective administration of the tournament by announcing in advance every essential detail of the tournament. Thus, during the course of the tournament, the host forensics director, as tournament director, makes no decision regarding the operational procedure of any participant.

A. Information in the Tournament Schematic

The tournament schematic contains the following information:

1. Which affirmative team will meet which negative team in each round of the tournament.

2. Who will judge each debate.

3. Where each debate will take place.

4. The time at which each debate will take place.

In the elimination tournament, the schematic cannot fully designate items 1 and 2 for the elimination rounds; rather, it indicates the method that will be followed in determining these assignments.

The tournament schematic is carefully prepared in advance by the tournament director. Prudent tournament directors prepare several schematics in advance. If they expect thirty colleges for a tournament, they prepare schematics for 27, 28, 29, as well as 30 colleges. Thus a last-minute cancellation will not upset the plans, as a suitable schematic will be immediately available. The importance of care in the preparation of a tournament schematic cannot be overemphasized—an error in the schematic may cause serious difficulty and delay. At the opening of the tournament, each team or unit is designated by a control number, drawn at random, which determines the operational procedure to be followed throughout the tournament. Since such a system is absolutely impartial, the teams of the host college may participate in the tournament on an equitable basis with all other participants.

When teams travel a considerable distance to attend a tournament, it is desirable to use geographic division for the drawing of control numbers for the tournament schematic. This assures that teams from neighboring colleges will not meet one another—they probably have many opportunities to meet without traveling to a distant tournament—and provides an opportunity for all teams to meet opponents from other parts of the country. The participating teams might, for example, be divided into five geographic areas, each having an equal number of teams. The teams from the Northeastern area might be assigned numbers 1 through 10. A team from that area would draw one of these numbers at random. The schematic would be so arranged that teams from this group would meet two teams from the Mid-Atlantic (11–20), two teams from the Midwest (21–30), two teams from the West (31–40), two teams from the South (41–50) and not meet any teams from its own immediate geographic area.

B. Essentials of the Tournament Schematic

Although a tournament schematic may be prepared in a number of ways, it should meet the following essentials:

1. No team should meet any other more than once in the preliminary rounds.

2. No team should be judged by its own director.

3. No team should be judged by the same judge more than once.

4. No team should be judged by a judge whose team they will meet in the course of the nonelimination rounds.

5. In a unit tournament, no team should ever meet a team representing its own college.

These simple requirements may be met in all tournaments except those involving a very small number of teams and a relatively large number of rounds.

On pages 350–351, there is a sample schematic of a six-round team tournament in which thirty colleges participated. Since this was a *team* tournament, it will be noted that each college entered a team—i.e., two debaters—and that each team debated alternately on the affirmative and the negative. For example, team 1 debated as an affirmative in Rounds I, III, and V and as a negative in Rounds II, IV, and VI.

It is an easy matter to adjust the schematic of a team tournament to provide for consecutive rounds of judging—for instance, even-numbered judges might be assigned to judge in Rounds I, II, and III and left free for Rounds IV, V, and VI. This convenience is often appreciated by judges who may wish to observe their own teams, attend committee meetings, or undertake other duties during a tournament. Sometimes it may be desirable to arrange the schematic so that the judge or one of the teams remains in the same room throughout the nonelimination rounds, thus reducing the amount of traffic between rounds. This is a convenience if all rooms are desirable, but it should be avoided if some marginal facilities (e.g., too small rooms or rooms with poor acoustics) must be used.

The use of octa-final elimination rounds is increasingly popular. On page 349, there is a sample schematic for octa-final elimination rounds, which may be used after eight (or any other even number) preliminary rounds in an elimination tournament to determine a champion. The teams are *ranked* 1 to 16 on the basis of (1) decisions won, (2) high quality rating points, and (3) low rank. It must be noted that the *rank numbers* shown on page 349 are different from *control numbers*. Thus the team with *control number* 29 in the schematic for preliminary rounds shown on pages 350–351 might be the only undefeated team in those rounds—it would thus be assigned *rank number* 1 in the schematic for elimination rounds shown on page 349. The teams are arranged in brackets as shown on the schematic. (The acum number for octas is 17; if the higher ranked team wins in each case the acum number is 9 for quarters, 5 for semis, and 3 for the final round.)

Sample Schematic: Six-Round Tournament

Round I			Round II			Round III		
Aff.	*Neg.*	*Judge*	*Aff.*	*Neg.*	*Judge*	*Aff.*	*Neg.*	*Judge*
1	2	15	4	1	16	1	6	17
3	4	17	6	3	18	3	8	19
5	6	19	8	5	20	5	10	21
7	8	21	10	7	22	7	12	23
9	10	23	12	9	24	9	14	25
11	12	25	14	11	26	11	16	27
13	14	27	16	13	28	13	18	29
15	16	29	18	15	30	15	20	1
17	18	1	20	17	2	17	22	3
19	20	3	22	19	4	19	24	5
21	22	5	24	21	6	21	26	7
23	24	7	26	23	8	23	28	9
25	26	9	28	25	10	25	30	11
27	28	11	30	27	12	27	2	13
29	30	13	2	29	14	29	4	15

Sides in each debate in the elimination rounds are determined as follows: (1) if the teams have met previously, they reverse sides; (2) otherwise they toss a coin—the winner of the toss having choice of sides.

The American Forensic Association's *Standards* stipulates that "(the judge) should be available to judge at least one round after his team has been eliminated, if requested." The request is almost invariably made and typically three neutral judges are assigned to each elimination round except the final where five judges are frequently used.

On page 352 we have a schematic for a four-round tournament in which thirteen units participated. Since this was a *unit* tournament, it will be noted that each college entered a unit—i.e., four debaters, two of whom debated as an affirmative team and two of whom debated as a negative team throughout the tournament. For example, College 1 has both affirmative and negative teams in each round.

The principles of concurrent variation exemplified in these schematics may be applied to schematics involving various numbers of teams or units. In unit tournaments, the elimination rounds leading to a championship may be conducted in exactly the same manner as previously indicated for the team tournament, except that the record of the unit is considered in selecting the four teams to enter the semifinals and in determining their placement in the elimination brackets. In some tournaments, the semi-final round is omitted and the teams proceed directly to the final round; in other tournaments, quarter-finals or octa-finals precede the final round.

When the number of teams participating in a tournament is sufficiently

Round IV			Round V			Round VI		
Aff.	*Neg.*	*Judge*	*Aff.*	*Neg.*	*Judge*	*Aff.*	*Neg.*	*Judge*
8	1	18	1	10	19	12	1	20
10	3	20	3	12	21	14	3	22
12	5	22	5	14	23	16	5	24
14	7	24	7	16	25	18	7	26
16	9	26	9	18	27	20	9	28
18	11	28	11	20	29	22	11	30
20	13	30	13	22	1	24	13	2
22	15	2	15	24	3	26	15	4
24	17	4	17	26	5	28	17	6
26	19	6	19	28	7	30	19	8
28	21	8	21	30	9	2	21	10
30	23	10	23	2	11	4	23	12
2	25	12	25	4	13	6	25	14
4	27	14	27	6	15	8	27	16
6	29	16	29	8	17	10	29	18

	Round I			Round II	
Aff.	*Neg.*	*Judge*	*Aff.*	*Neg.*	*Judge*
1	2	7	1	4	11
2	3	8	2	5	12
3	4	9	3	6	13
4	5	10	4	7	1
5	6	11	5	8	2
6	7	12	6	9	3
7	8	13	7	10	4
8	9	1	8	11	5
9	10	2	9	12	6
10	11	3	10	13	7
11	12	4	11	1	8
12	13	5	12	2	9
13	1	6	13	3	10

	Round III			Round IV	
Aff.	*Neg.*	*Judge*	*Aff.*	*Neg.*	*Judge*
1	5	13	1	3	5
2	6	1	2	4	6
3	7	2	3	5	7
4	8	3	4	6	8
5	9	4	5	7	9
6	10	5	6	8	10
7	11	6	7	9	11
8	12	7	8	10	12
9	13	8	9	11	13
10	1	9	10	12	1
11	2	10	11	13	2
12	3	11	12	1	3
13	4	12	13	2	4

large to justify it, the elimination rounds may begin at the sextodecimo level. The principle is the same as shown on page 349 and the bracketing is 1 vs. 32, 2 vs. 31, and so on. In some unit tournaments, the two teams entering the final round are chosen on the basis of team rather than unit record. However, because this method makes it possible for two teams from the same unit to meet in the final round, it is not widely used.

The method of determining which teams enter the elimination rounds may be seen in the following example. Positions are assigned in accordance with the sample schematic of the elimination rounds considered earlier.

Team	*Wins*	*Points*	*Rank*
A	6	324	
B	6	312	
C	5	300	23
D	5	300	25
E	5	294	
F	5	288	

Team A is assigned to position 1 and team B is assigned to 2; reference to rank is unnecessary as team B has lower points than team A. Teams C and D are tied in both wins and points; therefore, reference to rank is necessary. Team C is assigned to position 3 and team D to position 4. Further reference to E and F is unnecessary if only a semi-final elimination round is used. The same method may be used for the eight teams entering a quarter-final round, the sixteen teams entering an octa-final round or the thirty-two teams entering a sextodecimo round. The sample ballot shown on page 317 provides a method of recording decisions, rank, and quality-rating points. Some additional or alternate methods of tie breaking include (1) the highest total of the "middle" debates (i.e., the debate with the highest number of points and the debate with the lowest number of points are disregarded in this procedure) or (2) the highest median number of points. These latter procedures provide protection against unusual circumstances.

IV. Selective-Pairing Tournaments

The selective-pairing procedure is used primarily in the team tournament and represents a departure from the predetermined random-pairing systems indicated above. In selective-pairing tournaments, teams as *assigned* opponents on the basis of their win-loss records and in some cases on the basis of win-loss records and quality points. Two methods of selective pairing — group pairing and power pairing — are in general use, while the third method — challenge pairing — is gaining some attention.

A. Group Pairing

When this method is used, the participating teams are usually requested to submit their season's record in advance of the tournament. On the basis of an evaluation of this record, teams are classified as "above average," "average," or "below average." The tournament schematic is then drawn in such a way that each team meets an equal number of teams from each classification.

B. Power Pairing

When this method is used, the records of the teams are evaluated after a certain number (usually two) of nonelimination random-draw rounds. In subsequent rounds, an effort is made to pair teams of equal ability — that is, at the end of the second round a team that had won two debates would be assigned to meet another team that had won two debates. If there was not an even number of teams with two wins, the team with two wins and the lowest number of quality points would be assigned to meet the team with one win and one loss and the highest number of quality points, and so on.

This method may become time consuming and complicated. Very careful records must be kept to assure that each team has an equal number of affirmative and negative rounds and that there is no duplication of judges or opponents. This requires the preparation and publication of a schematic for each round. There may be a considerable time lag between rounds.

The increased availability of computers on college campuses provides a solution to the time-lag problem. A *properly programmed* computer can make and print pairings in a few seconds, can store instructions about "forbidden pairings" and "forbidden judges" in its memory bank, and can print final results in a minute or so.

The key to the use of a computer is proper programming. The computer can make pairings in microseconds, but it will only do *exactly* what it is programmed to do. The prudent tournament director will work with a computer programmer for some time in advance of the tournament to make sure that all contingencies are provided for in the program and will have the computer put through several "dry runs" in advance of the tournament to be sure that all the "bugs" are out of the system. Computer users have coined the word "GIGO" to express this problem: Garbage In, Garbage Out. If poor data or poor programming is fed into the computer, the "print out" will be "garbage."

C. Challenge Pairing

When this method is used, certain teams are allowed to select their opponents. The organization of the challenge-pairing tournament is as follows:

1. In the first round, team control numbers are assigned by a random drawing. Sides are determined by tossing a coin—the winner having choice of sides.

2. After each round, the teams are divided into two power groups. All winning teams from the previous round are assigned to the High Power Group, and all losing teams are assigned to the Low Power Group. Teams in the lower half of each group are allowed to "challenge" any team ranking above them. The same method of ranking is used as was described earlier for use to determine which teams enter elimination rounds. In round two, only rank and points are considered; in subsequent rounds, the wins, rank, and points are considered. The lowest ranking teams in each group are permitted to "challenge" first, the next challenges second, and so on. The "challenging" team is permitted to choose the side it will defend.

3. If any team wishes to challenge the same team twice, it must reverse sides in the second debate.

4. No team is permitted to debate another team more than twice. The tournament director shall, if necessary, make arbitrary "challenge assignments" to enforce this provision.

5. Before the start of the last nonelimination round, the top teams are announced to all the participants (i.e., the sixteen teams with the best records if the tournament has octa-final eliminations). The next sixteen teams that have a mathematical chance to replace any of these teams in the octas are given an opportunity to challenge any of the top sixteen teams, the lowest ranking of the second sixteen having first choice, and so on. The remaining teams in the tournament challenge among themselves in the usual way.

6. Judging assignments are made in a separate room, thus the judges are not informed as to who is the challenger or whether the teams are in the High or Low Power Group.

This method must be conducted with efficiency and dispatch to avoid unwelcome time lags. Often it is desirable to permit challenging during only some of the rounds in a tournament and to schedule these rounds after overnight or meal breaks, thus permitting the necessary preparations to be made during natural free time in the schedule.

V. Tournament Schedule

The tournament schedule is a carefully constructed timetable listing the various events of the tournament. The schedule must take into consideration travel requirements of the participants, availability of facilities on campus, meals, and various social events that may be a part of the tournament. The tournament schedule should be prepared in tentative form and distributed to the participants several weeks in advance of the tournament; and a final copy of the schedule, including any last-minute changes, should be distributed at the start of the tournament. Following is the schedule of a team tournament that provides for eight rounds of nonelimination debate and for octa-final elimination rounds. (The schedule should indicate the buildings and rooms in which the various events will be held.)

Thursday

9:00 A.M.	Registration opens, Coffee hour
11:00 A.M.	Registration closes
12:00 Noon	Orientation, Distribution of schematics
12:30 P.M.	Round I
2:15 P.M.	Round II
4:00 P.M.	Coffee break
4:30 P.M.	Round III
6:15 P.M.	Round IV
9:00 P.M.	Reception for debaters
9:00 P.M.	Reception for directors

Friday

8:00 A.M.	Continental breakfast
9:00 A.M.	Round V
10:45 A.M.	Round VI

12:30 P.M.	Lunch
2:00 P.M.	Round VII
3:45 P.M.	Round VIII
6:30 P.M.	Tournament banquet
7:30 P.M.	Awards and announcements
	(Awards are presented to the high ranking debaters—usually the top ten—of the preliminary rounds, and announcement is made of the sixteen teams to enter the octa finals and of the judges who will serve in the octa finals.)
9:00 P.M.	Reception for debaters
9:00 P.M.	Reception for directors

Saturday

8:30 A.M.	Announcement of pairings for octa-final round
9:00 A.M.	Octa-final round
10:45 A.M.	Announcement of pairings for quarter-final round
	Distribution of results of preliminary rounds
11:00 A.M.	Quarter final round
12:45 P.M.	Lunch
1:45 P.M.	Announcement of pairings for semi-final round
2:00 P.M.	Semi-final round
3:45 P.M.	Announcement of pairings for the final round
4:00 P.M.	Final round
5:45 P.M.	Presentation of awards

This schedule has been found highly satisfactory during a number of years of actual use. Naturally, any schedule must be tailor-made to fit the requirements of the tournament and the availability of space. Some tournaments, such as the National Tournament of Delta Sigma Rho–Tau Kappa Alpha, extend from Sunday to Wednesday and require so many classrooms that they can usually be held only during the spring vacation of the host college. Considerations of classroom availability, and, during the energy crisis, of Sunday gasoline station closings, have led to some tournaments being scheduled on Friday, Saturday, and Sunday or Saturday, Sunday, and Monday.

VI. Tournament Summary

The tournament summary is a report showing the wins and losses, rank, quality points, and opponents of each team in each debate of the tournament. The tournament summary is usually duplicated and distributed, together with the ballots for each debate, at the conclusion of the tournament. Thus the debaters may study the judges' critiques of their debates and compare their achievement with that of other students while the details of the debates are still fresh in their minds. The following is a segment of a tournament summary—one that may be extended to any number of rounds and to any number of participants.

College	Round I				Round II				Round III			
	D.	Rk.	Pt.	Opp.	D.	Rk.	Pt.	Opp.	D.	Rk.	Pt.	Opp.
9. Western U.	W			10	L			12	W			14
Hornung		1	20			4	20			2	17	
Bochin		3	17			2	22			1	20	
10. Atlantic U.	L			9	L			7	W			5
Adams		4	16			4	18			3	21	
Brown		2	18			2	22			2	22	
11. Midwest U.	W			12	W			14	W			16
Sharmin		3	19			2	22			2	21	
Tally		1	30			1	23			1	25	
12. Southern U.	L			11	W			9	W			7
Laino		4	18			1	24			3	23	
Rufo		2	29			3	21			1	26	
13. New Eng. U.	W			14	W			16	W			18
Kwarciany		1	23			1	27			1	26	
Langer		3	17			2	23			3	20	

In the above segment of a tournament summary, the name of each college is preceded by its control number, and the following abbreviations are used: "D" represents decision, "W" represents won, "L" represents lost, "Rk." represents rank, "Pt." represents quality points, "Opp." represents opponent, and the number listed thereunder is the control number of that team's opponent in that round.

VII. Tournament Administration

To achieve its full potential as an educational method, a tournament must be preceded by careful planning, implemented by adequate facilities and preparation, and operated with precision by a well-trained staff. Preparation for major debate tournaments usually begins a year in advance. The administration of a tournament moves through three phases.

A. Planning Phase

In the planning phase, the date of the tournament must be set; the format of the tournament must be determined; the schematics of the tournament must be drafted; the various publications, such as the instruction sheets, programs, and schedules, must be drafted; guest speakers must be selected; and social events must be planned.

B. Implementation Phase

In the implementation phase, the various supplies must be secured, awards purchased, publications printed, and stenographic arrangements completed; student personnel must be selected and trained, reserve judges secured, space requirements reserved, and publicity prepared. At least two months prior to the tournament, invitations should be issued giving the general outline of the tournament. Many directors issue invitations in the preceding spring or early fall. At least one month prior to the tournament, general information pamphlets should be issued giving explicit details of the tournament and stating the regulations under which the tournament will operate.

C. Operational Phase

In the operational phase, the previously made plans are executed. During this phase, the director should keep his schedule free to meet such contingencies as may arise. Usually the director will establish a number of student committees to assist in the operation of the tournament. Although the number, nature, and responsibilities of these committees will vary from one situation to another, the following list is representative of the committees:

1. *Registration Committee:* Responsible for registering the participating delegations as they arrive on campus.

2. *Hospitality Committee:* Responsible for executing all social programs planned in connection with the tournament.

3. *Publications Committee:* Responsible for preparing all publications issued before, during, and after the tournament.

4. *Statistical Control Committee:* Responsible for preparing all statistics of the tournament. They receive their raw data in the form of ballots from the Ballot Control Committee and prepare summaries that will be issued by the Publications Committee.

5. *Ballot Control Committee:* Responsible for providing for each debate chairmen-timekeepers, who also deliver a ballot to the judge at the start of the debate and return the completed ballot to a central headquarters at the close of the debate.

6. *Contest Operations Committees:* If the tournament includes contests other than debate, such as extemporaneous speaking or original oratory, it is desirable to establish a separate committee—to serve in a capacity similar to that of the Ballot Control Committee for debate—for each additional contest.

7. *Other Committees:* Depending upon the local situation, a number of other committees may be needed. On some campuses, it is necessary to establish a housing committee, a transportation committee, and other committees to meet specific local needs. A small tournament may be operated by a director and one or two competent student helpers; a large tournament may require scores of student helpers organized into many committees and subcommittees. At a recent national tournament, over one hundred students served on committees, and seventeen faculty members served as committee chairmen or co-chairmen.

In today's complex industries, penny-ante mistakes often escalate into million-dollar fiascoes. In similar fashion, a petty error can upset a tournament. At one tournament, a student typist made an error in copying a schematic. As a result, the judges for Round II were assigned to judge the affirmative teams they had just judged in Round I. The tournament ground to a halt when the error was discovered. Everyone waited with growing irritation while the harried tournament director drafted, duplicated, and distributed a new schematic.

Every tournament director is aware of Murphy's First Law: "If anything can possibly go wrong, it will," and the prudent director prepares tournament plans with scrupulous attention to detail. An educational opportunity as important as a tournament should be free from defects. A tournament staff that has administered a successful tournament can feel a well-justified glow of pride.

Exercises

1. If circumstances permit, plan and conduct a debate tournament in class. This may extend over several class meetings.

2. Prepare a tournament schematic for a fifteen-unit, three-round tournament. Make sure that your schematic meets the essentials of a good schematic considered in this chapter.

3. Prepare a tournament schematic for a twenty-team, six-round tournament. Make sure that your schematic meets the essentials of a good schematic considered in this chapter.

Chapter 23

Parliamentary Debate

Whenever a group finds it necessary or desirable to have formal debate, some rules for that debate must be provided to ensure order, efficiency, and impartiality. The law courts have special rules for debates conducted in the courtroom; the governing body of each city, town, or village conducts its debates under a special set of rules; civic, social, and business organizations have special sets of rules governing debate, as do the state legislatures and Congress. Parliamentary debate permits a large number of persons to participate and provides a means for a large group to reach a decision.

Parliamentary debate derives its name from the ancient parliaments of Britain. The details of parliamentary debate, however, vary from one group to another. The rules of debate for the British Parliament are different in many ways from the rules of debate in the American Congress. The rules of debate in the Senate, for example, are far too complicated and specialized for general use by other organizations. In fact, they are different in important aspects from the rules of debate in the House of Representatives. All well-conceived rules of parliamentary debate, however, have a common nature and certain common purposes.

Parliamentary debate provides for the orderly and efficient conduct of business. It does so by considering one matter at a time and by disposing of each matter before going on to another.

Parliamentary debate assures a decision. It does so by requiring that every motion must be acted upon in some way. Once a motion has been introduced, it must be passed, defeated, or postponed. A postponement, of course, is a decision *not* to pass a motion at the present time.

Parliamentary debate protects the rights of the majority. It does so by providing that the decisions of a sufficient number of members must prevail.

Parliamentary debate protects the rights of the minority. It does so by giving the minority many important privileges. For example, any member, without the necessity of securing a second, has the right to be heard on many important matters; only two members are required to introduce any motion; and one-third of the members plus one can exercise important restraints.

Parliamentary debate is impartial. Since the rules of procedure apply equally to all members, each member has an equal right to be heard and has equal voting power.

I. Sources of Parliamentary Debate Rules

Actually there is no one set of rules for parliamentary debate, although there are a body of commonly accepted practice and some legal requirements. As has been indicated, the two Houses of Congress do not debate under the same rules. The faculty and student governments of a university undoubtedly operate under different rules of parliamentary debate; and even two different clubs probably conduct their debate under somewhat different rules. Where, then, do the rules of parliamentary debate come from? Members of each group must adopt or create their own rules. If the decisions made by the group are of particular importance—for example, the decisions of a legislative body or a corporation—prudence dictates that those conducting the meeting have at hand expert parliamentarians familiar with general usage and attorneys familiar with the special laws applicable to the particular organization. For example, state laws, which differ considerably from one state to another, often dictate the methods of voting that must be used by corporations. For the average group, however, the problem is simpler. It is usually sufficient that its members follow one set of commonly accepted practices and make provision for their special needs. The rules of parliamentary debate for the average group come from five sources: (1) the constitution of the organization; (2) the bylaws of the organization; (3) the standing rules of the organization (these are recorded in the minutes of the organization); (4) the agenda of the meeting (although it is not necessary, it is often convenient to have an agenda); (5) a stipulated source.

With the exception of national and state legislative bodies, very few organizations attempt to write their rules of parliamentary debate in full. Rather, most organizations provide a set of rules to take care of their most obvious needs and special requirements and then stipulate some source as the basis for rules not otherwise provided. Small groups, for instance, could stipulate the rules printed on pages 366 and 367 as the source of their rules. Larger groups, or groups likely to be confronted with complicated problems, would select one of the various books devoted entirely to parliamentary procedure as the stipulated source of their rules.

Sometimes the special requirements of an organization make it desirable to set aside common usage in parliamentary practice. Groups that meet annually or infrequently often find it desirable to take from the motion to adjourn its customary privileged status and give it the lowest possible priority. This provision is usually unnecessary for groups that meet weekly, but it is often advisable for groups that meet only at infrequent intervals or in situations where a hastily passed motion to adjourn might seriously inconvenience the organization. Although deviations from common practice are sometimes desirable or necessary, they should be made infrequently and only after careful consideration of all of their implications.

II. Order of Business

The usual order of business for an organization using parliamentary procedure follows a clear, logical pattern.

The Call to Order: The call to order is usually a simple announcement by the chair: "The meeting will be in order" or "The National Convention of the Democratic [or Republican] Party is now in session."

The Roll Call: There is a roll call only if one is required by the rules or customs of the organization. A roll call is a useful device in a larger organization; most smaller organizations find it unnecessary.

Reading of the Minutes of the Last Meeting: The minutes are usually read by the secretary in smaller organizations, although this reading may be omitted by unanimous consent. Larger organizations, and many smaller organizations as well, find it convenient to have the minutes printed or duplicated and distributed to the membership. Once the minutes have been presented, they may be corrected, amended, or accepted.

Reports of Standing Committees: Most organizations have various committees that are established by the constitution or whose duties continue for a long period of time, such as the executive committee or the finance committee. These committees report at this time.

Reports of Special Committees: Most organizations also have various committees that are appointed to serve for a shorter period of time or to deal with a special matter, such as a special fund raising committee or the committee to recommend a site for next year's convention. These committees report at this time.

Unfinished Business: Unfinished business is that business not completed at the previous meeting. For example, if a motion was on the floor at the time the previous meeting adjourned, that motion now comes before the house as unfinished business. A motion that was postponed at a previous meeting, by a motion to postpone temporarily or "lay on the table," may be brought before the assembly at this time by a motion to resume consideration or "take from the table." The motion to postpone to a specified time often specifies that the motion shall come before the assembly as unfinished business at the next meeting.

New Business: Once the unfinished business has been disposed of, the floor is open to new business.

Miscellaneous: The last matter of business includes announcements and other miscellaneous items that may come before the group, such as "The executive committee will meet at eight o'clock" or "Members wishing to obtain tickets for the annual outing should see Bill Smith after this meeting."

Adjourn: Once the business of the meeting is completed, the chair may ask for a motion to adjourn. Such a motion may, however, be introduced earlier.

Larger organizations, or organizations that have many items of business to consider, find it convenient to prepare an *agenda*. An agenda is a special order of business, drawn up in advance of the meeting, which takes precedence over the usual order of business. The agenda may be changed by passing a motion setting a special order of business. The agenda often includes a detailed statement of the order in which reports will be presented and motions considered. When an organization's meetings extend over more than one day, it is particularly desirable to indicate in advance which matters will be considered on each day.

III. Presenting Motions

When motions are in order, a member who wishes to make a motion must first secure recognition from the chair. To gain recognition, the member rises and addresses the presiding officer: "Mr. Chairman" or "Madam Chairman." The chair grants recognition by addressing the member: "Joe" would suffice in an informal group; "Mr. Smith" or "The delegate from Ohio" in a more formal group. If the member's name is not known the chair may ask, "Will the member state his name?" The member replies, "Joe Smith, delegate from Ohio." In granting recognition, the chair replies, "The chair recognizes Mr. Smith from Ohio." (The chair always speaks in the third person; never, "I recognize . . .")

When several members seek recognition at the same time, the chair must decide which one to recognize. In granting recognition, the chair should consider the following factors:

1. Priority should first be given to the maker of the motion.

2. Priority should be given alternately to speakers favoring and opposing the motion if they are known to the chair. If the chair does not know which speakers favor or oppose the motion, he or she may state, "The chair will recognize a speaker favoring [or opposing] the motion."

3. Priority should be given to a member who has not spoken previously.

4. If none of the other considerations apply, the chair should, if possible, recognize the member who first sought recognition.

Once a member has gained recognition he or she states the motion by saying "I move that . . ." In many organizations a member is required to give the secretary a written copy of the motion at the time it is introduced. The secretary has the privilege, should it be necessary, of interrupting a member to request a restatement of the motion so that it may be entered into the minutes accurately.

Before a main motion may be debated, it must be seconded by another member. Any other member, without the necessity of being recognized, may state, "I second the motion." If the motion is not seconded immediately, the chair may ask, "Is there a second?" If there is no second, the chair announces, "The motion is lost for lack of a second." The motion is then no longer before the house and a new motion is in order. If the motion is seconded, the chair announces, "It has been moved and seconded that . . ." and then recognizes the proposer of the motion to speak on that motion.

IV. Precedence of Motions

In the interests of order and efficiency, there is a definite order of precedence of motions. As shown in the table on pages 366 and 367, the main motion has zero, or lowest, precedence, since it may be introduced only when no other business is before the house. Once a main motion is before the house any of the other motions, when appropriate, may be applied to it. The highest precedence—1—is given to a motion to fix the time of the next meeting, and the other privileged motions follow this motion in precedence. The incidental motions rank after the privileged motions in precedence but have no precedence among themselves; they are considered in the order that they arise. The subsidiary motions follow the incidental motions in precedence and have a definite order of precedence among themselves. The table of precedence lists the motions most frequently used in parliamentary debate and the preferred rules applying to these motions. Some of the rules may be modified by special circumstances.

V. Purposes of Motions

The four types of motions—main, subsidiary, incidental, and privileged— have different purposes. These are outlined in detail below.

A. Main Motions

Main motions bring substantive proposals before the house for consideration and decision. Main motions are the core of the conduct of business; they are the most important and most frequently used motions.

General Main Motion: To bring new business before the meeting.

Reconsider: To stop all action on a motion previously voted until the motion has been reconsidered. This motion may be made by any member (unless the rules of the organization specifically establish some limitation), but it may be made only the same day as the original motion was passed or on the next business day of a convention —*not* at the next weekly or monthly meeting or at the next convention. A motion to reconsider cannot be applied to a matter that has left the assembly. For example, if a motion has been passed authorizing the treasurer to pay five dollars to the Scholarship Fund and if the treasurer has already paid that money, the motion cannot be reconsidered. If carried, the motion to reconsider places the motion previously voted upon in the exact status it had before it was voted upon. If defeated, the motion to reconsider may not be renewed.

Rescind: To cancel an action taken at some previous meeting. This motion may be made at any time when other business is not before the meeting; it cannot be applied to a matter that has left the assembly.

Resume Consideration (Take from the Table): To bring a temporarily postponed motion (a motion that had been laid on the table) before the meeting in the same state that the motion held before it was postponed temporarily.

Set Special Order of Business: To set a date or time at which a certain matter will be considered.

B. Subsidiary Motions

Subsidiary motions are alternative aids for changing, considering, and disposing of the main motion. Consequently, they are subsidiary to the main motion.

Postpone Temporarily (lay on the table): To postpone consideration of a matter. This device may be used to allow more urgent business to come before the house or to allow time for some members to gather additional information before voting. It is also a way of "sidetracking" a matter in the hope that it will not be taken up again.

Vote Immediately (previous question): To close debate and bring the matter before the meeting to an immediate vote.

Limit or Extend Debate: To set, or extend, a limit on debate on a matter before the meeting.

Postpone to a Specified Time: To delay action on a matter before the meeting until a specified time.

Refer to Committee: To refer a matter before the meeting to a committee. If applied to an amendment, this motion also takes the main motion with it. It may be used to secure the advantage of having the matter studied more carefully by a small group, or to delay action on the matter.

Refer to the Committee of the Whole: To refer a matter to the committee of the whole, in order to debate the matter "off the record" and in the greater informality of the committee of the whole.

Amend an Amendment: To amend an amendment to a motion before the meeting. Most organizations find it advisable to prohibit an amendment to an amendment to an amendment.

Amend: To change a motion. A motion to amend may take any of four forms: (1) amend by striking out, (2) amend by substitution, (3) amend by addition, or (4) amend by dividing the motion into two or more parts.

Postpone Indefinitely: To suppress the main motion to which it is applied without the risk of adopting the main motion. This device is sometimes used to identify, without the risk of adopting the motion, who favors and who opposes it.

Table of Precedence of Parliamentary Motions

Once a main motion is before the meeting, any of the following motions, when appropriate, may be made. In the following table the motions are arranged from the strongest—1—to the weakest—o. A stronger motion takes precedence over any weaker motion and becomes the business before the meeting.

Precedence Number		Interrupt Speaker?	Require a Second?	Debatable?	Vote Required?	Amendable?	Subject to Referral to Committee?	Subject to Postponement?	Subject to Reconsideration?
	Privileged Motions								
1.	Fix time of next meeting	No	Yes	No	Maj.	Yes[1]	No	No	No
2.	Adjourn	No	Yes	No	Maj.	No	No	No	No
3.	Recess	No	Yes	No	Maj.	Yes	No	No	No
4.	Question of privilege	Yes	No	No	Chr.	No	No	No	No
	Incidental Motions								
	Incidental motions are of equal rank among themselves; they are considered in the order they are moved.								
5.	Appeal decision of the chair	Yes	Yes	Yes	Maj.	No	No	Yes	Yes
5.	Close nominations	No	Yes	No	$\frac{2}{3}$	Yes[1]	No	No	No
5.	Division of the house	Yes	No	No	None	No	No	No	No
5.	Object to consideration	Yes	No	No	$\frac{2}{3}$	No	No	No	No
5.	Parliamentary inquiry	Yes	No	No	None	No	No	No	No
5.	Point of order	Yes	No	No	Chr.	No	No	No	No
5.	Suspension of rules	No	Yes	No	$\frac{2}{3}$	No	No	No	No
5.	Request for information (Will the speaker yield for a question?)	Yes	No	No	Chr. or Speaker	No	No	No	No
5.	Withdraw a motion	No	No	No	Maj.	No	No	No	No

Subsidiary Motions

Motion								
6. Postpone temporarily (lay on the table)	No	Yes	No	Maj.	No	No	No	No
7. Vote immediately (previous question)	No	Yes	No	$2/3$	No	No	No	No
8. Limit or extend debate	No	Yes	No	$2/3$	Yes	No	No	No[4]
9. Postpone to a specified time	No	Yes	Yes	Maj.	Yes	No	No	No[4]
10. Refer to committee	No	Yes	Yes	Maj.	Yes	No	No	No[4]
11. Refer to the committee of the whole	No	Yes	Yes	Maj.	Yes	No	No	No
12. Amend an amendment	No	Yes	Yes	Maj.	No	Yes	Yes	Yes
13. Amend	No	Yes	Yes	Maj.	Yes	Yes	Yes	Yes
14. Postpone indefinitely	No	Yes	Yes	Maj.	No	No	No	No

Main Motions

(Main motions are of equal rank among themselves. They have zero precedence since they may not be considered when any other motion is before the house.)

Motion								
0. General main motion	No	Yes	Yes	Maj.	Yes	Yes	Yes	Yes
0. Reconsider	Yes	Yes	Yes	Maj.	No	No	Yes[3]	No
0. Rescind	No	Yes	Yes	$2/3$[2]	Yes	Yes	Yes	Yes
0. Resume consideration (take from table)	No	Yes	No	Maj.	No	No	No	No[4]
0. Set special order of business	No	Yes	Yes	$2/3$	Yes	No	No	Yes

[1] Although the motion is not debatable, the amendment may be debated.
[2] Only a majority is required if previous notice has been given.
[3] May be postponed to a specified time only.
[4] Motion may be renewed after a change in the parliamentary situation.

C. Incidental Motions

Incidental motions arise only incidentally out of the business before the house. They do not relate directly to the main motion but usually relate to matters that are incidental to the conduct of the meeting.

Appeal Decision of the Chair: To secure a reversal of a ruling by the chair.

Close Nominations: To prevent nomination of other candidates. Voting is *not* limited to those candidates who have been nominated.

Division of the House: To require a standing vote.

Object to Consideration: To prevent consideration of a matter.

Parliamentary Inquiry: To allow a member to ascertain the parliamentary status of a matter or to seek parliamentary information.

Point of Order: To demand that the chair rule on an alleged error, mistake, or violation of parliamentary procedure.

Suspension of Rules: To suspend rules to allow procedure contrary to certain rules of the organization.

Request for Information: To allow a member to ask the chair—or, through the chair, the speaker who has the floor—for information on a matter before the meeting.

Withdraw a Motion: To prevent action on a motion before the meeting.

D. Privileged Motions

Privileged motions have no direct connection with the main motion before the house. They relate to the members and to the organization rather than to substantive proposals. They deal with such urgent matters that they are entitled to immediate consideration. Privileged motions would be main motions except for their urgency. Because of their urgency, they are given the privilege of being considered ahead of other motions that are before the house.

Fix Time of Next Meeting: To fix a time at which the group shall meet next.

Adjourn: To close the meeting. This motion is also used to prevent further consideration of a matter before the meeting.

Recess: To suspend the meeting temporarily.

Question of Privilege: To request the chair to rule on a matter relating to the privileges of the assembly or the privileges of an individual member.

VI. Unanimous Consent

To expedite business on a routine or obviously desirable matter, any member may ask that approval for a certain course of action be given by unanimous consent. The chair will then ask, "Is there any objection?" and then, if no objection is made, "Hearing none, it is so ordered." If any member objects, the required parliamentary procedure must be followed.

Exercises

1. Prepare a list of the organizations to which you belong that conduct their business through parliamentary debate. Evaluate the effectiveness of each group in parliamentary debate.

2. From your experiences in groups that conduct their business through parliamentary debate, can you recall an instance when the will of the majority was defeated by a minority better versed in parliamentary procedure? Prepare a brief report of this instance.

3. Select a proposition of policy for parliamentary debate and hold a debate on this proposition in class.

4. Conduct a debate using the same arrangement suggested in exercise 3. This time, by prearrangement with the instructor, select a small group of students who will seek to secure passage of the proposition; select a second small group of students who will seek to defeat the proposition. The majority of the class will be uncommitted on the proposition at the start of the debate.

5. Conduct a debate using the same arrangement suggested in exercise 4. This time, the supporters of the proposition will be instructed to use every possible parliamentary motion in order to "railroad" the passage of the proposition. The opponents of the proposition will be instructed to use every possible parliamentary motion in order to obstruct or defeat passage of the proposition. The class will probably encounter some difficult problems in this exercise. In working their way out of these problems—with some help from the instructor, who will serve as parliamentarian when needed—the class will gain practical experience in parliamentary procedure.

6. Arrange to conduct a model congress in class. Elect a speaker and a clerk. Your instructor will serve as parliamentarian. Before the class meets each student will prepare a bill on a subject that would be suitable for consideration by the Congress of the United States at the present time. Prepare enough copies of your bill for each member of the class and for your instructor. Distribute copies of your bill at the first meeting of the class as a model congress. Prepare bills in the following form:

a. They must be typewritten, duplicated, and doublespaced on a single sheet of white, $8\frac{1}{2}$" x 11" paper.

b. The first line shall consist of these words: "Congress Bill Number _____."

c. The second line shall consist of these words: "by (your name)."

d. Commencing with the third line, the title of the bill must be stated, beginning with the words AN ACT and containing a statement of the purpose of the bill.

e. The text of the bill proper must begin with the words: BE IT ENACTED BY THE MODEL CONGRESS. The material following must begin with the word "That." Each line of the material which follows must be numbered on the left margin of the page, beginning with "1."

f. Every section shall be numbered commencing at one. No figures shall be used in the bill except for the numbers of sections and lines. No abbreviations shall be used.

g. The following form is an illustration of the prescribed form for drafting bills:
Congress Bill Number _____
by John Doe

AN ACT to make the United States energy independent by the year 2000.
BE IT ENACTED BY THE MODEL CONGRESS
1. Section 1. That the . . .
2. . . .
3. . . .
4. Section 2. That also . . .

The First Presidential Debate

September 26, 1960, is a unique date in American history. That day marked the first debate between Presidential candidates. Unquestionably more people witnessed this than any previous debate in history. In the United States an audience of more than seventy million followed the debate as it was broadcast on three television and four radio networks. The debate was also carried on a Canadian television network and, with appropriate translations, was broadcast a day or two later in Germany, Japan, and other countries. It had a significant influence not only on the outcome of the campaign, but it also set important precedents in the United States and around the world. The debate subsequently assumed further historic importance as other unique characteristics were added. This was the second time that two men, both of whom later became Presidents of the United States, met in debate.[1] One, the youngest man ever elected to the office, was assassinated, and his followers looked back on his 1,036 days in office as a Camelot.[2] The other, the only President in our history to resign, left office after 2,027 days under a cloud of scandal.

The debaters were Democratic candidate, Senator John F. Kennedy, and Republican candidate, Vice President Richard M. Nixon. Both men were undisputed masters of efficient political machines. By 1956 both had begun well-planned campaigns to win the Presidency in 1960. Each conducted flawless pre-convention drives. Kennedy won seven out of seven primaries and received his party's nomination on the first convention ballot. Nixon so thoroughly dominated his party that no real opposition developed, and his nomination was conceded long before the convention opened.

On Election Day, (November 3) 1959, a group of speech professors began to organize The Committee on the 1960 Presidential Campaign to call upon the candidates for the Presidency to meet in debate in the tradition of Lincoln and Douglas. Initially the committee consisted of all the past presidents of the American Forensic Association and most of the past presidents of the Speech Association of America. The movement quickly gained momentum and was endorsed by the American Forensic Association, Delta Sigma Rho–Tau

---

[1] The first was in 1947 at McKeesport, Pennsylvania, when Nixon and Kennedy, both freshmen Congressmen, debated the merits of the then highly controversial Taft-Hartley Act before an audience of 150 to 200.

[2] After the then popular Broadway musical about the mythical, perfect, but short-lived and tragic court of King Arthur at Camelot.

Kappa Alpha, and the Ohio Association of College Teachers of Speech. These organizations named additional members to the committee.

The committee contacted all those in public life who, early in 1960, were mentioned as potential Presidential candidates. Kennedy endorsed the project, indicated that he would be glad to debate if nominated, and stated his belief that such debates would be "both educational and fruitful for the American people." All of the other then potential candidates, with one exception, replied to the committee endorsing the idea of debates. The exception was Richard M. Nixon. His administrative assistant replied to the committee, called the idea "worthwhile," but declined to endorse the proposal.

The committee contacted newspaper editors, columnists, television network executives, public officials, and others prominent in public life seeking support. The idea of Presidential debates captured the public's imagination. Soon editorials, columns, and articles appeared supporting the idea. Television networks indicated their willingness to cooperate. Finally, in the summer of 1960, Congress passed a special law repealing, for 1960, the "equal time" requirement. Until this requirement was repealed the stations and networks were obligated to give all minor parties equal time with the Democratic and Republican candidates.

Kennedy welcomed the debates and as early as August confided to a friend that he would win the election in the debates.[3] Nixon's advisors were sharply divided on the debates, and his campaign manager, Leonard Hall, took the unusual step of announcing publicly that he was not present when Nixon made the decision to debate.[4]

Both men were effective debaters and both had experienced considerable success in campaign debate. Nixon began his political career by winning a seat in the House of Representatives largely as a result of a series of debates with his incumbent opponent, Jerry Voorhis. Kennedy won his first seat in the Senate largely as a result of a series of debates to which he was challenged by his incumbent opponent, Henry Cabot Lodge.

Nixon had acquired a further reputation as a debater as a result of his famous "kitchen debate" with Russian Premier Khrushchev.[5] During the 1960 campaign Republican orators pointed with pride to Nixon as "the man who stood up to Khrushchev."

Kennedy participated in two "debates" prior to his nomination. He "debated" Senator Hubert Humphrey during the West Virginia primary campaign and he "debated" Senate Majority Leader Lyndon Johnson before the Texas delegation during the Democratic convention. Actually these were more pleasant exchanges of opinion that debates. Kennedy expressed his

---

[3] See: *Time*, November 7, 1960, p. 29.

[4] "Meet the Press," November 6, 1960.

[5] In 1959, Nixon and Khrushchev engaged in a well-publicized informal debate in the kitchen of a model American home at the United States exhibit in Moscow.

esteem of Humphrey and Johnson, stressed his disagreements with Nixon, and pledged himself to support whomever the Democratic Party chose as its candidate. The form of debate was an effective method of gaining an audience. The real purpose of the participants was to present themselves as able candidates and at the same time to avoid any clash that would make it impossible for the loser to support the winner after the nomination. The debates between Kennedy and Nixon were another matter. The preliminaries were over. These were the championship rounds and the Presidency was at stake.

Four debates were agreed upon, and the dates were set as September 26, October 7, 13, and 21. As the debates went on, Kennedy, sensing that he was winning, called for a fifth debate. Nixon did not agree.

The first, and most important, of the four debates originated in Studio One of the Columbia Broadcasting System's Chicago station, WBBM-TV. By agreement between the candidates the first debate was limited to domestic affairs. Both debaters, however, found it easy to bring in certain foreign problems. It was also agreed that the speakers should use no notes during the debate. The format of the debate provided that each candidate would make an opening statement of eight minutes and a closing statement of approximately three minutes. The remaining portion of the hour-long debate was devoted to questions. A panel of four newsmen, in turn, asked questions alternately of the debaters. The debater to whom the question was addressed was permitted two and a half minutes to reply and his opponent was permitted one and a half minutes for rebuttal. The debaters were not permitted to cross-examine one another. Kennedy won the toss of a coin, which gave him the opening and closing statements.

The format used might best be described as a highly specialized type of joint press-conference debate. Although it left much to be desired and is clearly inferior to the types of debate considered earlier in this book, it was at least a step in the right direction. For the first time in American history it brought Presidential candidates together on the same platform, at the same time, before the same audience, to debate some of the issues of the campaign. It provided the American people with the best means of rational decision making thus far available in any Presidential campaign.

The moderator of the program was Howard K. Smith, then a CBS newsman. He read the rules of the debate and presented the debaters.

The Kennedy-Nixon Debate of September 26, 1960

Mr. Kennedy: Mr. Smith, Mr. Nixon: In the election of 1860 Abe Lincoln said the question was whether this nation should exist half slave or half free. In the election of 1960 and with the world around us, the question is whether the world will exist half slave or half free, whether it will move in the direction of freedom, in the direction of the road that we are taking or whether it will move in the direction of slavery. I think it will depend in great measure upon what we do here in the United States, on the kind of faith we build, on the kind of strength that we maintain.

We discuss tonight domestic issues, but I would not want any implication to be given that this does not involve our struggle with Mr. Khrushchev for survival. Mr. K is in New York, and he maintains the Communist offensive throughout the world because of the productive power of the Soviet Union itself.[6]

The Chinese Communists have always had a large population, but they are important and dangerous now because they are mounting a major effort within their country.

The kind of country we have here, the kind of society we have, the kind of strength we build in the United States will be the defense of freedom. If we do well here, if we meet our obligation, if we are moving ahead, then I think freedom will be secured around the world. If we fail, then freedom fails.

Therefore, I think the question before the American people is, are we doing as much as we can do? Are we as strong as we should be? Are we as strong as we must be if we are going to maintain our independence and if we are going to maintain and hold out the hand of friendship to those who look for assistance, to those who look to us for survival.

I should make it very clear that I do not think we are doing enough, that I am not satisfied as an American with the progress that we are making. This is a great country, but I think it could be a greater country; and this is a powerful country, but I think it could be a more powerful country.

I am not satisfied to have 50 percent of our industrial mill capacity unused. I am not satisfied when the United States had last year the least rate of economic growth of any major industrialized society in the world, because economic growth means strength and vitality.

It means we are able to sustain our defense. It means we are able to meet our commitments abroad. I am not satisfied when we have nine billion dollars worth of food, some of it rotting, even though there is a hungry world and even though four million persons wait every month for a food package from the government which averages five cents a day per individual.

I saw cases in West Virginia, here in the United States, where children took home parts of their school lunch in order to feed their families. I don't think we are meeting our obligations towards these Americans. I am not satisfied when the Soviet Union is turning out twice as many scientists and engineers as we are.

I am not satisfied when many of our teachers are inadequately paid or when our children go to school on part time shifts. I think we should have an educational system second to none.

I am not satisfied when I see men like Jimmy Hoffa in charge of the largest union in the United States still free.[7] I am not satisfied when we are failing to develop the natural resources of the United States to the fullest.

Here in the United States, which developed the Tennessee Valley and which built the Grand Coulee and the other dams in northwest United States, at the present rate of hydropower production that is the hallmark of an industrialized society, the Soviet Union by 1975 will be producing more power than we are. These are all the

[6] Khrushchev, commonly called "Mr. K" in newspaper headlines, was in New York attending a United Nations meeting in his capacity as head of the Russian delegation.

[7] James Hoffa was head of the Teamsters Union. A Senate Committee, of which President Kennedy was then a member, had investigated charges of corrupt practices involving Hoffa and the Teamsters Union.

things I think in this country that can make our society strong or can mean it is standing still.

I am not satisfied until every American enjoys his full constitutional rights. If a Negro baby is born, and this is true of Puerto Ricans and Mexicans in some of our cities, he has about one-half as much chance to get through high school as a white baby, he has one-third as much chance to get through college as a white student. He has about a third as much chance to be a professional man, about half as much chance to own a house. He has about four times as much chance that he will be out of work in his life as the white baby.

I think we can do better. I don't want the talents of any American to go to waste.

I know that there are those who say that we want to turn everything over to the government. I don't at all. I want the individual to meet his responsibility, and I want the states to meet their responsibilities. But I think there is also a national responsibility.

The argument has been used against every piece of social legislation in the last 25 years. The people of the United States individually cannot develop the Tennessee Valley, collectively they could have.

A cotton farmer in Georgia or a peanut farmer or a dairy farmer in Wisconsin or Minnesota cannot protect himself against the forces of supply and demand in the marketplace, but working together in effective governmental programs he can do so.

Seventeen million Americans who are over 65 live on an average Social Security check of about $78 a month. They are not able to sustain themselves individually but they can sustain themselves through the Social Security System.

I don't believe in big government but I believe in effective governmental action, and I think that's the only way that the United States is going to maintain its freedom. It is the only way in which we are going to move ahead. I think we can do a better job.

I think we are going to have to do a better job if we are going to meet the responsibilities which time and events have placed upon us. We cannot turn the job over to anyone else. If the United States fails, then the whole cause of freedom fails, and I think it depends in great measure on what we do here in this country.

The reason Franklin Roosevelt was a good neighbor in Latin America was because he was a good neighbor in the United States, because they felt that the American society was moving again. I want us to recapture that image.

I want the people in Latin America and Africa and Asia to start to look to America to see how we are doing things, to wonder what the President of the United States is doing and not to look at Khrushchev or look at the Chinese Communists. That is the obligation upon our generation.

In 1933 Franklin Roosevelt said in his inaugural that this generation of Americans has a rendezvous with destiny. I think our generation of Americans has the same rendezvous. The question now is, can freedom be maintained under the most severe attack it has ever known?

I think it can be, and I think in the final analysis it depends upon what we do here. I think it is time America started moving again.

Mr. Smith: Now the opening statement by Vice President Richard M. Nixon.

Mr. Nixon: Mr. Smith, Senator Kennedy:

The things that Senator Kennedy has said many of us can agree with. There is no question but that we cannot discuss our internal affairs in the United States without recognizing that they have a tremendous bearing on our international position.

There is no question but that this nation cannot stand still because we are in a deadly competition, a competition not only with the men in the Kremlin but the men in Peking. We are ahead in the competition, as Senator Kennedy I think has implied, but when you are in a race the only way to stay ahead is to move ahead, and I subscribe completely to the spirit that Senator Kennedy has expressed tonight, the spirit that the United States should move ahead.

Where then do we disagree? I think we disagree on the implication of his remarks tonight and on the statements that he has made on many occasions during his campaign to the effect that the United States has been standing still.

We heard tonight, for example, the statement made that our growth in national product last year was the lowest of any industrial nation in the world. Now last year, of course, was 1958. That happened to be a recession year, but when we look at the growth of GNP[8] this year, a year of recovery, we find it is 6.9 percent and one of the highest in the world today. More about that later.

Looking then to this problem of how the United States should move ahead and where the United States is moving, I think it is well that we take the advice of a famous campaigner: Let's look at the record.

Is the United States standing still? Is it true that this Administration, as Senator Kennedy has charged, has been an Administration of retreat, or defeat, of stagnation? Is it true that as far as this country is concerned, in the field of electrical power, in all of the fields that he has mentioned, we have not been moving ahead?

Well, we have a comparison we can make. We have the record of the Truman Administration of seven and a half years, and the seven and a half years of the Eisenhower Administration. When we compare these two records in the areas Senator Kennedy has discussed tonight, I think we find that America has been moving ahead.

Let's take schools. We have built more schools in these last seven and a half years than we built in the previous seven and a half years, for that matter in the previous 20 years.

Let's take hydroelectric power. We have developed more hydroelectric power in these seven and a half years than was developed in any previous Administration in history.

Let us take hospitals. We find that more have been built in this Administration than in the previous Administration. The same is true of highways.

Let's put it in terms all of us can understand. We often hear gross national product discussed, and in that respect may I say that when we compare the growth in this Administration with that of the previous Administration, then there was a total growth of 11 percent over seven years. In this Administration there has been a total growth of 19 percent over seven years. That shows that there has been more growth in this Administration than its predecessor. But let's not put it there, let's put it in terms of the average family.

What has happened to you? We find that your wages have gone up five times as much in the Eisenhower Administration as they did in the Truman Administration.

What about the prices you pay? We find that the prices you pay went up five times as much in the Truman Administration as they did in the Eisenhower Administration.

---

[8] Gross National Product.

What's the net result of this? This means that the average family income went up 15 percent in the Eisenhower years as against 2 percent in the Truman years.

Now, this is not standing still, but as good as this record is, may I emphasize it isn't enough. A record is never something to stand on, it is something to build on, and thus building on this record I believe that we have the secret for progress. We have the way to progress. I think first of all our own record proves that we know the way.

Senator Kennedy has suggested that he believes he knows the way. I respect the sincerity in which he makes this suggestion but, on the other hand, when we look at the various programs that he offers, they do not seem to be new; they seem to be simply retreads of the programs of the Truman Administration which preceded him, and I suggest during the course of the evening he might indicate those areas in which his programs are new, where they will mean more progress than we have had.

What kind of programs are we for? We are for programs that will expand educational opportunities, that will give to all Americans their equal chance for education, for all of the things which are necessary and dear to the hearts of our people. We are for programs in addition which will see that our medical care for the aged is much better handled than it is at the present time.

Here again may I indicate that Mr. Kennedy and I are not in disagreement as to the aim.

We both want to help the old people. We want to see that they do have adequate medical care. The question is the means. I think the means that I advocate will reach that goal better than the means that he advocates.

I could give better examples for whatever it is, whether it is in the field of housing or health or medical care or schools or the development of electrical power. We have programs which we believe will move America, move her forward and build on the wonderful record that we have made over these past seven and a half years.

Now, when we look at these programs, might I suggest that in evaluating them we often have a tendency to say that the test of a program is how much you are spending. I will concede that in all these years to which I have referred Senator Kennedy would have the federal government spend more than I would have it spend.

I costed out the cost of the Democratic platform. It runs a minimum of $15,200,-000,000 more than we are presently spending to a maximum of $18,000,000,000 more than we are presently spending.

Now, the Republican platform will cost more, too. It will cost a minimum of a billion more to a maximum of $4,900,000,000 more than we are presently spending.

Now, does this mean that their program is better than ours? Not at all, because it isn't a question of how much the federal government spends. It isn't a question of which government does most.

It is a question of which Administration does the right thing, and in our case I do believe that our programs will stimulate the creative energies of 180,000,000 free Americans. I believe the program that Senator Kennedy advocates will have a tendency to stifle those creative energies.

I believe, in other words, that his programs would lead to the stagnation of the motive power that we need in this country to get progress.

The final point that I would like to make is this:

Senator Kennedy has suggested in his speeches that we lack compassion for the poor, for the old, and for others that are unfortunate.

Let us understand throughout this campaign that his motives and mine are sincere. I know what it means to be poor. I know what it means to see people who are unemployed. I know Senator Kennedy feels as deeply about these problems as I do, but our disagreement is not about the goals for America, only about the means to reach those goals.

Mr. Smith: Thank you, Mr. Nixon. That completes the opening statements, and now the candidates will answer questions or comment upon one another's answers to questions put to them by correspondents of the networks. The correspondents:[9]

Mr. Vanocur: I am Sander Vanocur, NBC News.

Mr. Warren: I am Charles Warren, Mutual News.

Mr. Novins: I am Stuart Novins, CBS News.

Mr. Fleming: Bob Fleming, ABC News.

Mr. Smith: The first question to Senator Kennedy from Mr. Fleming.

Mr. Fleming: Senator, the Vice President in his campaign said you are naive and at times immature and he has raised the question of leadership. On this issue of leadership, do you think your experiences in government are comparable?

Mr. Kennedy: Yes, because the Vice President and I have served in the Congress together. In 1946 we both served on the labor committee. I have been there now for 14 years, the same period of time he has. So that our experience in government is comparable.

Secondly, I think the question is, what are the other programs that we advocate? What is the party record that we leave?

I come out of the Democratic Party, which in this century has produced Woodrow Wilson and Franklin Roosevelt and Harry Truman, which supported and sustained these programs which I have discussed tonight.

Mr. Nixon comes out of the Republican Party. He was nominated by them, and it is a fact through most of these last 25 years that the Republican leadership has opposed federal aid for education, medical care for the aged, development of the Tennessee Valley, development of our natural resources.

I think Mr. Nixon is an effective leader of his party. I hope he would grant me the same. The question before us is, which point of view and which party do we want to lead the United States?

Mr. Smith: Mr. Nixon, would you like to comment on that statement?

Mr. Nixon: I have no comment.

Mr. Smith: The next question, Mr. Novins.

Mr. Novins: Mr. Vice President, your campaign stresses the value of your eight-years' experience, and the question arises as to whether that experience was as an observer or as a participant or an initiator of policymaking? Would you tell us, please, specifically what major proposals you have made in the last eight years that have been adopted by the Administration?

[9] Each of the correspondents was seen on camera as he introduced himself.

Mr. Nixon: It would be rather difficult to cover the eight years in two and a half minutes. I would suggest that these proposals could be mentioned: First, after each of my foreign trips I made recommendations that have been adopted.

For example, after my first trip abroad, I strongly recommended that we increase our exchange programs, particularly as they related to exchange of persons, of leaders, in the labor field and in the information field.

After my trip to South America I made recommendations that a separate inter-American lending agency be set up which the South American nations would like much better than to participate in the lending agencies which treated all the countries of the world the same.

I have made other recommendations after each of the other trips. For example, after my trip abroad to Hungary, I made some recommendations with regard to the Hungarian refugee situation, which were adopted, not only by the President, but some of them were enacted into law by the Congress.

Within the administration of the President's committee on price stability and economic growth, I have had the opportunity to make recommendations which have been adopted within the administration, and which I think have been reasonably effective.

I know Senator Kennedy suggested in his speech in Cleveland yesterday that this committee had not been particularly effective. I would only suggest that, while we do not take the credit for it—I would not presume to—that since that committee has been formed, the price line has been held very well within the United States.

Mr. Kennedy: Well, I would say on the latter, that is what I found somewhat unsatisfactory about the figures, Mr. Nixon, that you used in your previous speech when you talked about the Truman Administration.

Mr. Truman came to office in 1944, and at the end of the war, and difficulties that were facing the United States during this period of transition, 1946, when price controls were lifted; it is rather difficult to use the overall figures, of using those seven and a half years, and comparing them to the last eight years. I would prefer to take the overall percentage record of the last 20 years of the Democrats and the eight years of the Republicans to show an overall period of growth.

In regard to price stability, I am not aware that that committee did produce recommendations that ever were certainly before the Congress from the point of view of legislation in regard to controlling prices.

In regard to the exchange of students—I mean Africa—I think that one of the most unfortunate phases of our policy toward that country was the very minute number of exchanges that we had.

I think it is true of Latin America also. We did come forward with a program of students for The Congo of over 300, which is more than the federal government allowed from all of Africa. So that I don't think that we have moved, at least in those two areas, with sufficient vigor.

Mr. Smith: The next question to Senator Kennedy from Mr. Warren.

Mr. Warren: Senator Kennedy, during your brief speech a few minutes ago you mentioned farm surplus. I would like to ask this. It is a fact, I think, that the Presidential candidates always make promises to farmers. Lots of people, I think, don't understand why the government pays farmers for not producing certain crops, or paying farmers if they overproduce for that matter. Let me ask, sir, why can't the farmer operate like the businessman who operates factories. If an auto company over-produces a certain model car, Uncle Sam doesn't step in and buy the surplus. Why this constant courting of the farmer?

Mr. Kennedy: Because I think if the federal government moved out of the program and withdrew its support, then I think you would have complete economic chaos. The farmer plants in the spring and harvests in the fall.

There are hundreds of thousands of them. They really are not able to control their market very well. They bring their crops in, or their livestock in, many of them about the same time. They have only a few purchasers that buy their milk or their hogs, a few large companies in many cases.

Therefore the farmer is not in a position to bargain very effectively in the market-place. I think the experience of the twenties has shown what a free market can do to agriculture. If the agricultural economy collapses, then the economy of the rest of the United States sooner or later will collapse.

The farmers are the number one market for the automobile industry of the United States. The automobile industry is the number one market for steel.

So if the farmer's economy continues to decline as sharply as it has in recent years, then I think you have a recession in the rest of the country. So I think the case of the government intervention is a good one. Secondly, my objection to present farm policy is that there is no effective control to bring supply and demand into better balance.

The dropping of the support price in order to limit production does not work, and we now have the highest surplus, nine billion dollars' worth.

We have had a higher tax load from the Treasury for the farmer in the last few years with the lowest farm income in many years. I think this farm policy has failed. In my judgment the only policy that will work will be for effective supply and de-mand, and that can only be done through governmental action.

I therefore suggest that in those basic commodities which are supported that the federal government, after endorsement by the farmers in that commodity, attempt to bring supply and demand into balance, attempt effective production controls, so that we won't have that 5 or 6 percent surplus which breaks the price 15 or 20 percent.

I think Mr. Benson's program has failed, and I must say that after reading the Vice President's speech before the farmers, as he read mine, I don't believe that it is very much different from Mr. Benson's; so I don't think it provides effective con-trol. I think the support prices are tied to the average market price of the last three years, which was Mr. Benson's theory. I therefore do not believe that that is a sharp enough breach from the past to give us any hope of success for the future.

Mr. Smith: Mr. Nixon, any comment?

Mr. Nixon: I, of course, disagree with Senator Kennedy insofar as his suggestion as to what should be done on the farm program. He has made the suggestion that we need to move in the direction of more government controls, a suggestion that would also mean raising prices that the consumers pay for products, and imposing upon the farmers controls on acreage even far more than they have today.

I think this is the wrong direction. I don't think this has worked in the past. I do not think it will work in the future. The program that I have advocated is one which departs from the present program that we have in this respect.

It recognizes that the government has a responsibility to get the farmer out of the trouble he presently is in because the government got him into it, and that is the fundamental reason why we can't let the farmer go by himself at the present time.

The farmer produced these surpluses because the government asked him to through legislation during the war. Now that we have these surpluses, it is our responsibility to indemnify the farmer during that period that we get rid of the surplus.

Until we get rid of the farmer . . . until we get the surpluses off the farmers' backs, however, we should have a program such as I announced which will see that farm income holds up, but I would propose holding that income up not through the type of program that Senator Kennedy has suggested, which would raise prices, but one that would indemnify the farmer, pay the farmer in kind from the products which are in surplus.

Mr. Smith: The next question to Vice President Nixon from Mr. Vanocur.

Mr. Vanocur: Mr. Vice President, since the question of executive leadership is a very important campaign issue, I would like to follow Mr. Novins' question.

Now, Republican campaign slogans — we see them on signs around the country as we did last week — say it is experience that counts. That was over a picture of yours, sir — implying that you have more governmental, executive, decision-making experience than your opponent.

Now, in his news conference on August 24, President Eisenhower was asked to give one example of a major idea of yours that he adopted. His reply was, and I am quoting: "If you give me a week I might think of one; I don't remember." That was a month ago, sir, and the President hasn't brought it up since.

I am wondering, sir, if you can clarify which version is correct, the one put out by Republican campaign leaders or the one put out by President Eisenhower.

Mr. Nixon: Well, I would suggest, Mr. Vanocur, that if you know the President, that was probably a facetious remark.

I would also suggest that insofar as his statement is concerned, that I think it would be improper for the President of the United States to disclose the instances in which members of his official family had made recommendations, as I have made them through the years to him, which he has accepted or rejected.

The President has always maintained, and very properly so, that he is entitled to get what advice he wants from his Cabinet and from his other advisers without disclosing that to anybody, including, as a matter of fact, the Congress.

Now, I can only say this: Through the years I have sat on the National Security Council, I have been in the Cabinet, I have met with legislative leaders, I have met with the President when he made the great decisions with regard to Lebanon, Quemoy, Matsu and other matters, the President has asked for my advice. I have given it. Sometimes my advice has been taken, sometimes it has not.

I do not say that I have made the decisions and I would say that no President should ever allow anybody else to make the major decisions. The President only makes the decisions; all that his advisers can do is to give counsel when he asks for it.

As far as what experience counts and whether experience does count, that isn't for me to say. I can only say that my experience is there for the people to consider, Senator Kennedy's is there for the people to consider. As he pointed out we came to

Congress in the same year. His experience has been different from mine. Mine has been in the executive branch, his has been in the legislative branch.

I would say that the people now have the opportunity to evaluate his as against mine, and I think both he and I are going to abide by whatever the people decide.

Mr. Smith: Senator Kennedy.

Mr. Kennedy: I will just say this, on the question of experience: The question also is what our judgment is in the future and what our goals are for the United States and what ability we have to implement those goals.

Abe Lincoln came to the Presidency in 1860, after a rather little-known session in the House of Representatives, and after being defeated for the Senate in '58, and was a distinguished President.

There is no certain road to the Presidency; there are no guarantees that if you take one road or another that you will be a successful President. I have been in the Congress for 14 years; I have voted in the last eight years when the Vice President was presiding over the Senate as one of his responsibilities.

I have met decisions over 800 times on matters which affected not only the domestic security of the United States but as a member of the Senate Foreign Relations Committee.

The question really is, which candidate and which party can meet the problems of the United States that will make the decision.

Mr. Smith: The next question to Senator Kennedy from Mr. Novins.

Mr. Novins: Senator Kennedy, in connection with these problems of the future that you speak of and the program that you enunciated earlier in your direct talk, you called for expanding some of the welfare programs for schools, for teachers' salaries, medical care and so forth; but you also called for reducing the federal debt, and I am wondering how you, if you are President in January, would go about paying the bills for all this.

Mr. Kennedy: I am not advocating the reducing of the federal debt, because I don't believe you are going to be able to reduce the federal debt very much in 1961, '62, or '63, and if you have the obligations which we are going to have to meet. And, therefore, I have never suggested we should be able to retire the debt substantially or even at all in 1961 or '62.

Mr. Novins: I think in one of your speeches you suggested reducing the interest rate would help.

Mr. Kennedy: No, not reducing the debt; reducing the interest rate. In my judgment, the hard money, the tight money policy, fiscal policy of this administration has contributed to the slowdown in our economy which helped bring the recession of '54, which made the recession of '58 rather intense, and which has slowed somewhat our economic activity in 1960.

What I have talked about is, however . . . the kind of programs that I talk about, in my judgment are fiscally sound medical care for the aged, which I would put under Social Security.

The Vice President and I disagree on this. The Javits-Nixon or the Nixon-Javits program would have cost, if fully used, 600 million dollars by the government per year and 600 million by the states. The program which I advocated, which failed by five votes, is medical care for the aged tied in with Social Security and would have been paid for through the Social Security System and the Social Security tax.

Secondly, I support federal education and federal aid for teachers' salaries. I think that's a good investment. I think we are going to have to do it, and I think to keep the burden further on the property tax, which is already strained in many of our communities, it will provide, it will insure, in my opinion, that many of our children will not be adequately educated and many of our teachers not adequately compensated. There is no greater return to an economy or to a society than an educational system second to none.

The question of developing of natural resources, I would pay as you go. The power revenues would bring back sufficient money to finance the project in the same way as the Tennessee Valley.

I believe in the balanced budget, and the only conditions under which I would unbalance the budget would be if there was a grave national emergency or a serious recession; otherwise, with a steady rate of economic growth, and Mr. Nixon and Mr. Rockefeller in their meeting said a 5 percent economic growth would bring by 1962 ten billion dollars extra in tax revenue — whatever is brought in I think we can finance the essential programs within a balanced budget, if business remains orderly.

Mr. Smith: Mr. Nixon, a comment?

Mr. Nixon: I think what Mr. Novins is referring to was not one of the speeches of Senator Kennedy but the Democratic platform which did mention cutting the national debt. I think, too, that it should be pointed out that, of course, it is not possible, particularly under the proposal that the Senator has advocated, either to cut the national debt or to reduce taxes. As a matter of fact, it will be necessary to raise taxes.

Senator Kennedy pointed out that as far as his one proposal is concerned, the one for medical care for the aged, that that would be financed out of Social Security. That, however, is raising taxes for those who pay Social Security.

He points out that he would make pay-as-you-go be the basis for our natural resource development, which I also supported generally. However, whenever you appropriate money for one of these projects you have to pay now and appropriate the money. While they eventually do pay the debt, the government has to put out the money this year.

So, I would say that all of these proposals Senator Kennedy has made result in one of two things:

Either he has to raise taxes or he has to unbalance the budget. If he unbalances the budget, that means you have inflation, and that will be, of course, a very cruel blow to the very people, the older people, that we have been talking about.

As far as aid for school construction is concerned, I favor that, as Senator Kennedy did in January of this year. When he said he favored that rather than aid to teacher's salaries, I favored that because I believe that's the best way to aid our schools without running any risk whatever of the federal government telling our teachers what to teach.

Mr. Smith: The next question to Vice President Nixon from Mr. Warren.

Mr. Warren: Mr. Vice President, you mentioned schools. It was just yesterday I think you asked for a crash program to raise educational standards, and this evening you talked about advances in education.

Mr. Vice President, you said it was back in 1957 that all salaries paid to school teachers were nothing short of a national disgrace. Higher salaries for teachers you added were important and if the situation wasn't corrected, it would lead to national disaster. Yet you refused to vote in the Senate in order to break a tie vote when that same vote, if it had been yes, would have granted salary increases to teachers.

I wonder if you can explain that to me.

Mr. Nixon: I am awful glad you got that in because, as you know, I got into the last of my other questions and wasn't able to complete the argument.

I think the reason that I voted against having the federal government pay teachers' salaries was probably the very reason that concerned Senator Kennedy when, in January of this year, in his kickoff press conference, he said that he favored aid for school construction, but at that time did not feel that there should be aid for teachers' salaries. At least, that's the way I read his remarks.

Now, why should there be any question about the federal government aiding teachers' salaries? Why did Senator Kennedy take that position then? Why do I take it now? We both took it then and I take it now for this reason: We want higher teachers' salaries, we need higher teachers' salaries, but we also want our education to be free of federal control.

When the federal government gets the power to pay teachers, inevitably, in my opinion, it will acquire the power on such standards to tell the teachers what to teach. I think this would be bad for the country, I think it would be bad for the teaching profession.

There is another point that should be made. I favor higher salaries for teachers but, as Senator Kennedy said in January of this year, and in the same press conference, the way that you get higher salaries to teachers is to support school construction, which means that all the local school districts in the various states then have money which is free to raise the standards for teachers' salaries.

I should also point out this: Once you put the responsibility on the federal government for paying a portion of teachers' salaries, your local communities and your states are not going to meet the responsibility as much as they should. I believe, in other words, that we have seen the local communities in the states assuming more of that responsibility.

Teachers' salaries, very fortunately, have gone up 50 percent in the last eight years as against only a 34 percent rise for other salaries. This is not enough. It should be more. But I do not believe that the way to get more salaries for teachers is to have a federal government get in with a massive program.

My objection here is not the cost in dollars; my objection here is the potential cost in control and eventual loss of freedom for the American people by giving the federal government power over education, and that is the greatest power a government can have.

Mr. Smith: Senator Kennedy's comments?

Mr. Kennedy: When the Vice President quoted me in January 1960, I did not believe that the federal government should pay directly teachers' salaries, but that was not the issue before the Senate in February. The issue before the Senate was that the money would be given to the states, the states then could determine whether the money would be spent for school construction or teachers' salaries.

On that question the Vice President and I disagree. I voted in favor of that proposal and supported it strongly because I think that that provided an answer to our teachers for their salaries without any chance of federal control, and it is on that vote that Mr. Nixon and I disagreed, and his not breaking the tie vote defeated the proposal.

I don't want the federal government paying teachers' salaries directly, but if the money would go to the states, the states could then determine whether it should go for school construction or for teachers' salaries.

In my opinion, then, you protect the local authority over the school board and the school committees. And, therefore, I think that was a sound proposal and that is why I supported it and I regret that it did not pass.

Secondly, there have been statements made that the Democratic platform would cost a great deal of money and that I am in favor of unbalancing the budget. That is wholly wrong, wholly in error, and it is a fact that in the last eight years the Democratic Congress has reduced the appropriations requested by over ten billion dollars. That is not my view, and I think it ought to be stated very clearly in the record. My view is that you can do these programs and they should be carefully drawn within a balanced budget if our economy is moving ahead.

Mr. Smith: The next question to Senator Kennedy from Mr. Vanocur.

Mr. Vanocur: Senator, you have been promising the voters that if you are elected President, you will try and push through Congress bills on medical aid to the aged, a comprehensive minimum hourly wage bill, federal aid to education. Now, in the August post-convention session of the Congress, when there was at least held up the possibility you could one day be President, and when you had overwhelming majorities, especially in the Senate, you could not get action on these bills.

Now, how do you feel that you will be able to get them in January if you couldn't get them in August?

Mr. Kennedy: We did pass in the Senate a bill to provide $1.25 minimum wage. It failed because the House did not pass it, and the House failed by 11 votes, and I might say that two-thirds of the Republicans in the House voted against the $1.25 minimum wage, and a majority of the Democrats sustained it, nearly two-thirds voted for the $1.25.

We were threatened by a veto if we passed the $1.25 minimum. It is extremely difficult with the great power that a President has to pass any bill when a President is opposed to it. All that the President needs to sustain his veto of any bill is one-third plus one in either the House or the Senate.

Secondly, we passed a federal aid to education bill in the Senate. It failed to come to the floor of the House of Representatives. It was killed in the rules committee.

And it is a fact, in the August session, that the four members of the rules committee who are Republicans, joining with two Democrats, voted against sending the aid to education bill to the floor of the House. Four Democrats voted for it.

Every Republican in the rules committee voted against sending that bill to be considered by the members of the House of Representatives.

Thirdly, on medical care for the aged, this is the same fight that's been going on for 25 years, and we wanted to tie it in with Social Security. We offered an amendment to do so. Forty-four Democrats voted for it, one Republican voted for it, and we were informed at the time it came to a vote that if it was adopted, the President of the United States would veto it.

In my judgment, a vigorous Democratic President, supported by a Democratic majority in the House and Senate, can win the support for these programs.

But if you send a Republican President and a Democratic majority in, the threat of a veto hangs over the Congress, and in my judgment you will continue what happened in the August session, which is a clash of parties and inaction.

Mr. Smith: Mr. Nixon, a comment.

Mr. Nixon: Well, obviously, my views are a little different. First of all, I don't see how it is possible for one-third of a body, such as the Republicans have in the House and Senate, could stop two-thirds if the two-thirds are adequately led. I would say, too, that when Senator Kennedy refers to the action of the House Rules Committee, there are eight Democrats on that committee and four Republicans.

It would seem to me again that it is very difficult to blame the four Republicans for the eight Democrats not getting something through that particular committee.

I would say further to blame the President in his veto power for the inability of the Senator and his colleagues to get action in this special session misses the mark. When the President exercises the veto power, he has to have the people behind him, not just a third of the Congress, because let's consider it.

If the majority of the members of Congress felt that these particular proposals were good issues, the majority of those who were Democrats, why didn't they pass them and send them to the President and get a veto and have an issue? The reason why these particular bills and these various fields that have been mentioned were not passed was not because the President was against them, it was because the people were against them, it was because they were too extreme. And I am convinced that the alternate proposals, that I have, that the Republicans have, in the field of health, in the field of education, in the field of welfare, are not extreme, because they will accomplish the end without too great cost in dollars or in freedom, that they could get through the next time.

Mr. Smith: The next question to Vice President Nixon from Mr. Fleming.

Mr. Fleming: Mr. Vice President, I take it, then, you believe that you can work better with Democratic majorities in the House and Senate than Senator Kennedy could work with Democratic majorities in the House and Senate?

Mr. Nixon: I would say this, that we, of course, expect to pick up some seats in both the House and the Senate. We would hope to control the House, to get a majority in the House in this election. We could not, of course, control the Senate.

I would say that a President will be able to lead, a President will be able to get his program through, to the effect that he has the support of the country, the support of the people. Sometimes we get the opinion that in getting programs through the House and Senate, it is purely a question of legislative finagling, and all that sort of thing.

Really whenever there is a majority of people for a program, the House and the Senate respond to it, and whether this House and Senate in the next session is Democratic or Republican, if the country will have voted for the candidate for the Presidency and for the proposals that he has made, I believe that you will find that the President, if he were a Republican, as it would be in my case, would be able to get his program through that Congress.

Now, I also say that as far as Senator Kennedy's proposals are concerned, that again the question is not simply one of a Presidential veto stopping a program, you must always remember that a President can't stop anything unless he has people behind him, and the reason President Eisenhower's veto has been sustained, the reason the Congress does not send up bills to him which they think will be vetoed is because the people and the Congress, the majority of them, know the country is behind the President.

Mr. Smith: Senator Kennedy.

Mr. Kennedy: Let's look at the bills that the Vice President suggests were too extreme. One was a bill for $1.25 an hour for anyone who works in a store or a company that does a million dollars a year business. I don't think that is extreme at all. And yet nearly two-thirds to three-fourths of the Republicans in the House of Representatives voted against that proposal.

Second was the Federal Aid to Education Bill, because of the defeat of the teachers' salaries, was not a bill that was extreme. In my opinion, the fact of the matter is, it was a bill that was less than you recommended, Mr. Nixon, this morning in your proposal. It was an extreme bill. And yet we could not get one Republican to join — at least I think four of the eight Democrats voted to send it to the House, and not one Republican joined with those Democrats who were opposed to it.

I don't say the Democrats are united in support of the program, but I do say a majority are, and I say a majority of Republicans are opposed to it.

Third was the medical care for the aged which was tied to Social Security, which was to be financed out of the Social Security funds, and does not put a deficit on the Treasury. The proposal advanced by you and Mr. Javits would have cost six hundred millions of dollars. Mr. Rockefeller rejected it in New York. He said he didn't agree with the financing at all. He said it ought to be tied to Social Security.

So these are three programs which are quite moderate. It shows the difference between the two parties. One party is ready to move on these programs, the other party gives them lip service.

Mr. Smith: Mr. Warren's question for Senator Kennedy.

Mr. Warren: Senator Kennedy, on another subject, communism is so often described as an ideology, a belief that exists somewhere other than in the United States. Let me ask you, sir, just how serious a threat to our national security have these communists' subversive activities in the United States been?

Mr. Kennedy: I think they are serious. I think it is a matter that we should continue to give great care and attention to. We should support the laws of the United States as passed in order to protect us from those who would destroy us from within. We should sustain the Department of Justice in its efforts and the FBI and we should continually be alert. I think if the United States is to maintain a strong society here in the United States, I think that we can meet any internal threat; the major threat is external and will continue.

Mr. Smith: Mr. Nixon, a comment?

Mr. Nixon: I agree with Senator Kennedy's appraisal generally in this respect. The question of communism within the United States has been one that has worried us in the past; it is one that will continue to be a problem for years to come.

We have to remember that the cold war that Mr. Khrushchev is waging, and his colleagues are waging, is waged all over the world and is waged right here in the United States. That's why we have to continue to be alert.

It is also essential in being alert that we be fair, because by being fair we uphold the very freedoms that the communists would destroy. We uphold the standards of conduct which they would never follow. And in this connection I think that we must look to the future, having in mind the fact that we fight communism at home not only by our laws to deal with communists, the few who do become communists and the few who do become fellow travelers, but we also fight communism at home by moving against those various injustices which exist in our society which the communists feed upon.

And in that connection I again say, while Senator Kennedy says we are for the status quo, I do believe that he would agree that I am just as sincere in believing in my proposals for federal aid to education, my proposals for health care, are just as sincerely held as his. The question again is not one of goals. We are for those goals. It is one of the means.

Mr. Smith: Mr. Vanocur's question for Vice President Nixon.

Mr. Vanocur: Mr. Vice President, in one of your earlier statements you said we moved ahead, we built more schools, we built more hospitals. Now, sir, isn't it true that the building of more schools is a local matter for financing? Were you claiming that the Eisenhower Administration was responsible for the building of these schools or is it the local school districts that provided for it?

Mr. Nixon: Not at all. As a matter of fact, your question brings out a point that I am very glad to make. Too often in appraising whether we are moving ahead or not, we think only of what the federal government is doing.

Now, that isn't the test of whether America moves; the test of whether America moves is whether the federal government, plus the state government, plus the local government, plus the biggest segment of all, individual enterprise, moves.

We have, for example, the gross national product of approximately 500 billion dollars. Roughly a hundred billion dollars to a hundred and a quarter of that is the result of government activity. Four hundred billion, approximately, is the result of what individuals do.

Now, the reason the Eisenhower Administration has moved, the reason that we have had the funds, for example, locally to build the schools and the hospitals and the highways, to make the progress that we have, is because this Administration has encouraged individual enterprise, and it has resulted in the greatest expansion of the private sector of the economy that has ever been witnessed in an eight-year period, and that is growth. That is the growth that we are looking for, it is the growth that this Administration has supported in the past.

Mr. Smith: Senator Kennedy?

Mr. Kennedy: I must say the reason that the schools have been constructed is because the local school districts were willing to increase the property taxes to a tremendously high figure, in my opinion almost to a point of diminishing returns, in order to sustain the schools.

Secondly, I think we have a rich country, and I think we have a powerful country. I think what we have to do, however, is have the President and the leadership set before our country exactly what we must do in the next decade if we are going to maintain our security, in education, in economic growth, in development of natural resources.

The Soviet Union is making great gains. It isn't enough to compare what might have been done eight years ago or 10 years ago or 15 years ago or 20 years ago. I want to compare what we are doing with what our adversaries are doing so that by the year 1970 the United States is ahead in education, in health, in building, in homes, in economic strength.

I think that is the big assignment, the big task, the big function of the federal government.

Mr. Smith: We have completed our questions and our comments and judgments, and we will have the summation time. There will be allowed three minutes and 20 seconds for each candidate.

Mr. Nixon, will you make the first summation?

Mr. Nixon: Mr. Smith, Senator Kennedy: First of all, I think it is well to consider where we really do stand with regard to the Soviet Union in this whole matter of growth. The Soviet Union has been moving faster than we have, but the reason for that is obvious. They started from a much lower base.

Although they have been moving faster in growth than we have, we find, for example, today, that their total gross national product is only 44 percent of our total gross national product. That's the same percentage that it was 20 years ago. And as far as the absolute capacity is concerned, we find that the United States is even further ahead than it was 20 years ago.

Is this any reason for complacency? Not at all, because these are determined men, they are fanatical men, and we have to get the very most out of our economy. I agree with Senator Kennedy completely on that score. Where we disagree is in the means that we would use to get the most out of our economy.

I respectfully submit that Senator Kennedy too often would rely too much on the federal government, on what it would do to solve our problems, to stimulate growth. I believe that when we examine the Democratic platform, when we examine the proposals that he has discussed tonight, when we compare them with the proposals that I have made, that these proposals that he makes would not result in greater growth for this country than would be the case if we followed the program that I am advocating.

There are many of the points that he has made that I would like to comment upon. The one in the field of health is worth mentioning. Our health program, the one that Senator Javits and other Republican senators as well as I supported, is one that provides for all people over 65 who want health insurance the opportunity to have it if they want it. It provides a choice of having either government insurance or private insurance but it compels nobody to have insurance who does not want it. His program under Social Security would require everybody who has Social Security to take government health insurance whether he wanted it or not, and it would not cover several million people who are not covered by Social Security at all.

Here is one place where I think that our program does a better job than his.

The other point that I would make is this: This downgrading of how much things cost. I think many of our people will understand better when they look at what happened during the Truman Administration when the government was spending more than it took in. We found savings of over a lifetime eaten up by inflation. We found the people who could least afford it, people on retired incomes, people on fixed incomes, we found them unable to meet their bills at the end of the month.

It is essential that a man who is President of this country certainly stand for every program that will mean growth, and I stand for programs that will mean growth and progress. But it is also essential that he not allow a dollar spent that could be better spent by the people themselves.

Mr. Smith: Senator Kennedy, your conclusion.

Mr. Kennedy: The point was made by Mr. Nixon that the Soviet production is only 44 percent of ours. I must say that 55 percent in that Soviet Union is causing a good deal of trouble tonight. I want to make sure that it stays in that relationship. I don't want to see the day when it is 60 percent of our production, 75, and 80, and 90 percent of ours—with all the force and power that he could bring to bear in order to cause our destruction.

Secondly, the Vice President mentioned medical care for the aged. Our program was an amendment to the Kerr Bill. The Kerr Bill provided a means for all those who were not on Social Security. I think it is a very clear contrast. In 1931 when the Social Security act was written, 94 out of 95 Republicans voted against it, and Mr. Landon ran in 1936 to repeal it. In August of 1960, when we tried to get it again, this time for medical care, we received the support of one Republican in the Senate on this occasion.

Thirdly, I think the question before the American people is they look at this country and they look at the world around them. The goals are the same for all Americans. There is a question; there is an issue.

If you feel that everything that is being done now is satisfactory, if the relative power and prestige and strength of the United States is increasing in relation to that of the communists, that we are gaining more security, that we are achieving everything as a nation that we should achieve, that we are achieving a better life for our citizens and gaining strength, then I agree I think you should vote for Mr. Nixon.

But if you feel that we have to move again in the sixties, it is the function of the President to step before the people and present the unfinished business of our society as Franklin Roosevelt did in the thirties, the agenda for our people, what we must do as a society to meet our needs in this country and to protect our security and hence the cause of freedom—as I said at the beginning, the question before us all that faces all Republicans and Democrats is, is freedom in the next generation possible or are the communists going to be successful? That is the great issue.

And if we meet our responsibilities, I think freedom will succeed. If we fail to move ahead, if we fail to develop such military and economic and social strength here in this country, then I think that the tide could begin to run against us, and I don't want historians ten years from now to say these are the years when the tide ran against the United States. I want them to say these were the years when the tide came in, these were the years when the United States started to move again.

That's the question before the American people and only you can decide what you want, what you want this country to be, what you want to do with the future.

I think we are ready to move, and it is to that great task if we are successful that we will address ourselves.

Mr. Smith: Thank you very much, gentlemen. This hour has gone by all too quickly. Thank you for permitting us to present the next President of the United States on this unique program.

I have been asked by the candidates to thank the American networks.

This debate dramatically illustrated the importance of ethos. The appearance of the debaters and their conduct during the debate cannot be found in the text. These factors, however, had an enormous impact on the viewing audience.

Prior to the debate an important issue advanced by the Republicans was the charge that Kennedy was "youthful, immature, and lacking in experience." This issue was effectively destroyed in the first debate. The debaters clashed briefly on this issue during the debate. More important, however, was Kennedy's "image" during the debate. It might be noted here that "image" is merely the Madison Avenue advertising word for ethos. Those who saw the debate described Kennedy as "alert, aggressive, cool." His responses were characterized as "crisp, decisive." He was clearly able to "stand up to the man who stood up to Khrushchev."

The networks offered the services of their makeup men to both debaters. Kennedy declined and appeared without makeup. Nixon declined and was made up by a member of his own staff. In addition, Nixon's aides insisted that special lighting be provided for their candidate. Kennedy accepted the lighting provided by the network. The combined effect of the makeup and lighting gave Nixon an appearance described as "drawn, haggard, sick." His appearance was so unfavorable that some Republicans insisted he had been "sabotaged" until it was revealed that his own staff had provided the makeup and lighting. His manner was described as "nervous, ill at ease, defensive." Many felt that Nixon created a much better impression on radio listeners, who could not see him, than he did on television viewers.

Who did the better debating? The Committee on the 1960 Presidential Campaign, a group well qualified to speak on this subject, expressed the judgment that Kennedy did the better debating by a vote of twenty to six, with one member undecided.

Who made the greater political gain in the debate? All but one of the committee expressed the judgment that Kennedy made the greater political gain. The one recording his vote as "undecided" pointed out that political gain was difficult to measure. A group of professional politicians concurred with the majority of the committee. On the day following the debate nine Democratic governors gathered at Hot Springs, Arkansas, for the Southern Governors' Conference and sent Kennedy a hearty telegram of congratulations. Prior to the debate they had been at most lukewarm for Kennedy, and some had withheld their endorsement.

How did the debates affect the election? Many will agree with the judgment of the *New York Times* that the debates were "the really decisive factor" in the election.[10] The public opinion polls gave Nixon a slight lead at the start of the campaign. Kennedy's popularity steadily increased as the debates progressed and reached a peak shortly after the fourth debate. Nixon put on an intensive drive during the last days of the campaign, making extensive use of the enormously popular incumbent Republican President Eisenhower and almost, but not quite, overcame Kennedy's lead.

After the four debates were over, editorial writers and television executives generally hailed them as tremendously useful instruments of Ameri-

[10] See: *New York Times,* November 6, 1960, Sec. 4, p. 1.

can politics. Although many called for an improvement in the format of the debates, most thoughtful observers expressed the hope that debating would become an established part of Presidential campaigns.

The precedent set in the debates was felt far beyond the United States. The Japanese instantly seized upon the idea of debates and, within a month of the fourth Kennedy-Nixon debate, incumbent Premier Hayato Ikeda arranged television debates with his opponents, Saburo Eda and Suehiro Nishio. Other countries, too, gave serious thought to the possibility of making debates a part of their national election campaigns.

Kennedy strongly favored making debates a regular part of Presidential campaigns and on several occasions stated publicly that he would debate in 1964. Had he lived to try for a second term, debating might have become a firmly established part of Presidential campaigns. In 1964 and 1968, there was widespread support for Presidential debates and both the Senate and the House passed, by large majorities, bills suspending the "equal time" requirement and thus permitting television debates. There were slight differences in the legislation passed by the two Houses, however, and in both years the matter was referred to joint conference committees, where the bills died.

Whether or not we will have debates in future Presidential campaigns will probably depend upon public opinion. Nixon reported that the pressures for debates in 1960 were "irresistible."[11] While debates may not always fit into the campaign plans of the candidates, there is no question that they have an enormous impact on the public and that they are the most effective way of informing the public about the candidates and the issues.

Exercises

The following exercises may be used for review or your instructor may select from among them for discussion, quiz, or examination questions.

1. Identify the issues introduced into the debate by Kennedy.

2. Identify the issues introduced into the debate by Nixon.

3. Identify the issues introduced into the debate by the newsmen.

4. What did Kennedy do to build ethos in the debate? Cite specific passages from Kennedy's speeches that were apparently intended to build his ethos. Do *not* consider those aspects of ethos that would be apparent only to a viewer or a listener.

5. What did Nixon do to build ethos in the debate? Cite specific passages from Nixon's speeches that were apparently intended to build his ethos. Do *not* consider those aspects of ethos that would be apparent only to a viewer or a listener.

6. Which debater was more successful in building his ethos? Justify your answer.

[11] Richard M. Nixon, *Six Crises* (Garden City, N.Y.: Doubleday & Co., 1962), p. 323.

7. Each debater sought to reduce his opponent's ethos by associating his opponent with unpopular persons or matters. Cite specific passages illustrating this from each debater's speeches.

8. What motivational appeals did Kennedy use? Cite specific passages from his speeches of as many different types of motivational appeals as you can find.

9. What motivational appeals did Nixon use? Cite specific passages from his speeches of as many different types of motivational appeals as you can find.

10. Which debater made the more effective use of motivational appeals? Justify your answer.

11. Find an example of the use of the dilemma.
a. Who used the dilemma?
b. How was it stated?
c. What reply was given?
d. Was the reply effective? Justify your answer.

12. The proposition of this debate was, in effect, "Resolved: That the Democratic candidate should be elected President."
a. What type of affirmative case did Kennedy use?
b. What type of negative case did Nixon use?

13. Although the debaters spoke without notes, they devoted long and intensive thought to planning their opening and closing statements and to preparing their position on all possible questions. Which debater's statements revealed the more effective speech composition? Justify your answer.

14. Which debater made the more effective use of evidence? Justify your answer.

15. Which debater made the more effective use of reasoning? Justify your answer.

16. Which debater made the more effective use of refutation? Justify your answer.

17. Who did the better debating? (You need not agree with the majority of The Committee on the 1960 Presidential Campaign — there were distinguished professors voting with the minority.) Justify your answer.

For Further Reading

Students interested in the background and evaluation of the first Presidential debates may wish to consult the following:

The American Forensic Association, *The Register*, Vol. 8 (Winter 1959), p. 3.

Lionel Crocker, "The First Presidential Television Debate," *The Speaker*, Vol. 43 (November 1960), pp. 11–17.

Austin J. Freeley, "The Presidential Debates and the Speech Profession," *Quarterly Journal of Speech*, Vol. 47 (February 1961), pp. 60–64.

Austin J. Freeley, "Who Won the Great Debates of 1960?" *The Register*, Vol. 9, No. 3 (1961), pp. 29–30.

Sidney Kraus, ed., *The Great Debates* (Bloomington: Indiana University Press, 1962).

Herold Ross, "Laboratory in Persuasion," *The Gavel*, Vol. 43 (November 1960), p. 2.

Frank Stanton, "The Case for Political Debates on TV," *New York Times Magazine*, January 19, 1964.

Television in Government and Politics, A Bibliography (New York: Television Information Office, 1964).

Raymond K. Tucker, "The Nixon-Kennedy Debates and the Freeley Committee," *The Gavel*, Vol. 43 (March 1961), pp. 47–48 and 52.

An Intercollegiate Debate

The debate presented here is an example of contemporary intercollegiate debate. The debaters, at the time they participated in these debates, were about the age of the average college student.

Except for the correction of obviously unintentional errors, the text of this debate is as close to a verbatim transcript as was possible to obtain from tape recordings. Thus, the style of speaking characteristic of the extemporaneous method has been retained. Citations of evidence and authorities are, of course, subject to the usual omissions and errors of the extemporaneous method. Even Presidential candidates — as may be seen in Appendix A — make an occasional mistake under the pressure of debate. In studying these debates, it should be remembered that many of the classical models of the great argumentative "speeches" are not verbatim transcripts of the speech. The "text" of Patrick Henry's famous "Liberty or Death" speech, for example, was actually written by Henry's biographer, Wirt, some fifty years after Henry gave the speech.

As you read the text of this debate, you will find that the speakers have made extensive use of judicial notice (considered in Chapter 6) in citing evidence. You may indeed wonder whether the documentation of much of the evidence is so fleeting as to fall below the desideratum for the argumentative speech. The level of documentation *is* below the level acceptable for general argumentation. Yet, as we saw in our earlier consideration of judicial notice, this type of documentation is often accepted in the final round of a tournament, as it was by the panel of judges for this debate.

The explanation is simple: the students were adapting to the highly specialized audience found at the final round of a national tournament. The four debaters, the panel of judges, and the varsity debaters in the audience who had participated in the previous rounds of the tournament were all knowledgeable about the available evidence. All of them had been doing research on the subject for seven or eight months; there was a considerable body of evidence that was common knowledge to the forensic community. Thus, a fleeting reference to the source by judicial notice was sufficient to establish much of the evidence for this special audience.

Time is precious in a debate, and given the choice between citing four pieces of evidence incompletely or two pieces of evidence completely, the experienced debater, in this situation, would take the risk of incomplete citation. The "in group," the experienced judges and debaters, would understand why this was done and, for better or worse, accept it in this situation.

This premium on time, as may be seen in this verbatim transcript, sometimes causes the debater to use fractured language or to fail to provide the audience with referents for the points being made. As we have seen earlier (pages 276–277), there are differences between oral and written styles. These speeches, except for the first affirmative constructive, are not the polished rhetoric of the ivory tower—composed and rewritten at leisure—they are the rhetoric of debate—created and delivered in the intense pressure of a final round. A contributing factor to these stylistic faults is the speed at which debaters speak. Such speed is often a cause for criticism of contemporary educational debate. Yet rapid delivery has a real-world parallel. Kennedy's aide Sorenson, commenting on the first presidential debate, noted with evident approval, that Kennedy's ". . . rapid-style delivery crowded more facts and arguments into each severely limited time period than Nixon could answer."[1] This, of course, is precisely the motivating force behind the rapid delivery of college debaters. College debaters, however, have escalated their speed beyond the rate of presidential debaters. One judge clocked the second affirmative in this debate at 228 words per minute in his constructive speech and at 245 words per minute in rebuttal. Fractured language and stylistic faults are almost inevitable at such speeds. Judges understand why this happens, and some are willing to overlook it in these special circumstances.

The average student or average member of the public in the audience, however, would probably be disturbed by this virtuoso performance and might well find the debate too exotic to follow readily, just as the novice is blinded by the speed of jai alai or completely misses the subtleties of a masters chess match. Thus, the student is reminded of the importance of audience analysis and adaptation. If the audience consists of knowledgeable experts, the citation of evidence by judicial notice and the use of high speed delivery may be acceptable. If, however, the decision is rendered by a group of laymen, then more thorough documentation and more conventional delivery is essential. The skilled debater is able to identify and adapt to the needs of the audience.

The following debate was presented in the final round of the Heart of America Tournament.[2]

The debaters are first affirmative Mike Miller, University of Houston; first negative Joe Angland, Massachusetts Institute of Technology; second affirmative David Seikel of Houston; and second negative Larry Rosenbaum of MIT.

[1] Theodore C. Sorenson, *Kennedy* (New York: Harper & Row, 1965), p. 200.

[2] Reprinted by permission of Donn W. Parson, Director of the Heart of America Tournament, University of Kansas, Lawrence, Kansas.

Resolved: That executive control of United States foreign policy should be significantly curtailed

First Affirmative Constructive Speech

David and I are resolved that the executive control of the United States foreign policy should be significantly curtailed. By way of definition, control is the discretionary power to act in the administration of foreign policy. Specifically, we seek to curtail the President's Commander-in-Chief power to conduct military interventions; that is, to use military force in intrastate conflicts. Our justification for such change is founded upon the following three conclusions: Number one: On balance, military intervention is unwarranted. It is unwarranted because the political coloration of the third world does not affect vital U.S. security interests. In the economic sphere, Charles Woolf of the Rand Corporation said in 1967 that the United States is in no way dependent for goods or raw materials from the underdeveloped world, for she can either produce them herself or obtain them from other sources.

In the military sphere, the countries of the third world need not threaten American security. Consider Edwin Reischauer of Harvard in 1967, that the world already has such a military balance of terror between the two great powers that the military strength of other countries has relatively little bearing upon the balance of power and becomes a matter of only localized significance. Empirical examination of our postwar intervention sustains our conclusion. Concerning Latin American intervention, Arizona political scientist Clifton Wilson wrote in 1968: "The occupation of Santo Domingo and the invasions of Guatemala and Cuba were hardly justified by any real or immediate threat to the security of the United States." Concerning our actions in the Middle East, the *Harvard Law Review* of June 1968 concluded that there was no threat requiring a response to protect the integrity of the United States. And finally, concerning Vietnam: George Kennan of Princeton University told the Senate Foreign Relations Committee in 1966, "Even a situation in which South Vietnam was controlled exclusively by the Viet Cong would not present dangers great enough to justify our direct military intervention." On balance, we suggest that military intervention is unjustified by any threat to our vital security interests.

Number two: On balance, military intervention is ineffective. It is ineffective in determining the outcome of revolutionary activity. This was explained by Stanley Hoffman of Harvard in 1968 when he noted that the possibility of preventing by military force a communist takeover through subversion depends upon the political capacity for resistance within the society. No amount of substitution of American military power will suffice. Again consider our specific intervention. In Guatemala in 1954, for example, our intervention was irrelevant to the eventual outcome. According to Norman A. Bailey of the Georgetown Center for Strategic Studies, writing in 1966: "The Arbens regime was overthrown not by the rebels who in ten days had not advanced more than ten miles into Guatemala but rather by a junta of its regular army headed by Colonel Diaz." What did the 1958 Lebanese intervention accomplish? Richard Nolte of the Institute of World Affairs noted in 1964 that the only visible result was the demise of the Shamoon government upon whose behalf we had intervened in favor of a neutralist government led by one of the rebels. And finally by a Lebanese repudiation of the Eisenhower doctrine. The disastrous failure at the

Bay of Pigs hardly needs retelling to show its lack of efficacy. In 1965, the United States intervened in the Dominican Republic ostensibly to stop the spread of communism in the hemisphere. However, as Ronald Steele of the American Political Science Association observed in 1967, "If there was no communist problem in Santo Domingo before the United States landing, there is one now. Moreover, the American intervention strengthened the appeal of communist movements throughout the hemisphere." Finally, concerning Vietnam, Samuel Huntington of Harvard concluded in 1968 that the frustration of the war in Vietnam is that the soldiers cannot win it militarily and the Administration cannot win it politically. Our position here is best summarized by Alexander Eckstein of the University of Michigan, writing in 1968: "History knows no instance where national identity, national integration, and national stability were built on the backs of foreign troops."

Conclusion number three: On balance, military intervention is wasteful. Please recall our foregoing analysis. First, that intervention is unjustified by any threat to our vital security interests. Second, that even if utilized military intervention will likely be ineffective in achieving its objectives. Logically, therefore, an investment of resources in an unnecessary or ineffective policy is by definition wasteful. As UCLA's William P. Gerberding wrote in 1966, "Any defensive policy against communism must be viewed at the tactical level, where cost versus gains becomes the primary consideration, and utilizing such criteria, cost versus gains, consideration of past, present, and future interventions affirms our analysis of waste. In the interventions of the past, Guatemala, Lebanon, the Bay of Pigs, and the Dominican Republic, the United States expended, according to official estimates, approximately $1-billion and 30 lives. Recall the ineffectiveness of each intervention demonstrated in the proof of the second contention. Hence we submit that there has been waste in the past. And Charles Lerche of American University in 1964 concurs that "Support for one or both sides in guerrilla war has not produced gains proportionate to its risk." Consider now the present intervention in Vietnam. Recall that, as indicated by Mr. Kennan, "If we could win in Vietnam, it wouldn't be worth the cost." Recall Mr. Huntington; "There is little prospect for success in the immediate future." Hence we submit that our Vietnamese intervention is wasteful in both monetary and human resources. Monetarily, according to the Department of Defense, we have spent over $80-billion on the war with projected expenditures this year of from $25- to $30-billion. Far more important is the needless human death and suffering that has been wrought by the war in Vietnam. American casualties number in the hundreds of thousands, including over 30,000 killed. The latest issue of *U.S. News & World Report* indicates that even if some Americans are withdrawn this year, another 8,000 will lose their lives before the decade ends. Worse still is the effect upon the people we are supposedly defending in Vietnam. Professor Wilson, previously cited, in 1968 reported that we are killing at least four to ten times the civilians as that of enemy troops. Compare these losses to our gains, as does Edwin Reischauer in 1967: "The cost in American lives and wealth has proved far higher than anyone should have accepted for the objectives achievable through this war."

Finally, consider the spectre of future interventions. One might hope that the President would be more prudent in his use of military force, but David and I suggest that inherent in executive office is the proclivity for the use of military intervention best described by Henry Steele Commager in 1968 of Amherst College: "The possession of power generates the conditions for its use exemplified by Vietnam and Santo Domingo. The bloody stalemate in Korea did not prevent a Vietnam and our disastrous failure at the Bay of Pigs did not proclude our invasion of the Dominican Republic." We conclude, as does Senator J. William Fulbright in 1967: "Whatever safeguards are devised, they must be institutional rather than personal, rooted in the constitution rather than in promises concerning the use of power." Otherwise we are only forced to concur, as did that noted source the *Kansas University Law Review* in November of 1967, that it would appear likely that similar conflicts would be waged again by the United States before the twentieth century ends. To assure that this grim prediction is not realized, we submit the following proposal, by means of all necessary legislation and constitutional amendment.

Number one, concerning our present intervention: Withdraw all military forces from Vietnam. Withdraw all military forces from Vietnam. Number two, concerning future situations: Permit the executive stationing and use of military force in two cases: (a) an unprovoked overt attack against an ally pursuant to a declaration of war against a state; (b) an unprovoked overt attack upon the United States territory or forces. Plank three: Prohibit paramilitary operations such as the Bay of Pigs. And number four: An independent regulatory commission with access to all necessary information and investigative resources will (a) determine the existence or non-existence of overt aggression; (b) determine the existence or nonexistence of a state for declaration of war purposes using the criteria of international law; (c) and third, act as the enforcement mechanism of the proposal.

David and I suggest, in summary, that the risking of public monies and the risking of human lives require that the powers of any administrative functionary be scrutinized for necessity and effectiveness. And it's because we find neither in the executive power to militarily intervene that we offer the resolution.

First Negative Constructive Speech

First of all, three questions relating to the gentlemen's plan: Number one, what enforcement mechanism are they going to utilize? Number two, is intervention by a foreign power the definition of aggression? And number three, will their plan permit the President to station troops abroad in areas where they are currently not now stationed or to increase force commitments? With those three questions in mind, now let's direct our attention to the gentlemen's analysis.

Now the gentlemen start by examining the present situation and claiming that because of the composite result of the three conclusions, we should withdraw the option of intervention. The basic philosophy Barry and I are going to hold throughout today's debate is that the option of intervention should not be foreclosed. We are going to suggest several reasons. We're going to consider the gentlemen's analysis and show that in the present system conditions don't warrant the elimination of the option but moreover, as we were informed by our friends from USC in the last round, even if it were true in the present system, we've got to be aware of the possibility of changes in the future. Because even if everything the gentleman said were true and even if all these conditions did exist, all that would call for would be the maintenance of the option of intervention; and then selectively analyzing each situation. If what the gentleman said is true then we wouldn't intervene today because that is bad, but ten years from now when situations might be different, then we might intervene. We're going to argue that the gentlemen haven't called for the elimination of the option.

Contention number one: They argue that on balance the American intervention is unwarranted. Number one: we don't think that their analysis of "on balance" is justified. If the gentlemen show that in some cases intervention is unwarranted, in other cases it is warranted, then we should preserve the option to intervene in those cases where it is warranted. They don't establish the universality of their indictment. Arguing on balance isn't sufficient. At best that would call for selectively refraining from intervening in areas where importance wasn't very crucial. Number one, they argue economically the areas of the world aren't very important and secondly militarily. First of all, what about the economic sphere? First of all, we'd like to point out the gentleman didn't exhaust the possibilities. There was also political importance. Roger Hilsman pointed out politically and economically the underdeveloped world is important to us. He argued in 1966: "It would be unrealistic and dangerous to withdraw from Southeast Asia. Under present circumstances, withdrawal would turn the area over to communism which we cannot afford. Politically, economically, strategically, and psychologically the United States stake in Asia is high." We argue, then, economically and politically we are justified.

Secondly, the gentlemen claim that militarily our intervention isn't justified because these areas are irrelevant to the world balance of power. We choose to disagree. Consider first the area of Asia. Fred Green writes in 1965, "Serious dangers would ensue from the forcible establishment of unified power systems centered on China. To an important degree, the physical security of the United States would be impaired by such an aggregation of power." We claim in the area of Asia, that Asia is vital. But number two, with regard to Asia, we argue that even though it is vital today, it is going to be even more vital in the future. Which is just one example of a changing condition which can apply to the affirmative's analysis and show why the option shouldn't be foreclosed. Russel H. Fifield wrote in 1963: "The overall strategic importance of Southeast Asia, moreover, is likely to increase rather than decrease in the years ahead. For the foreseeable future the United States must hold fast as a bulwark against communist expansion." We argue that Asia is crucial, but number two, the cruciality is increasing.

Secondly, consider Latin America. Charles Woolf of Rand Corporation argued about the significance of Latin America when he commented: "Of all the underdeveloped countries, those whose value in a general war context would be the greatest are in Latin America. For example, we might envision a scenario with communist nuclear missile sites in Cuba, Mexico, and the Dominican Republic." Mr. Woolf then claims that Latin America is important because of the possibility of them posing a direct threat to the United States in a general war context. We reject the gentlemen's first contention and claim that the option to intervene is valid. They turn to some specific examples. They say that in Latin America, Santo Domingo, and Guatemala there is no real threat to the United States. Consider the evidence we've given you already about Latin America being important. Consider second that the gentlemen never considered the reason to intervene was to stop communist expansion. The presumption of the entire contention is that the only reason we think of intervening is to prevent the communists from getting ahead. Barry's going to talk about that later on. Just put it down on your flow so you don't think I skipped the gentleman's argument. We're going to contend that it's irrelevant.

Second contention: The gentlemen argue that, on balance, the military intervention is ineffective. They argue that indigenous factors determine the outcome. They then proceed to consider the examples. Insofar as the gentlemen are trying to establish a warrant for universal and generic change, the crucial factor is going to have to be the generic argumentation. We'll get to the examples later on but right now consider the general argument. The gentleman reads a piece of evidence, and he says that indigenous factors determine the outcome. We'd like to argue by counter example and also by positing reasons. Let's presume, number one, that there is an inefficient military in the country. We claim by intervention we can enable the military to overcome the opponents when otherwise they wouldn't. This is the point of Frank Armbruster, director of guerrilla warfare studies at the Hudson Institute, when he wrote in 1968: "The current nationalist Malaysian government is in existence today because thousands of foreign troops stepped in to rescue the native government from certain defeat at the hands of an active revolutionary force. The government forces had shown little capability to cope with the communists." Note the implication for the gentlemen's analysis. They claim indigenous factors are determinant. Consider Malaysia. Before the intervention, the communists were winning. After the intervention, we shifted the tide. We were able to overcome the opposition. We reject the gentlemen's point.

But number two, we argue that we can increase insufficient force ratios. Consider the following: The gentlemen say indigenous factors are determining that the majority of people oppose the communist efforts then we're not going to have any problem. Let's presume that 75 percent of the people oppose the insurgency. There you have a three to one ratio. However, the strategems of guerrilla warfare dictate that a three to one ratio is not going to be sufficient. The point was made by Seymour Deishman of the Institute for Defense Analysis when he wrote in 1965: "It appears that in any unconventional war in which the defenders are to be successful, the force ratios must favor the defenders by factors varying from five to almost twenty to one." So secondly, by intervening we can shift the force ratio to an acceptable level. But thirdly, the presumption that the gentlemen make is that by intervening we cannot shift the indigenous factor. We claim by our interventions we can create situations which didn't exist, we can change the indigenous conditions which the gentlemen claim were determining.

Our third argument is going to be that we can curb terrorism. Note the point made by Frank Armbruster once again in 1968: "Even when the guerrillas lack a strong popular cause, if insurgents show they have the strength and resolve to impress their will on the people by terror tactics, the people are likely to listen to what they have to offer." The gentlemen claim indigenous factors will determine but by intervening we can change the indigenous factors because by curbing terrorism we can change the amount of people willing to support the communists.

But fourthly we'd like to cite another reason why we can change indigenous factors; that is, we can foster urbanization. It is known in the theories of advocates of people's wars that communist insurgency can be most successful when a country is in a very rural, undeveloped stage. Our intervention shifts the focus of the nation from the countryside into the city, thus making it less susceptible to advances. Samuel P. Huntington writes in *Foreign Affairs*, July 1968: "In an absent-minded way the United States and Vietnam may have stumbled upon the answer to wars of national liberation. The effective response is to force-draft urbanization and modernization which rapidly brings the country in question out of the phase in which a revolutionary movement can hope to generate sufficient strength to come to power." Our fourth reason, then, we foster urbanization. We reject the gentlemen's point in general then. We claim that indigenous factors are not determinate and if the gentlemen cannot establish that point in a generic sense, they have no call for the resolution because, then, our intervention could be effective.

They talked about the Dominican Republic. They said there was no reason for us to intervene in the Dominican Republic. Consider again, they're presuming the only reason was to stop communism. We deny the point. Georgetown University's Special Report of the Center for Strategic Studies comments in 1966: "American actions in the Dominican Republic had four objectives: they were number one, the protection of American and other foreign lives; number two, the halting of violence; number three, the prevention of a communist seizure; and number four, the opening of an option to the Dominican people to choose their leaders in a free election." All these objectives were obtained. We'd like to claim the intervention in the Dominican Republic was a benefit.

Number two, the gentlemen talk about Lebanon. They say we shouldn't have intervened there. Eleanor Dulles points out in *Foreign Policy in the Making*, 1968: "The objectives of the United States in this instance were to end aggression, to halt panic, and to preserve political stability and freedom for Lebanon and Jordan were met. The cost of this accomplishment was slight in comparison with the ends achieved." We maintain both in general and in the specific examples the option to intervene is warranted. The gentlemen talked about Vietnam. They said we cannot win militarily and our policymakers aren't winning politically. Now wait a second. We've prevented the communists from winning militarily, and all we have to do is get a few better policymakers and then maybe we can get a better political settlement than we could have gotten otherwise. The gentleman begs the question.

Consider the gentleman's third contention: On balance, military intervention is wasteful. They talked about the loss of money in Vietnam. Well, granted there is a significant loss in Vietnam. However, we're going to dispute the significance of the other interventions. Collectively, they cost $1-billion and 30 lives. Now look. We've already shown there are many reasons for intervention, among them the preservation of American lives and the protection of American business. We're going to claim that it's a very insignificant harm. The only significance comes in Vietnam. We're going to reject the theory that there will be Vietnams in the future. They say there will because after all we didn't stop fighting after Korea and the Dominican Republic and other situations like that. You know why? In both cases we won. The only example the gentleman gave us of the case we lost is the Bay of Pigs, where we spent a few dollars sending people down to Cuba and that wasn't much of an expense. Vietnam has taught us a lesson: We shouldn't get engaged in large wars. We'd like to document the point, number one, the President's not going to want to intervene. Samuel Huntington writes: "Recent experience of recurring U.S. intervention makes no more Vietnams a likely guideline for the American future." Then number two, there are no other places like Vietnam where such a protracted conflict will result. George Lisker writes: "Presently we can see on the horizon no actual or potential concentrations of energy comparable to the Hanoi-NLF coalitions." Reject the gentleman's theory. We call for preservation of the option to intervene.

Second Affirmative Constructive Speech

The gentleman asked three questions. Enforcement would be through constitution and statutory prohibition and, if necessary, criminal sanctions against commanders in the field. Secondly, the intervention by other powers would not constitute aggression but only the crossing of a border by foreign troops. Thirdly, the stationing of forces in bases—we can't have any additional stationing or increase in present deployments without that declaration of war.

Consider the gentleman's philosophy that we have a permanent change for a temporary situation. He's going to have to demonstrate the probability of such changes and, until he does, we can justify ours.

Consider the first contention: On balance, military intervention is unjustified. Here the gentleman says, on balance, it is justified because we should pick out the good ones and stay away from the bad ones. He's opting for selective intervention but can't demonstrate that in advance we can apply the criteria of cost versus gain. We can't apply the criteria of cost because we can't predict escalation. The *Harvard Law Review* of June 1968 points out: "The unpredictability of rushing troops to Lebanon, the constantly revised predictions about the nature and extent of our involvement in Vietnam, indicate that it can no longer be said with any degree of assurance that the commitment of troops to combat under any conditions is unlikely to result in major conflict." We can't estimate the cost because we can't estimate the escalation. We can't estimate the gains because we can't predict success as Mr. James C. Thompson of Harvard notes in 1968: "Yet here we move into the jungle growth of ignorance, poor intelligence, wishful thinking, and competing constituencies within the U.S. government. For embracing the key question of our chances for success, we bring to bear human frailty and human illusions, qualities that repeatedly led us astray in Vietnam." For this reason I ask you to conclude with us and Professor Morgenthau of Chicago in 1968 that obviously, as others have said, it is quite impossible to lay down abstract principles to tell you under what conditions you ought to intervene and under what conditions you ought not to intervene. The gentleman says we can have the executive implement such a program, not denying the inherent proclivity for the use of that military intervention. It can't be selected.

Consider then that he talks about the political factors. He says that in fact we have a political rationale. Now why is that important? He reads one quotation saying that we ought to intervene for political purposes, not demonstrating that we can selectively intervene and accomplish only political goals. He's simply dealing in ambiguities. We suggest that the criteria for intervention should be a threat to vital U.S. security interests and look what the gentleman does. He suggests that politically, in fact, we can't have all these countries in Southeast Asia go communist, not demonstrating that that would be the result. For example, if the U.S. withdrew from Vietnam, it would provide the best barrier to the expansion of Chinese communism according to Ronald Steele, Congressional Fellow of the American Political Science Association in 1967. "A strong unified Vietnam, even under communist control, would be a better barrier to Chinese expansion than a divided Vietnam fighting a civil war with foreign intervention." Stillman and Pfaff of the Hudson Institute discount the likelihood of an effective North Vietnamese aggression in the area because of nationalism in 1966 and William C. Johnston, Professor Asian Studies at Johns Hopkins, concludes in February of this year: "Because of China's foreign policy failures, and the turmoil over cultural revolution, regardless of what happens in South Vietnam, the other nations of Southeast Asia will try to resist communist influence." I suggest even that one particular allusion to the political factor is not significant or relevant.

Consider now the economic criteria. The gentleman doesn't demonstrate any vital economic resources that the United States has to intervene to protect. He says, now wait a minute, Asia might have some great power threat in the future. He doesn't demonstrate they have the potentiality to upset the nuclear balance of power which Professor Reischauer has said is the basis of our security. Hear once again Professor Reischauer: "The United States is so extremely rich and strong and so far away from Asia we would not be threatened by the kind of military power Asia could develop. We are not dependent in any way on Asia." We couldn't be threatened by that kind of power they develop.

What about Latin America? The gentleman says we can't have any missile bases in Latin America because that threatens our security, not demonstrating that missile bases in Latin America upset the vital nuclear balance of power, which they simply don't. Take the example of when we did have the base—Cuba in 1962. Roswold Kirkpatrick, deputy secretary of defense, November 12, 1962, points out in alluding to the Soviet missile buildup in Cuba. He said, "I don't believe we were under any greater threat from the Soviet Union's power taken in totality after this than before." Hanson W. Baldwin of the *New York Times* explains why in 1967. "Missiles flown from Cuba could have no effect upon the hundred or so Strategic Air Command bombers armed with nuclear weapons that are always in the air. Nor could they knock out the nation's Polaris submarine fleet hidden submerged in the waste of waters or the Navy's aircraft carriers or ships." The gentlemen don't relate their analysis to our specific contentions about the nuclear balance of power on which we depend for our security. The gentlemen suggest with respect to the overall net that we must be concerned about the third world. I deny the point and so does Bella Bellasa, advisor with the International Bank for Reconstruction and Development in 1967: "With the availability of intercontinental and submarine based missiles, the importance of military bases in the less developed countries is on the decline. Nor do these bases have much significance for the deployment of conventional forces." In conclusion, then, economically and militarily we have no threat to vital U.S. security interests. Note the gentleman doesn't examine a single one of the specific examples. He simply says perhaps we have other purposes for intervening. I deny the point and so does Herbert Dinerstein of the Washington Center for Foreign Policy Research in 1967: "At present, however, the purpose of intervention is either to prevent a communist regime from coming to power or to unseat an existing regime." Hence, it's unjustified on balance.

Secondly, on balance, military intervention is ineffective. Now notice that in spite of the gentleman's four basic lines of reasoning, he doesn't deny that the crucial determinant of the outcome of a revolutionary struggle is the indigenous condition. First of all, he talks about such things as an inefficient military, directs us to the Malaysian example. Note that's not even an American intervention. But secondly and more importantly, Malaysia was a unique exception to this analysis. William Gerberding of UCLA in 1966 points out; "In Malaysia there were three favorable conditions which may not be present in some future struggle. In the first place the guerrillas were Malayan Chinese and therefore were more readily identifiable and less acceptable to the rest of the Malayan population. Moreover, the guerrillas in Malaysia had a permanent border through which they could be supplied and replenished. Finally the counter-guerrilla Malayans were promised their independence by the British and this incentive is no longer available in most of this decolonized world." The point being, the reason those British military forces were effective was because they tied it to a promise of decolonization, something which is unique to Malaysia and cannot be generalized around the world. Secondly, he talks about the increase in insufficient force ratios. Notice, we can supply military assistance. More important, what doesn't he prove. He doesn't prove that even that 20 to 1 ratio is going to be effective. More importantly, he doesn't apply the criteria of cost versus gains to that force ratio. Take the example Vietnam, gentlemen, and apply your general analysis to a specific intervention situation. Thirdly, he talks about curbing terrorism. I say that's irrelevant because if they use terrorism it causes it to backfire. Turn to John S. Pusty, Professor of Political Science at the Air Force Academy in 1965: "An important element in the defeat of the Malayans, Philippine, and Greek communist insurgencies was the fact that the terrorist operations against the people backfired. Instead of insuring consolidated support through fear, terrorism engendered antipathy toward insurgents and thus alienated a significant portion of the masses." No significant problem.

Lastly the gentlemen said that we made a big boo-boo in Vietnam and found out how to beat counter-revolutionary warfare because we have urbanization. I deny the point. We can't even protect the cities in Vietnam according to Professor Schonbrun in 1968: "The Tet offensive demonstrated that there is no part of the country under effective control of the Saigon regime or even secure under allied protection." Mr. Goldstein, Professor of International Relations of the City University of New York, concludes in the summer of '68; "The U.S. responded to the Tet offensive with all available firepower to clear the adversary forces out of the cities. The destruction was vast and tragic as at Bien Tray, where a U.S. officer made a classic comment: "We had to destroy the town to save it.' " I suggest urbanization isn't necessarily effective.

Consider the analysis then. Can they show that outside force can determine the outcome of the conflict? They read a lot of generalized evidence never demonstrating the specific analysis. I suggest we should conclude with Edwin O. Reischauer in 1968 when he points out: "The history of the last 15 years has also shown the key to success in subversive movements in Asia is not the degree of foreign instigation and support but the level of local discontent and willingness to participate." Ted Draper of the Stanford Institute in 1967 concludes: "In the end the political, social, and economic conditions in these countries will determine the outcome of the political struggle more than U.S. political, economic, or military power." Consider then that, in effect, the gentlemen direct us to the example of Lebanon. I suggest that, in fact, we actually precipitated rather than diminished the instability. Turn to Stephen B. Carsetts of Notre Dame in 1961: "The application of the Eisenhower doctrine in Lebanon contributed to the outbreak of the civil war, not the preservation of peace and brought deep resentment to the United States."

He says look at the Dominican Republic. All right, let's look at all four purposes. The saving of lives — Professor Draper points out that the President didn't need about 25,000 troops to evacuate about 5,000 American civilians who were being successfully evacuated anyway. The quelling of violence — Clifton Wilson of the University of Arizona in 1968 again points out that "No lives were lost till the shooting started after we intervened. We actually promoted the violence." What about the prevention of a communist takeover? We encouraged communist infiltration. The gentleman doesn't deny the point. Last, we go to Dominican elections in 1966. According to Richard J. Barnett who points out that "In the context of continued intimidation by the military and strong U.S. support for Balagier, strongly influenced the result against Bosch. They weren't even free elections."

Consider lastly, on Vietnam. He says we can provide a better settlement. Notice, he doesn't guarantee a military success. More importantly, he doesn't guarantee a political success, but most importantly of all it's not worth the cost, so why should we stick around for another ten years wasting those billions of dollars and hundreds of lives to try to get a quote "better settlement." Consider then that it's ineffective.

Thirdly, I suggest that, on balance, military intervention is wasteful. We said that it was only $1-billion and 30 lives. I suggest that 30 lives are significant when you view the gains which were nonexistent, minimal, or ineffective and for that reason we applied the ratio and the analysis of cost versus gains. He then suggests the fact that we're going to have a lesson learned from Vietnam because there we were unsuccessful. Number one, I suggest that doesn't necessarily refute the previous situations, such as the Bay of Pigs, when we were unsuccessful. More importantly, that standard, according to Chester Cooper of the IDA would not be very permanent. He points out in 1968 that "the kind of standard likely to emerge after Vietnam will have a life expectancy of only 5 years or so." Secondly, he says there could be no more Vietnams because there are no similar situations. I suggest we were darn lucky in 1965 in the Dominican Republic to have avoided a Vietnam, and so did Professor Draper of Stanford in 1968. He tells us that we could have easily had another Vietnam in the Dominican Republic in 1965. If we did not, it was not because of us. We owe our good luck there to our opponent, to the man we decided to cheat of victory. We could have had another one and we're lucky. We can't predict in advance. That's why we reject selective intervention. In the option, we say, on balance, it's wasteful and should be eliminated.

Second Negative Constructive Speech

You know, I think for the purposes of this debate I'm going to dispense with my usual point-by-point spread attack and attempt to discuss with you what's going to happen in the light of Houston's plan. Now the first thing I'd like to mention, however, is the way David ended his speech. You'll notice that he read evidence telling us we might have had another Vietnam in the Dominican Republic. In fact, his evidence said we probably would have. Couple that with what he said at the beginning of his speech—selective intervention—you can't tell in advance (a) the cost, (b) the success, or (c) whether it's going to escalate or not. I'd claim that's inherently contradictory if he's going to tell you on one hand you can't tell if it's going to escalate. On the other hand, he says, well, in the Dominican Republic it would have escalated if they'd fought back. I think the gentleman's contradictory.

Number two: Look at the affirmative plan in relation to solving the need. Their need is eliminating intervention against internal subversion. I'd claim they're not going to be able to solve their need because they aren't going to be able to distinguish between aggression and subversion. Let's develop this along a four-point analysis.

Number one: There is a historical precedent which shows that people have always disagreed on whether things have been aggression or subversion. We've never been able to come up with a workable definition. The point was made by Rollin Stromberg of the University of New Mexico in 1963: "No one has yet been able to define aggression. Exhaustive efforts lately by the UN special committee have always led to a blind alley. The special committee finished its work in 1956 without reaching a definition, having labored on the problem since 1953. Before that the International Law Commission had the job. In the 1920s Geneva went through a similar process.

After all this, it seems safe to say that a general definition of aggression will never be adopted." Historically, they haven't been able to do it. Let's look at some reasons why.

Number two: The only time you might be able to make such a definition is when you have an absolute peace–war dichotomy. That doesn't exist in present conditions. Stanley Hoffman, the affirmative source, in *Gulliver's Troubles*, 1968: "The very idea of aggression corresponds to a neat peace–war dichotomy in international relations and to a situation of domestic stability. Its applicability to an era of neither peace nor war is highly dubious since the collapse of so many of the rules of international law dealing with civil or interstate war."

Number three: Look to an empirical example: Vietnam. Now I have about five sources in my file box that say that Vietnam is internal subversion and five sources that say it's external aggression. The point is, they disagree over one specific example. How are the gentlemen going to be able to eliminate such disagreement or perhaps even wrong decisions under the affirmative plan?

Number four: Note what they're going to tell you. They say it's the presence of foreign troops that's going to define this aggression. Now in Vietnam, in Southeast Asia, the situation is particularly relevant because the Chinese and the North and South Vietnamese all look alike. Now how the devil are we going to be able to tell whether someone in black pajamas in South Vietnam is Chinese or North Vietnamese. We don't know. Under the affirmative plan they won't be able to tell either, and I say it's pretty disadvantageous if the Chinese can infiltrate 200,000 men in black pajamas that look like North Vietnamese and we won't be able to stop them. I claim the affirmative plan is not going to be able to solve the affirmative need.

However, let's look at something else. Now Joe told you that the gentlemen presumed that the only reason we might want to intervene is to stop a communist takeover. I'd claim, as you might suggest, that there are other reasons. But please note the burden the gentlemen from Houston have taken upon themselves. They've said, for the future, we will never intervene again. Now they've got to show then that in the future there will never be any reason to intervene. Not merely that we're not successful against communist uprisings but rather that there will never be any reason. I have a few which I might suggest.

Number one: We want to keep the option to intervene open in order to manage the dissemination of nuclear weapons. First the evidence, then the analysis. The point was made by George Liska, of the Washington Center for Foreign Policy Research, in *War and Order* in 1968: "One reason for keeping American capacity and propensity to intervene intact is that both will be useful in managing dissemination. Either by employing intervention to bar nuclear acquisition where it would be clearly premature in terms of economic and political maturity or by conspicuously withholding intervention to accelerate progress toward nuclear and other self-sufficiency in the interest of regional stability." Now look how this is helpful in two ways. Number one, actual intervention. If a government decides it can't defend itself and requests U.S. help and the U.S. doesn't help, then the government might develop nuclear weapons. If the U.S. decides this is good, we can hold back intervention. If we decide it's bad, we can send them our troops. Number two, there's the threat of intervention. If we maintain the threat of intervention, then our credibility of defending these countries would also keep them from developing nuclear weapons if they believed it. If we don't have that threat, and if they can't depend on the U.S. to defend them, then they might go ahead and develop them. Note Mr. Liska says it's a two-way situation. We might want some people to have nuclear weapons; we might want to keep others from doing it. The option of intervening might be one way in which we might control it.

Reason number two that we ought to maintain the option to intervene is in order to control the amount of conflict in the world. Now my previous source, Mr. Liska, wrote an entire book on this, *War and Order*. The overall conclusion of the book is that the amount of conflict in the world is constant. What he suggests we do is continue to fight such small wars, so that we don't have to fight big ones in the future. This is not a domino theory; you might even call it an anti-domino theory. Listen to what Mr. Liska says in 1968: "The United States is rather restricted in its options. It can choose to fight important but still limited engagements, such as that in Vietnam, at a relatively early stage of dislocation in the regional structure of power and will. Or it can choose to retrench until such time as it may have to fight a bigger war or face more diffuse and even less forcible elements of disorder under less favorable conditions." Fight the small wars; avoid having to fight the big ones, because the sum of conflict is constant. There is still going to be some conflict in the world. We'll have to fight the big ones under that affirmative plan.

Number three: We need to keep the option to intervene open to protect American lives and property. First, let's look to history. Senator Fulbright said, in 1967: "Most of the cases which have been cited as authority for the President's sending troops abroad are cases where the use of our troops was limited to the protection of American citizens or of American property." Let's look to a specific example: The Dominican Republic. In *Intervention and Revolution* Professor Richard J. Barnet said in 1968: "Bennet's hysterical cable arrived at 5:30 Wednesday, April 28. In sum, the situation in Santo Domingo had collapsed, the police could not keep order, American lives were in danger." We went in, as Joe showed you, to protect American lives. But note that Houston can't answer this by saying in the past we haven't been able to do it. If at any point in the future it might become necessary to send American troops to protect American lives, then we damn well better have that option to intervene open to go in and protect American citizens. I think that's another reason to protect that option to intervene.

Number four: We want to keep the option to intervene open to deter Soviet and Chinese support of internal subversion. The point is they won't give major support at present to internal subversion in another country when there's a serious threat of United States intervention because there's too great a risk of escalation. Amatai Etzioni in *Winning without War*, 1964— please note his analysis: "The central change that has occurred is not in Soviet society or its expansionist goals, although these have changed, but what is considered a high or a low risk. Acts such as outright invasion and armed subversion which in the first postwar years could have been carried out with some degree of impunity and thus were low risks would now almost surely trigger a war and hence are considered high risks." They won't do that because they know there's a serious threat of United States intervention, which might escalate into a major war. We keep the option and the threat of intervention open, and we prevent it with the present system.

However, let's take a look at one additional consequence of the affirmative plan and that's their withdrawal from Vietnam. I'd claim that's going to be disastrous for two reasons. First, there's going to be a systematic liquidation of several million South Vietnamese. Now the point was made by Herman Kahn of the Hudson Institute in *Foreign Affairs*, 1968. "A purge of substantial numbers of the 3-million armed forces, government officials, 1-million Montgnards, 2-million Hao-Hao, 2-million Catholics, and a million Cao Dai would follow a unilateral withdrawal from Vietnam by the U.S." Historic precedent from Bernard Fall in 1966: "An estimated fifty to one hundred thousand Vietnamese were being killed by land reforms in the North during the period of 1954 to 1956." Now look. The gentlemen can't get up there and tell you that there are only a few thousand marked men, because marked men are only the ones they have the names of and they're going to get rid of immediately. What we're telling you is that all these many millions of people who are presently opposing the North Vietnamese are just going to get slaughtered when we pull out and I'd say that's disadvantageous if several million of them go.

Number two: Withdrawing from Vietnam is going to increase the proliferation of nuclear weapons. Recall I told you before we no longer can control it by using or withholding our threat of intervention. Under the affirmative plan we're going to see some countries develop nuclear weapons. Let's look to India. Irving Kristol in the *New York Times Magazine*, May of 1968: "Can anyone doubt that, dominoes or no dominoes, the immediate consequence of an American withdrawal from Asia will be India's arming itself with nuclear weapons?" Henry Kissinger in *Look*, August of 1966: "The long-term orientation of such countries as India and Japan will reflect to a considerable extent their assessment of America's willingness and ability to honor its commitment. For example, whether or not India decides to become a nuclear power depends crucially on its confidence in American support. A demonstration of American impotence in Asia cannot fail to lessen the credibility of American pledges in other fields." With India and Japan, we're going to increase that proliferation. Withdrawing from Vietnam is disadvantageous. We have to keep the option of intervention open even if we only use it once in the next hundred years. The affirmative plan can't tell the difference between aggression and subversion. That in light of Joe's devastating attack on the affirmative need would urge us to ask you to reject the affirmative resolution.

First Negative Rebuttal

We should preserve the option to intervene because the gentlemen don't demonstrate what conditions will be like for the future. They say its incumbent upon us to show it's going to change. No. If at best, if everything they're saying is true, we should retain the option to intervene and if Dave and Mike advise the President in every particular situation and let him know if the situation is true. If nationalism is still strong, if indigenous factors are still determinant. We think it's incumbent upon them. We'd suggest something which is subject to change which the gentlemen talked about: nationalism. Louis Snyder writes in 1968: "Nationalism reflects the chaos of history itself as a historical phenomenon. It is always in flux, changing according to no preconceived patterns." No preconceived pattern; therefore, we shouldn't have this overall abolition of all intervention. We reject the gentlemen's theory.

Number one: On balance, intervention is unwarranted. I talked about the political and economic implications and I turned to Mr. Hilsman. The gentlemen respond, well, we didn't show we intervened selectively. That's not my point here. Our selectivity argument is an overall analysis which says, granting everything the gentlemen say in the entire first speech, we should still retain the option and just refrain from intervening if situations are like this. Right now in just refuting what they have to say directly. And that point the gentlemen didn't challenge. However, they did say it's contingent upon Vietnam falling and the Middle East being taken over by our enemies. They say a strong Vietnam will be a barrier to communism. What if the Chinese communists support revolutions somewhere else in Asia? Moreover they say, wait a second, the nationalists, the people in Asia are not going to go along with China. If we'd pull out, they're not going to let themselves be taken over. Well, the Asians don't think so. *Washington Post*, November 4, 1968: "Cambodian Chief of State Prince Sihanouk said today he would welcome the continued presence of the Americans in Southeast Asia." An American withdrawal from the Far East would mean virtual Chinese takeover of the regime since the weight of China would be too heavy. "If the United States pulled out of Southeast Asia," Sihanouk went on, "he would retire and ask Mao Tse Tung to take over my country." We reject the gentlemen's theory.

But next, we turn to the military implication. Number one, I contend that Asia is important. The gentlemen turned to Mr. Reischauer. Now the gentleman said Mr. Reischauer didn't think Asia was crucial. Recall I already turned to Mr. Fifield who said it was. More importantly, I turn to a second source which said it too was in flux. The importance of Asia was going to increase rather than decrease in the years ahead. And to that point Dave wasn't responsive. But, however, what is Mr. Reischauer's view of the whole? We'll grant that, according to Reischauer, Asia isn't very important today, but even he doesn't argue universally. He goes on to say, "The oil of the Middle East and our heavy investment in Latin America may make these areas of special economic interest to the United States." Even though Asia isn't similar, even their own source doesn't argue in the generic sense.

Moreover, the gentleman argues that Latin America won't be under any greater threat from Russia if the Russians do go in and put missiles. It's possibly true. However, I would suggest we'd be under greater threat from Latin America. The point: not that they think they can defeat the United States in a war but recall the horrors, the dangers of proliferation itself. Either irrationality or accidental war, or if there were any problems when we try to protect American lives, we wouldn't be able to. They'd have the options of using these weapons.

Next we talked about other reasons for intervention. Barry considered them. Barry alluded to loss of lives. Consider again, if you will, the gentleman's second contention.

Here they say, on balance, military intervention is ineffective. Number one: I say *inefficient* military. They turn to Malaysia. Now look what they admit. They say there were three unique characteristics of Malaysia which make that an exception. All right. Let's retain the option to intervene and see if there are some other three characteristics which make another area unique. And so we can intervene. The fact that some factors could make a particular intervention an exception mitigate against the rationale for overall withdrawal of the concept of intervention.

Number two: I talked about force ratios. The gentleman said, well, can you show they'd win if they got the correct force ratio? I demonstrated the fact that what you need is a 20 to 1 ratio. All we have to do is go over the ratio and, according to Mr. Deischman, you normally will be able to win.

Number three: I said you need to curb terrorism. He said, look in Greece and Malaysia—terrorism alienated the populace; therefore, we don't have to curb terrorism. The reason was that, in those three nations, the fact was they had a very strong army which forced the insurgents to use a high level of terrorism. Richard Barnett writes: "The only decisive victories over insurgents have been in Greece, Malaysia, and the Philippines. And these were attributable to political factors, combined with a military superiority of at least 10 to 1. We'd claim those prove our point.

Next, urbanization. The gentleman said we can't make the cities safe. That wasn't our point. We're not talking about terrorism here; we're talking about changing the economic condition of the country, making it less susceptible to takeover that way. Dave's not responsive. The examples, once again, the Dominican Republic. Said you didn't need 25,000 lives—troops to save the lives. No, but the first 400 did a good job.

Number two, he argues, well, no lives were lost until we intervened. Fine, we intervene quickly enough as situations start to break out. He asserts that that disputes our argument. It doesn't. Number three, he said it would encourage a takeover. No, it was going to go communist then. It's not communist now. Fourth, he said we influenced the outcome of the election against Bosch, so it wasn't fair. What he's saying is that we got what the United States wanted. We got the pro-United States man elected. I'd claim that's a reason to intervene.

Consider the third contention: On balance, it's wasteful. I argued that the only harm was in Vietnam. Number one, the President's not going to want to intervene in Vietnam. Well, five years from now that's going to go away. We'd like Mike to explain why, why the situation is going to change. He doesn't give me the reason; I can't refute the analysis. I argued there would be no similar conditions. He said the Dominican Republic. I'd like him to show how that could escalate to a conflict like Vietnam. I'd like him to show how covert activities could escalate to a conflict like Vietnam. I claim there's no rationale for the resolution.

First Affirmative Rebuttal

Barry says we've got a contradiction. We say you can't predict in future success in escalation, and then he says we predict future Vietnams. No. We say any intervention can become a Vietnam. Any one might, and you can't predict which one will; and that's the crucial argument, and the gentleman really doesn't show any contradiction. Next, he says that you can't distinguish between aggression and subversion. We gave the criteria: the use of foreign troops. The gentlemen's only argument was sometimes they're racially indistinguishable. Tom Ferrar of Columbia in 1967: "Foreign forces cannot move into war zones in substantial numbers without being identified, even where they're racially indistinguishable, because in order to avoid being shot by their own units they have to carry accouterments identifying them."

Number two, the gentlemen prove that at best we can't go into a situation, not that we will go into a situation, so we still meet our need and the gentleman really has no point here. Number three, the gentleman talks about the future necessity for military intervention. First, to preclude the use of nuclear weapons by certain states and to manage proliferation. Now recall, he gives no examples of where we want to promote proliferation or how we would do it. He says there are two ways we can stop it. First of all, we can threaten intervention and thus give credibility, so they won't proliferate. Now when was the last time you ever heard about nuclear weapons being used in a war of subversion? The gentleman never really explains how that's the case. Number two, He says that we can have a controlled amount of conflict.

Now we intervene etcetera, etcetera, to prevent future conflicts. Now wait a minute. You can't predict the degree of escalation. Perhaps we went into Vietnam in 1954 to fight a small war. It's a mighty big one right now. The gentleman doesn't show us how we can predict escalation. Number three, the gentleman says we need to protect lives. He talks about the Dominican Republic. Recall. They were being evacuated anyway, that was in the second affirmative constructive. The gentleman doesn't deny it. He says in the future consider the circumstances. Dean Rusk, *U.S. News*, January 29, 1962: "In most circumstances, the attempt to use force to protect American citizens cannot secure the people who are being threatened. Even if that situation arises, it won't be successful."

The gentleman then has two disadvantages to withdrawing from Vietnam. One is the liquidation of the people. I suggest therefore that we sell them boat tickets and, when we pull our troops out, they can go with us. Number two: I suggest that will not take place. David Schoenbrun of Columbia in 1968: "There is no reason to believe that the NLF will want to have another bloodbath. They have every reason to try to win over the people, to rebuild the shattered country and win respect, not to eliminate people."

All right, consider finally the proliferation disadvantage. He says it's harmful in Asia. I deny it; so does Fred Green in 1968 of Williams College: "Over the long run, the United States would find that proliferation among its Asian allies and friends would make for more harmonious relations with them easier to attain." I suggest no disadvantage.

Return with me to the case. First of all, the gentleman says we have to show the situations won't change in the future. No. We show that they won't change for the foreseeable future and that's important because we're weighing cost versus gains. The gentleman then says I opt for selective intervention. At no time does he try to predict escalation. At no time does he try to predict success. So how can he utilize that selective intervention policy? Consider the first contention.

On balance, military intervention is unjustified. The gentleman has basically four arguments. He says first of all the situation is not such. We have political stakes in Asia. Now what he said was a quote—we have political stakes in Asia. We ask why the gentleman doesn't point that out. Number two, He says the Chinese communists can export revolution. Does he ever prove that will be successful? No, he doesn't. Then he says Asia may change in the future. Recall the statement of Mr. Reischauer. "No matter what kind of power they get in the future, they can't affect United States security." And the gentleman doesn't deny the point. Then he says the Latin Americans can get missiles, and they can threaten the United States. Wait a minute. The Soviet Union controls the missiles in Latin America. They didn't give them to the Cubans and, besides, deterrence posture is going to work on Latin Americans just like they do on the Soviet Union. I don't think they're that stupid.

Consider now the second reason for eliminating the option. On balance, military intervention is ineffective. The gentleman says look at Malaysia. We have three factors which might recur again. Now I want to emphasize the Malaysian intervention was lucky, not predicted. They didn't predict those factors, they just happened to be there. We can't base it on that particular situation. He talks about the necessity for manpower. Says a 20 to 1 ratio is needed. All right, so what? He doesn't indicate that a 20 to 1 ratio can be successful. Third, he talks about the idea of terrorism. And he says terrorism backfires where the government has a large army. One of the examples David gave you was Malaysia, where they said they had a weak army in the first negative constructive. Fourthly, he talks about urbanization and says he's talking about economic stability this time. Recall, if you blow up the city, you don't have much economic stability, and that's what they did in the Tet offensive. He drops the example on Lebanon. He turns back to the Dominican Republic. Recall, the communist threat is expanded, if anything. Number two, those people were being evacuated anyway. Number three: We influenced the election against Mr. Bosch; and, number four and finally, the gentleman can't show that promotion of stability.

Finally, consider future interventions. Recall — we could have had a Vietnam in the Dominican Republic. The gentleman says why. Remember the gentleman's evidence? If you have a guerrilla war, it takes 20 to 100 times as many men to suppress it. Number two, he says the situation will change. Recall that situation changes for only five years.

Finally, the gentleman at no time ever really shows us that we can avoid a Vietnam but more important never turns to any example in this case and shows us any significant gain. We feel the costs outweigh the gains.

Second Negative Rebuttal

Joe begins by telling you that conditions might change. He proves that nationalism is definitely changing and even may change against us. The gentleman gets back up with his same point and says, but look, we can't tell if it's going to escalate or not. First of all, that doesn't refute that nationalism is changing, but secondly Joe asked him, please Mike, show us how covert operations may escalate into Vietnam. He refuses to do that. I'd say it's a little late for David.

On balance, military intervention is unwarranted, they tell us. Joe talks about political importance but the gentleman says, what political stakes do we have in Asia? Remember Joe's example of Sihanouk saying that he wanted the United States being there. That's certainly political. Mike doesn't refute it. But next Joe goes on to show how Asia's vital. He says it's vital today. It's going to be more vital in the future. The gentleman doesn't deny this. Recall further, Joe goes to their own source, Mr. Reischauer, who says other areas of the world are vitally different from Asia. The gentleman doesn't answer that. Latin America. Talking about the threat of nuclear weapons. The gentleman says, first of all, the Soviet Union controls these countries. All right, what if they develop the nuclear weapons in the future? But further, the gentleman talks about deterrence theory. Now remember Joe told you what the problem would be. What if there's an accident. Or a miscalculation. We all remember from the high school topic that that doesn't deter nuclear war. Further, we went to the second contention.

They tell us, on balance, military intervention is ineffective. Joe says look, let's retain the option to intervene and look to the example of Malaysia. The gentleman says it's unique and comes back up here and asserts that we couldn't predict those factors. Remember one of the factors, the promise of decolonization. It sure sounds to me like we could have predicted that. That was there. We can predict it. Keep the option open. Joe talks about the size of the force ratio. The gentleman says prove it will be effective. Joe told you in his rebuttal that's what Mr. Deischman said. The gentleman said prove it again. Terrorism backfires. Joe says but look in those three examples we had a strong army. He turns to the example of Malaysia. But recall in Malaysia they did have the strong army because the British sent their troops in, and that's when it came about. Urbanization. Joe says we can change the economic conditions. The gentleman says, yeah, but they'd blow up the cities. That doesn't deny that if we put them in the cities they can modernize and get out of the stage where wars of liberation can hurt them. Please note that Mike reasserts David's argument on the four points in the Dominican Republic. Doesn't deal with Joe's answers which were indeed sufficient.

Third, on balance, military intervention is wasteful. Joe says it's certainly not very significant. But secondly Joe says, look, why is this theory going to change? Why are we going to have future Vietnams? The gentleman doesn't deny that. He says we could have had an escalation in the Dominican Republic. Joe says how could they do that. The gentleman says the force ratios argument. Further, remember Joe's challenge, show how covert operation can escalate. He doesn't want to do that.

Let's go to my analysis. Note the contradiction. I said they say you can't tell in advance. Then read evidence saying the Dominican Republic would. He gets up and says any intervention can escalate, but we don't know which ones they're going to be. Now that's pretty contradictory to his reading evidence which says the Dominican Republic would. I think the gentleman loses the argument: Can't define aggression. He doesn't deny the historical precedent. He doesn't deny the peace-war dichotomy. He doesn't deny that Vietnam is presently considered some by some and some by the other. But fourth, I tell you they all look alike. The gentleman says, well look, they can be identified by their own army so they don't shoot at each other. Okay they can all come in wearing uniforms—suppose they all wear uniforms—we still aren't going to know who they are. I don't think the gentleman's analysis is responsive.

Reasons to maintain the option to intervene. This is crucial. Manage the dissemination of nuclear weapons. He says, why do we need nuclear weapons against subversion? No, the point is, we can send our troops in if necessary to blow up their nuclear forces. That's intervention, and the gentleman doesn't answer the point. Number two, controlled conflict. The gentleman says Vietnam is a big war. It may be a big war, but it is not the kind of general nuclear war we'd have to fight. That's what Mr. Liska was referring to. Third, I told you protecting lives and property. He says, well look, in the Dominican Republic they were being evacuated anyway. Yeah, well they weren't all out, that's why we had to send the additional troops. Secondly, he says they won't be successful which is incredibly contradictory with his telling you we were successfully evacuating them in the Dominican Republic which he doesn't deny. Fourth, deter Soviet and Chinese support of revolution. The gentleman refuses to talk about it. Harm in Vietnam. Systematic liquidation. They won't want another bloodbath. Why? Because they want the support of the people. But if they can't get it from those Hao-Hao and Cao Dai, who are now opposing them, then they're going to kill them all and the gentleman doesn't deny that. Increased proliferation. The gentleman says, look, wait a minute, it's going to be helpful if our allies in Asia have nuclear weapons. Now what did he say up above? He said show us some situation where we might want to have people get nuclear weapons. I think he contradicts himself on that. And he doesn't deny that they're going to get those nuclear weapons. The affirmative case doesn't solve the need. We have to retain the option to intervene, in light of the fact that even in the present system we aren't going to have future Vietnams and, further, under the affirmative plan we wouldn't be able to intervene for all these other reasons. Even if only once in the next 200 years.

Second Affirmative Rebuttal

I'd like to begin with the issue of selectivity. Recall the evidence from the *Harvard Law Review* that says you can't predict the degree of conflict in any use of force. Recall Professor Thompson saying you can't predict success. The gentleman claims my quote about the Dominican Republic didn't apply. Yes, it did. We could easily have had another Vietnam in the Dominican Republic in 1965. And if we did not it was not because of us. We owed our good luck there to our opponent, the man we decided to cheat of victory. It didn't say we could tell in advance what would happen in the Dominican Republic. It didn't say we would have had another Vietnam. It said we could have had another Vietnam and we were lucky, and that's the whole point—we didn't predict in advance, hence, the gentlemen's analysis is irrelevant.

Secondly, that we can't distinguish aggression from subversion. Look, Mike says if you're using foreign troops you can recognize them because they have identifying accouterments. The gentleman says something about uniforms, not denying according to Professor Farris that they can be distinguished. I suggest that that's basic answer.

Next, consider other reasons. Now look, you're going back to balance all those other reasons against the predictability and the lack of success. Number one, managing nuclear proliferation. He says we can send the troops in to blow up nuclear installations. Now doesn't that sound to be rather dangerous, something we can't predict because they might use those nuclear weapons against us and get that automatic nuclear war these gentlemen are concerned with? To control the amount of conflict. He says we're going to have a general war. Number one, you can't predict the degree of escalation in any use of armed force and that's something the gentlemen have never denied. To protect lives. We found out, in the vast majority of cases, we couldn't be successful. The gentleman says your Dominican evidence contradicts that. No, it says the Dominicans were evacuating them for us and that they can be successful. More importantly, you can't predict in advance when you intervene with some troop to protect lives what the eventual conflict will be. That's the crucial distinction. Deter Soviet and Chinese support. Once again the predictability argument applies here. That's something the gentlemen didn't answer. We can't predict when we intervene, such as in Vietnam, the ultimate dimensions of the conflict. Hence we can't weigh it on the basis of cost versus gains to justify that intervention.

Next consider the harm from Vietnam. He talked about liquidation. I suggested he's merely asserting that they're going to want to liquidate all those people. We found that they're going to make the most attempts possible to get them on their side. We can evacuate those few that are marked.

Increasing proliferation. He said there was a contradiction. No, there wasn't. We said, on the one hand, why will they want nuclear weapons against subversion but on the other hand, if proliferation does occur in some countries it's going to result in more harmonious relations. That wasn't a contradiction. He merely asserted it.

Consider the affirmative case structure. The gentlemen talk about the possibility of change and that nationalism is changing. Did they ever demonstrate that we can evaluate it on the basis of predictability in specific situations if it's in such a state of flux? That's a good reason why we can't predict in advance. It's in such a state of flux we don't know what's going to happen when we go in and that's why we should forego that option. He says, how can covert operations turn into it? We're not concerned with covert operations. We're concerned with military intervention, which the gentleman doesn't come to grips with.

Number one, on balance, military intervention is unjustified. He talks about political considerations. Here I suggested that in those specific situations that we would have the best barrier to the expansion of communism, that North Vietnam shouldn't succeed and that these countries themselves will resist it. He gives us one country, Cambodia. If Cambodia goes to the communists, where's the threat to U.S. security interests? The gentleman doesn't demonstrate it.

Economically, he talks about Asia and the Middle East not defending his position on Asia. And I would suggest that because Latin America and the Middle East, in fact, were subsumed under the first affirmative speech when Mr. Wolfe said none of these minerals or materials are vital to our security interests. He talked, secondly, about the military aspects. Recall they've never demonstrated the crucial issue — that any of these factors is going to upset our security interests based on second strike nuclear deterrence potential. He talks about bases in Latin America. Then he shifts ground. He admits the bases don't threaten our security. What about proliferation? Here we're going to have a situation in which the deterrent still applies. He asserts a quote not proving it. Recall the gentleman would want us to go in and intervene against these proliferaters, perhaps have an all-out nuclear war that way. I suggest no consistent analysis.

They've never denied any one of the five examples that there was no threat to our security. Let's consider, secondly, whether it's effective. Now the gentlemen say we can support inefficient militaries as in the Maylasia situation. Now look, we didn't predict in advance those three factors were going to be unique or successful. That was after-the-fact analysis. The crucial distinction is that we can't have those successful factors anywhere else because we've got no more colonies. Increase the insufficient force ratios. Once again it doesn't say that you can predict in advance the ultimate outcome of the conflict or the escalation of the conflict which is the crucial distinction. Curbing of terrorism. We said terrorism backfires in most of the cases. They said that's because they have large armies. In those two other cases, there was no foreign military intervention; hence they don't have that rationale. Urbanization. Let's say we can herd them all into the cities and have economic development. How, if we're blowing up the cities? Consider Guatemala, consider Lebanon dropped, consider the Bay of Pigs and the Dominican Republic. The gentleman said we repeated our arguments. That's right because all they were countered with was assertions. The lives were being saved. No shots were fired until we went in. We actually have an increase in communism. And we had that basic election which was rigged and didn't provide them that free choice. They talked about a better settlement in Vietnam and dropped the argument. On balance, it's ineffective.

Lastly, on balance, military intervention is wasteful. We're only going to have that new standard for about five years. The gentlemen ask why. It's because that inherent proclivity for the use of intervention will reassert itself after that point in time. Second, what about future situations in which we could have a Vietnam? The Dominican Republic.

And I'm going to leave you with this one question: If we accept everything the gentlemen have said as true, does it still justify the risk of just one more Vietnam — $100-billion and 30,000 lives — to gain anything they've said? I suggest, on balance, it doesn't.

Exercises

1. Evaluate each of the speeches from the point of view of speech composition. Which was constructed the best? Which was the easiest to follow?

2. What type of case did the affirmative use?

3. How did the affirmative design its case to achieve the optimum balance of offensive and defensive capabilities?

4. Are the three issues advanced in the first affirmative independent or interrelated? Which is the most important?

5. What is the negative's basic philosophy? Does the negative carry this argument?

6. How effective is the first negative's attack on each of the affirmative issues? Which side is ahead on each issue at the end of this speech?

7. What evidence do you find that the affirmative, in building its case, anticipated many of the negative attacks?

8. What examples can you find of the second affirmative extending the affirmative case?

9. What examples do you find of the second affirmative bringing the affirmative case into sharper focus?

10. The second negative claims an inherent contradiction to the affirmative case. How damaging is this contradiction? Which side wins this argument?

11. How effective were the second negative's workability arguments?

12. How effective were the second negative's disadvantages arguments?

13. Which team was ahead at the end of the constructive speeches?

14. What was the turning point in the debate, that is, the point at which it became apparent that one side had won? Justify your answer.

15. Using the ballot shown on page 317, prepare a ballot for this debate. Omit the evaluation of delivery.

16. Using the form shown on page 315, prepare a flow sheet of the debate. Hand the flow sheet to your instructor for evaluation of your ability to prepare a flow sheet. (Use two or three sheets of $8\frac{1}{2}'' \times 14''$ or larger paper; use fewer abbreviations than you would in a flow sheet prepared exclusively for your own use.)

17. Write a 500-word paper in which you answer the question: Which team did the better debating? Draw on your total knowledge of argumentation and debate, and cite specific instances from the debate to justify your answer.

National Intercollegiate
Debate Propositions

Following is a list of the national intercollegiate debate propositions from the academic year 1920–1921 through 1975–1976:[1]

1920–1921 (Men) *Resolved:* That a progressive tax on land should be adopted in the United States.
(Men) *Resolved:* That the League of Nations should be adopted.
(Women) *Resolved:* That intercollegiate athletics should be abolished.

1921–1922 *Resolved:* That the principle of the "closed shop" is unjustifiable.

1922–1923 *Resolved:* That the United States should adopt the cabinet-parliamentary form of government.

1923–1924 *Resolved:* That the United States should enter the World Court of the League of Nations as proposed by President Harding.

1924–1925 *Resolved:* That Congress should be empowered to override, by a two-thirds vote, decisions of the Supreme Court which declare acts of Congress unconstitutional.

1925–1926 (Men) *Resolved:* That the Constitution of the United States should be amended to give Congress power to regulate child labor.
(Women) *Resolved:* That the United States should adopt a uniform marriage and divorce law.

1926–1927 (Men) *Resolved:* That the essential features of the McNary-Haugen bill be enacted into law.[2]
(Women) *Resolved:* That trial by jury should be abolished.[3]
Resolved: That the Volstead Act should be modified to permit the manufacture and sale of light wines and beer.[4]

1927–1928 *Resolved:* That the United States should cease to protect, by force of arms, capital invested in foreign lands, except after formal declaration of war.

---

[1] See: George McCoy Musgrave, *Competitive Debate, Rules and Techniques,* 3rd ed. (New York: H. W. Wilson Co. 1957), pp. 143–145, for a list of intercollegiate debate propositions from 1920–1921 through 1956–1957; and E. R. Nichols, "The Annual College Question," *The Debater's Magazine,* Vol. 3 (December 1947), pp. 206–207, for a list of intercollegiate debate propositions from 1922–1923 through 1947–1948. Various issues of the *Quarterly Journal of Speech* and the *Speech Teacher,* as well as announcements issued by the Committee on Intercollegiate Debate and Discussion, publish the current intercollegiate debate proposition.

[2] Listed by Musgrave, *op. cit.*

[3] *Ibid.*

[4] Listed by Nichols, *op. cit.*

1928–1929 *Resolved:* That a substitute for trial by jury should be adopted.

1929–1930 *Resolved:* That the nations should adopt a plan of complete disarmament, excepting such forces as are needed for police purposes.

1930–1931 *Resolved:* That the nations should adopt a policy of free trade.

1931–1932 *Resolved:* That the Congress should enact legislation providing for the centralized control of industry.

1932–1933 *Resolved:* That the United States should agree to the cancellation of the interallied debts.

1933–1934 *Resolved:* That the powers of the President of the United States should be substantially increased as a settled policy.

1934–1935 *Resolved:* That the nations should agree to prevent the international shipment of arms and munitions.

1935–1936 *Resolved:* That the Congress should have the power to override, by a two-thirds majority vote, decisions of the Supreme Court declaring laws passed by Congress unconstitutional.

1936–1937 *Resolved:* That Congress should be empowered to fix minimum wages and maximum hours for industry.

1937–1938 *Resolved:* That the National Labor Relations Board should be empowered to enforce arbitration of all industrial disputes.

1938–1939 *Resolved:* That the United States should cease the use of public funds (including credits) for the purpose of stimulating business.

1939–1940 *Resolved:* That the United States should follow a policy of strict economic and military isolation toward all nations outside the Western Hemisphere engaged in armed international or civil conflict.

1940–1941 *Resolved:* That the nations of the Western Hemisphere should form a permanent union.

1941–1942 *Resolved:* That the federal government should regulate by law all labor unions in the United States.

1942–1943 *Resolved:* That the United States should take the initiative in establishing a permanent federal union with power to tax and regulate commerce, to settle international disputes and to enforce such settlements, to maintain a police force, and to provide for the admission of other nations which accept the principles of the union.

1943–1944 *Resolved:* That the United States should co-operate in establishing and maintaining an international police force upon the defeat of the Axis.

1944–1945 *Resolved:* That the federal government should enact legislation requiring the settlement of all labor disputes by compulsory arbitration when voluntary means of settlement have failed.

1945–1946 *Resolved:* That the policy of the United States should be directed toward the establishment of free trade among the nations of the world.

1946–1947 *Resolved:* That labor should be given a direct share in the management of industry.

1947–1948 *Resolved:* That a federal world government should be established.

1948–1949 *Resolved:* That the federal government should adopt a policy of equalizing educational opportunity in tax-supported schools by means of annual grants.

1949–1950 *Resolved:* That the United States should nationalize the basic nonagricultural industries.

1950–1951 *Resolved:* That the noncommunist nations should form a new international organization.

1951–1952 *Resolved:* That the federal government should adopt a permanent program of wage and price control.

1952–1953 *Resolved:* That the Congress of the United States should enact a compulsory fair employment practices law.

1953–1954 *Resolved:* That the United States should adopt a policy of free trade.

1954–1955 *Resolved:* That the United States should extend diplomatic recognition to the communist government of China.

1955–1956 *Resolved:* That the nonagricultural industries should guarantee their employees an annual wage.

1956–1957 *Resolved:* That the United States should discontinue direct economic aid to foreign countries.

1957–1958 *Resolved:* That the requirement of membership in a labor organization as a condition of employment should be illegal.

1958–1959 *Resolved:* That the further development of nuclear weapons should be prohibited by international agreement.

1959–1960 *Resolved:* That Congress should be given the power to reverse decisions of the Supreme Court.

1960–1961 *Resolved:* That the United States should adopt a program of compulsory health insurance for all citizens.

1961–1962 *Resolved:* That labor organizations should be under the jurisdiction of anti-trust legislation.

1962–1963 *Resolved:* That the noncommunist nations of the world should establish an economic community.

1963–1964 *Resolved:* That the federal government should guarantee an opportunity for higher education to all qualified high school graduates.

1964–1965 *Resolved:* That the federal government should establish a national program of public work for the unemployed.

1965–1966 *Resolved:* That law-enforcement agencies in the United States should be given greater freedom in the investigation and prosecution of crime.

1966–1967 *Resolved:* That the United States should substantially reduce its foreign policy commitments.

1967–1968 *Resolved:* That the federal government should guarantee a minimum annual cash income to all citizens.

1968–1969 *Resolved:* That executive control of United States foreign policy should be significantly curtailed.

1969–1970 *Resolved:* That the federal government should grant annually a specific percentage of its income tax revenue to the state governments.

1970–1971 *Resolved:* That the federal government should adopt a program of compulsory wage and price controls.

1971–1972 *Resolved:* That greater controls should be imposed on the gathering and utilization of information about United States citizens by government agencies.

1972–1973 *Resolved:* That the federal government should provide a program of comprehensive medical care for all citizens.

1973–1974 *Resolved:* That the federal government should control the supply and utilization of energy in the United States.

1974–1975 *Resolved:* That the power of the Presidency should be significantly curtailed.

1975–1976 *Resolved:* That the federal government should adopt a comprehensive program to control land use in the United States.

1976–1977 *Resolved:* That the federal government should significantly strengthen the guarantee of consumer product safety required of manufacturers.

1977–1978 *Resolved:* That United States law enforcement agencies should be given significantly greater freedom in the investigation and/or prosecution of felony crime.

Index

Aaron, Hank, 291
"Acres of Diamonds," 291
Adams, John Quincy, 3
Administration of tournament, 357–359
Aesop, 287–288
Affirmative case:
  alternative justification case, 190–191
  building for optimum capability, 194–195
  comparative advantages analysis, 185–194
  criteria case, 190
  integrating, 182–185
  needs analysis, 179–185
  objectives of, 179
  outlines, 195–199
Agenda, 362–363
Ali, Muhammad, 291
Alternative justification case, 190–191
Ambiguity, 147
Ambition, 264
American Forensic Association, 18, 19, 312, 371
  statement of principles, 21
American Telephone and Telegraph Company, 20
Analogy:
  fallacies of, 146
  figurative, 119
  literal, 119
  reasoning by, 118–120
Analyzing opponent's case, 235
Andersen, Kenneth, 246
Animal Farm, The, 288
Anthony, Susan B., 18
Appellate debate format, 334–335
Arguing in a circle, 150
Argument:
  adopting opposing, 244
  irrelevant, 244
  structural model for, 138–142
  substituting bombast for, 152–153
  substituting person for, 152

Argumentation, *defined*, 1, 8
"Argument from authority," 83
Aristotle, 2, 7, 17, 137, 297, 310
Assertion, repeated, 151
Attitudinal inherency, 170–171
Audience:
  acceptance of evidence, tests for, 104–108
  analysis during speech, 271–272
  analysis of, 266–272
  attitude toward speaker, 268
  ballot for, 322, 323
  debate, 337–338
  heterogeneous, 266
  homogeneous, 266
  hostile, 270–271
  information about, 267–271
  and the occasion, 268
  participation, 288–289
  preferences, wants, and beliefs of American, 262–266
  priority of, 339
  and purpose of advocate, 269
  stereotype, 268
  "universal," 8
  what the advocate needs to know about, 268–269
Audio materials, 292–293

"backing," 139
Baird, A. Craig, 23
Baiting an opponent, 150–151
Baldwin, Charles S., 22
Ballot:
  American Forensic Association Form C, 317
  for audience decision, 322, 323
  for direct clash debate, 321–322
  educational tool, 320
  functions of, 319–320
  quality rating points, 316, 317, 319–320